# Knowledge in the Blood

# Knowledge in the Blood

## Confronting Race
## and the Apartheid Past

*Jonathan D. Jansen*

Stanford University Press
Stanford, California

Stanford University Press
Stanford, California

©2009 by the Board of Trustees of the Leland Stanford Junior University. All rights reserved.

The poem on p. v is reprinted from Macdara Woods, *Knowledge in the Blood: New and Selected Poems* (Dublin, Ireland: Dedalus Press, 2007), 101. Used with permission of the Dedalus Press, www.dedaluspress.com.

Library of Congress Cataloging-in-Publication Data

Jansen, Jonathan D.
  Knowledge in the blood : confronting race and the apartheid past / Jonathan D. Jansen.
    p. cm.
  Includes bibliographical references and index.
  ISBN 978-0-8047-6194-9 (cloth : alk. paper)--ISBN 978-0-8047-6195-6 (pbk. : alk. paper)
  1. University of Pretoria--Administration. 2. College integration--South Africa. 3. Educational change--South Africa. 4. Afrikaner students--South Africa--Attitudes. 5. College students, White--South Africa--Attitudes. 6. Racism in higher education--South Africa. 7. Post-apartheid era--South Africa. 8. South Africa--Race relations. I. Title.
  LG471.P7J36 2009
  378.68'227--dc22                                                      2008054140

Typeset by Bruce Lundquist in 11/15 Bell MT

## Time and the Ice-Fish

This is it now the lighthouse
any further we can not
than the sea-wall's end
like the others we must drop back

This week-end—in a day or less
they are turning the clocks back
and we will hear the cogs mesh
and the minutes beginning to tick

Because there is no respite
from the knowledge in the blood
this is a fearful country this
bleak landscape of the ice-fish

*Macdara Woods*

# Contents

# Acknowledgments

I DEDICATE THIS BOOK to my white Afrikaner undergraduate students. Yet I cannot write about white students without acknowledging my black students, about whom there is a different book to be written.

I acknowledge the incredible members of my staff: Yvonne Munro, Esther Schilling, Rinelle Evans, Alta Engelbrecht, Carol van der Westhuizen, Loyiso Jita, Everard Weber, Venitha Pillay, Chaya Herman, L. D. Beukes, Nkidi Phatudi, Christina Amsterdam, Thidziambi Phendla, Sarie Berkhout, Thea de Kock, Ina Joubert, Johan Beckmann, Jan Heystek, Carien Lubbe, Riekie van Aswegen, Lien Howatt, Chika Sehoole, Kobus Maree, Neil Roos, Johan Hendrikz, Saloshna Vandeyar, Gilbert Onwu, Erna Alant, Sarah Howie, Anita van der Bank, Irma Eloff, Annelie Botha, Johannes Cronje, Johan Conradie, Willie Potgieter, Helena Davidson, Selena Davids, Thuli Phaladi, Vinay Rajah, Ingrid Bester, and Gawa Pritchard.

I acknowledge my intellectual mentor, Professor Chabani Manganyi, and those critical friends on main campus: Niek Grove, Charles van Onselen, Robin Crewe, Christof Heyns, Christine Williams, Johan Kirsten, Maxi Schoeman, Janis Grobler, Christa North, Mary Crewe, Johan Nel, Antony Melck, Hein Willemse, "Doc" Breedt, Flip van der Watt, and Jerry Kuye.

This book would not have been possible without generous funding from the Fulbright Commission in South Africa, and in particular Mareka Chabedi and Mary Ellen Koenig; the Oppenheimer Memorial Trust; and the National Research Foundation.

I thank colleagues at the Carnegie Foundation for the Advancement of Teaching for giving me the physical and intellectual space as a Visiting Fellow to do the actual writing of this book: Ann Lieberman, Lee Shulman, Rose Asera, Cheryl Richardson, Judy Shulman, Kelly Vaughn, John Merrow, Luella Parker, Louise Kruszenski, Lisa Glenn, Sherry Hecht, and Charlene Moran.

Stanford University was the official home for my Fulbright attachment from late 2007 to early 2008: here I thank Martin Carnoy, Joel Samoff, Arnetha Ball, Sam Wineburg, David Abernethy, Jim Gibbs, Hans Weiler, Richard Roberts, Linda Darling-Hammond, Karen Fung, and Elliot Eisner. I thank our friends in the San Francisco Bay Area for providing that broader support network: David and Nancy Christie, Taiga and John Christie, Joyce Farrell, Brian Wandell, Adam Wandell, Ernie Liebermann, Rachel Samoff, Madhuri and Kran Kilpatrick, and Jewell Gibbs.

I had invaluable research assistance from Karen Harris, Bronwyn Strydom, and Ria Groenewald (University of Pretoria Archives); Faith Cranfield in Michigan; Clarisse Venter, Elsabe du Toit, Johann van Wyk (University of Pretoria Education Library); and the AP Archives in New York.

I first tested the ideas in this book at several universities. In this respect I thank Zimitri Erasmus and Melissa Steyn (University of Cape Town); Teboho Moja and Colleen Larson (New York University); Darren Clarke and his colleagues at Rutgers University; Labby Ramrathan and his colleagues at the University of KwaZulu Natal; Carol Ann Spreen and her students at the University of Maryland; Daniel Perlstein at the University of California at Berkeley; Paula Cordeiro, Cheryl Getz, and their colleagues at the University of San Diego; Deborah Ball, Jeffrey Mirel, Gary Krenz, and Julie Ellison (University of Michigan); and Tim Eatman (Syracuse University).

I am delighted to acknowledge my successive classes of doctoral students in education policy at the University of Pretoria who were subjected to the initial ideas that became this book: Samuel Isaacs, Gail Weldon, Tshepiso Matentjie, Franci Cronje, Thobs Gamede, Hersheela Narsee, Itumeleng Molale, Dan More, Mamolahluwa Mokoena, Zoleka Sokopo, Juliana Seleti, Beverley Damonse, Jerry Madiba, Muavia Gallie,

Helen Sidiropoulos, Hermenean Laauwen, Patricia Machawarira, Maggie Okore, Joy Papier, and Vanessa Koopman.

Books and families seldom go together. My wife, Grace, understood more strongly than anyone how important it was for me to write this account of change at the University of Pretoria. My two exemplary children, Mikhail and Sara-Jane, always seemed to have that puzzled look ("You mean they're paying you to write a book? Don't you have real work?"). Yet they too understood what I was passionate about and, in their own quiet and unexpressed way, as becomes teenagers, always supported my scholarly pursuits.

Finally, I am indebted to the editors at Stanford University—Kate Wahl, senior editor; Joa Suorez, editorial assistant; Mariana Raykov, production editor; and Tom Finnegan, freelance copyeditor—and to my South African editor, Richard Proctor-Sims.

Jonathan D. Jansen
Stanford University
July 2008

# Abbreviations

| | |
|---|---|
| ANC | African National Congress |
| ATKV | Afrikaanse Taal- en Kultuurvereniging (Afrikaans Language and Cultural Association) |
| CNE | Christian National Education |
| DA | Democratic Alliance |
| DRC | Dutch Reformed Church |
| FF+ | Freedom Front Plus |
| HEQC | Higher Education Quality Committee |
| HNP | Herstigte Nasionale Party (Reconstituted National Party) |
| KKNK | Klein Karoo Nasionale Kunstefees (Little Karoo National Arts Festival) |
| NKP | Normaal Kollege Pretoria |
| NP | National Party |
| PAC | Pan Africanist Congress |
| SAQA | South African Qualifications Authority |
| SRC | Student Representative Council |
| TRC | Truth and Reconciliation Commission |
| UCT | University of Cape Town |
| UDW | University of Durban Westville |
| UP | University of Pretoria |
| YSDP | Young Scholars Development Program |

# Glossary of Afrikaans Words, Names, and Phrases

*Aardklop*   the name of an arts festival

*Afrikaanse Taal- en Kultuurvereniging, die*   the Afrikaans Language and Cultural Association

*baasskap*   racial domination

*bakkie*   a light truck

*barmhartig*   compassionate

*Beeld*   an Afrikaans daily newspaper circulating in the northern provinces

*beleefdheid*   courtesy, politeness

*bode*   a messenger

*Boere, die*   (literally) the farmers; a name for the Afrikaner people

*Boeredrag*   traditional Boer clothing

*boerekos*   traditional Afrikaner food

*'n Boer maak 'n plan*   a farmer (or Boer) will make a plan or come up with an idea

*Boesmans, die*   (literally) the Bushmen or San; sometimes used pejoratively to refer to colored people

*boetie op die grens*   little brother on the border

*Broederbond* (also *Afrikaner Broederbond)*   (literally) "a band of brothers"; a secret cultural and political society with membership limited to male Afrikaner adults

*Burger, Die*   an Afrikaans daily newspaper circulating in the southern provinces

*dekaan*    a dean

*dominee*    a minister of religion in one of the Dutch Reformed Churches

*dorp*    the downtown area

*drafstappie*    a fast walk, a trot

*Engelse, die*    the English

*gatvol*    fed-up

*goeie môre*    good morning (a greeting)

*Herstigte Nasionale Party, die (HNP)*    the Reconstituted National Party

*Hervormde Kerk, die*    the Reformed Church (one of the Dutch Reformed Churches)

*jeugweerbaarheidsprogramme*    youth preparedness programs

*Junior Rapportryers*    junior dispatch riders (a traditional Afrikaner cultural body)

*jy and u*    the familiar and formal "you"

*kafferboeties*    a derogatory word for a white Afrikaner who sides with a black person or the black community

*Klein Karoo Nasionale Kunstefees, die (KKNK)*    the Little Karoo National Art Festival

*kollegas*    colleagues

*koshuis*    a university residence or dorm

*laagering*    (literally) forming a defensive ring of wagons during the "Great Trek"; or (figuratively) a closing of Afrikaner cultural ranks

*Loftus Versfeld*    the name of a rugby football stadium in Pretoria

*lokasie, die*    the (usually black) township

*Nederduitse Gereformeerde Kerk*    Dutch Reformed Church

*Nie Langer*    No Longer (title of an Afrikaner patriotic song)

*Nkosi Sikilel' iAfrika*    God Bless Africa; considered the unofficial national anthem of South Africa during the Apartheid years; see also *Volkslied*

*Normaal Kollege Pretoria (NKP)*    Pretoria Normal (Education) College

*onderdaniges*   subordinates

*oom*   uncle

*oorvoorsiening/ondervoorsiening*   oversupply or undersupply (of academic staff)

*opbouende kritiek*   constructive criticism

*opdrag*   command

*opleiding vs onderwys*   training vs education

*Oppiekoppie*   the name of a rock festival

*Ossewa-Brandwag, die (OB)*   (literally) the ox-wagon fire-watch; a neo-Nazi group with Afrikaner membership in the Second World War

*Rapport*   the leading Afrikaans national Sunday newspaper

*regstelling*   affirmative action

*rooi gevaar*   the Red threat (Communism); see also *Roomse gevaar* and *swart gevaar*

*Roomse gevaar*   the Roman Catholic threat

*Skip, die*   the Ship (a symbol of the University of Pretoria)

*Stem, Die*   see *Volkslied*

*stryddae*   fetes

*suiwer*   pure

*swart gevaar*   the Black threat (menace)

*tannie*   aunt

*Tukkies*   a nickname for the University of Pretoria

*veldskole*   veld (field) schools

*verengelsing*   Anglicization

*verraaier*   traitor

*Volk*   the (Afrikaner) people

*volkekunde*   anthropology

*Volksblad*   an Afrikaans daily newspaper circulating in the central provinces

*volkseie skole*   schools reserved for Afrikaner people

*volksfeeste*   folk festivals

*Volkslied, die*   the (old) South African national anthem
("Die Stem van Suid-Africa"/"The Call of South Africa")

*volksliedjies*   folk songs

*volksmoorde*   ethnic murders

*volkspele*   folk festivals

*Volkstaat, die*   the idea of a separate state for the Afrikaners

*voortbestaan*   survival

*Voortrekkermonument*   the Voortrekker monument outside the city of
Pretoria, built in 1938 to mark the centenary of the "Great Trek"

*Voortrekkers*   (historically) those who trekked away from the Cape
Colony in the "Great Trek" of the 1830s; (today) a youth movement
for boys and girls, along the lines of the Boy Scouts and Girl
Guides

*woordfees*   an Afrikaans word festival

# Knowledge in the Blood

# Prologue: Bearing Witness

> The dynamics of power trouble all our doing and all our knowing.
> Knowledge is always contingent, always standing above an abyss.[1]

IT WILL NEVER HAPPEN AGAIN. This is the first and only generation of South Africans that would have lived through one of the most dramatic social transitions of the twentieth century. Nobody else would be able to tell this story with the direct experience of having lived on both sides of the 1990s, the decade in which everything changed.

I am fortunate, in this sense, to be part of the South African generation that lived under and after Apartheid. I was especially privileged to have been able to teach young South Africans in both periods, at high schools prior to 1985 and at universities since that time. Raised as a conservative evangelical Christian from birth, my life changed during the Apartheid years as I witnessed firsthand the courage and cost of resistance on the part of my students; they formed my political consciousness as I grappled with a denominational perspective that ruled out activism by insisting that "your citizenship is in heaven."[2] It was during those years of teaching in the rural Western Cape coastal town of Vredenburg and inside the urban ruins of District Six[3] in Cape Town that the grinding poverty, the forced relocations, and the decency of revolt first touched my life, through my students.[4]

In the course of graduate studies in the United States, starting in 1985, I found myself joining the anti-Apartheid movements and assuming leadership in student movements in that country, where young people insisted that American universities divest from companies doing business

in South Africa.[5] For the first time, I met student leaders and senior political officers of the banned African National Congress (ANC), and here
I found some of the most insightful, analytical, inspired voices of struggle
that people inside South Africa were deprived of. It was, ironically, outside South Africa that I discovered a theoretical and political language
about liberation struggles and the centrality of education in the resistance
project. Once again, it was my fellow South African as well as progressive American students who gave me a conceptual lens for making sense
of personal experiences of oppression.

When I returned to South Africa in 1991, Apartheid was beginning
to disintegrate. After a short stint working with nongovernmental organizations from my base in Johannesburg, I joined the University of
Durban Westville (UDW) on the east coast of the country in 1994. Here
was a troubled institution in which discourses of anarchy and struggle
fused into a destructive chaos that almost collapsed one of the more
promising of the black universities.[6] But it was intellectually an exciting
period, nonetheless, and as dean of education at UDW I started to teach
and engage black university students about the meaning of struggle and
the trajectory of change in a country that was about to hold its first-
ever democratic elections.

It was in this former university for South Africans of Indian descent
that I saw, for the first time, the real dilemmas of racial interaction, racial
intolerance, and racial camaraderie among African and Indian staff and
students.[7] It was here that I found how race and ethnicity could be invoked by and among black people for very destructive political interests.
For example, being "African" could be cited to demand privilege against
"Indians"; being "Indian" could be asserted to retain social distance from
the "African." Nevertheless, this was an expectant youth looking to and
beyond the end of Apartheid, and I observed, even as I taught and led,
how important it was to be guided by the pain, the idealism, and the
aspirations of students.

## Entering

What completely changed my life was the next stop in my journey, which
took me out of the world of black struggles into the heart of whiteness.
As one of only a handful of senior black administrators at what was then

South Africa's largest residential university, I found myself in the midst of a white, conservative, and affluent public institution that, until 1989, did not admit black people onto its main campus.[8]

The University of Pretoria (UP) was one of the key Apartheid institutions for higher learning and one that fulfilled its white nationalist duty with considerable fervor for more than a hundred years.[9] This was the place where the loyal civil servants of the white state were steadfastly churned out year after year. It was the site for the production of Apartheid *dominees* (ministers of religion), trained to find theological justification for white rule. It was where Apartheid's anthropologists were trained to assign ethnic and racial predictabilities to human cultures through a subject called *volkekunde* (anthropology). It was the home to leading sociologists whose views of a racially ordered society gave scientific status to government policy. It was a place where political scientists justified Apartheid rule premised on racial hierarchies of human existence. And it was the base from which historians impressed Afrikaner nationalism on public understandings of the past.[10]

The system of Apartheid depended on the few Afrikaner universities, including Pretoria, to generate the fraught knowledge and the loyal expertise that would sustain the system of racial separateness and racial dominance in every sphere of society. A university for Pretoria was an idea first championed by the colonial secretary, General J. C. Smuts, an international statesman who later led the Union of South Africa to establish, as a founder member, the League of Nations, predecessor to the United Nations. Among its distinguished graduates it included prime ministers, international business moguls, chief executives of major financing institutions (including the governor of the Reserve Bank), leading judges, famous cultural leaders, world-renowned researchers, and at least four Springbok rugby captains.[11] Originally an English-medium and later bilingual university, Pretoria was gradually appropriated by Afrikaner nationalism and became the training ground for generations of white Afrikaner youths in their exclusive language, Afrikaans.[12] At the center of its emblem, unchanged to this day, sits the powerful symbol of the ox wagon, representing those who made the long and dangerous "trek" from the more liberal Cape to occupy this northern territory and establish the Transvaal province, its capital city Pretoria, and its race-regulating institutions.[13]

It was this venerable Afrikaner institution that I joined in the middle of 2000 as its first black dean of education. This was a completely new experience for me, having worked up to this point teaching and leading only in black schools and black universities. Yet I was excited about working in a completely new terrain, attracted as I always am by challenges that render me a stranger and intruder into a new culture.

The first suggestion of what I could expect at Pretoria came unexpectedly. At a presentation I made to the Parliamentary Portfolio Committee on Education in Cape Town a few months before taking up the Pretoria job, a white Afrikaner colleague from my prospective Faculty of Education[14] was in attendance at these hearings and congratulated me on my appointment as dean. "The faculty was fully supportive of your selection," she said. "You know why?" At that moment I anticipated responses that might have included my experience as dean in other places, my Stanford Ph.D., my research publications and leadership, and the other kinds of things that should count in choosing academic leaders. "It's because you speak Afrikaans," she offered. I did not have the guts to tell her that Afrikaans was not my first language, that I had not spoken the language actively for a long time (there was little Afrikaans in Durban, where I was based for five years), and that when I tried it was a very shaky Afrikaans. Her response certainly got my attention about what mattered in this citadel of Afrikaner power; yet even then I could not have anticipated *how much* the language mattered.

I was asked to come to UP by its charismatic vice-chancellor and principal, an agricultural economist of some distinction and a worldly man, having worked at the World Bank and been called on to advise Mandela's government on economic policy. Dr. Johan van Zyl was a powerful, smart, and young Afrikaner, with his roots in the city and the university, having done all his degrees at Pretoria. He was also a political entrepreneur who read the signs of change and decided, at a considerable pace, to transform UP in light of the new realities surrounding it.[15] Whether he had a deep sense of social justice I am still not sure, but what he did have was an uncanny mind as a strategist, and he was going to position this university opportunistically within the new political ecology that surrounded it.

I felt comfortable with this man, despite an offer from another prestigious university at a higher level of appointment. But it was the complexity and unfamiliarity of the change problem at Pretoria, and its seeming determination to transform, that gave me a sense that here I could actually do things that might contribute to making this a truly South African university. Van Zyl departed all too soon thereafter to head a major Afrikaans insurance company in Cape Town, but he left an indelible mark on the institution. He was cautious in his assessment, though: "I have turned the ship around; the problem is it is still floating in the same direction." The administrative headquarters of the university is called *Die Skip* (the Ship), after the design of the building.

Central to van Zyl's strategy was to bring senior black leaders into the institution, including deans, and this is how I got there. There was a problem, though; he was obliged to do an interview in an open process even though he had his candidate in mind. I showed up for this process and was the first to be interviewed, followed by three other academics, all white Afrikaners from the Faculty I was to lead. Immediately after my interview, van Zyl invited me to his office to discuss the financial terms and logistical arrangements, while his colleagues continued to conduct the interviews with my competitors.

I raise this incident since it speaks volumes about the kind of university that is Pretoria. Here the leader at the top of this very hierarchical institution has all the power. Even though he formally reports to and is appointed by the University Council, there is a tremendous amount of trust invested in the leader to take charge and make decisions that would, in most cases, simply be ratified by the governing authority. Though this was procedurally in bad taste, and certainly challengeable on legal grounds, few would bat an eyelid as the chief executive negotiated an appointment with a new dean while selection interviews were still under way with other candidates for the same position.

This is the environment into which I came in June 2000.[16] There were other black people, of course, but mainly in gardening, security, and tearooms, and always under the authority of a white person. The faculty was white, except for one or two junior staff who came in just before me as the university decided to open its doors to accommodate the new South Africa. All the professors were white, all the heads of department were male, and all the white administrative staff were Afrikaners.

When I walked into my office, the white secretary jumped around in anxiety, grabbing papers without purpose, and moving behind her desk as if she had just seen a ghost. It was the second unnerving experience in a matter of moments, for just before then I had walked down a plush corridor with the walls on each side carrying large portraits of stern and austere Afrikaner men, the former deans of this Faculty. They seemed to look right through you, and I wondered at that point what black students would feel and think if they had to negotiate this clean, cold, and intense white space.

I was in strange territory indeed.

To understand why this was an unlikely place for me to find myself as an employee, let alone as dean, it is important to understand a little bit about my biography.[17]

I came into the world at a time when the oppressive regime of laws of the newly installed Apartheid government was beginning to bite. Like so many black families, my own suffered the trilogy of losses—the power of the franchise, the security of property, and the cohesion of community—that did serious damage to the self-esteem of those negatively classified as "nonwhites." In fact, in the year I was born (1956) blacks were finally struck off the common voters' roll. During the decades that followed, whole communities were regularly uprooted and dispersed to places like the windswept Cape Flats in order to clear prime living areas for white residence. As I stood teaching about ecological conservation in my biology classroom, my high school students stared out the windows watching the heavy-duty tractors bring down the last of their homes in the well-told story of "forced removals" from the historic inner city in Cape Town called District Six.

My experience of growing up on the edges of survival in the gang-ridden townships of Cape Town was intense, and it bred within me a deep anger and resentment toward whites. By the time I was introduced to the philosophy of black consciousness, I found this assertive thinking that made black identity and black power central to its ideological tenets much more appealing than the nonracialism of Nelson Mandela's African National Congress. I had firm views about white privilege and a very clear understanding about redistribution from white hands back to the original inhabitants of the land.

My friends reminded me that I had sworn never to teach in a white university. Yet here I was, intrigued by this foreign place, with its overwhelmingly white body of students and staff, and a familiar but uneasy language. Like many black South Africans, I felt uncomfortable with Afrikaans; this was, after all, the language that the oppressor forced upon black schools and that led to the massive student uprising of 1976. Around me, the artworks, people, photographs on the walls, architecture, textbooks, seating patterns, formal dress, ways of speaking, and medium of communication—all told the same story about authority, hierarchy, identity, culture, masculinity, and power.

There was one difference, though, and this was that despite my being black I was also dean. This meant, at UP, an instinctive deference and submission to the leader—something I had not seen anywhere else in my previous roles as an academic head. This created a tension for some colleagues, especially older men: the difficulty of accepting a black man and the obligation of respecting a faculty dean. I became aware of an authority to speak on the basis of position alone, not because of any personal qualities, demonstrated experience, or moral standing. "You need not ask us what to do," confided one colleague. "We expect you to tell us what we should do."

It was clear to me that initiating anything at this stage would be a bad idea. I needed to listen. So for three months I did just that: listen to students, to academics, to heads of departments, to workers in the common rooms, to parents, to communities, and to other deans and professors in the university. This was the beginning of my personal transformation, a process that would continue for seven years as I started to reach below the surface features of institutional certainty, cultural assertion, and moral pretense. What I saw was a fearful people, anxious about personal futures and institutional fate; concerned about jobs and security; nervous about "transformation" and what it might portend; and aware of the fragility of language, custom, and culture. Everywhere around me, I witnessed a community struggling to come to terms with loss and change.

## Immersion

At UP I have had some of the most profound and life-changing experiences that any human being could expect to face in one career. This intense interaction with white Afrikaners as teacher, leader, manager, administrator, preacher, sports fan, workshop presenter, advisor, and counselor generated the data from which this book is composed.

I spent hours with white university students, together with and separately from black students, behind closed doors and in open forums, talking about the past and the future. I visited their homes and attended their churches. I addressed them at Afrikaans youth camps once set aside for Afrikaners and still looking ominously all-white. I signed up as a fan of the local rugby team, the Blue Bulls, and perched myself with students and colleagues in *die losie* (the spectator box) at *Loftus Versfeld* (the Bulls' home ground) for every home game as I adopted the marketing slogan "my blood is blue."

I visited the schools of my university students to understand the social and cultural processes that bring white Afrikaans students into university with such powerful memories about the past and such dismal anticipation of the future. I did countless workshops and presentations to white high school students, in general, and to Afrikaner youths in particular. I listened carefully to their anxious and sometimes angry questions.

I visited the principal of every Afrikaans high school in and around Pretoria, insisting on one-on-one meetings to discuss their concerns about education broadly and the training of teachers in particular. Some of these meetings were very intense, especially with principals of the elite public schools, who made sure I understood that my charge was to retain the Afrikaans language; these were angry middle-aged men.

I also worked with the principals of white Afrikaner schools who signaled their deliberate intent to transform their schools. This got me into the most intense spaces, emotionally and politically, where parents, teachers, school governors, and managers grappled openly with the problem of how to retain the best knowledge of the past and yet transform such knowledge for greater inclusiveness. These schools, as I wrote in several places,[18] worked against the grain of their social and cultural biographies by opening themselves fully to the prospects of a new South Africa. The mission of these schools was not simply to grant access to black students but to bring in black teachers and extend the curriculum in pursuit of a broader cosmopolitanism.

I spoke at, attended, and participated in heated debates and contro-
versies at Afrikaner cultural festivals from the *Klein Karoo Nasionale
Kunstefees* (KKNK) in the southern Cape to *Aardklop* in the northwest of
the country. I addressed what was until recently a racially exclusive and
socially offensive organization, the Broederbond (now reconstituted as
the Afrikaner Bond),[19] where I found only men, a massive old Bible, and
a routine of Afrikaner rituals on a very dark night in a poor suburb in
the north of Pretoria; once there, I genuinely feared for my life. I also
spoke at meetings of longstanding cultural institutions of the Afrikaner
such as the *Afrikaanse Taal- en Kultuurvereniging* (ATKV),[20] and I addressed the Afrikaans churches in their various expressions of Dutch
Reformed theology.[21]

I had hundreds of white Afrikaner parents pass through my office
at UP. In this culture, parents take a direct interest in their children's
university education and regularly visit with their children to discuss
everything from academic grades to campus adjustment. This is no different from the kind of interaction occurring between parents and learners in the school context. No other grouping of South Africans has such
an intense parent-child interaction at the university level. The parental
meetings provided direct insight into the knowledge and memories of the
first generation, of those who lived under, benefited from, and advanced
the cause of Apartheid over the past three or more decades.[22]

The parents, always respectful of the dean, would often engage me
directly on complex and difficult issues regarding their children, the
university, and the society. Nowhere was this interaction more intense
than when parents expressed themselves about loss of the Afrikaans
language as the sole medium of instruction at Pretoria, and the consequences for their children.

I frequently addressed parents at schools through meetings organized
by school governing bodies. I walked and talked with parents in the malls
around Pretoria. I addressed men's groups and women's groups, often
organized by parents of my students. I advised parent assemblies on how
to open their schools, and on the dangers of racial isolation. I addressed
thousands of Afrikaner parents at school prize givings and special events
from Pretoria to Cape Town, including visits to parents in deep rural
areas of the country. I addressed parents (and often grandparents) when

they showed up every year for the twin events of orientation (called Open Day) in midyear and the official welcoming of new students at the beginning of the following year.

I communicated with Afrikaners through an invited column for the newspaper *Beeld*, in which I wrote a regular monthly article that both affirmed the positive things in Afrikaans culture and community and criticized the negative things such as racism and *baasskap*[23] that threatened to derail our democracy.[24] I spoke about the good things happening in Afrikaans schools, such as the strong learning and teaching culture, and the bad things, such as keeping out black children and teachers under the pretense of protecting language rights. I drew attention to those principals, teachers, and students who lived their lives against the grain of Afrikaans conservatism, who broke with tribal mentality, and who exemplified the kind of decency that should mark post-Apartheid society. This column attracted widespread attention, and it led to many emails and letters from readers.

I sat through and participated in countless university meetings at all levels discussing issues of "employment equity," given the lack of progress in the appointment of black academics generally and especially in middle and senior management positions. I sat in the senate[25] and on the council,[26] as the senate representative. Both gave me unique insights into the mind of the institution with respect to knowledge of the past and anxieties about the future. I was at one time advisor to the university principal, in a small group of about five persons, on what South Africans call *transformation*[27] as it applies to higher education. I led research into the institutional culture of UP and would regularly be asked to offer an experiential and analytical account[28] on the state of race, identity, and culture among the citizens of this large organization.

I taught students in the classroom, undergraduates (mostly by invitation) and postgraduates (mostly by assignment). This is where I would gain direct experience of student anxieties about knowledge of the past and their struggles with knowledge of the present. Invariably, discussions in class would flow over into confrontations and questioning in my office. Students, perhaps too intimidated to meet the dean in his office, would send handwritten notes or emails conveying their concerns, their hurts, and their aspirations. Students used the arrangement instituted when I became dean—that first-years could see me without an appointment—to full effect in the early morning and late afternoon. The students I taught would invite me to their schools to observe their professional work while they were on "teaching practice." Since my teaching is and has always been interactive, this approach opened up spaces for dialogue, sometimes hurtful and angry, but always honest and engaging.

I lived with the students outside the classroom. I took them to movies, sometimes en masse, especially the first-year students. I sat with them on the campus lawns and ate with them in the cafeteria, always talking about change. Living together in the residences more than learning together in the classroom often caused racial tensions to boil over—and for good reason since, historically, "the residence as a spiritual home for many students became more important than their university."[29] The residences are where I collected the raw emotions of white and black students. It was the residential conflicts between young men that led to a series of after-hours workshops with white and black boys, separately, that yielded crucial insights into knowledge, memory, and identity.

I invited ten first-year students every week to sit down with me for lunch. There were several goals here: to convey the idea that the dean's office and that of his leadership team were accessible spaces for students; to induct first-years into a new way of thinking about authority; to bring together black and white students in a social and less formal setting, often for the first time in their lives; and to signal the kinds of expectations we held about the embrace of race, language, and culture within this single space, one faculty with its own campus within a large university. It is for this reason that the instruction given was that five of the students should be black and five white, for without this requirement they would come by tribe.

Of course I had another job, doing the routines of administration and management that so many deans actually thrive on and that many think to be their only labor: conducting meetings, defending budgets, allocating resources, implementing work schedules, promoting academics, revising curricula, disciplining staff and students, communicating with parents, recruiting prospective undergraduate and postgraduate students, deliberating on succession, advertising and filling vacant posts, fighting for air conditioning and parking spaces, and that most sublime of decanal duties, signing staff leave forms.

Every one of these seemingly mundane events was an opportunity to understand how this strange institution worked, and what happened to such an ordered environment when someone threw the proverbial wrench into the works. Through the many days of frustration, especially in moments when logic gave way to authority in this centralized structure, I took solace in the fact that I could record these events, especially critical incidents, and that I could discuss their meaning with fellow black and white intellectuals who were similarly energized about making this ethnic institution a truly open university.

These are the data, from richly variegated sources, that come together in this account of living history. The case, loosely framed, is UP and its extension into families, schools, churches, sports fields, festivals, and other living spaces that radiate from and reflect back onto this prestigious Afrikaans institution.

Perhaps the most testing of my leadership experiences was the restructuring processes that constantly loomed over and threatened the Faculty of Education and the university itself.

## Restructuring

When I arrived at UP, the senior management had already decided to incorporate the small and ineffectual Faculty of Education under the larger Faculty of Humanities, a treatment not uncommon in other South African universities at the time.[30] The new administrative handbooks were in print and had Education relegated to the status of a school under Humanities. This threatened loss of academic identity and stand-alone status was traumatic for the academic staff in Education. The appointment of a new dean was a temporary reprieve, and this might have contributed some support for the new leader.[31]

But then something quite dramatic and unforeseen happened. The minister of education announced that colleges of education,[32] nondegree-granting institutions that prepared elementary school teachers, would be rationalized. Most were closed down, and a few were incorporated into faculties of education of nearby universities. As it turned out, UP was to absorb the nearby all-white Afrikaans teacher training college, called *Normaal Kollege Pretoria* (NKP).[33] Deracializing the white Faculty of Education was set back, for now another cast of all-white lecturers, steeped in the fundamentalist dogma of Apartheid teacher education,[34] had to be absorbed into a university environment that was in the throes of change. This incorporation[35] saga was to become a receptacle into which white trauma and white loss would be poured.[36] I was to observe directly this crushing of identity and the intense anxiety—especially among older Afrikaner women who had long enjoyed job protection in all-white colleges inside all-white suburbs—suddenly finding themselves at the mercy of a black provincial government that could instantly deploy them to black townships.[37] The background symbolism was overwhelming: a new black dean was to make decisions about older and younger white Afrikaners—about who would stay and who would go.

Once the college was incorporated, and the old Faculty had moved onto the beautiful terrain of the former college of education, the organizational reframing of the new structure had to take place. This involved decisions about new staffing, inherited resources, choice of departmental leadership, the kinds and numbers of academic departments, a new curriculum—in short, an unprecedented scale and intensity of change that my colleagues had never been part of.

For years, in the decades since 1948, Afrikaner nationalist sentiment was successfully installed and defended in white Afrikaans schools and universities. There was an everyday character of normality in white university life generally and in the preparation of teachers in particular. The curriculum was never questioned, only obeyed. The authority of the leader was paramount, and any dissent was punished swiftly and abruptly. There was no racial tension, for white lecturers taught white students about white society with a white curriculum. The whites were from the same cultural and religious base, broadly speaking, and so there was very little concern about or need to engage *difference*. Everybody communicated in Afrikaans, the textbooks and lectures were in the same language, Afrikaans-only symbols and signboards appeared everywhere, only Afrikaans students were admitted, and with few exceptions only Afrikaans-speaking lecturers were hired.

Men were promoted and women applauded. Men were professors and most women were secretaries and entry-level "lecturers."[38] Students, even university students, were children whose parents might be called at home if their offspring missed a class. Many students at the time called their lecturers *Oom* (Uncle) and *Tannie* (Aunt). Discipline was strict. Those who made the tea in the faculty kitchen, tended the gardens, and removed the dirt were black. Those who gave orders, supervised their work, and disciplined their labors were white. Whites were in charge and blacks were said to be happy. There were seldom any serious protests in this environment, no student revolt against tuition fee hikes or living conditions. For the most part, stability and peace reigned on the campuses of UP; there was little conflict.

This occluded space had seldom seen or experienced fundamental change. The practice of teaching and learning was deemed universal and scientific, unencumbered by and unconscious of the broader politics and pedagogy of Apartheid. In fact, the teachers, students, and administrators inside this insular space assumed normality; everything they did made sense to them and to those looking in. The reputation for delivering solid and committed teachers into the surrounding schools was something left undisturbed for a long time. The people who worked here exuded professionalism and dedication to the task. Schools worked because of them. Change?

Then, without warning, change was everywhere. Jobs long guaranteed for white men and women were under threat. The college, originally built as a protected enclave for the training of white Afrikaner teachers, would now close and its staff and buildings would be incorporated into UP.[39] There was talk of "equity" everywhere, and so the threat, real or imagined, was black people and, for the college lecturers, also university people. The curriculum had to change, not only in response to a broader and more inclusive vision of ideas, people, and history but also in response to new regulations in teacher education coming from the government. College lecturers, who had long built their identity on the ability to train future teachers, were now themselves faced with the need for being trained in their new role as university academics; and in this unfamiliar role, they had also to become researchers.

Classes had to be taught in Afrikaans and in English, given the gradual changes in the demography of the undergraduate class as more and more black students started to come into the Faculty. This was a very, very difficult transition; several of the Afrikaans-speaking academics were simply not competent to teach in any other language, and now it was English, the language of the British, the colonialists. There were emotional and political hurdles to scale here, along with linguistic ones.[40]

These changes in substance were to be accompanied by changes in symbolism: departmental designations that betrayed old Apartheid epistemologies had to be renamed and the titles of courses had to reflect a new set of social realities on the outside of this once-settled, segregated space. Even teaching and assessment methods were rendered suspect; these too had to change.

Initially, I led this process of change, and as more and more like-minded scholars were hired from the outside, they too started to take forward this leadership at the departmental level. In these intense interactions with attendant but suspicious colleagues, much was learned about the meaning of change in this institutional and national context. I did several months of intensive research training for all the former college staff who were hired to teach at the university. This itself was a challenge, since college staff typically taught in the mornings and left for home in the early afternoon. I also led the training in advanced university teaching, again confronting willing attendees, but by this time my colleagues had started to challenge (albeit cautiously) the new approach to pedagogy and assessment.

The point to amplify is that this was not simply change within the context of normal organizational life, the cycles of change and restructuring that tend to overwhelm universities everywhere. This was university change in the context of a country that was itself transforming dramatically in the aftermath of Apartheid. What happened inside took its cue, and gained legitimacy, from what was happening outside. What happened outside heralded clear expectations about what should happen inside.

But this was also change in one Faculty inside a large organization, UP. So what I tried to do with the Faculty leadership was constrained or enabled by the kinds of changes and levels of support that were available within the university's senior management.

UP is a top-down, hierarchical organization with all authority vested in a single leader at the apex; it is an authority that can ignore senior executives in making final decisions. Entire meetings can be conducted with one man speaking. In this organization, the unions, students, and other stakeholders have little authority in final decisions; this authority vests in the institutional leader. Here the Senate, the highest academic body, functions mainly to approve, not to challenge, debate, or overturn executive decisions; this body will never seek to reverse what comes from the top.

Another mark of organizational culture is that potential and even severe managerial crises are privately handled, seldom making it into a public forum or the media (except for student protests). In this context, middle management is technically competent and delivers on a tight schedule, a fixed budget, and firm performance outcomes, using exact data on most managerial functions. Management is founded on predictability, and sudden changes in the external environment create serious crisis and instability; such changes are eventually managed in a highly disciplined fashion. At UP there are reliable data on every management event, but the data answer narrow managerial and operational questions only.

Understandably, ordinary managerial processes are slowed down in this hierarchical system because nobody is trusted to make a final decision at any level without the whole system knowing about it (as an example, appointment of new staff). Everyday managerial decisions at UP are based on consensus; more precisely, decisions are engineered or channeled toward consensus. Voting is rare, and always in a noncontested context. Also, loyalty to the leader is the only kind of loyalty allowed; criticism carries direct penalties, and this engenders a deeply apologetic culture in the discourses of approach among staff.

There is superficial *beleefdheid* (politeness) in the UP management culture, but it conceals a vicious capacity for managerial assault on *onderdaniges* (subordinates). In cases of possible conflict or in order to convey authority, management comes in the form of the ubiquitous *opdrag* (authoritative instruction). The management culture is oriented toward conflict avoidance; direct confrontation is rare, and when it happens it causes bewilderment; the opdrag suffices as resolution. Stakeholders trust management to act responsibly and in the best interests of the institution; a deeply held subservience accepts and allows for a paternalistic role through management.

Management behavior at a place like UP derives from long-established traditions that have their roots in a mix of civil service and authoritarian political cultures, and that lend predictability to processes of governance and administration. Management discourses revolve around issues of efficiency, *belyning* (alignment), order, compliance, and control. Management decisions, once taken, are represented as unified (even when they are not); this enables a strong central role for executive authority.

Management in this culture is therefore highly successful in achieving hard targets—such as financial stability—but struggles with the soft targets—such as institutional transformation. To fail, in this management context, is to bring shame on oneself (*ek het droog gemaak*, "I messed up"); and therefore the most common response to failure is to blame downward. Here the protests of dominant groups center on *the politics of displacement*: what we used to enjoy we no longer can, because of change.

This summary shows both the strength and the hardiness of this well-entrenched organizational way of doing things, as well as its dilemmas when new people and new ideas from outside the cultural frame begin to enter this kind of university. Responsiveness to the government requirement that the university open its doors to blacks is largely the kind of reaction of such an institution to external authority under any circumstances. What happens after access is allowed is another matter.

The process of change at UP was and remains an extremely complex transaction. On the one hand, senior management is eager to be seen responding to state imperatives with its directives for transformation; on the other hand, however, it enacts these intentions within a conservative institutional culture and a rigid organizational bureaucracy. As dean of education, it took me some time to understand these complex realities, such as the institutional approach to planning.

Well-meaning strategic plans were developed and refined for months, sometimes years. New organization charts enticed with a flat structure that promised to delegate authority to lower levels, to instill broader ownership of change, and to foster the values of an incipient democracy. Profound statements of intent set out clear targets for achieving racial equity commitments, especially among staff. Paragraphs appeared about changing the institutional culture in ways that welcomed all campus dwellers into the university community. Brochures showed smiling white and black faces on a serene, beautiful campus.

The reality was very different. Every time the university took stock of its equity gains, it would find that it fell far short, and at one time it actually hired more white men than any other category of employee—the one group overrepresented in the employ of the institution. Black staff, once hired, would often leave soon afterward, making the equity profile even bleaker.

## Negotiating Change

It was within this context that the Faculty of Education sought to accelerate transformation against the grain of organizational culture and political inertia. As a leader bent on transforming this white university, my task required patience and demanded political skill working with conservative colleagues. It could not be done without seeking allies and making pacts at all levels. It required time to be spent investing from below and building cultures and allegiances that would support new initiatives. It called for courageous action with respect to hiring new staff from outside the institutional culture. It meant hard work convincing powerful people in the organization that the changes proposed in Education worked in the university's favor. It demanded building the confidence of external constituencies, especially schools and parents, so that there was a continued flow of students—the most important funding unit—into the university from the traditional white community.

This requires some explanation. No black student in South Africa intends to become a teacher. Black high school graduates would rather stay unemployed than study teaching, if becoming a teacher were their only study option. The reason is simple. Black schools are, with few exceptions, chaotic and unstable places that deliver poor results with mediocre teachers following an unpredictable timetable. After twelve years of such apprenticeship of experience, teaching is the most unattractive profession of all to black students.

White students have the opposite experience, coming from stable schools with qualified and committed teachers working in a pleasant physical environment and where the full range of cultural and sporting activities makes for a strong and holistic education. Whatever the content of curriculum and cultural transmission, these students identify strongly with teacher role models from an early age, and many have a vision of becoming such a teacher in their own career. This is especially true of white Afrikaans students, who come from a community with very deep commitments to education that have yet to be fully understood in educational inquiry.[41]

The change problem in this context had multiple dimensions. There was the obvious financial concern: a neglect of the transmission belt for white students (the Afrikaans schools) would collapse the Faculty since students would and could choose other Afrikaans institutions. This meant that shifting the language policy toward English too quickly would alienate Afrikaans students, who have always constituted at least 80 percent of the undergraduate class. This meant therefore that changing the equity profile of the staff could also not proceed too rapidly since this would invariably bring in black academics, who could teach only in English. This also meant that the only way in which to break the racial cycle of reproduction was to begin aggressive recruitment of reluctant black students, for at base this would enable the other dimensions of change to be introduced. In the meantime, all these change variables had to be held in constant interplay.

This book cannot therefore be a story about linearity, strong-willed leaders, an overriding moral correctness of change, and muscling in on the racial and cultural order of a large university; it is, rather, about the struggle for change and what that does to people. Most important, it is about how white Afrikaner students experience this change and what it means for them in terms of remembering an inherited past and acting on an uncertain future.

## Insider / Outsider

The instrument is the researcher, as the textbooks on qualitative research put it, and this requires reflection on my personal position and racial identity within the institutional context. I was and still am an outsider to UP. It was not simply that I came from the outside. It was that I constantly felt myself to be an outsider. To be sure, I was generally accepted warmly by my colleagues at all levels of the university, and I can recount only a few occasions of direct confrontation on anything serious. It is, however, not only what individual people did or did not do in response to my presence as academic or researcher or dean. It was, rather, the ensemble of actions, symbols, rituals, and routines together conveying the message that I was from somewhere else. The paintings on the walls, the traditions of greeting, the ceremonies of prayer, the repertoire of the choir, the linguistic expressions, the formalities of dress, and the language of bodies communicate who is in and who is out.

Being an outsider was, however, also about regnant epistemologies within the institution, the kinds of knowledge that were strange and distant, sometimes offensive. I did not understand the positivist impulse applied to decision making and the deployment of a rigid organizational logic that substituted for genuine deliberation. I could not access the kind of science that accepted the world as given, fixed, and knowable. I was stirred, often irritated, by the language of certainty, the dogma of predictability, the sure-mindedness that governed everyday thought and practice. It was the link between knowledge and authority that disturbed most—knowledge graded for truth depending on who was speaking and how high up the hierarchy the speaker was located.

Knowledge was, and still largely is, white knowledge. There has never been, at an institutional level, an engagement about the meanings of received knowledge. This does not mean that there are not individuals and even departments in which knowledge has been the subject of intense contestation and change. But in the university as a whole, *institutional knowledge* has not been rendered problematic in the course of South Africa's otherwise remarkable social transition. If transformation were going to happen at all, it would have to happen at the level of knowledge.

Not to recognize radical theory or even liberal progressive thought, if that were your only life, is to feel extremely alienated within a conservative institution. Not being able to engage feminist thinking or post-Marxian analysis or critical pedagogy within the everyday intellectual life of an institution is to feel left out. Recognizing knowledge only as narrow instrumentality or meaningless abstraction is not only nerve-racking; it also works to deaden the intellectual impulse and to render the incoming campus dweller foreign.

As outsider, though, I was also determined to be an insider, however incomplete that process and ambition would always be. I tried to improve my facility in Afrikaans. I attended formal and informal institutional events to demonstrate interest. I made sure I listened to and embraced all. As indicated earlier, I made myself part of the religious, cultural, social, intellectual, and even political lives of Afrikanerdom in order to lessen distance and allow me to lead with greater responsiveness to students and staff, parents, and community. I knew that I could not be an insider, in the fullest sense; but I was not going to stand on the sidelines and either bemoan outsider status or withdraw from engaging on the inside.

This was hard, emotional work, and my soul felt it. It was also difficult political work, an endless confrontation with power. It was in the course of these struggles that I came across the insightful depiction of this insider-outsider dilemma in Debra Meyerson's term *tempered radicals*.[42] These are people who have different values from their organizations but who nevertheless try to influence change while walking the tightrope between conformity and rebellion. Expressed colloquially, they rock the boat but stay in the boat. I too found myself tempered by the organizational culture, history, and politics and yet within it, pushing for a deeper and radical change of the place.

It should be said, though, that I learned to enjoy the position of outsider. By holding up the workings of the institution as a foreign subject, I was able to see things that those who had lived there all their lives, and for whom the institution was originally intended, could not. Outsider status, the stance of not-being-at-home, yields valuable analytical advantage, and it is from this vantage point that my analysis proceeds.

Being an insider, of course, risks losing one's own identification within a dominant institutional culture. Sometimes black or women leaders do that, with disastrous consequences. Buying in comes at a huge cost, for the outsiders who lose their identity on the inside can be ejected as easily as they are drawn in. In a crisis, outsider identity can be used as a target, the reason for excluding and removing. "You don't really understand this place," I often heard, and without further explanation this shuts up the outsider eager to be drawn in.

The perception of insider or outsider status rests in part on the subjective understanding of the newcomer, and it is also attributed or bestowed on the newcomer by the insiders. When I invited the grounds staff—

those maintaining the beautiful landscape surrounding the campus—to my office for an introductory lunch with their new dean, all the workers were black and the supervisor, as usual, was white.

"What are the kinds of challenges you face as workers at Pretoria?" I asked.

The white supervisor rose to his feet and in front of a huge audience of only black workers said, "Well, Professor, things are going well on this campus, but you know how lazy these blacks are." In an instant, the supervisor had separated me, a black dean, from my fellow citizens, the black workers, and made me a conspiring insider. There was also the white colleague who came to me after one of my research training sessions and politely and with good intent said, "You keep referring to yourself as black, but I do not see you as black; you are one of us." The first respondent had to receive a public but gentle reprimand, in front of the other workers, for obvious racism. The second respondent did not require a response. In both cases, I became aware of the dangers of an insider status bestowed on myself as black dean, not always with harmful intent.

This book will convey the tensions between being an insider and remaining an outsider. The stories and analysis will show the slipping between the two, the desire to be part of the lives of people whom I serve and yet being constantly and often unconsciously reminded that I was, in the end, an outsider. Throughout, this tension is seen as productive and one that brings the capacity for a kind of analytical engagement that would not be possible by taking the position of either an angry outsider or an unreflective insider. It enabled me to bear witness.

## Conclusion

Bearing witness carries a powerful and personal meaning. *Witness* reminds me of my evangelical roots, and the responsibility for telling truthfully and fearlessly what I saw, what happened, and how things changed. It requires me to bear witness to the prior condition of racial blinkeredness and the new state of being able to see a common humanity. *Bearing* suggests heaviness, a burden on your back—and that it was. It remains difficult to talk about my students, for many of those intense, fearful, angry, and anxious exchanges were very personal, for them and for me. This heaviness tested my physical, emotional, spiritual, and intellectual being in ways that I had never encountered before as a teacher and leader in schools and universities. The only reason I could come out of this once-in-a-lifetime experience more fully human was because my students were always there: encouraging, directing, inspiring, and lifting me. In my most difficult moments living through this conservative, white university, there would always be a note under the door, a short email, a reassuring smile, a double-fisted handshake, a thank-you.

# 1    Loss and Change

Through a single announcement, an entire knowledge framework, a way of life and thought, was thrown into disarray.[1]

The nightmare . . . is not knowing what's true. Imagine if you had suddenly learnt that the people, the places, the moments most important to you are not gone, not dead, but what is, had never been. What kind of hell would that be?[2]

The price of sanity for Minnie Pretorius, of suddenly seeing things the way they really are, would be complete breakdown and despair.[3]

ONE COUNTRY, at the tip of a troubled continent, becomes the last of the former colonies and the last of the settler states to yield on white minority rule.[4] Some thought it would never happen; others held it would happen only through a bloodbath with innumerable casualties on both sides. The academic prophets of the time framed ominous questions: "Can South Africa survive?"[5] "Hope for South Africa?"[6] "Endgame in South Africa?"[7] As the internal conflict escalated, studies warned of "time running out"[8] and "five minutes to midnight."[9] But happen it did; Apartheid eventually came to an abrupt and ignominious end.

As the end of the 1980s approached, the unrelenting pressure from outside and the stubborn resistance from inside forced the Afrikaner elites into negotiations as they realized that not changing would eventually cost them more than trying to sustain a system that had become anachronistic in a postcolonial world. The political scientists continue to contest what exactly brought the end of Apartheid and the transition to democracy.[10]

It is important to remember that not too long before the 1990s South Africa was in good company. There were other states in the North and the South where racism and racial rule were enshrined in policies and laws. But times had changed. As the old order of colonial rule in the Third World and legalized discrimination in the First World started to unravel, South Africa stood alone as a "pariah"[11] among democratic states. It stood its ground for what seemed an interminably long time, even after the independence of the last two regional states, Zimbabwe in 1980 and Namibia in 1990.

Secret negotiations started with the principal liberation movement, the ANC, long before ordinary South Africans got to know about them. Quiet meetings with imprisoned black leaders inside the country and exiled leaders outside the country continued at the initiative of corporate leaders, academics, diplomats, and secret emissaries of the Apartheid government. You would not have known about these clandestine meetings at the time, for the brutal hand of state repression was still making itself felt inside the black townships of South Africa. But in addition to "secret diplomacy," the so-called go-between activities[12] and track-two diplomacy[13] were both crucial to the process of transition in that they "reduced threat perceptions among white participants . . . and helped create a sense of negotiation possibility complementary to decision-makers' sense that negotiations were necessary."[14]

White public anger was trained on those meeting openly with the enemy,[15] and eventually news leaked out about the more secret meetings, but nothing could alter the fact that the Apartheid regime was talking to the banned ANC. Frederick Willem (known more commonly by his initials, F. W.) de Klerk, the last of the white presidents, did what his obstinate predecessor (P. W. Botha) lacked the courage to do: he unbanned the liberation movements, eased repulsive race laws, and freed political prisoners. In the political phraseology of the time, he crossed the Rubicon.

Many whites would like it to be known that these political reforms happened on their own terms, that these changes were possible once

blacks were mature enough to rule, once black leaders accepted that violence was not the answer, and once the Communist threat was no longer
real after the fall of the Berlin Wall. Whites would have done this anyway; it was just a matter of waiting for the right time. This is the self-
congratulatory argument of former Defense Minister Magnus Malan in
his autobiography *My Life with the South African Defense Force*.[16]

Of course this was a fiction, a belated justification for what had become inevitable. Sanctions worked, bringing pressure on the faltering
economy of the Apartheid state and threatening the one other thing
that white elites cared about: their material welfare as a group. Boycotts
worked, keeping South Africa out of major international academic, social,
and sporting events. To be sure, all kinds of sanction-busting activities
were funded and pursued by the Apartheid state.[17] Support started to dry
up from the last of the regimes that winked at South African Apartheid.
For years, the leaders of the United States and the United Kingdom had
complained about Apartheid racism and the exploitation of black people
with a slap on the wrist for the white rulers, but they were willing to
tolerate such backwardness for the sake of some broader geopolitical
interests, or as some then argued, some common racial interests.

But even within those Western states that preferred "constructive
engagement"[18] to outright condemnation of racist rule, their own citizens
were standing up and demanding that their government withdraw support and that their business communities remove investments from South
Africa. Isolated at the tip of a continent, surrounded by liberated states,
paralyzed by internal resistance, and under growing demand for change
from Western powers, Apartheid could not hold out any longer. When
F. W. de Klerk stepped up to the podium in Parliament to end Apartheid on February 2, 1990, he was not acting alone. The announcement
was a calculated decision of the white elites: act now or lose everything.
One thing the white and black elites feared in equal measure was what
would happen if the international icon of political liberation and human
decency, Nelson Mandela, died in prison. It would be the beginning of
the end; a bloodbath might become a reality after all.

In the event, Nelson Mandela is released, but not before some of his
imprisoned comrades are first freed—"to test the waters," some said.
Initial negotiations start—"talks about talks," the overly cautious nego-

tiators called it. Outside the smoke-filled rooms of the official negotiating forum, violence peaks[19]—"the last kicks of a dying horse," said the expectant liberators. Yet this violence propels negotiations, underlining the risk of nonsettlement of the race question.[20] What South Africa now becomes is neither the product of a revolutionary overthrow of the Apartheid state nor a reforming of the Apartheid system. The new country lies somewhere in between, the product of a negotiated settlement. This simple fact will determine the depth, pace, and direction of the change trajectory that follows the first democratic elections in 1994, which the ANC wins decisively with 62.7 percent of the national vote.

There are clear victors from this negotiated settlement, and as time goes by the rigid clauses and negotiated understandings that protect white privilege begin to dissolve as the new nationalists take office under the impressive leadership of Nelson Mandela. The sun sets on protective clauses, and former white rulers complain of betrayal of negotiated agreements on the part of the black elites.[21] Eventually things settle as the terms of the endgame finally dawn on those who ruled with impunity for so long.

Within a short time, power changes hands. It comes as a huge shock to ordinary white citizens. They thought that their leaders would take them into negotiations without giving up too much; that they would continue to enjoy economic privileges, land and language rights, and educational and cultural preservation. The more ambitious among them, the hard right, even expect a "volkstaat"[22] (a separate homeland for Afrikaners) to emerge from the settlement. White elites still quibble among themselves about who sold out whom in those short but intense negotiations.[23]

The black elites waste no time in consolidating power. Parliamentary majorities steer through landmark legislation over the protests of the new political minority, whites. Compromise positions, such as a white second deputy president, become meaningless when the one so positioned, F. W. de Klerk, leads his National Party out of the Government of National Unity as he adjusts to the reality of political defeat.[24] Black and white members of the ANC, on the other hand, are required to support the party line in the new Parliament; some conscientious objectors leave and others are pushed out, but the newfound power of the victors must be enforced.[25] Few expect the overwhelming political authority the ANC will gain within the government and the country. White power, at least in the political domain, has come to an end.

Few countries produce more laws, more "White Papers," more policy positions—a raft of symbolic statements that promise to transform, at its roots, the devastating legacies of Apartheid. Money comes from everywhere to make these ambitions possible, with donors seeking a foothold in this most promising of capitalist states in the developing world. Traditional lenders, including the World Bank, push hard to secure their own influence but are held at arm's length—a cockiness that the new state with its relatively strong economy can afford. Blacks are in power, and things look very, very hopeful.

It is not enough to entrench political power in the formal structures of government, such as Parliament. It is also important to bring to life all kinds of new symbols to draw attention to the changing ownership of the state. Museums and monuments flourish, calling on the new nation to remember the black struggles of the past. New holidays come to life remembering dates in the liberation calendar: Human Rights Day (March 21), Freedom Day (April 27), Youth Day (June 16), and National Women's Day (August 9).[26] The old holidays of Afrikaner nationalism disappear from the calendar, and even their one solemn remembrance recalling the Battle of Blood River—the Day of the Vow—is given broader meaning as the Day of Reconciliation (December 16).

Blacks are in control.

Yet all is not lost to the defeated. Whites are allowed to keep their schools, set their own fees, appoint teachers,[27] decide on their languages, and determine their own admission policies. Museums are not knocked down; the Voortrekker Monument retains its prominence on a hill overlooking the founding city of the "trekkers," Pretoria; the monument of Cecil John Rhodes, the arch imperialist of the region, continues to overlook the University of Cape Town; and the burial sites of the Boers still enjoy prominence in Bloemfontein. Land is not seized and transferred from whites. There are no Nuremberg-type trials for the defeated, no official harassment for those who implemented the vicious policies of Apartheid. What is offered, instead, is a commission, one seeking truth and reconciliation, a necessary experiment that achieves little of either.

Ordinary white South Africans are not fooled. They no longer have exclusive power. Jobs favor blacks. Promotions favor blacks. Appointments and contracts in the public sector favor blacks. The pressure on companies and universities to hire blacks over whites is unrelenting, and potentially costly. Stories are legion of better-qualified whites being overlooked in favor of less-qualified blacks. It is, after all, a black country.

Of course, the consequences of the negotiated settlement are more nuanced than often presented by the defeated. Whites remain better qualified, on average, than blacks. White graduates find jobs more easily than black graduates. The private sector remains dominated by white economic power. Boardrooms remain overwhelmingly white, and decisions about employment and directorships still favor whites (and white males in particular). Whites have accumulated assets on the back of race that yield advantage to successive generations into the foreseeable future. Whites remain, at least in economic terms, much better off on average than black people—a completely foreseeable outcome given the soft terms of transition.

But the empirical status of transition is not what impresses whites. It is the psychological state of being defeated that clouds any interpretation of what is happening in a country where everybody—the black peasant and the white capitalist—has the same vote.

The little twists and turns of the transition compound the feelings of defeat. It is the odd provocation by a leading voice in the presidency claiming that the struggle was about black people in general and Africans in particular.[28] It is the occasional statement of the minister of land affairs about the need to redistribute farmlands to black farmers that raises vivid images of the collapse of Zimbabwe right next door—and that under a black government. It is the constant reminders of black sports administrators and black politicians that quotas must remain in place and that not enough is being done to transform sports such as rugby, touching one of the most sensitive cultural properties of white emotion. It is the pressure on schools to integrate, on universities to appoint more black academics, on boardrooms to hire more black directors. It is a presidential initiative called "the Native Club," where the black intelligentsia assembles to complain about the still-enriched white minority, that raises fears and compounds loss.

When these things happen, feelings of defeat are magnified, and any calm and reasoned appeal to the statistics on race and employment has little meaning when the emotions of loss and change are so palpably felt among the defeated.[29] The victors, on the other hand, are caught up in the throes of winning; nobody pays attention to the pain of losing. "Why should they matter?" assume the victors. "This is our time." Whites were rotten, they brutalized the original peoples of the land, they mercilessly stood by as their leaders with their armies of police and infiltrators deprived mothers of their children, men of their wives, families of their loved ones, all to keep in place an evil system called Apartheid. "They had their time. Who cares about their loss?"

Slowly, even the symbolic recognition of whites through public acts—such as the ground-moving gesture of Nelson Mandela to pull the white captain's number 6 rugby shirt over his head at the emotional Rugby World Cup finals in Johannesburg in 1995—begins to fade. Streets, towns, and cities become unrecognizable as African names displace Afrikaner names. Objections are lodged inside Parliament, and whites take to the streets to protest—something new to most white South Africans, still unaccustomed to the liberties they now enjoy in a democratic state. Those who now object against Afrikaner-to-African name changes often forget that such changes happened in the reverse throughout the 20th century;[30] the protests are about the here and now. But it does not matter; a majority of blacks in the new Parliament ensures that a preferred policy or law or even street name is eventually pushed through.

To be sure, there is recourse to higher authority, and some landmark court reversals of decisions of black political and administrative authority make headlines.[31] But such victories are few, and they are reversible as new laws and refined political strategies overcome temporary reprieves. In the end, the legal challenges do not matter much, for the courts are reluctant to involve themselves in "administrative matters," the things governments are responsible for.

There are those among the new black elite who remember what it means to be politically powerless, and who try to give expression to an inclusiveness that soothes white fears. Some of them even suggest that employment equity, South Africa's version of affirmative action, might require a termination date.[32] This kind of ideological slippage is cannon fodder to black nationalists eager to enhance their political reputations among the majority; discriminating in favor of blacks cannot have an end date—ever. How can a system of white power and privilege that took three and a half centuries to entrench itself be overcome in slightly more than a decade?

Whites read the signs and recognize that the game is up, that with the passage of time their privileged position will be lost forever. Their claim to political voice is already permanently silenced in the new arrangement. Truth and myth mix readily in these narratives of defeat, producing a compelling story about loss.

## Afrikaners, Afrikaans

Nowhere is this sense of defeat more palpably felt than among the majority (60 percent) of whites, the group called Afrikaners. These descendants of mainly Dutch settlers of the 17th century have a moving story to tell of conquest over the English and the blacks in equal measure. Their stories are told with unfettered admiration by the historians of Afrikaner nationalism, such as Herman Giliomee in his massive tome *The Afrikaners*.[33] A disparate group of white settlers from Europe comes to the southernmost tip of Africa, overcomes the elements and the imperialists, establishes a strong tribal identity, and founds one of the longest-surviving and only white nationalist party on the harsh soil of another continent.

They did not leave, as did so many other settler communities in Africa, when white rule ended. Settlers either fled back to the motherland, as from Kenya to England and Mozambique to Portugal, or their numbers were so small that they became unrecognizable within black nationalist landscapes, as in Namibia and Zimbabwe. But even there, at the slightest hint of trouble these already small numbers of whites began to seek solace in the home country. They carried two passports; they could leave on a whim.

Not so in the case of many Afrikaners. They regard South Africa as their home. They have nowhere to go. They resent their English counterparts, those with dual citizenship. Surely no European country would consider such passport status with Afrikaners. It is inconceivable that Belgium or the Netherlands or France would make such primordial connections today to the descendants of the early settlers. Nor would these hardened farmers, teachers, and businessmen require such descendant recognition from Europe; they are African, children of the soil. If they leave at all, it will be the way others leave, including black South Africans to Australia or New Zealand, not by pull of heritage or birthplace but simply as entrepreneurs seeking new ventures, or as African citizens seeking a better life elsewhere, or, let it be said, as white supremacists unwilling to live under black rule. For the majority, however, such migration is either undesirable or unaffordable. They are staying put. This is the land on which they have established their past, and on which they will make their future.

It is, however, not just the conquest of the blacks, once deemed uncivilized savages not worthy of human status, that fueled Afrikaner nationalism. It was the defeat at the hands of Great Britain at the turn of the previous century (1899–1902) that continues to occupy the historical memories of the Afrikaner. The ignominy of the English concentration camps, in which thousands of Afrikaner women and children were starved to death, carries powerful memories into the present. People name their children after Boer heroes from that war, and after place names that mark the graves of those who died in two shameful wars at the end of another century. The *Anglo-Boer War*, say the old history textbooks. The *South African War*, say the new school texts, recognizing that this war involved more than a conflict between two white tribes.

It was this experience of trauma and loss, the feelings of inferiority, and the dread of economic insecurity that constitute the ethnic mobilization thesis of Giliomee and others when they explain the rise of Afrikaner nationalism and the emergence of Afrikaner identity in the 20th century. In these processes, educational institutions would come to play a crucial role.[34]

It is the memory of defeat at the hands of the English and the continued hegemony of English institutions and English power long after the South African War that in part explains the defense of the Afrikaans language. Current generations tell readily of social humiliation at the hands of English speakers, of being regarded as dirty, forced to speak the colonial language, and marginalized as a language grouping long after the first defeat.

For the Afrikaner nationalist historian, these hardy people, the Afrikaners, raised themselves from poverty and defeat to establish a new nation in which they ruled. They used powerful symbols to overcome what not so long ago, less than a hundred years, constituted a Carnegie Commission of Investigation on the Poor White Question in South Africa (1932). Defeated the first time, in that other war, economic times were hard long after the attempt to create a settlement between Afrikaner and Brit in the Union of South Africa in 1910.

The cultural facility they used to uplift themselves from poverty and despair was education, and within it the Afrikaans language. *"Afrikaans was a broodsaak"* (Afrikaans was a bread necessity), said one of their major poets and intellectuals.[35] No other nation has so quickly taken a rudimentary language formed through the interaction of European languages (principally Dutch) with indigenous tongues and created such a powerful new language, Afrikaans. This emotional narrative that carries the Afrikaans language explains why South Africa remains the only country that erected a monument to a language.[36]

It is against this background that the emotional claim of its foremost academic protagonist must be understood as he reflects on Afrikaner history:

The poor were 40–50 percent of the Afrikaner community and without Afrikaans they were powerless, without meaning, doomed to poverty and backwardness, doomed to worthlessness, ready to be forgotten—people without language and without hope. I wish to make the claim that Afrikaans as language of communication and as official language did more to uplift the Afrikaners than work reservation.[37]

It was indeed the connection between the state and language that enabled Afrikaans to be the connective tissue binding together a disparate and desperate group of people. The achievement of white nationalist rule in 1948 under the banner of Apartheid placed power firmly in the hands of the Afrikaners, and this opened up all kinds of possibilities to consolidate white rule in the form of a more virulent Afrikaner nationalism. To this day, for Afrikaners "the strongest sense of a unifying, defining 'essence' is their language, Afrikaans."[38] Yet it was not enough to establish a new language; it was important to ensure that the language was dominant. Afrikaans, with English, was declared a national language. It was made compulsory in schools—a fatal mistake that contributed heavily to the weakening of the white nationalist state starting in the 1970s. Suddenly, white and black children were taking Afrikaans as an official language.

It was the language of officialdom; no one could obtain a birth certificate or a passport without going through the administrative center of Afrikaner nationalism, the city of Pretoria. It was the language of economic transaction, the language that enforced subservience. It was the language that shaped social relations, especially in rural areas; blacks would quickly learn to speak Afrikaans out of economic necessity as farm laborers, store hands, or domestic workers.

To ensure that Afrikaans gained hegemony in the broader society, the language appeared everywhere. No public sign appeared anywhere without showing two languages, Afrikaans and English, often in that order. Whether it was directions to a suburb off a major highway, or a sign indicating public toilets, or the names of public cemeteries, Afrikaans appeared alone or alongside English. Road names changed to celebrate Afrikaner heroes. Hospitals and highways, malls and airports all received Afrikaans designations.

Though defeated on the battlefield by the British, Afrikaners nevertheless emerged to take control not just of the political and economic apparatuses of power but, more successfully, of social and cultural power. Yet at the back of the Afrikaner mind remained the constant memory of that defeat, of *die Engelse*, and how they humiliated a proud tribe. Any attempt, therefore, after the second defeat to once again threaten these potent symbols of resurrection and self-definition, such as Afrikaans, was bound to stir something deep within the collective psyche of the Afrikaner.

As Apartheid crumbles in that "single announcement," the sense of loss is complicated by a sense of shame. In her landmark work on whiteness, Melissa Steyn summarizes their post-Apartheid dilemma insightfully:

For Afrikaners—whatever the ethical issues may be—the end of the Old South Africa cannot but be accompanied by feelings of loss . . . [and] there is certainly an element of shame and guilt—of disgrace—that attaches to the social positioning of the Afrikaner.[39]

## White Spaces, Contested Change

With the transition from Apartheid to democracy in 1994, Afrikaners lose the battle for Afrikaans in the public domain—that is, in state departments and in government facilities, from post offices to railways, from airports to streets. The command language of Afrikaans loses its sure footing as black nationalists take over political power, except in three cultural spheres: schools, churches, and universities.

With the second defeat, the struggle for Afrikaans and to some extent Afrikaner protectionism is now restricted to these three spheres. Of the three, the churches are the most secure; they are the only space in which Afrikaners can be left alone to be white and Afrikaans without interference; they remain the only arena that is, in many cases, still all-white and all-Afrikaans in the new South Africa; true, there is external pressure to change from the broad church community, and there are voices of conscience within the mainstream Afrikaner churches pressing for a broader sense of mission and for recognition by world bodies that once ejected them from the international faith community;[40] but it is entirely up to these churches, once indistinguishable from the state, to decide whether and when they will change at all.

Not so with schools, or not entirely. White schools are institutions under pressure; whereas the period of early transition came with an understanding that schools could control their own destiny as far as teachers and students were concerned, white control has increasingly become a focus of government attention. By setting their fees prohibitively high and by deciding for themselves on crucial matters such as language and admission policies, white middle-class schools effectively keep their schools and their teachers white.

The Afrikaans language has an interesting utility in such contexts. White schools that decide their language policy and in particular the medium of instruction will be only Afrikaans make an important assertion that cultural rights are protected by the Constitution of South Africa.[41] It is the right of the schools to choose their language policy, and on paper mother-tongue instruction enjoys official support in South African education.[42] However, anyone who reads this decision of white Afrikaans schools as a simple cultural assertion around language rights is seriously mistaken. No doubt there are some whites for whom this is nothing other than a language issue, but for many there is a more compelling political agenda.

Since most black students do not speak Afrikaans, and most black teachers cannot teach in this language, Afrikaans becomes a respectable way of keeping out black people without the burden of having to make nasty racial arguments. For this reason, schools in some of the major cities of South Africa remain all-white as far as students are concerned, and all-white as far as teachers matter. Here, perhaps, one finds a neat-and-tidy solution to an otherwise explosive problem. Rural white schools do not have this facility at their disposal. These schools are typically undersubscribed, and even though they too insist on claiming language rights and teaching only in Afrikaans, it is a failing position when there are overcrowded black schools in the area with parents demanding access to the empty classrooms inside these white schools.

Some spectacular legal and political challenges[43] have arisen around these rural white schools, but it is simply too much for a black government, no matter how deep its conciliatory impulses, to concede to white privilege with such blatant inequality staring its poor constituents in the face. How some of these institutions then change is quite absurd, with two schools on one campus—effectively, English and black on one side and Afrikaans and white on the other.[44] But the resentment is palpable and the conflict simmers just below the surface of these racially divided schools.

So the government has started to flex its racial muscle. The argument is that schools have a responsibility to respond to the spirit and substance of education policy. Schools must be integrated; black teachers must enjoy access to white schools. The government wants to review the decisions of school governing bodies around teacher appointments, and not simply approve the lists and the recommendations made to the head of education in each province.[45] The practice with respect to teacher appointments is that schools recommend a candidate from their shortlist and the provincial head of education approves. This administrative routine has to stop, says the government.

This is tricky terrain.

In technical terms, these relatively small numbers of white schools deliver high standards of scholastic performance. Built on decades of advantage, they have accumulated resources and built internal capacities that give white children a decisive head start in the academic race. These schools make national averages respectable, thereby saving face for black politicians who struggle to defend the miserable standing of South African schools in international achievement tests. White schools also pay their own way and, though nominally public, raise their income stream through very high tuition fees, which keep poor black students out but relieve the state of having to resource white schools at the same level as their black counterparts.

In political terms, however, all-white schools with all-white teachers more than a decade into a nonracial democracy are an eyesore to black nationalists. They make a mockery of the struggle for change, and their privileged standing in a sea of poverty drives politicians to become more and more aggressive about changing white schools. But how can this be done without white flight into the even more protected sphere of private schooling, leaving a large mass of mediocre public schools over which the state has to preside?

Whites hold on desperately to this last political space in which to defend race, culture, and language. All around, the defeat is emphatic, the sense of loss pervasive. But even educational space is constricting, and it is a matter of time before black nationalists also overwhelm this arena and force the issue of change and integration in white schools.

## On the State of Being Defeated

It would be a mistake, however, to cast all whites (or for that matter all Afrikaners) as expressing a monolithic response to defeat.[46] Among Afrikaners, there are at least three responses to history, transition, and the future. Not too many decades ago, Afrikaners were united in the defense of Apartheid. There was simply no way in which Apartheid could be sustained without such overwhelming support, and this included the support of English-speaking whites in South Africa. More and more Afrikaners represent a diverse group culturally, religiously, economically, and of course politically.[47] Nevertheless, there are major tendencies of social thought among Afrikaners that can be distinguished.

*Nothing Happened*

The first group of Afrikaners are those who believe that nothing out of the ordinary happened. What happened was quite simple: there was an orderly transition in which power was shared with blacks once they were ready for change and once geopolitical conditions allowed. This peaceful transition was planned all along, and when the time was right and blacks capable enough, the handover took place in a responsible manner.

Apartheid, for this group, was not an offense, let alone a crime against humanity. It was a well-intended experiment that might have had one or two weak points but overall was a brilliant scheme for keeping racial order and peace. One of the more astounding examples of this reasoning can be found in a collection of articles[48] in honor of one of the architects of Apartheid and the one politician most responsible for giving substance to Apartheid education: former Prime Minister Hendrik Frensch Verwoerd. Family, friends, artists, and academics line up to justify the face of Apartheid; what emerges is a warm, loving man with no hostility toward black people. He was the one person who understood the needs of "blacks" and who defended South Africa against hostile enemies at home and abroad. One hundred years after his birth (September 8, 1901), thirty-five years after his assassination,[49] and seven years after the end of Apartheid, a collection of respectable people could find nothing wrong with a past shaped so emphatically by a man born in another country, the Netherlands.

In this perspective, therefore, there was no oppression. In fact, blacks were given voting rights at various historical points and they had representation (through whites) in the government. Eventually they even had their own "houses" within central government, the House of Representatives for coloreds, and the House of Delegates for Indians.[50] The state provided separate homelands for rural Africans, allowing self-determination for different ethnic groups. The problem of course was the agitators, who were inspired by external agents, the Communists, determined to take over South Africa and destroy Western civilization and culture in their evil, atheistic schemes.

The role of the state was to protect Christian and white civilization externally from *die rooi gevaar* (the Red threat, Communism) and its fueling internally of *die swart gevaar* (the Black threat). In this understanding, there were no torture chambers, there were no mass shootings of peaceful protestors, there were no exploitative labor practices, there were no racist social policies, there were no exclusionary social laws, and there was no dispossession of land and property. What whites achieved was on the basis of their own hard work in a barren land through superior skills.

When black South Africans cynically remark that after 1994 there were no whites who ever supported Apartheid, this is the group they refer to: those who claim that nothing really happened.

### Something Happened—Now Get Over It

The second group of Afrikaners recognizes and might even concede that *some* bad things happened during the course of white rule. In defense of an otherwise rational and acceptable system based on self-determination, there might have been some excesses, but even these must be seen against the backdrop of the external and internal threat to peace and stability in the country.

The members of this group are conscious of and alert to the international criticism of Apartheid, and although they believe that minor atrocities might have been committed by individuals doing their job, they also believe this criticism is exaggerated. This is not a small and insignificant group of white South Africans, especially among Afrikaners. They too believe that the Truth and Reconciliation Commission was a one-sided exaggeration of what happened, a new nationalist backlash aimed at doing little else but embarrassing whites and justifying black rule.

Still, something did happen, so "get over it" is the sentiment. There is anger here, resentment of those who both exaggerate and dwell on the past for political reasons. Nothing captures this sentiment more powerfully than the popular song among young white Afrikaners that enjoys prominence at Afrikaans festivals:

| *Nie Langer*[51] | No Longer |
|---|---|
| *Ek weet ons was verkeerd* | I know we were wrong |
| *Dit was op CNN, BBC en oral oral* | It was on CNN, BBC and |
| *op TV* | everywhere, everywhere on TV |
| *Die feite is nou op die tafel* | The facts are now on the table |

| | |
|---|---|
| *Kan ons asb aanbeweeg, meneer?* | Can we please move on, Sir? |
| *Want: ek sal nie langer jammer* | Because: I will not say sorry |
| *sê nie* (x2) | anymore (x2) |
| *Ek sal agter in die tou staan* | I will stand in the back of the line |
| *Ons reënboog op my mou dra* | Carry our rainbow on my sleeves |
| *Maar ek sal NIE langer jammer sê nie* | But I will NOT say sorry anymore |
| (x2) | (x2) |
| | |
| *Die feit dat ek nie altyd saamstem nie* | The fact that I do not always agree |
| *Maak my nie 'n racist nie.* | Does not make me a racist. |
| *So gaan soek die balk in jou eie oog* | So look for the beam in your own eye |
| *Hou op geld mors op* | Stop wasting money on name |
| *naamsveranderings* | changes |
| *Daar's mense sonder huise, kinders* | There are people without houses, |
| *sonder kos* | children without food |
| *Wie's nou die sondebok?* | Who is now the guilty one? |
| *Ek sal nie langer jammer sê nie* | I will no longer say sorry anymore |
| (x5) | (x5) |

This desire to move on is common among this large group of Afrikaners. It can be read as impatience with the constant harking back to the past among black people. It could also be read as embarrassment at having to deal with their role as whites in the ugly past. Either way, for this group the past should be dealt with factually and quickly: something happened, sorry, move on, and deal with the real problems facing South Africa.

These "real problems" are cast as resource problems. It is about taking state monies and giving them to those without food and shelter. It is wasteful to spend these limited resources on changing the names of towns and cities, streets, and buildings, from their Afrikaans, Apartheid, or colonial names to reflect the contributions of struggle heroes and stalwarts. Use the money for the poor, or you make yourself the new perpetrators, the new ones guilty of wrong. Whatever you do, there will be no more apologies.

"No Longer" is, of course, much more than a song; it is a powerful sentiment among many white South Africans. It is a sentiment that falls between the stools of straight denial and full confession. It grudgingly concedes a half-mistaken past but wants to get on with the future. It does not want to carry the past burden of oppression but instead insists that the new rulers direct their attention to the present burden of poverty.

But there is a third group.

### Terrible Things Happened

There are at least three strains of response among those who concede that terrible things happened.

*The Activists*    This is a small group of whites in South Africa who recognize that what happened under Apartheid was terrible, and it was wrong. They readily concede that atrocities were committed, and they willingly step forward to acknowledge they were wittingly or unwittingly part of the system that allowed such atrocities to happen.

In this group there is immediate concession of privilege, that what they have is a direct result of being treated differently as whites, and a consequence of the dispossession meted out against blacks. This group of whites does not need to be told that something happened; it readily owns up to a terrible past. Of course, this group, and indeed the other two, are not necessarily homogeneous.

There are those in this group who were always on the side of the struggle against Apartheid, whether in its radical form of armed resistance or in its more liberal form of peaceful dissent. In the former group are those whites who consciously joined the ANC in exile, and in the latter group are those who associated themselves with the broad goals of freedom through ANC-aligned structures such as the internal United Democratic Front or the whole range of white liberal associations (among others, the Black Sash[52] and the End Conscription Campaign[53]). In other words, there is a small contingent of white South Africans who always—that is, before 1994—took an active stand against Apartheid in one form or another.

This is a vocal group that spoke out loudly under Apartheid and speaks out passionately after Apartheid. Their one dilemma, especially among English-speaking whites, is that they sometimes forget they continue to benefit from the received privileges of the past and include in their number those who do not believe that *they* did anything wrong; it was other whites, the Afrikaner nationalists, those who exercised the racial vote under Apartheid. Many in this group did not vote under Apartheid's white democracy, refusing to legitimize a racially exclusive system.

*The Gradualists*   The gradualists are those who came to their position only after 1994, either as a result of the progressive revelation of atrocities committed under Apartheid or as a consequence of the progressive changing of their own understandings of what Apartheid really was about. As their knowledge about the past changed, this group slowly felt the embarrassment, shame, and guilt of what whites had done to blacks. The best illustration of this group is Leon Wessels, one of the last white cabinet members in the final Apartheid parliament, whose book *The End of an Era* has the moving subtitle, *The Liberation of an Afrikaner.*[54]

This is a group that does not necessarily want to speak about the past; its members are quiet but acknowledging of the terrible past. They will often work determinedly to correct wrongs, advance affirmative policies for the excluded, defend practices that include others, and even demonstrate considerable sensitivity toward blacks as they grasp the enormity of the terrible things that happened.

There is no dramatic change here, no Damascus Road experience, only gradual awareness and change in their knowledge about the past. It is a stressful experience for this group, coming to terms with the lies, the indoctrination, the misinformation that was their received knowledge throughout the Apartheid years. As they grapple with past deceits, they must make sense of new realities. It is an emotional whirlwind for such white citizens, a journey made all the more difficult by the decision not to speak openly about what happened and why it happened. The young journalist-intellectual Christi van der Westhuizen captures the complex emotions of knowing before and after the evil of Apartheid, in the voice of Leon Wessels:

I further believe that the political defense of "I did not know" is not available to me, because in many respects I believe I did not *want* to know . . . an entanglement exists between what you know, what you don't know and what you want to know.[55]

It is nevertheless in this group that the claim is most often made that they really did not know. They tell of a controlled media under Apartheid in which the news was sanitized in such a way that dramatic acts of resistance were not shown at all, and when they did appear they depicted criminals and terrorists inspired by external Communists bent on destroying their civilized, Christian way of life. They tell of controlled living spaces in which news of the plight of others, torture by the regime, imprisonment of children, and separation of families were simply not known to them.

*The Confessionalists*    This third group within the white community has had a direct and often traumatic encounter with the past; this hard knowledge remains deeply disturbing. They talk, they want to talk, in order to confront the demons within themselves and settle and reconcile with those whom they hurt and despised not too long ago.

People in this group are the ones who experienced the dramatic turnaround as a result of any combination of factors: critical incidents during the negotiations, the death of a loved one, meetings with the exiled or imprisoned leaders of the liberation movements. It was sudden, it was dramatic, and it was final.

Within this group are some of the leading politicians during the dying days of Apartheid, including Adriaan Vlok, the minister of police during the 1980s. It is hard to imagine a more unlikely candidate in this category. On his watch, thousands of black (and some white) activists were imprisoned, tortured, and killed during the most sustained wave of anti-Apartheid resistance during the 1980s. He epitomized the violent state, with chants of "Vlok off" heard in the many protests that dotted the urban centers of the country. He was responsible for suppressing the internal uprising, and he spared no instrument in his deadly arsenal, including poisoning, burning, beating, and assassinating any activists— men and women, children and adults—who dared to stand in the way of Apartheid rule.

Yet this is the same man who dramatically discovers God and truth. In a moment that will be remembered forever, he makes his way up to the Union Buildings, the seat of the new black government, and begs for forgiveness from the head of the presidency, Frank Chikane, for trying to kill him through poisoning. It was a murderous affair that almost cost this affable man his life as he traveled through Namibia and the United States winning international support for the struggle. His clothes were laced with poison, and for a long time it was difficult to establish why

Chikane had become so violently ill as he stood at death's door. Doctors in the United States, where he was during these near-fatal episodes, diagnosed poisoning, and Chikane survived, though barely.

Now in his offices in the Union Buildings he finds, on his knees, the man who set out to kill him.

Both Chikane and Vlok come from the same evangelical background, a theological world in which washing the feet of others is an expression of servanthood, submission, and humility. These common beliefs, albeit ones shaped in racially divided worlds, enable a commonness of purpose. Chikane forgives the former head of police and Vlok then asks him whether, in an act of contrition, he may wash his feet. Chikane hesitates but then allows Vlok to proceed.

It was Chikane's idea to make this event known more broadly, since he reckoned it would enable other whites to come forward and confess what they did during those years of oppression. But when he does this, all hell breaks loose, in a manner of speaking. Many blacks feel this is too little, too late; to forgive Vlok is to dilute the serious crimes committed by him and under his rule. Many whites feel this was unnecessary—yet another example of feeble white people submitting themselves to the reckless authority of black nationalists when in fact they had done nothing wrong; and if they had, so had those blacks during the war through terrible crimes such as the "necklacing" of suspected informers by burning them to death with oil-lit tires around their necks, and through the torture of suspected spies in the ANC camps in exile in places such as Quattro in Angola. For conservative whites, Vlok's act of washing his opponent's feet is both unnecessary and humiliating. It is perhaps this astounding act that, for the first time, symbolizes the completeness of the defeat of white rule and the demise of the old order.

And so Vlok travels across the country, addressing small groups and large, pleading for and receiving forgiveness. He devotes his free time to walking the streets of black townships and feeding small children. He commits his pension to feeding mothers whose children disappeared or were killed during his term as police minister. He preaches in churches with Chikane and others to tell of God's love and grace, and to seek forgiveness.

The Memories of the Defeated

What runs across the three categories of response to the past is a common experience of defeat. To radical whites—as small as this group is—this *defeat of a system* is a welcome event, the end of the tyranny of Apartheid. Liberal whites might share this view, but for them the defeat is qualified. Despite a liberal Constitution, there are not enough safeguards against the tyranny of black rule. It must be remembered that among the leading political lights in South African liberalism there are those who never foresaw a system of one man, one vote, as this gender-insensitive phrase was known on the streets of struggle and in the anxious business boardrooms and parliamentary chambers of the whites. Not too long ago, models of interracial government under such awkward terms as "consociationalism" were the subject of endless conferences and monographs on "power sharing."[56] The complete shift of power into black hands was not comfortable for many liberals, hard as they might pretend today to have always championed the cause of an unrestricted franchise.

For the ordinary white South African, and Afrikaners in particular, the transition remains a traumatic experience. From a psychotherapist's perspective:

South Africa is an intensely anxious society, living with many unresolved fears and collective fantasies, much repressed anger, guilt, and shame. Many black-white relationships are unstable and ambivalent. The necessary collective healing will have to go far beyond the superficial political processes of reconciliation, reparation, and truth-seeking about the past—urgent though these are.[57]

To understand why this is so, it is important to recognize "the reserves of social knowledge"[58] on which the memories and identity of the Afrikaner are built.[59] Their mythological knowledge of the past is one of proud restoration of a people under divine guidance who created South Africa. Such knowledge is one flowered with the heroes of Afrikanerdom: great poets, great scientists, great theologians, great intellectuals, great political leaders, great teachers, great literary figures, great rugby men, great universities, great schools. Knowledge of the past is embedded in rich and emotional narratives of the rise of Afrikaans as a language of science, a medium of teaching, a vehicle for learning the mother tongue, a powerful form for communicating the cultural, aesthetic, spiritual, romantic, economic, and political ideals of a chosen people. Important in this store of knowledge is not simply what is claimed but what is left out in "these processes of silencing" through "the fabrication of dominant myths."[60]

Their knowledge of the past is also one of bitter struggle against the colonialists, the English, and the Communists, this last group readily substituting for black resistance. Their knowledge of the past is one of self-determination, lifting themselves from the humiliation of the Anglo-Boer wars and the desperate poverty that followed. Their knowledge of the past is one of defending this elect tribe of Afrikaners from constant external threats such as the decadent West and Soviet imperialism. Their knowledge of the past is one of sacrifice to establish the Afrikaner community and protect the country from internal agitators and external threat.

Then come the 1990s, and despite a whites-only referendum[61] that gives the National Party the authority to begin negotiations with blacks, nobody in this group expects things to go so far. Nobody expects that negotiations will, in the end, be the simple handover of power to a black majority. In short, nobody expects defeat of such proportions and the eventual collapse of the formidable political machinery represented in the once-mighty National Party.[62]

Suddenly, such treasured knowledge of the past is shattered; this received knowledge, handed down faithfully from one generation to the next, is officially negated with the stroke of a negotiator's pen. This is extremely difficult and traumatic for ordinary Afrikaners, for whom a hitherto uncomplicated, straightforward, and uncontested knowledge of the past has governed their lives. They make unspeakable sacrifices when they release their sons on compulsory military duty to fight a war that they are told (and that they believe) is just. Their boys die in a long bush war defending the borders of South Africa, pursuing the terrorists into the foreign lands of Namibia, Angola, Mozambique, Botswana, Swaziland, Zimbabwe. Their men come back injured, physically and psychologically, from those encounters. But it is not only the losses in the bush war far away; it is also the policemen and officers who lose their lives quelling internal revolt or who are disfigured in the struggle to maintain law and order.[63]

South Africa has an elite settlement. Nobody bothers to tell ordinary people, the masses of this white tribe of Africa on which the Afrikaner elite built their prestige and power, that whatever they think is true is not. There is a trauma here that has yet to be studied and understood in all its hurt and complexity,[64] a problem Peter Marris places his finger on:

It may be harder to recover from loss if the meaning of what has been lost was never satisfactorily resolved. Its ambiguities, or our ambivalence toward it, complicate the task of reconstituting the enduring meaning of the lost relationship for the future. There may, for instance, be a residue of conflict and anger which cannot now be worked out in a living relationship. Trying to deal with that conflict retrospectively may make it harder to work out what sense to make of the future.[65]

It is a traumatic loss that expresses itself in bitter writings in the mainstream Afrikaans media, especially in the major print media such as *Rapport, Die Burger, Beeld*, and *Volksblad*, ignoring for a moment the more outrageous right-wing prints such as *Die Afrikaner*. From letters to the editor to the lead newspaper editorials to the invited writers, there is a deep resentment not only of the new government but of the old government for relinquishing power in such a careless manner. These media pages are soaked with stories about the threat to the identity of the Afrikaner; the demise of the Afrikaans language; the targeting of Afrikaans schools; the end of the Afrikaans universities; the collapse of the major political party of the Afrikaners; the loss of jobs (to blacks); and the end of Afrikaans-named cities, towns, and streets. No matter what good happens in the new black government, the Afrikaans press will see a downside.[66]

It is a constant lament from one day to the next, and from one set of weekend papers to the following weekend's release. The tone is bitter, resentful, angry. With predictable frequency, this loss is attributed to the weak-kneed white politicians who betrayed the knowledge, culture, and identity of the Afrikaner for thirty pieces of silver.

In this context of fragility, and the demise of reliable landmarks of cultural and social conviction, any sign or symbol of restoration is desperately clutched in the quest for a lost past. And so the "De la Rey" phenomenon. A musician, Louis Pepler (known by his stage name as Bok van Blerk), stumbles across a song that even he could not have imagined would have created so much following and caused such controversy. With its catchy tune and powerful lyrics, van Blerk, the consensus goes, was less interested in political revival than in turning around his financial fortunes. But this is not about van Blerk; it is about how the song is received in the white Afrikaans community and among youth in particular.

The song calls on a hero from the South African War, one General Koos de la Rey, to come and lead the Boers of today in their struggles against overwhelming adversity:

*De la Rey*[67]

*De la Rey, De la Rey*

*Sal jy die Boere kom lei?* (Will you come and lead the Boers?)

*De la Rey, De la Rey*

*Generaal, Generaal*

*Soos een man sal ons om jou val* (Like one man we will fall around you)

*Generaal de la Rey*

The backdrop is the war against the English, and powerful accompanying visuals in the music video show Boer women and children in concentration camps as the song calls for "a nation that will rise up again." At Pepler's performances, the old Apartheid flag is waved in the crowds; at others, young people respond by lustily singing the old Apartheid anthem, *Die Stem van Suid-Afrika* (The Call of South Africa). Whatever Pepler might have intended, this song absorbs and reflects among many Afrikaners the fears, the anxieties, the anger, and the confusion.

Just beneath this loud bravado, however, lies a much deeper set of emotions about loss and change. It is about a people unprepared for the suddenness of transition. It is about the disruption of a once-simple narrative about the past. It is about the travail of giving up privilege and power to those who only yesterday were tarnished as terrorists and enemies of the state. It is about deep feelings of racism and racial superiority being challenged in the demonstration of economic success and social stability, and having to face up to the intellectual and cultural prowess of those deemed backward and uneducated. It is, in the end, about the gradual recognition of defeat.

This sense of profound loss finds ready traction in the inevitable problems of transition facing South Africa, such as the spiraling crime wave, the HIV/AIDS pandemic, the poor quality of (most) schooling, the reports of corruption, the struggles for political position inside the dominant party, and the mismanagement of government portfolios such as Home Affairs and those dealing with electricity supply. The new state's sometimes clumsy and ineffectual response to these problems is what the defeated seize on either to prove the predictability of black behavior or to mourn some earlier, imagined euphoric state in which things were better.

A new book for Afrikaner youth acknowledges some of the excesses of Apartheid, but it then falls into a disturbing logical trap in which many whites find themselves caught:

This does not mean that everything would have been moonshine and roses for all the members of these [nonwhite] communities if there was no Apartheid. Quite the opposite, for the experiences from the rest of Africa indicate that they would probably have been worse off today if Apartheid was never there.[68]

For the defeated, none of these problems are connected to a divided past. None of the problems are located within the systematic inequalities visited upon black communities: deliberate underfunding of black education, destruction of the black family through the migrant labor system, brutalization of young people through state-sanctioned violence, dispossession of stable communities that created vast economic wastelands, or political creation of congested slum areas that over decades of Apartheid sowed the seeds of a violent public culture.

However legitimate the complaint, the lament of the defeated is simply another way of uttering a deep sense of alienation and loss, and this lies at the root of the continuing malaise of defeat and the growing awareness of a troubled knowledge that white citizens have to deal with.

### Conclusion

Against this backdrop of loss and change, white students step into schools and enter universities with a powerful knowledge of the past. With such knowledge, they also carry the emotions of defeat and uncertainty received from, and alive among, their parents. That students are not empty vessels is one of the fundamentals of educational thought; accordingly, psychologists of learning instruct that the most important thing about teaching is to determine what the learners already know.[69] This profound wisdom is, however, often applied only to the domain of conventional subject-matter knowledge, such as mathematics or science or geography. It is seldom applied in the context of knowledge of a personal and traumatized past.

# 2   Indirect Knowledge

How are experiences of historical catastrophe transmitted to
its literal and figurative inheritors? How should we remember
experiences that are close to us, but which are not really ours?[1]

The paradoxes of indirect knowledge haunt many of us
who came after.[2]

"How," asks the education historian Sam Wineburg,
"is historical knowledge transmitted across genera-
tions?" and "What is the role of schooling in that transmission?"[3] While
leading and teaching at UP, I noticed quite early on that my white students would often express very firm views about the past, hold rigid
views about the present, and convey (especially among the men) fatalis-
tic views about the future. It was especially their firm knowledge about
the past that puzzled me. How could young people, still young children
around the time of Nelson Mandela's release from prison, recall so vividly events and experiences from the past? How did they know? Who
told them? Where did they get this knowledge? The same was true for
my black students. They too would have been children in the last days
of Apartheid and gained any social consciousness only well into the
first years of democracy. Yet my black students had clear views about
Apartheid, about the role of whites within that past, and the effects of
discrimination on blacks within history. But it was not merely that these
post-Apartheid students had knowledge of the past that puzzled me; it

was that they held this knowledge firmly, personally, and emotionally. For a long time I mulled this over without a clear sense of the phenomenon and how to name it.

During these musings, and while browsing in a large bookstore, I came across a work with exceptionally insightful building blocks for a conceptual framework within which I could approach this observed problem. It was Eva Hoffman's *After Such Knowledge* (2004), subtitled variously but for the version in hand *A Meditation on the Aftermath of the Holocaust*.[4] This is one of many books on the second generation of Holocaust survivors, those children whose families lived through and often perished in the *Shoah*. Told in biographical form, *After Such Knowledge* re-presents the experiences of the children of Holocaust victims by foregrounding the knowledge problem handed down over generations. Conscious throughout the reading and rereading of this evocative monograph of the differences between these two great events of the 20th century, the Holocaust and Apartheid, I nevertheless found powerful strains of knowledge and experience among the second generations of both cataclysms. Suddenly, my observations started to come together into preliminary lines of thought that would lead to greater confidence of explanation about the origins and consequences of knowledge within my target group: white Afrikaner students.

This chapter therefore moves through a discussion of a complex but critical set of conceptual propositions and problems regarding the transmission of historical knowledge about national, communal, and familial events into the minds and hearts of second-generation children.[5] The conceptual framework is built on the key construct of *indirect knowledge*, taking Hoffman's initial propositions and elaborating them into an interpretive schema for reading the data represented in the individual chapters. Hoffman's construct of indirect knowledge is linked to other empirical accounts and conceptual frameworks on the transmission of especially traumatic knowledge and memory from one generation to the next. In the process, a more elaborate conceptual framework on indirect knowledge is developed than is available in existing literatures, and this is contextualized within the specific conditions of South Africa, Apartheid, and the transition to democracy.

### Paradoxes

How does one explain the powerful knowledge held by post-Apartheid children about events they did not witness themselves and about experiences they never directly had? Hoffman calls this *the paradoxes of indirect knowledge.*[6] Not having been there, as in the case of second-generation Holocaust children, they nevertheless behave as if they were, for those events

> overshadow and overwhelm our own lives. But we did not see them, suffer through them, experience their impact directly. Our relationship to them has been defined by our very "postness," and by the powerful but mediated forms of knowledge that have followed from it.[7]

Several things are important in this perceptive formulation of second-generation knowledge. First of all, it is about *knowledge* and not about experience or trauma or pathology.

Second, it is about *indirectness,* again an important observation in that it points immediately to sources; that is, if this knowledge is carried so powerfully among the nonpresent, where exactly did it come from? What is it about indirectness that nevertheless gives it such powerful resonance within the lives of the second generation, as if this were direct knowledge?

Third, it is about *transmission.* How did this direct knowledge become indirect knowledge? What are the mechanisms for transmission, and how do they work intergenerationally? Knowledge runs along a crooked line from one generation to the next, never smooth, often interrupted, but always connecting generations that were there with those who were not.

Fourth, it is about *influence.* How does this received or inherited knowledge affect children, the second-generation recipients of knowledge of something they were not a part of? That there is an impact is not contestable; that the post children are affected in powerful ways is not in question in any of the literatures on any kind of memory, traumatic or otherwise. The question is, What does this knowledge do to the generation of children who come after?

Fifth, it is *relational,* in that there cannot be knowledge of a child without knowledge of an adult, even in the absence of a physical parent.

For this reason, the familial relationships between the first and second generations are intense, emotionally charged, and often destructive. At the heart of these family ties is a complex knowledge relationship about how the same past is known by the first and second generations.

Sixth, it is *mediated* knowledge. None of this knowledge is received without passing through any number of mediations that lie between historical events as they happened then, and as they are received now by the second generation. In different cultures and for different events, the nature and range of mediating agents will obviously vary, and this adds to the intellectual value of seeking out these operations within specific contexts.

Seventh, it is *paradoxical* knowledge. How can you know something you did not witness? This of course raises questions about the authenticity of knowledge and about the knowability of distant events. It generates complex philosophical and moral questions about "not having been there" and how this manifests itself in secondhand knowledge. But beyond these questions lies a more important problematic: this is knowledge nevertheless that carries emotions and memories, which have real effects on the lives of the second generation.

Eva Hoffman does not dwell on the conceptual thicket that comes with such moving ideas. She travels smoothly and eloquently, yet painfully, through the pages of narration about second-generation knowledge, casting along the way these powerful constructs without exploring them on their own terms. What she leaves in the process of telling is nevertheless a rich tapestry of ideas on the basis of which a conceptual framework for indirect knowledge can be more fully developed and understood.

### Comparisons

The literary base from which my South African work on indirect knowledge derives is mainly that which deals with the second-generation children of the Holocaust, the offspring of the victims as well as those of the perpetrators. This bringing together of work on children of Apartheid and children of the Holocaust is fraught with conceptual, methodological, cultural, and political difficulties, and it therefore requires a cautionary note.

Apartheid is not the Holocaust, and the Holocaust is not Apartheid. These are two distinct events in their origins, content, trajectory, and outcomes. This has not stopped authors from linking the two cataclysms, whether in the form of Jocelyn Hellig's sensitive portrayal in *The Holocaust and Apartheid*,[8] or in the shrill polemic of Lawrence Langer in his chapter "Memory and Justice After the Holocaust and Apartheid,"[9] or in Michael Simpson's more deliberate comparisons of Apartheid and other national atrocities in "The Second Bullet."[10]

Theoretical writings warn, however, about the historical and political minefield of comparison, as do Levi and Rothberg in their rich set of edited papers under the title *Uniqueness, Comparison, and the Politics of Memory*.[11] Uniqueness, their collection argues, must not be set in opposition to historicization, and they note that a supposedly unique event might hold various meanings according to the contexts of the time, and across time. One massive atrocity, such as the Holocaust, could have divergent meanings when the target for repression and elimination is Jews or Gypsies or homosexuals or Slavs, even at the hands of the same brutalizing force.

I therefore approach the comparison softly, without collapsing the two events into one account of human suffering and without claiming uniqueness for either event. In between sameness and uniqueness lie undeniable points of comparison when it comes to the narrower subject of what received knowledge does to the second generation.[12] There are common issues of silence, denial, aggression, irritability, externalization, shame, and guilt that call for discussion, if not direct comparison, on the meanings and effects of received knowledge.

There are of course major tensions in comparing the knowledge and experiences of the children of victims and perpetrators. The obvious and first response is to deny such comparison; it is morally unacceptable, the hard version of the argument goes, to compare the suffering of one group to that of another, and this probably explains why, until recently, there was almost no literature on the knowledge of children of the perpetrators in Nazi Germany. The softer version of this argument allows comparison but cautions against assigning moral equivalence to the sufferings of perpetrators and victims. Fair enough, but then the tricky question becomes whether the same moral compass applies in comparing the suffering of children of the perpetrators and children of the victims. Surely the former cannot be held accountable for what their parents did. Or can they, and if so, to what extent and how?

These are without doubt intricate moral and philosophical questions. As the South African experience shows, the flight from responsibility is indeed one of the more common expressions among children of Apartheid perpetrators: whatever happened in the past happened. "We were not responsible for it and we cannot therefore be punished for it. We therefore demand the same access as blacks to jobs in the economy or places in higher education or financial support for studies."

The question of moral equivalence applied to the suffering of the children of perpetrators compared to children of victims is not something I try to address at this point. What I do, rather, is reveal the data and then make the argument that the children of perpetrators suffer directly and intensely, sometimes with devastating consequences, for something they did not do. The qualitative meanings of the suffering of the inheritors of knowledge on each side of the divide can be dealt with only after the case material has been presented.

### Contexts

Taking heed of the caveats about simple comparison between two cataclysms, one must nevertheless note important differences between the Holocaust and Apartheid that have a direct bearing on the knowledge and memories of the second generation.

First, the Holocaust was an intensely traumatic event that sought the mass extermination of a people in a relatively short period of time; this is why it is called genocide. This does not mean there was not a long history of persecution against the Jews; it simply means that an unprecedented level of mass violence was visited on the Jewish people in a concentrated period. Apartheid, on the other hand, was an institutionalized policy of racial oppression that preceded 1948 all the way back to the arrival of the colonists in the 17th century and continued as racial discrimination and economic exploitation over centuries. True, the practice of racial oppression was intensified through a dense architecture of racist laws and policies when the Afrikaner nationalists came to power in 1948, but in many ways it was a continuation of other forms of racial hatred and discrimination.

Second, South Africa did not experience mass extermination of black people; nor was such an outcome the intended policy of the white minority regime. Rather, the goal of Apartheid was separate development, that is, keeping blacks contained within their own separate areas and out of the privileged white spaces. Again, this does mean many thousands of South Africans did not die, directly and indirectly, as a result of Apartheid; it is simply the point that this was not the founding rationale of this policy. In both cases, however, state policy was founded on racial contempt for what were regarded as subhumans.

Third, the Holocaust drove Jews out of Europe into remote parts of the world and triggered in part establishment of the state of Israel. This is a crucial point because it meant that for the children of the victims and the children of the perpetrators, the post-Holocaust period essentially meant dealing with the terrible past in isolation. It is a point made insightfully in the introduction to the play version of the book *Born Guilty*, where a German professor explains:

You see, the problem in West Germany is that we remembered in the absence of the victims. It was a discourse between the perpetrators and their children alone. We were not forced to listen, and we are not forced to listen to the voices of the victims.[13]

In the South African experience the victims and the perpetrators had to live together and together make sense of the experiences of defeat and victory. White South Africans are indeed "forced to listen" to the victims on television, in documentaries, through public memorials, on public holidays, in newspapers, on the streets, and, most important, inside the classrooms of integrated educational institutions. It will be shown later that this state of being forced to listen evokes intense emotions from the perpetrators and their children, not always with constructive social or educational outcomes.

Blacks and whites had always lived together under Apartheid, albeit in a master-servant relationship. After 1994, blacks and whites continued to live together even though historical patterns of segregation keep many black people in residential and social isolation from their white counterparts. Many white Afrikaans schools still remain white, but in most schools and universities black and white students increasingly live and learn together; black and white faculty teach together; and black and white South Africans engage, at least formally, the same curriculum.

Fourth, although economic relations still largely reflect inequality, political power now rests in the hands of the black majority. The defeated are the minority and the former victims are the majority. This is important since it means the stories of the past get told through the eager instruments of new state power. From the perspective of the former victims, there certainly is not a loss of memory, but a feverish remembrance of the terrible past. In the case of postwar Germany, the stories of National Socialism were also told, by Jewish survivors, but outside the authority of state power and the borders of the defeated state.

Fifth, in the case of the Holocaust the defeat of the Nazi state was resounding and clear. The Allies and the Soviets claimed victory, occupied the territory of the Nazis, arrested the major leaders and soldiers of this racist state, set up the Nuremberg courts to try the Nazis for crimes against humanity, executed and imprisoned those found guilty, required reparations from the Germans, and subjected the defeated to a process of denazification. In the case of Apartheid, the end came through a negotiated settlement in which the terms of transition favored reconciliation over recompense and peace over retribution. A few of the most vile of the perpetrators at the lower end of the command order were tried and imprisoned, but even they were given a way out provided they told the truth and it could be proved that they acted under the authority of their political masters. In other words, in these two contexts the culture of the defeated could be *expected* to be different.[14]

What these crucial differences suggest is that who remembers and how people remember is tied to the history of oppression, the nature of the state, the character and extent of the crimes, and the terms of transition. The knowledge of the second generation is directly connected, as will be shown, to these sensitive but real differences in the social, historical, and political terrain on which these two horrific events came to an end.

## Perpetrators

To comprehend the nature of the knowledge carried down to the second generation, it is important to have clarity about the identity of those who handed down such knowledge, that is, the perpetrators. Who were they?

The simple answer might be those who carried out the atrocities. But the persons at the end of the chain of command, or even those in command of a military unit under Apartheid, might claim—as they do—that they were simply doing their duty. Indeed, on this argument several of the big men from the military and police machinery of Apartheid received amnesty or were understood to be relieved of responsibility. The problem with confining the conception of perpetrators to the armed forces or the police and reservists invariably directs attention away from the political command, those who gave the orders. But is it only the issuing of specific orders that made the politicians in the Apartheid cabinet responsible? Surely the mere fact that these men created the atmosphere in which widespread atrocities were committed requires that they be held culpable.

Yet it was more than the creation of fearful and intimidating environments that allowed intolerable acts of cruelty. It was that these men had designed and defended a system that relegated black people in their millions to lives of poverty, restricted the victims to their racial and ethnic reserves, and thereby ensured they were cut off from essential and adequate social services when disease started to eat away at the most vulnerable. These men elaborated a system of laws and policies that visited wide-scale dispossession of land and deprivation of citizenship on the majority of the population. And these men installed the machinery of oppression that arrested those who revolted, peacefully or otherwise, and detained, killed, maimed, and tortured the resisters until Apartheid was declared by the United Nations to be a crime against humanity.

Even so, the identification of the perpetrators cannot be restricted to politicians who designed and enforced Apartheid, or to those who acted on military command or responded to political demands to defend the system. After all, South Africa was a white democracy in which every white person could vote and elect the party that governed and, by obvious extension, created the laws and policies regulating the lives of every black South African. It would be disingenuous, in this context, to portray white citizens as innocent bystanders to Apartheid; white people created, defended, and nurtured the system of racial rule from its inception, and returned the dominant party, the all-white National Party, to government with every election since D. F. Malan first captured power in 1948 from the more liberal-minded whites on an election platform called *Apartheid*.

A multigenerational inequality gap was secured for decades if not centuries to come, as a result of this massive empowerment of whites at the expense of the black majority. White South Africans kept this system in place until defeat was no longer avoidable. In this sense, every white South African was a perpetrator of, and inside, this evil system of Apartheid. Here the dictionary is helpful in rendering a modest if limited meaning of the word: "someone who perpetrates wrongdoing,"[15] or even more broadly, "to be responsible for; commit."[16]

The difficulty with this conception of white culpability is that white South Africans do not necessarily hold such knowledge of the past. This is a critical point, for to assume that the past as just described has the same meaning, especially for Afrikaners, is to fail to understand the content of the knowledge transmitted to the second generation. For example, in an ongoing controversy fourteen years into the new democracy, one of the white Afrikaner churches, desirous of rejoining an international alliance of reformed churches, was instructed to first renounce Apartheid. This brought internal anguish: "it depends which Apartheid we must renounce," said one of its leaders.[17] What this striking retort reveals is a still-contested view of what happened and therefore of what, if anything, there is to be remorseful about.

The knowledge many Afrikaners hold of the past, and therefore transmit to the second generation, can be understood only by accessing the belief systems that carry this knowledge. Knowledge does not transmit as neutral, technical, fact-based information from one generation to the next; it is embedded within dominant belief systems that give the knowledge meaning, emotion, and authority. The contemporary Afrikaner belief system[18] about the past is based on a number of arguments:

That Apartheid was, in general, a reasonable policy at the time, with good intentions; it was an attempt to create an orderly society among the races

That the implementation of Apartheid might have had some unintended consequences, but the attack on it is exaggerated; in fact, had it not been for Apartheid, blacks would probably be worse off—like blacks elsewhere on the continent

That there might have been some atrocities, but this was the result of some bad apples within the police and the military who were acting on their own and not under orders

That the real segregation and the basis for segregationist policies came not from the Afrikaners but from the English, years before

That the Afrikaners are also products of a struggle, against British colonialism, and in addition that the Afrikaners worked their way out of poverty through hard work and dedication, tilling the land, and not by expropriation from blacks

That they created out of nothing their own language; made their people literate; produced leading intellectuals, businessmen, and politicians; crafted their own universities; and established a strong economy—all in the face of constant threat

That the Afrikaners also built modern South Africa, giving it the kind of infrastructure and economy without which the country would simply be another Third World basket case

That whatever excesses might have happened under Apartheid, it must be remembered that the country was under threat from Soviet and Cuban Communists, who threatened Western civilization and Christianity at the southern tip of Africa; in other words, Afrikaners saved all South Africans from the much more terrible fate of godless Communism,[19] while the country was also under constant threat from liberation movements

That Afrikaners are being treated as scapegoats for all the sins of the past; they were not the only ones to benefit from Apartheid or the only ones who did wrong things,[20] a realization forcing Afrikaners to push back assertively because they are just *gatvol*[21]

That blacks also did terrible things, attacking whites, burning people alive, using children for political purposes, and committing black-on-black violence

Finally, that when the time was right, whites could enter into negotiations with blacks about the future; but first the Berlin Wall had to fall (that is, Communism was no longer a threat) and blacks had to renounce violence (that is, liberation was no longer on the agenda); the only problem was that the negotiations gave too much away as Afrikaner leaders capitulated to blacks.

There was once more virulent strain of this knowledge when, at the height of Afrikaner nationalism, beliefs about this superrace were expressed in terms of God's chosen people on a civilizing mission to enter unpopulated lands and establish Christianity among the subjugated who needed constant reminders that equality with whites was not for them.[22]

Although no longer in the public domain, this kind of knowledge finds expression in right-wing forums such as Radio Pretoria and publications of the otherwise defunct Herstigte Nasionale Party.[23] As Willem de Klerk put it, the superrace concept, "while no longer displayed as such, yet the mentality—even though packaged differently and more carefully—is still alive and kicking."[24]

While such views are probably a minority position within Afrikanerdom, they still receive space in current publications by some of the more prominent administrators of Apartheid.[25] A more sanitized version replaces racism and nationalism with culture. This move is poignantly captured by Suren Pillay, who observes "a complex shift from racialised claims of 'supremacy' to ethnicised claims to 'protection,' in so doing re-racializing 'whiteness' and re-inscribing difference through the language of 'culture.'"[26]

What there has not been in Afrikanerdom, therefore, is any public sense of defeat of a system, or any lament about the destructive force that kept Apartheid in place before and since its baptism under Afrikaner nationalism in 1948. The closest concession came from the last white President, F. W. de Klerk, in a revealing submission to the Truth and Reconciliation Commission (TRC):

Apartheid was wrong. I apologize in my capacity as leader of the National Party to the millions of South Africans . . . who suffered as a result of discriminatory legislation and policies. This apology is offered in a spirit of true repentance, *in full knowledge* of the tremendous harm that Apartheid has done to millions of South Africans [emphasis added].[27]

There are several important revelations in this apology. First, it is an apology. This is rare, and very few Apartheid masters went this far.

Second, it is an apology for specific things: not for killing, torturing, and maiming people, but for the inappropriate laws and policies that did harm to black people. Third, it is for the speaker an expression of *full knowledge* of the consequences of Apartheid.

This limited and cautious apology was clearly not acceptable to the victims. As Giliomee recounts the reception of this apology within the TRC, "What it [the TRC] also wanted to hear was that the State Security Council, of which de Klerk had been a member, had authorized or condoned the murder and torture of state enemies."[28]

Such broader terms for an apology from the leader of the Apartheid government were not forthcoming; in fact De Klerk would go on to deny any criminal role for his state machinery or himself.

What is crucial for the argument on knowledge transmission is that this apology, limited as it was, did not go down well with Afrikaners in general. There was widespread condemnation that the leader had shown this kind of weakness in the first place, having already surrendered the country to the black majority. In other words, this brief and limited concession of what Apartheid was and what it did was not received as clear and uncontested knowledge of the past. For such reception in the second generation, the mechanisms of transmission were much more complex than the voice of one (De Klerk) referred to in many circles as a *verraaier* (traitor) of his people.

Even so, this apology is what De Klerk and some of his colleagues considered to be submission *in full knowledge* of what Apartheid did to blacks. Here the outgoing white leadership faced a dual dilemma: knowledge was incomplete as far as many blacks were concerned, while it was also without foundation as far as many whites were concerned. Suddenly, the Apartheid that De Klerk speaks about had no supporters. Afrikaners detached themselves from the leaders, who alone were now responsible for Apartheid. No whites supported Apartheid, especially not the Apartheid that some of the leaders now regret.

This incapacity to acknowledge the terrible past is a threat to the long-term prospects for democracy and stability in South Africa. For "how can interpersonal trust increase across former conflict lines if one side ignores the fate of the other? And how can reconciliation take place if past discrimination is not accepted as principally wrong and evil?"[29]

There is rich theoretical precedent for what Jeffrey Herf calls *Divided Memory*[30] when he sets out to explain the very different interpretations of the Nazi past in the two successor German states in the postwar period and later in a unified Germany. Herf argues that memories split because of the distinctive histories, ideologies, and interests that shaped memory of the past in these two states. In East Germany, the Nazi past and the Holocaust were subject to a process of *universalization*, a nasty by-product of capitalist exploitation. In West Germany, the terrible past was subject to *internalization*, a function of an emerging liberal democracy there after the war. In Austria, on the other hand, the same past was the focus of *externalization*, crimes committed by those from elsewhere.

What Herf does not offer are explanations for such divided memory within one group of people, the perpetrators, and this clearly constitutes grounds for theoretical and empirical work yet to be done, especially in South Africa. Are whites divided in their knowledge of the past because of their differential class status within the same community? Did white leaders willfully manipulate knowledge of the past knowing that to concede murder and torture could possibly lead to criminal prosecution? Is this divided memory among Afrikaners a still-continuing contestation about Apartheid, its origins, causes, and effects? If so, how is knowledge of the past resolved, if at all, within such community? One might find partial answers to these hard conceptual issues by examining how and with what content knowledge travels between living generations.

## Children
### Nazi Children

There are volumes of writing on the Jewish second generation, the children of Holocaust victims, those killed and those who survived, those who were "hidden" through exile and those who lived through the terror. It started perhaps in the late 1970s with Steinitz and Szonyi[31] and around the same time as Helen Epstein,[32] whose work is regarded as seminal in first giving us the concept of the second generation. Then came many others, among them Aaron Hass,[33] Ellen Fine,[34] and of course Eva Hoffman.[35] These references exclude the rich studies of literary and cinematic responses of and to the second generation.[36]

Initially and perhaps understandably, little thought was given to the children of the perpetrators and their knowledge and experiences of that terrible past. "It had never occurred to me," concedes Julie Goschalk, "that the Holocaust might have impacted the lives of the descendants of the perpetrators."[37] When Dan Bar-On[38] started his seminal study he too found a hole in the literature: "I could uncover hardly a word about the perpetrators and their children. Was it that the children remained unaffected by their parents' past, or was it that nobody had tried to find out?"

Since then a literature on children of the perpetrators has mushroomed, starting with Peter Sichrovsky in 1988[39] followed by Bar-On,[40] Gerald Posner,[41] Heimannsberg and Schmidt (which encompasses children and grandchildren of active Nazis[42]), Gertrud Hardtmann,[43] Gita Sereny,[44] and Alan and Naomi Berger (which includes children of victims and perpetrators).[45] What is particularly disturbing are the vivid responses of angry children of Nazis recounted in such works as those by Anna Rosmus[46] or Barbara Roger[47] or Liesel Appel,[48] and perhaps the most heart-rending of responses, that of Sabine Reichel.[49]

Several important observations can be made across this literature on the children of both victims and perpetrators. This summary focuses on children of the perpetrators.

First, the range of responses of children of perpetrators is very *diverse*, from those who deny any knowledge of past atrocities to those who own up to full knowledge of the same, and in between there are various degrees of ownership and acceptance of knowledge of what happened. There is not a single response—and this is important—because to speak of postwar German children as a single experience or voice is to miss variations in understanding and knowledge of the Nazi past.

Second, *denial* of past knowledge is, within this variegated response, the most common experience recorded in these many accounts of the children of perpetrators. For some, this is a genuine account that results from parents not talking, a pervasive response of perpetrators who seldom talked directly or at all to their children. For others, there is clearly awareness of a terrible past, but it is not a knowledge that yields easily to psychotherapy or to ordinary interviews.

Third, among those who deny that they know, there is an intense *irritability* at being questioned about knowledge of the past. One interview after another across these studies with children of perpetrators reveal tense moments, the early termination of an interview, and deep discomfort bordering on aggression. The children, whether they know or not, are placed in the invidious position of having to defend or deny their parents, with serious emotional consequences. It is difficult in this voluminous data to establish knowledge of parent-perpetrator crimes, but what nevertheless emerges is irritability, defensive anger, even hostility, on the part of the children.

Fourth, the data on the second generation, the children of perpetrators, reveal a deep sense of *shame* among the offspring, whether or not knowledge of the past is conceded. This is very different for the victims' offspring: "The children of survivors can look up to [their] parents with pride and admiration. The children of the perpetrators see themselves reflected in the eyes of evil."[50] This shameful knowledge, whether it is suppressed or acted on, explains to some degree the awkwardness, the inarticulateness, and the silence among the children of the perpetrators.

Fifth, among the children of the perpetrators who accept this awful knowledge, there is *intense reaction* expressed as blinding rage against one or both parents, or as intense activism as a form of corrective action to the past knowledge, or as complete paralysis in the face of this terrible knowledge. The arrival of this knowledge leads to incalculable loss, as Appel found: "I am now an orphan [since] that horrible day that I learned that my beloved parents were Nazis."[51]

Sixth, the more common response among children of the perpetrators is, as with their parents, a deafening *silence* in the face of revealing knowledge. It is a contemplative period, the difficulty of coming to grips with their parents as perpetrators, even murderers, or simply as onlookers, bystanders, and beneficiaries: "Against . . . this knowing, stands the silence."[52] Silence is not the absence of sound; quite the contrary, it is the enforced quiet as the loudness of disturbing knowledge crashes in on all the senses. It is "the unthought known," which Gordon Wheeler describes as "all that which is felt, and known, and which colors the world, but which cannot be spoken."[53]

Seventh, apart from the intense reaction against revealing knowledge, another more common response was *indifference*, expressed in withdrawal of responsibility. What happened is in the past, and so "with a shrug of the shoulders the young repudiate any imputation of responsibility for the infamous behavior of their elders."[54] Indifference is not the result of lack of knowledge; it is often a response to shameful knowledge, a protective shield. In their classic study, the Mitscherlichs called this "the inability to mourn . . . the result of an intensive defense against guilt, shame, and anxiety."[55]

### Apartheid's Children

What is striking from the account of horrific knowledge and the responses to it in the children of the perpetrators of Nazi atrocities are the many similarities—and important differences—among Afrikaner children whose parents upheld Apartheid. The problem of knowledge and memory of course predates Apartheid atrocities in South Africa. Indeed, for the children in this study there is an all-important event that first defined their knowledge of a more distant past, and that shaped their identities as powerfully as Apartheid.

The South African War (to the perpetrators and their children, it is the Anglo-Boer War) between the Boers and the British at the end of the nineteenth century resulted in about 26,000 Boer dead, the majority women and children (22,000). This searing event, in which concentration camps were established with troubling images of starving and dying Boer inmates staring out from behind these fences, continues to leave an indelible mark on Afrikaner identity and remains central to their knowledge of the past. But this too is indirect knowledge, "a past not available in any direct sense to memory."[56] Yet no other historical event is represented more powerfully in the memory and emotions of contemporary Afrikaners—none of whom were there—than this conflict; indeed, "some are still fighting that war."[57]

Far more than a recent atrocity (Apartheid), the South African War constitutes the postmemory of the Afrikaner, such postmemory being defined as "the experiences of those who grow up dominated by narratives that preceded their birth."[58] This humiliation and defeat at the hands of the English, and the devastating poverty that followed, fueled the ethnic mobilization of Afrikaners, deepened the sentiments around Afrikaans and inspired the anti-English prejudice that remains to this day.

The white Afrikaner children of Apartheid display many of the same responses as the children of the Nazi perpetrators. There is a wide diversity of responses, for the Afrikaners of the twenty-first century are more fragmented in ideology, interests, and politics than ever before; it is for this reason that many resist the monochromatic[59] depiction of the group.[60] Yet it is true that the majority of Afrikaners, and certainly the children of those described here, represent a dominant response to the past and knowledge of it.

There remains deep denial about a criminal Apartheid past among white Afrikaner children and their living parents. There is no sense of crimes committed or of personal responsibility among the parents or the children. There is, rather, firm justification for what happened if the issue is pushed for a response. The Communist threat, internal agitation, protection of Christian values, the threat from regional states that offered a launching pad for revolutionaries, the refusal to lay down arms and accept Apartheid reforms, and the barbarism of the revolutionaries—all justified the total strategy to keep South Africa safe and retain law and order. To understand this denial of Apartheid as a crime against humanity, it is important, as indicated earlier, to understand the belief system in which the knowledge of a particular Apartheid is embedded.

To probe this Apartheid past, therefore, is to provoke considerable irritability, an aggressive and hostile response that could be quite dangerous if not done in the right circumstances and with the necessary build-up to the event. There is among the children, as with their parents, a feeling of being targeted, that blacks, having got what they wanted in terms of power, still want to harass whites into yielding more. Already, quotas favor blacks in jobs and sports; why then continue to rant and rave against those newly dispossessed?

There is among Afrikaner youth, also, a widespread silence everywhere. Nobody ever raises the Apartheid past, and if someone does it creates the irritability referred to earlier. It is as if nothing happened, and as if history started in the 1990s. But this silence is easily ruptured whenever Afrikaner youth are confronted with that past and have no way of escaping the engagement that comes from living, working, and learning with black South Africans.

Such reaction is intense, confrontational, and extremely hostile. What breeds this hostility is that the Afrikaner youths see everything collapsing around them. They see a future that is dark. Whereas their parents enjoyed job security—all, of course, through hard work and perseverance—such certainty is no longer guaranteed. The slightest change in the social climate spells impending doom, and the Afrikaans media know that milking such primordial ethnic fears sells newspapers. For this commercial reason, the major Afrikaans daily *Beeld* and the Sunday paper *Rapport* will run screaming headlines about vicious murders of white people over and over again.

Crime is therefore not simply an attack on everybody, black and white; no, crimes are examples of *volksmoorde* (ethnic murders), a deliberate targeting of whites. The shift in language policy at a university is not simply a pragmatic response to include black and other non-Afrikaans speakers; it is read as an attack on the last vestiges of Afrikaner culture and heritage. Nobody feels this sense of loss and emasculation more directly than the future head of the household, the young white Afrikaner man.

In relation to the historical context of the South African War, the course and triumph of Afrikaner nationalism that established Apartheid, the political mythology of a total onslaught against South Africa during the last decades of white rule, and the negotiated settlement that ended minority rule together explain this racial bravado, or what Barbara Masekela insightfully read as "a quality of embarrassing boastfulness and pride."[61] There is no outward sense of humiliation and defeat, real as that was in the political realm. There is, however, considerable indifference among Afrikaner youth to an atrocious past as it affected their black peers in the second generation whose parents came through it.

And so, unlike German perpetrators, Afrikaners did not seek to break all affective ties to the past.[62] Rather, the past was reasserted and embellished in an attempt to reclaim what is perceived as threat and loss.

How exactly is this knowledge transmitted, and what clues exist within the transmission mechanisms about the nature and content of indirect knowledge?

## Transmission

More than any other group, the Afrikaner child is a product of an intense set of closed circle interactions that establish and reinforce identity, memory, and knowledge of the past. This is still a culturally cohesive formation of people bound together closely through ties of history, language, culture, and struggle. The lines of transmission for knowledge therefore run much more linearly than in any other social grouping, such as English-speaking white South Africans or any one of the black communities in the country. Peter Lambley was among the first to capture this phenomenon through structured observation:

The Afrikaner child, like children everywhere in their different communities, is brought up on Afrikaner values and perspectives of life. But, unlike other children, the Afrikaans child finds these same values expressed uniformly at every level of his society. . . . At school he hears this from all his teachers, he reads it in all his school books. At home his parents reiterate the same values—if there is any conflict between school and home it is usually over [the] degree of adherence to the same values, not over different sets of values. As the child grows up, he hears the same ideas expressed at church, on the radio and on television, reads them in Afrikaans newspapers, magazines, comics and in Afrikaans novels, plays and at the cinema.[63]

Nonetheless, as elsewhere, "the modes of transmission . . . are multiple, complex, and mediated by numerous variables."[64] They include both informal means of transmission such as food, stories, songs, friends, and speaking the native language, as well as formal means such as educational, religious, political, cultural, and charitable.[65] But seldom is this cohesion as strong, the lines of transmission so direct, as in the Afrikaner community.

It is important to understand this cultural cohesiveness in the Afrikaner community, which, even though increasingly vulnerable to strain and fracture, still falls back on itself under external threat. Language rights can be invoked in an instant to dissolve political or class differences in this community. Any perceived threat to culture and identity leads unreflexively to closing of the cultural ranks, a phenomenon still referred to as *laagering* in reference to those defensive maneuvers during the Great Trek of Afrikaners when the Voortrekkers circled the ox wagons against the threatening enemy.[66]

What are these encircling influences that enable such powerful lines of knowledge transmission across generations, and in this case to the first generation of Afrikaner children born after Apartheid?

*Family*

The first and tightest of these concentric circles surrounding the young child is the family,[67] which is a tight and cohesive group with clear lines of authority, and an early mechanism for "intergeneration congruency" between the political attitudes of parents and children everywhere.[68] But this is particularly strong among Afrikaner families.[69] The father is the head of the household. The woman is to be obedient to her husband, and she is constituted as the emotional center around which the socialization of the Afrikaner child proceeds.[70]

The child is subject to strict parental authority in which punishment to the body is required by scripture. This authority over the child extends to the broader family and the community at large. Boys and girls refer to any other (white) adult as Oom (Uncle) and Tannie (Auntie), a longstanding familial tradition extending into the present. There is no talking back in this familial culture; children are told what to do, and whether it makes sense or not they are required to fall into line.

Such intense authority over the child extends into the adult years, and so it is not uncommon that parents will accompany their children into the office of the professor or the dean to sort out some minor administrative matter or academic concern of a twenty-year-old student. In these circumstances, the parent often leads and concludes the discussion, with the university student talking about his concerns only when prompted by the parent.

The authoritarian grip over the child must not be interpreted as lack of concern and affection for the child. Demonstration of affection within a highly controlled and structured family environment has no consistent equal within other South African families. This strong love for their children therefore translates into a deep and abiding interest in all aspects of the child's life.

Parents are with their children all the time, at sporting events, cultural festivals, youth camps, and church events. Parents show up en masse, sometimes with grandparents, at university opening and closing ceremonies. There is constant interaction over the telephone when children move away from home to take up residence at university. The family, in Afrikaner culture, lies at the center of the socialization of the child. It is the primary site for transmission of first knowledge, the intimate or fairy-tale knowledge[71] that lays the foundation for any future understandings of self, of community, of history.

The family transmits to children the continuity of justificatory knowledge from the past to the present. This is evident in the astounding testimony of Afrikaner youth leaders at the Johannesburg Children's Hearing of the Truth and Reconciliation Commission:

As young Afrikaners, we are proud of our cultural heritage and we are proud of the role that we play in this country. And we believe that our struggle was imbedded in core values *that we learnt in our families* and our struggle will come to the fore every time these values are endangered [emphasis added].[72]

The home was not only a place in which children were taught by words; it was the sphere in which they gained crucial master knowledge about how to behave toward the black domestic worker, the black gardener, and the black passerby. As elsewhere, "what children were allowed to see within their homes was often even more powerful than what they were allowed to hear."[73]

### Church

The Afrikaner churches, in particular the mainstream Dutch Reformed Church, were the prime instrument of the theological justification for Apartheid. In the church, fervent prayers were heard for *Boetie op die Grens* (Little Brother on the Border), who was fighting the black terrorists and shielding the Afrikaners from godless atheism. The church took away doubt about the racial order, advanced the white nationalist[74] cause, and constantly reminded churchgoers about memories from a persecuted past. Such messages were transmitted in the language of the *Volk* (the nation-people) and in the idiom of God's similarly chosen and suffering people in the Old Testament, the children of Israel.[75]

Afrikaners attend church, and children attend from an early age through *Sondagskool* (Sunday School) and the myriad of church-related activities and events that serve as the moral compass for white families.

The Afrikaner churches were a powerful transmission line for Apartheid politics and policies, and any dominee (minister) who strayed from the party line would find himself (only men at the time) without a church to lead—and worse, as the example of the Reverend Beyers Naude demonstrated so powerfully. This son of Afrikaner nationalism stood up gradually to the evils of Apartheid and was banned from the church and imprisoned in his home by the state. The church and the state were inseparable organs of white oppression, with the church functioning not only to convey positive values about white supremacy but also to institute negative threats against white disobedience.

In the churches, white Afrikaner youths would find Afrikaners compared by the dominees to the children of Israel struggling through the wilderness of oppression and being led by God to the promised land. Even though few churches would trumpet this kind of dogma in such undiluted form today, the underlying themes of ethnic uniqueness, self-preservation, struggle against others, and lamentation of oppression continue to mark this theology. When the Afrikaner child therefore receives knowledge from the past through the tight bonds of the Church, it is a knowledge of a glorious past of struggle and achievement against the odds, a knowledge of a troubling present that still threatens families and faith, and an absent knowledge about the horrors of Apartheid. Most important, it is an ecclesiastical knowledge that complements perfectly the familial knowledge transmitted during the early years, tightening the stream of transmission.

### Sport (Rugby)

Every Saturday morning and after every school day, thousands of white elementary and high school boys can be found running on a rugby field playing the great game. Every Afrikaans school has a rugby field, if no other sporting facility. Almost every Afrikaner boy plays rugby at some stage of his childhood. It is a powerful social circle in which identity is tied to achievement on the rugby field. When one enters the almost all-white, almost all-Afrikaans rugby stadium called *Loftus Versfeld* in Pretoria, it becomes immediately clear that this game is much more than rugby. It is an event of tremendous social and cultural significance for the Afrikaner. It is, of course, at base a sport, and so the normal travails and joys of losing and winning are the same as with sports everywhere. But there is something more, for this is the sport in which power, nationalism, and masculinity are projected and entrenched in Afrikanerdom.[76]

Here stories of a golden past filter smoothly across the seats around the newcomer. There are stories of Afrikaner men who represented the Volk in their battles at home and abroad. Matches against England take on special significance, for here old wars are fought afresh. Matches against the South African English south, Western Province, from where the hardy Afrikaners trekked to establish a more conservative north, also take on added significance. Rugby, here, is inextricably tied to identity. A dominee attracts attention, and some controversy, for wearing a rugby shirt from a victorious provincial game during his preaching in the Sunday service after a game. Families attend, not just single men. When losing, the hurt is palpable. "Like a funeral," says a Loftus faithful.

It is therefore the one social space in which the most intense racial conflicts can be observed. When black sports administrators and politicians seek to cleave open the racial exclusivity of rugby at the highest levels of the game, they run into a massive defense of all-white or white-dominant teams by white administrators and the white public. "Quota" remains a swear word in Afrikaner circles: it avoids the unpleasant word "race" itself but still has the same meaning. "Take rugby out of politics," is the new mantra, as if politics did not construct rugby as a nationalist playground for Afrikaner power.

The second generation walks into this minefield and hears complementary voices: the one set of voices speaks emotionally to a sense of racial identity through a recurring representation of knowledge of great Afrikaner rugby players who conquered the world, of great rugby victories over the enemy, of momentous occasions (like when the famous stadium collapsed), of myths (the one side of the field runs downward), and of administrative legends of the game (like "Doc Craven"). The other set of voices speaks with similar emotion about an assault on this racial heritage and cultural identity, the game of rugby. It is no coincidence, therefore, that angry songs such as "De la Rey" make their way forcefully into the repertoire of rugby songs sang lustily at places like Loftus.

This third concentric circle, binding the childhood identity of Afrikaner children and adolescents, runs with the same firm certainties of knowledge and memory as the family and the church. Unlike the family and the church, however, rugby is the one sphere within which there is a direct threat to racial dominance and exclusivity, and where any threat to this position is read as synonymous with all other historical threats to white minority culture, prestige, and power.

### Schools

The fourth circle of socialization is the Afrikaner school, still largely white and Afrikaans in many public institutions around the country,[77] and where, then and even now, "we learned in excruciating detail about the Voortrekker and Afrikaner heroes." More than rugby, these schools are under even greater threat to their exclusivity, though this perceived danger hits the working-class white schools much more directly than it does the middle- and upper-middle-class Afrikaans schools.[78] For complex political reasons, the government insistence on deracialization has been less forceful in white public schools than in the case of rugby and other sports such as netball and cricket.

Unlike the other circles of influence and sites of transmission for knowledge, the school is the only institution formally sanctioned to transmit official knowledge to children. It was understood by the founding fathers of Apartheid education that the school was crucial to intergenerational transmission of racialized knowledge, for "youth can faithfully take over the task and vocation of the older generation only when it has acquired through instruction in history a true vision of the origin of the nation, and of the direction in that heritage."[79]

Schools have, then[80] and now,[81] faithfully conveyed powerful master symbols of Apartheid ideology to one generation after another of Afrikaner children. In the words of the distinguished education scholar, Edmund King, "Schools . . . are but the expression of the Afrikaner-dominated cultural totality."[82]

In a centralized school system with a centralized curriculum, one would expect a black government to ensure that the official knowledge codes so transmitted would meet the demands of a more open society and a more inclusive democracy. Ordinarily, this would be the case.

The problem is that, unlike the curriculum under Apartheid, there is no state surveillance mechanism (such as the infamous inspection system) to check on the classroom routines and knowledge dispensed by every teacher for purposes of compliance.

Schools are, to a large extent, left to themselves as conveyors of knowledge to the next generation. The sole instrument for content accountability is the grade 12 end-of-school examinations; they apply only to the later grades and do not prohibit teaching other knowledges in the lower grades. Although an anti-inspection culture persists through the black teacher unions because of the terrible experience of these quasi-political agents (the school inspectors)[83] under Apartheid, such resistance has the effect today of relieving white schools of responsibility for what knowledge they actually transmit in the classroom.

This does not, however, imply that teachers can be micromanaged and controlled in terms of knowledge taught, for even under the most intense periods of surveillance during Apartheid black teachers found ways of transmitting a broader curriculum that conveyed values of freedom, democracy, and change.

Still, in white Afrikaans schools the transmission mechanisms for white knowledge are relatively untouched by the enormous changes in the social world surrounding schools. In recent research, Thobekile Gamede observed content teaching in two schools, one white and one black, using the same curriculum regarding two critical events in struggle history (the Sharpeville Massacre of 1960 and the Soweto Uprising of 1976). She found that what was actually taught in the two schools was light years apart. The white school reduced this segment of the curriculum to the bare minimum of information in teaching overshadowed by European history; the black school used an extended period of time to bring in the details of the emotions, politics, and drama of social change inspired by and through these two events.[84]

A tight concentric circle of school knowledge reinforces a clear and consistent message about knowledge of the past that, up to this point, has not been fundamentally disrupted. Even so, the mere possibility of a symbolically open curriculum has driven right-wing families into home schooling and private school options in a minority of Afrikaner homes.[85]

*Cultural Networks*

Nothing transmits historical and social knowledge in a more explicit and emotionally charged form than the host of cultural festivals and celebrations that have flourished in South Africa after 1994.[86] There has always been a rich array of cultural organizations to transmit the Afrikaans language, symbols, rituals, and traditions to youth, including the *Afrikaanse Taal- en Kultuurvereniging* (ATKV), the *Voortrekkers, Veldskole* (veld schools), and the *Junior Rapportryers.* Such traditional bodies continue today, though some with less attraction; but alongside these undiluted forms of knowledge transmission has sprung up a forceful array of new celebratory forms, from the *Klein Karoo Nasionale Kunstefees* (KKNK) with its "exhausted focus on the Afrikaner"[87] to the *Oppiekoppie Rock Festival,* the *Aardklop Arts Festival,* the *Woordfees* (Word Festival), and many others. Here Afrikaans music, poetry, and politics mix freely in a very assertive though not uncontested display of racial and cultural power.

This latter-day assertion of cultural presence (we are still here) is a response to being declared invisible in the social and political domain. This is what the Mitscherlichs call *mourning* (as opposed to *melancholia*), the loss of something with which one had an intense emotional relationship.[88]

At these events, knowledge of the past is brought to the surface again and presented in nostalgic celebration of former heroes and events, recalling past struggles and achievements among the new generation. There are endless debates about whether these cultural events are "political" or not. The atmosphere is often tense, the dialogue fierce, and the underlying question of *Who is more Afrikaans?* is always present if not directly expressed.

Nothing is more strenuously asserted and lamented at these events than the Afrikaans language. Seminar after seminar, speaker after speaker, in poem and song, remonstrate against the threat to Afrikaans and by implication the *voortbestaan* (survival) of Afrikaner culture and identity. With such recollection, deep and primordial animosities are stirred, and emotional knowledge of a lost past is powerfully conveyed to young Afrikaners.

Cultural events are often held in remote rural areas; this in itself is a politics of location since the ideal of the Afrikaner rustic working the land in these small towns and on distant farms forms part of the mythology of Afrikanerdom and the essential knowledge of the past. But culture is also conveyed in schools through drama, poetry, and music in the extracurricular program of an Afrikaans institution. Central to the broader curriculum of every Afrikaner school is *Die Revue*, an evening concert in which Afrikaans children present Afrikaans music, drama, poetry, and theatre as a fixed item on the annual school calendar. Here too, a powerful transmission of knowledge of history, language, and culture is conveyed in the school as cultural arena.

It is, however, also at these events that the beginnings of rupture occur, the questioning of certainty. The odd black speaker raises "the other side," although this is almost always a black Afrikaans speaker. The odd white speaker makes the argument for a broader and more incorporating culture, one less racially and even culturally exclusive. A black child wins the Afrikaans prize for speaking the language. The cynics claim this broadening of access to Afrikaner culture is a political act designed to increase the numbers that stand up for something that can no longer make demands, and be heard, on purely racial grounds. Nevertheless, for the most part, these *suiwer* (pure) transmissions of cultural knowledge are smoothly conveyed into the anxious, sometimes angry, and receptive minds of Afrikaner youth.

### Peers

The final social circle that binds Afrikaner youth together and conveys common knowledge of the past is the peer groups within which white children and adolescents assemble. In no other social group in South Africa is racial exclusivity so rigidly maintained than among Afrikaner youth. In these all-white, all-Afrikaans peer groups, a powerful set of social and historical stories, received knowledge, is shared and reinforced in an emotionally intense closed circle.

These closed Afrikaans circles are often gendered, with boys coalescing around male interests that reflect, reproduce, and reinforce the gender hierarchies of the family, the church, and the school. The all-white families, the all-white churches, the all-white schools, the all-white school sports, and the all-white festivals predictably deliver all-white friendship circles in this Afrikaner community. Here a dangerous knowledge is received and repeated, unchallenged, and often with disastrous consequences.[89]

It is this powerful transmission belt for historical knowledge that explains "the rage against alterity"[90] at both ends of the conveyor: the adults (parents, dominees, cultural organizers, teachers) as the senders and the children as the receptors of this knowledge. This conceptual representation of the specific forms and sites of knowledge transmission in the Afrikaner community is unique in its content and intensity, but it fits within other conceptual schemata that seek to explain the intergenerational mechanisms of transfer in an integrated way. So, for example, in Danieli's integrated framework:

An individual's identity involves a complex interplay of multiple spheres or systems. . . . These systems dynamically coexist along the time dimension to create a continuous conception of life from the past through the present to the future.[91]

Danieli's framework cannot explain two things. First, it does not differentiate between open and closed systems in the intergenerational transmission of knowledge. Here the study by Wineburg and his colleagues is instructive on transmission of historical knowledge about the Vietnam War among American schoolchildren.[92] In this open system, there is a distinction between the "lived history" of the parents and the "available history" of their children because the knowledge influences at play are multiple, diverse, and loosely connected. Thus, children learn more about the Vietnam War from films representing one kind of knowledge (protests against) than from the more contested and nuanced accounts of the war which their parents lived through. From the Wineburg study, it becomes clear that there are marked differences between the open systems of a democratic society and the closed systems of an authoritarian state.

Second, Danieli cannot explain the traumatic separation or disjunction between group (ethnic) knowledge and national (official) knowledge among Afrikaners. In his framework, the national identity is simply another form of extending personal identity; but when these two circles shatter and separate, what happens among Afrikaners is a defensive falling back on the group knowledge and identity that suddenly has to contend with, and even contest, the national version of past events. This leads to intensification of group knowledge and identity, and the beginnings of its fragmentation as it is forced to confront hitherto unheard knowledge.

## The Primacy of Knowledge

Memory carries emotions such as fear, anxiety, pride, and hurt. It also carries knowledge. Much of the literature on the second generation focuses on emotions and their traumatic effects and not on knowledge; this is a crucial limitation in the extensive research on the receivers of transmitted knowledge. This is perhaps not surprising, since many of the studies on the receptor generation come from psychologists and psychotherapists who report on their work with the traumatized from a mental and emotional health perspective. This book narrows the focus of inquiry in line with the rare approach of Auerhahn and Laub (1998): "We have shifted the focus away from value-laden judgments of psychological health to the issue of knowledge . . . it is through this lens that we attempt to examine the intergenerational effects . . . of trauma."[93]

The focus on knowledge, and specifically indirect knowledge, concerns itself with what is known, how it is known, and how such knowledge is expressed in the second generation. Of course this knowledge is embedded in, and affected by, emotions. But emotions and knowledge are not the same. The stories of the past as held by parents and other adults, and how this information relays down to the second generation through closed circles of influence (the biblical text in church, the curriculum text in schools, the cultural texts of festivals, the domestic scripts of the family, the public texts of memorials and monuments), are knowledge constructs. Similarly, the interruption of secure knowledge produces human responses that are also "essentially a kind of knowledge, interacting with all the other kinds of knowledge which make up our struggle to overcome uncertainty."[94]

Knowledge so conceived implies culpability. To know or not to know about an atrocity, whether one committed it or not, has legal consequences and, importantly, personal and familial consequences. This focus on knowledge enables analysis founded on questions such as: What did they know? How did they know? What did they do with such knowledge? How was it transmitted from the direct receiver as indirect knowledge to the second generation?

Knowledge of a terrible or glorious past is of course not only transmitted in words. Even if there is silence and "this knowledge was not passed on openly in the family narration, it nevertheless exists"[95] in the bodies, actions, and responses of the parents who transmit it. This is the powerful contribution of Christa Wolf's writing on being a German child in Nazi Germany, where "the family functions as the privileged locus of scenes of transmission,"[96] and where "silences are themselves passed on both consciously and unconsciously from generation to generation,"[97] and in which context children achieve "a certain knack for knowing when to deflect one's 'curiosity from dangerous areas.'"[98]

It is also the question of whether knowledge, so conceived, disables the ability to distinguish emotional reaction from the facts of the situation. So the hard question asked repeatedly in South Africa—How can whites claim they did not know about atrocities?—is a moot point, for as elsewhere "even if knowledge . . . was available early on, the proregime belief made it seem like . . . propaganda."[99]

## Conclusion

In one of the most astounding exchanges at the Truth and Reconciliation Commission, this problem of knowledge and what it allows the perpetrators to see and not see is vividly on display when young Afrikaners present their case.[100]

**Interviewer** (himself an Afrikaner)
How is it possible that we didn't know anything [of what was happening] or did nothing about it? Do you have a perspective on that?

**Young Afrikaner**
War as such is a crime against humanity, there are no victors. I had personal knowledge because I saw it, certain of these actions that took place, I saw the result of bodies being burnt [by blacks], I had knowledge of that. I didn't have knowledge of orchestrated efforts of [security and police] forces that I served to incite such incidents.

**Interviewer**

You say that you saw bodies that were burnt, what did you think was the reason for that, who burnt them?

**Young Afrikaner**

I didn't have to think of what the reason was, it was quite clear. I did my service in the Vaal Triangle and at that stage it was in the midst of the whole issue, in the 1990s and it was Black on Black violence. That it could have been incited from another force, well we have evidence for that now. But I have personal knowledge of well let's refer to it as violence between ethnic groups, Black ethnic groups in the Vaal Triangle, I saw that.

**Interviewer**

You never saw some kind of an orchestrated effort from the government?

**Young Afrikaner**

No, I never experienced it as such and I think the evidence came as a shock.

This is a rare but crucial exchange with young white Afrikaners. It demonstrates how knowledge of the same event, an atrocity, is interpreted through ideological lenses that permit only preferred meanings even when faced with the brutal facts of what really happened. Many Afrikaner youths and their parents continue to hold this knowledge of a barbaric black people over whom the security and police forces did nothing else than to impress law and order in the unstable townships. This sense of what happened remains undisturbed knowledge among Afrikaners, and it explains the contempt from many within this community for the Truth and Reconciliation Commission, and the difficulty of accepting even the moderate terms of transition from Apartheid.

To understand such transmission and how it shapes and affects the daily lives of the children of the perpetrators, we now turn to actual experiences of Afrikaner students at high school and university, recorded as I lived, talked, taught, led, and learned from them over a period of seven years.

# 3    Sure Foundations

We must strive to win the fight against the non-White in the
classroom instead of losing it on the battlefield.[1]

To understand the nature, content, and intensity
of knowledge transmitted to the second generation,
it is crucial first to grasp the knowledge received by the parents or the
first generation, those Afrikaners who actually lived through, upheld,
enforced, and defended Apartheid during the years of white nationalist rule. Then, with Afrikaner nationalism in its most virulent expression, the transmission belt for knowledge was even more intense and
extended because in addition to the family, school, and church the mass
media (radio, television, print, and even cinema[2]) and the state machinery (ministerial speeches, government policies) added to the robustness
of what was transmitted to the children.

In rare South African scholarship on "the intergenerational transmission of Apartheid and the life-world of Afrikaner children," Joyce
Hickson and Susan Kriegler (1996)[3] identified at least six influences on
the young: the Afrikaner Broederbond, the Federation of Afrikaans Cultural Organizations, the Dutch Reformed Churches, the South African
media and in particular the state broadcaster, Christian National Education (CNE), and textbooks. There is some overlap here, while other
critical transmission influences are curiously missing (for instance, the
Afrikaner family and powerful socialization through national service
in the South African Defense Force), but what Hickson and Kriegler

point out—on the basis of their counseling experiences—is that compared to other groups

issues for the Afrikaner are complex. Infused in the identity are the authoritarian ideology of Afrikaner nationalism and the intergenerational transmission of white domination. In a rapidly changing society, feelings of guilt, shame and confusion may be presenting concerns. Fear about one's own role in the new South Africa may add to a host of self-doubts. For many Afrikaner clients, early ethnocentric conditioning has resulted in anxiety and fearfulness, feelings of alienation, and a distorted racial-cultural identity development. Fear about the future is a dominant concern.[4]

A review of research at the time showed that

in other less racially divided societies there is evidence to show that white ethnocentrism may decrease somewhat in degree through later childhood, whereas in South Africa ethnocentrism may increase in conformity with racist social norms. Afrikaner children appear to be more prejudiced toward blacks than English-speaking children, *mirroring the established findings from adult research* [emphasis added].[5]

Three major analyses[6] of Apartheid textbooks have demonstrated how the first generation received their knowledge, a transmission line that reinforced patriarchy, rigid authoritarianism, extreme ethnocentrism, white pride, racial exclusivity, out-group rejection, and the naturalness of white rule and black subjugation.[7] It was, moreover, the parents who lived through what Gavin Evans[8] called the militarization of white South African schooling, where:

once a week over 300,000 white South African youths leave their school uniforms at home and come to class in military browns. For an hour or more a week they will learn the basics of army drill, how to shoot and more advanced forms of "military preparedness".... This school cadet programme ... [served] to mould the consciousness of white pupils and to educate them to accept the national priorities of an increasingly militarised state.[9]

In addition to the school cadet program, other complementary activities ensured that a tight transmission of knowledge was constantly impressed on the minds and hearts of white children; such programs included the veld schools (*veldskole*) in what was then Transvaal province, youth preparedness programs (*jeugweerbaarheidsprogramme*), civil defense exercises, school guidance programs, and the "emergency terrorist plan."[10] In addition to these formal curricular events, there were a host of informal education activities with the same socialization intent, including *volkspele* (folk dances), *stryddae* (fetes), *kermisse* (bazaars), and of course *volksfeeste* (folk festivals).[11] What is crucial in this powerful socialization role of formal and informal educational programs is not only that they transmitted knowledge of the truth so intensely to the inside of this insular grouping of Afrikaner youth but that they also shut out alternatives. Thus recalls an Afrikaner from his childhood:

Racist ideology went unchallenged because we never heard dissenting voices: it seemed to be rational, and it seemed to serve the interests of all of us. . . . Not a single parent or teacher believed in a non-racial society. The facts seemed to be clear.[12]

It was this combination of closing in with dogma and keeping away alternatives that led Stanley Cohen to observe that "the essence of white consciousness in Apartheid South Africa was a continuous shutting out of what seemed 'obvious' to any outsider."[13]

What was the knowledge being transmitted? It was knowledge of black people as terrorists and Communists and of white people as Christian and civilized. It presented black people as a threat to the very existence of white people. Through this mix of activities, children again gained knowledge of fear, the distrust of difference, the defense of privilege, and the acceptance of military-type authoritarian discipline as normative in school and society. If other circles of influence worked softly to reinforce the closed experience of Afrikaner children, this aggressive military approach to their socialization sealed any chances of dissent. For the first generation, "socialized in all-Afrikaner schools and universities, informed exclusively by Afrikaans newspapers and sanctified by at least nominal religious adherence, the life of racial privilege was taken for granted and assumed to be natural."[14]

It should not surprise therefore that with these closed circles of interconnecting influences the chain of transmission from the first generation to the post-Apartheid generation of Afrikaner children kept the knowledge of the past, present, and future firmly intact, and that such knowledge was couched in the intense emotions of fear, anger, anxiety, hostility, and defensiveness. On this claim the research is unequivocal: that as young South Africans made the transition from the Apartheid era to the post-Apartheid period, not only did their racial attitudes and orientations remain largely undisturbed but "political change has produced an increase in racism in the most threatened group, the whites."[15]

If this thesis is correct—that the second generation will express in their attitudes and behavior this indirect knowledge of the past—then it should be demonstrated most clearly in the undergraduate university years, that is, when most white Afrikaans students are, for the first time, exposed to learning and living with black students. The thesis will be tested in this and the next chapter, but the purpose of this introduction is simply to uncover the nature of *direct* knowledge as impressed on and received by the parents of white children and youths living after Apartheid, knowledge that would make its way down to their children as indirect knowledge.

### On the Playground

As I walk through the gates of one of the oldest Afrikaans high schools for boys in South Africa, a venerable institution within its community,[16] I become conscious of the stares and the whispers of these young adolescents as their gaze turns toward this sole black person on their campus—apart from the cleaners and gardeners. Some move closer as I make my way up the long path that connects the school gate to the principal's office. One or two venture an unmistakable racist comment; others speak to friends in unwelcoming tones intended for my ears: "*wat soek hy hier?*" (what is he looking for here?).

When I come anonymously into white Afrikaans schools, I find this kind of treatment common, especially from the white boys. When I come in introduced as the dean at Tukkies, the treatment is very different, for then these same boys would scrape and bow in elaborate greetings and signs of respect.

I return to the school for a photo shoot with some of these boys for a progressive Afrikaans magazine on the topic of leadership for change; the reaction is of course different. But I sense the discomfort among the boys, the difficulty of being spontaneous as children tend to be when an unknown person enters the schoolyard. I try to engage them during the shoot, and some try, but I notice how they look around for approval from their peers; this is not easy for them. For most of these white Afrikaner boys, this is the first time they encounter a black authority figure so close to them. Slowly, the narrative of whiteness and the knowledge of others are no longer as secure.

White girls also give you "the look," but they are less likely to make racist or unwelcoming comments. At the white English boys' high school up the road, the treatment is completely different. There the boys greet with a lively "Good morning, sir!" The English school has been integrated for years, and has even had black boys in the leadership of the student body. There are one or two black teachers on the staff, and black parents are visible in the school halls. This does not mean that white English schools do not have racial incidents from time to time; it simply means that these schools have experienced racial interaction and cross-racial friendships for some time, making it easier for white and black school boys in this context to get along. But the student body at the Afrikaans high school is almost all white, with no black teachers, as is the case with its sister school. The boys' school and the girls' school are separated, as if by design, by the Dutch Reformed Church, which in turn sits across the road from the great rugby stadium, Loftus Versfeld, and just down the road from UP and the surrounding Afrikaans homes. Within steps of each other, all the major socialization agents of Afrikaner youth huddle together in this intense urban space.

Years before, I would have reacted to their comments and made sure that these white Afrikaans boys knew what I thought about them, and then I would have raised hell in the principal's office. Now, I find this useful information, offering an understanding of why they find it so difficult to adjust to racial diversity in the residences when they eventually come to UP. I am also, throughout, conscious of their loss of power and of the misery of defeat.

I realize early on that these students come from insular and closed white environments where family, church, school, and peer group reinforce their sense of white exclusiveness. In these closed circles of influence the narrative is solid and uninterrupted: blacks are taking over everything, are killing whites, are corrupt, take jobs from whites, are favored through quotas in medical school enrollments, are treating whites unfairly. Blacks in government, the narrative continues, are undermining Afrikaans culture, language, and history by changing the names of streets and towns and by allowing English to dominate within the former Afrikaans universities. Blacks should be spending this money on the poor. The charges are obviously exaggerated, but in the confusion of loss "identity requires difference in order to be, and it converts difference into otherness in order to secure its own self-certainty."[17]

The problem with these stories is not that they happen, but that they are largely uninterrupted by counternarratives. The closed nature of these concentric life circles and reinforcing stories is no longer hermetically sealed as during the days of Apartheid. There are no Apartheid state media now that feed interpretation of resistance and uprising from blacks as terrorism and tribalism; *then* the state media were a major vehicle for racial reassurance among white Afrikaner youths.

The state media, now in black hands, offer different interpretations of the past, present, and future, and this is new to young Afrikaners. There are other counternarratives now—including the erection of new monuments and museums to memorialize a black nationalist past. This too is challenging and begins to break the stranglehold of singular knowledge and uncontested meanings. When white Afrikaner students reach university, the closed circles of interaction are challenged by living and learning with black students and a few black professors. The closed circles of white interaction still interpret such disruptive knowledge from the media and monuments inwardly and conservatively, but at least such interpretation is no longer unchallenged. It also provokes reaction, which can be quite aggressive and angry, as the single story of an innocent past starts to unravel in front of their eyes.

What cannot be dismissed as easily, though, is what happens when the counternarrative is present in the form of a black dean from their historic university, where many of them will study, engaging them in their own language in a way that brings white and black stories into the open for discussion. This is where the trouble starts.

## On to Camp

The Afrikaans girls' school in Pretoria has an annual camp for grade ten children where students are exposed to broader topics than the school curriculum allows. Speakers talk about Afrikaans culture, about living in a democracy, about careers and life choices, and about self-awareness and personal development. A good friend on the staff, involved with Afrikaner youth development outside of schools, invites me to speak on the changes in the country and how white youth can respond. This friend has a more liberal streak than many of her colleagues, and I can only imagine what the invitation must have cost her. But this event was to fundamentally change my life and my disposition to Afrikaner youths and their families.

I try to connect with young people not only in their own language but in a cultural idiom that makes sense to them and that further enables social connection between speaker and audience. I start with some biography, telling them about my earlier years growing up in South Africa, the dispossession of family property given to whites, the struggles of my parents to give their children a decent life, the gangs and the violence that threatened in the townships where I grew up, the spiritual lives of my parents, my choice to become a Christian and an active preacher, my encounters with the brutality of Apartheid in the lives of the high school students whom I taught, and my hatred at the time for all things white. The story is interspersed with humor, and this keeps them attentive, but I sense clearly that the atmosphere is tense and that this workshop will have to be handled sensitively. The biographical sketch is a crucial introduction, for this will be the first time they hear such a story, so directly, from a black person and in Afrikaans. It lays the foundation for what will happen next.

I take out a Bible and paraphrase the story of *The Good Samaritan*, which in its Afrikaans translation has the powerful title *Die Barmhartige Samaritaan* (the Compassionate Samaritan).[18] It is the story told by Jesus to an inquiring lawyer who challenged him with the question, "And who is my neighbor?" Jesus then tells of a Jew who goes down from Jerusalem to Jericho, is attacked and robbed by thieves, and lies battered alongside the road. The story goes that a priest and a Levite pass by and ignore the man, but the Good Samaritan takes care of him, transfers him to a local inn, and pays the expenses for his care.

After outlining the bare essentials of the parable, I call on three girls to explain to their three hundred peers what the point of the story is. Like so many, they venture that this is about being kind to people—which is just what I want to hear. I then, with some dramatic performance, tell them that this is all wrong and that they, like me, have been totally misled. This is really a story about border crossings, about caring and relating "to those whom you think are different from you." How else, I ask them, can we explain the effort Jesus makes to identify the religious and ethnic identities of the main characters in the story?

This seems to work, first because it is a biblical story, which carries considerable legitimacy among these churchgoing children and their families; and second because it is a human story about things we all struggle with in this new South Africa. I then tell the packed and now very quiet audience that the single most important challenge they face to making it in the new South Africa is to move out of their white comfort zone and to embrace, not tolerate, their fellow human beings who, despite the accident of skin color, are in fact no different from them.

I am still working my way through the social implications of the Samaritan story for South Africa when the hand of a grade ten girl shoots up for attention. This kind of interruption of an adult is unusual in an Afrikaans school, but I am happy to find response. "Well, Professor," she starts, "I agree with what you say about crossing bridges and stuff. But tell me this, how do I cross bridges toward someone who looks like the people who almost killed my sister and me a few weeks ago in a violent car hijacking?"

In all my years of teaching, this is easily the most difficult question I have faced. It is direct, insightful and sophisticated. I am off-balance, and the experience of teaching tells me that this requires some reflection. "Let's take a break," I tell the expectant audience, they too sensing a potentially slippery moment. I move to a corner to think about what to say, but I am soon surrounded by about a dozen of the girls from this group, all probing and questioning, several quite emotional about what they had just heard—for the first time, said several of them. I abandon my quest for a quiet, reflective moment for dealing with the original question.

In these moments of high emotion, children tend to say things off-guard. One of the girls, who is clearly moved, says that when she sees this black man as a speaker, she starts to prepare herself for a lousy speech in English or an even lousier talk in Afrikaans. "But you speak our language so well," she offers. Another tells me about her racist father, and that what I say makes a lot of sense, *"maar u moet my pa ont-moet"* (but you must meet my father). Yet another tells me that she has a black friend and she would like to take her home, but what should she do since she knows her father will not allow such a visit. None of them speak about their mothers' attitudes; fathers loom large as racial gate-keepers in their homes.

It is at this point I realize that for some of these girls the transmission line carrying knowledge from parents to children is a lot less secure than I had assumed. There is tension here, a willingness to break away, at least for some of the girls, but there are powerful *resocialization* forces at work, as students of political socialization call it. At the heart of this tension stands the family and its patriarch. One of the teachers confides, as I make my way back to the front of the barn, "Don't worry, they are more *verlig* [enlightened] than their parents." I have to continue, and I do not know what to tell the original questioner.

"Listen, you asked a very good question, and I must be honest with you, I do not know how to answer you, but can I say the following?" I then tell a story about how, as a young high school student in grade eleven, I visit my grandparents' home in Montagu, a small and picturesque town in the rural Western Cape province. This is a place of powerful memory, where the family lost its property to whites under the Group Areas Act around the time I was born. This is the act that, his daughters insist, contributed to the psychosomatic blindness of my grandfather. By the time this knowledge reached me as a child growing up, I was angry with white people. It was with this anger that I traveled on a segregated railway bus to Montagu to visit my grandparents. Only now they were moved into *die lokasie* (the location, literally, or the township), away from the center of shops and tarred streets in *die dorp* (the downtown white area) where they used to live.

As I tell the story, there is complete quiet in the room, 100 percent concentration; the girls are absorbed and I am conscious of the need to retain, as hard as I can, a managed emotional voice, so that the story is not lost in this critical moment. It is hard, since I have not told this story before, not even to my closest family, and I certainly did not expect at the start of this workshop to share it with three hundred strangers.

I continue and tell how I am instructed by my grandmother to go down to die the *dorp* to buy a loaf of bread. As I walk back through the now-white town I carry my anger and hostility on my sleeve, conscious in the knowledge of what whites stole from my grandparents. Then, as if on cue, a brick comes flying across the road in my direction, clipping the back of my heel and hitting the sidewalk with a loud bang. In shock, I look up and see a smiling white boy, about my age, leaning over his gate and pretending that he has nothing to do with the flying brick. Angry before the brick came, I rush the boy, taller than me, and climb into him. His father, unfortunately, is at home, and even more unfortunately, is an off-duty policeman.

I am kicked and bundled into his car, not knowing where he is taking me, but sure that this is not going to be a pleasant afternoon. I am angry enough not to be scared. Every now and then he will throw a question at me, like, "Where are you from?" or more rhetorically, "Do you realize what you have done?" and I answer where I can. With every attempted answer, he slams his foot on the brakes, leans backward, and throws a punch in my direction. I only later figure out why he is doing this; I am required to intersperse my answers with that humiliating word "baas" (master, as in servant to master). He is certainly not going to get that out of me.

We end up at the Montagu police station, and this is where I start to become anxious, but I will not show this anxiety to him. Behind the main desk sits a huge man in uniform, looking half-disinterested. His off-duty colleague is pacing the floor, asking for permission to deal with me once and for all. I know what this means, for at that time and especially in the rural areas I have heard what happens to activists and to black people generally. The heat is building in the room; my heart pounds.

At this point, my aunt comes storming through the door and pleads with the police to let me go. I am from Cape Town, she says, and only visiting, and the family is expecting me back home. Her pleas work, and eventually I am released.

The room is dead quiet, and I notice several girls in tears, and also one of the teachers.

I turn toward the girl who asked the riveting question and say:

So you see, I too have this terrible knowledge of what happened to me, and all my life I have been struggling to cross this bridge toward people who look like you. And I must be honest, it is very difficult.

And so all I can ask of you is that you too try to cross the same bridge, from the other side, and maybe, just maybe, we will meet each other somewhere in the middle. For the sake of our country, we must at least try.

That is the end of the workshop, nothing more can be said; the message carries powerfully, and I am very aware of the fact that like some of these grade ten girls. I have made a major emotional crossing myself in those moments of engagement. Still in tears, we talk and talk after the workshop. At this moment I realize, for the first time, that these children are my children, and I will spend all my energy to help them make the transition across this difficult bridge.

There are a number of pedagogical observations to make about this rare encounter in a culture that still values silence over dialogue about the past. The first is that it is lodged within a cultural idiom familiar to these girls and to which they can relate; in other words, the political intrusion comes through the scriptures. The second is that the engagement transpires in Afrikaans, and this makes a vital difference, especially in terms of their ability to respond and their capacity to listen; a major emotional stumbling block is thus removed. The third is that they are being engaged with a senior authority respected by and brought in by their teachers; I am in no doubt that being dean at "their" university enables me to reach them in ways that would be more difficult otherwise. The fourth is that the engagement acknowledges personal weakness and struggles; I cannot and do not speak to them from the position of the accuser occupying the moral high ground; in such a scenario, I will simply be another black speaking head that threatens their already insular and fragile world. The fifth is that the engagement took them, as young people, seriously; their voices matter and their questions carry weight. Preaching to them would be the end of dialogue, especially about difficult topics such as racism and dispossession. The sixth is the use of humor interspersed throughout the engagement, and at critical points, so that this very serious topic is taken on in a relatively relaxed manner. And the seventh is that the dialogue encourages and models directness in speaking about difficult social issues.

The terms of the engagement are the platform from which to engage and disrupt received knowledge. There are still powerful resocialization forces at work within the circles of influence in which these girls live, but at least the dominant narratives about the past have been challenged directly, empathically, and responsively. It will, for at least some of those girls, constitute a turning point. Three years later, a family turns up at an address of the same kind to a major Dutch Reformed Church in Pretoria; it is the only family to bring their two children to this seminar. The mother comes to me afterward with the other members of her family in tow. "I wanted them to hear you; I was the teacher who sat at the back during that workshop with the Pretoria girls three years ago; it changed me, and I wanted them to hear you too."

## Withdrawing In

Below the political and intellectual radar of most observers of schools, socializing forces keep pulling white Afrikaner students back into the conserving narratives of the past. About four miles up the road from where the grade ten girls attend school in Pretoria, there is another Afrikaans school of considerable academic and sporting reputation. Known for producing great athletes, this school also remains largely white and all-Afrikaans after more than fourteen years of South Africa's nonracial democracy. The pattern of racial settlement remains undisturbed in this school as well, with disastrous social consequences for these young people.

So it is with some surprise that I receive an invitation to address the Voortrekker youth club of this high school one night. Driven in part by curiosity and in part by yet another opportunity to influence change, I accept the invitation. Surely any notion of a Voortrekker youth is anachronistic all these years after Apartheid. What on earth are the teachers doing with these young people in today's environment?

As I rush out of my office, it is already dark outside. I look at the invitation and discover that the event is not at the school but at the Voortrekker Monument itself, the huge monument to Afrikaner nationalism overlooking the city of Pretoria and in sight of schools and universities in the area. This is ominous, I think. It is very dark in the secluded area of the monument to which I am directed. Eventually I find the small arena but no students, only a small group of adults on the cold stone seats of the open-air amphitheatre. What is going on here? I wait for some time and then, suddenly, in this dark amphitheatre with only torches burning, from all sides come lines of students marching into the arena.

The young people wear the ties and scarves and clothing that mark them as Voortrekkers. Those who walk in front carry flags, not of the new South Africa but of the old Boer Republics. At this point I begin to think this is a serious mistake. Am I being ambushed by this archconservative event? Why was I not told about the procedures and the purposes of this archaic ceremony? It is a mistake coming here, I think.

As the leaders of the marching student body reach the center of the arena, everybody stands and an oath is taken with the leaders' hands placed on a huge Bible. Young people are admonished to stay true to Afrikaans and the ideals of the struggle of Afrikaners over the centuries. They are reminded of the Trek and the values of their ancestors. There is a solemnity in this ceremony, an orderliness that becomes as attractive as it is absurd. Then, despite my presence, the audience of mainly young people but also parents are invited to sing *die volkslied*—not the awkward but integrated national anthem of the new South Africa that brings together the struggle anthem of blacks with elements of the volkslied of Apartheid, but the old anthem.

Eventually I am invited to speak after a generous and elaborate introduction. I speak about the challenges of the new South Africa, the threat of cultural isolation, the need to rethink treasured symbols and traditions from the past, and the importance of coming to terms with black South Africans. It is a difficult talk, for on the one hand I do not want to dismiss out of hand this elaborate ceremony and appear disrespectful. But on the other hand, I cannot stand by and see yet another generation of young South Africans close in on culture and traditions that circle out the pressing reality of an integrated society. How does one teach in ways that retain the best of the ethnic traditions of the past and at the same time include a broader set of knowledges and memories

that enrich both? This is unexplored terrain in much of critical pedagogy, with its all-or-nothing approach to change.

The Voortrekkers are a defensive organization, concerned about
responding to loss and defeat, and conscious of the burden of having
served in the network of cultural influences that transmitted knowledge
of Apartheid symbols, traditions, and memories to generations of white
Afrikaner youth. Its leadership responds aggressively to the contested
role of the Voortrekkers:

Of course the Voortrekkers, with youth and adult members, are not perfect.
Naturally we also do not always do the right things. And of course those
intent on finding fault will find such faults among us . . . we refuse to adopt
an "excuse me that I live" attitude and to be forced into thinking that the
Voortrekkers are an embarrassment in the current South Africa. Our attitude
is precisely the opposite![19]

So for a segment of Afrikaner youth there continues to be exposure to
an organization that tries to retain the transmission role of knowledge
of the past. It continues to appeal to God and Afrikaans in its Constitution. But it also respects order and submission to the state even as it
advances culture, language, and ethnicity. Nominally open to all who
identify themselves as Afrikaners, in practice the Voortrekkers remain
a conservative and conserving organization for the transmission of
knowledge of a cleaned-up past.

### Reaching Out

In a minority of Afrikaans schools, the school leaders have taken a very
different route to engagement with old knowledge and new realities. In
schools in one of our research projects,[20] the principals led the change
and decided, with varying degrees of ambition, to bring black students
and staff into their schools, and to broaden at least the unofficial curriculum to include other knowledge and traditions.

My earliest experience in Pretoria was an invitation to an Afrikaans
high school on the western edges of the city. It was located in the poor
white suburb of Danville, and I prepared for a difficult visit. This was
the year 2000; emotions and politics were still raw among whites and
blacks alike. Yet here, in one of the poorest urban areas of white resi-

dence, the principal is proud to show me two couples: a black head boy and a white deputy-head boy, a white head girl and a black deputy-head girl. In the school prefect system still honored in white schools, these are the most senior responsibilities given to students, and they bring significant prestige and respect from students, parents, and teachers alike. It was not what I expected.

Some white schools went farther along this route. One was J. G. Strijdom High School in the south of Johannesburg, named after an Apartheid prime minister, which boldly changed its name to Diversity High. Often motivated in part by the need to increase student numbers, which whites alone could not sustain, these were mainly working-class schools.

Their plans for integration seem to work. White and black students learn in the same school environment. The informal curriculum includes soccer alongside rugby, gumboot dancing alongside Afrikaans *volkslied-jies* (folksongs), Indian dress with *Boeredrag* (traditional Boer clothing) on special evenings, and foods that reflect ethnic traditions. However awkward and sometimes superficial these efforts to advance racial integration seem to be, what cannot be faulted is the attempt to bring together students from diverse backgrounds and experiences.

Although examples of Afrikaans schools integrating are still rare, they exist in isolated parts of the country, calling on enormous courage from principals readily labeled *kafferboeties*, a despicable term meaning "nigger lovers" that was used over the decades whenever there was the slightest hint of a white Afrikaner siding with any black person.[21]

The sad outcome of these bold ventures is that invariably these white working-class schools desegregate over time from all-white schools into all-black schools; this is very different in, for example, the middle-class white schools, mainly English, where desegregation happens. As more and more black students come into white working-class schools, white students begin to leave gradually to all-white schools, and eventually working-class white parents no longer send their children to their traditional schools. This has been the trend in the schools in our research, and it has the effect of again leaving white Afrikaner children isolated from meaningful interaction with black children.

There seems to be little that can be done, by way of policy or political initiative in South Africa, to recognize these opportunities for bringing together white Afrikaans and black students. The sheer need to respond to the resource imbalances in black schools overrides political concerns with this major fault line between white and black youth, a neglect that could have serious consequences for future generations.

## Sure Foundations

Inside white Afrikaans primary schools, it is easy to understand how early knowledge establishes such a firm and binding commitment to language, culture, and Volk. I have yet to find more dedicated teachers and more involved parents than in these Afrikaans primary schools. Here the bond of language is firmly secured. It is here that the child is introduced to the foundations of custom, creed, and culture through generous and warm adults other than their parents. Until this primary terrain is witnessed firsthand, it is hard to understand the strength of the emotional connection to the past among white Afrikaans children by the time they reach university.

Entering such a primary school on the edges of the city of Pretoria, I am officially welcomed by the principal, an aging and retiring man who displays those old-world values that Afrikaners like to speak about. He is kind, generous, and warm, and even though he is way past retirement age, the parent community cannot conceive of this stalwart in the community ever leaving. So he stays on, grooming his successor but remaining as the solid father figure in the school and in the community; everyone is comforted by the genteel presence of this large and kind man. I immediately feel at home, and the table is spread for the dean from *Tukkies* with simple but elegantly prepared homemade *Hertzoggies*,[22] *koeksusters*,[23] and *boerekos* (traditional Afrikaner food). This is too neat, too well-prepared, and I ask permission to explore the playgrounds, to see what this school is really like. To my surprise, I am encouraged to wander.

As I enter the playground, there is a little boy no older than seven or eight years running across the tarmac with a message from one teacher to the next. He sees me, runs a wide arc, and stands to attention in front of me: *"Goeie môre, Oom"* (Good morning, Uncle). Stunned, I pat him on the head and return the warm greeting, *"Goeie môre, my seun"*

(Good morning, my son). He smiles and continues on his errand, running. I am slightly off-balance, still trying to get used to a white child calling a black man Uncle. Throughout that morning, whenever a child spots this stranger on the campus, the youngster rushes over to greet, and in this manner.

As I walk through the upper floor of this double-storey building, I take the liberty of entering a classroom. The teachers, without exception, welcome me and ask that I observe the lesson. The children jump to attention and greet the stranger in unison. Like children everywhere, these students enjoy interruptions of any kind, and especially by strangers. All of them smile warmly; one or two come to greet by hand. In this simple but colorful classroom, the teacher is on the floor and the children are on mats. This is not a wealthy school, but it has the basics from the subsidy they receive as a public institution. The teachers have made this an oasis of community for these little ones. For a moment I forget that this is an all-white school with all-white teachers and all-white students.

I do not have time to visit every classroom so I peer into every second class. Then something happens that is unlikely to be repeated at any other South African school. One of the teachers whose class I skipped comes running when she realizes that she is to miss out and pleads: *"Asseblief meneer, kom kyk tog ook wat ek met my kinders doen"* (Please sir, come and look also at what I am doing with my children). The South African teachers I know would freeze simply at the thought of having anyone observe or interfere with what they were doing; not here at this Afrikaans primary school.

Suddenly a figure comes running toward me: it is one of the younger teachers. I recognize her instantly; she is one of my undergraduate students on "teaching practice" in this school. She hugs me and says proudly to the principal: *"dis my dekaan"* (this is my dean). I am bewildered by all this warmth and care, and my oversensitive racial antennae tell me this was all planned; but it was not. The young student teacher begins to tell the principal about how her life changed at university as a result of our leadership and how her attitudes toward other people changed; she recommended her younger brother to also join us in the teaching program.

The evening comes and I return to give the main speech at the prize-giving ceremony of the school. There are prizes for everything from sporting and academic achievements to good behavior and community service. Both parents come. The arrangement is that every child receives recognition in some way, and so the ceremony goes on into the night. What strikes me as a veteran speaker at school prize-giving events is how different this one is in this Afrikaans primary school. "Come here, my dear child," says the presenter as she announces the winner in a category. The little child ascends the stage to enthusiastic applause and receives a long and sometimes tearful hug from the presenter. Eventually it is my turn to speak, and for once I am not going to hammer the school for its whiteness but compliment them for their warmth, and for creating such an emotionally rich and rewarding environment in which these South African children could experience wholeness.

What I see in this school is a far cry from the quasi-military environments critics of white schooling wrote about during the anti-Apartheid period.[24] This primary school ties an embracing certainty around these young children, which makes their learning an affirming experience and which gives them trust in their teachers, an extension of the close embrace of their parents. The foundational knowledge of these children is emotionally secured and socially reinforced in the primary grades in ways that will make the disruption of this sealed space very difficult into the future. It is also the kind of environment that secures a constant stream of future teachers from and back into this community; for the first time, I understood why more than 90 percent of my first-year undergraduate class are white Afrikaners and why more than 80 percent of that group want to teach in the primary school, and particularly in the first three years of schooling.

This warm and secure environment is nevertheless socially deceptive and culturally dangerous for these wonderful young children. It is an island separated from the realities of a changing South Africa. Isolated from the children of a black majority, these white children will face the kinds of difficulties that begin to surface in high school, break out into full confrontation at university, and lead to being social misfits in the world of work. Exposed only to white teachers, these white children begin over time to identify knowledge and authority with being white. By not learning about the richness of cultures, traditions, and beliefs among all South Africa's children, young white students are socially, linguistically, and culturally stunted, precisely because of the inward-looking nature of their socialization in the early years.

As with younger primary schoolchildren everywhere, there is initial innocence about others, lack of hard prejudice, and willingness to explore relations with their nonwhite peers. Yet even in the school described, where there is an effort made to teach children basic decency toward others, this kind of racial nurturing also breeds exclusivity and strangeness toward the outside world. So the kind of primary environment described represents a two-edged sword. On the one hand, it affords foundational certainty that gives white children a solid education and a personal confidence in themselves and their culture; on the other hand, this sense of foundational certainty acts as a social buffer against anything that threatens the constricting embrace of culture, language, and ethnicity. It explains why racial attitudes are so hard to change in later years.

## Into the Principal's Office

As I snake my way up the long path past these boys, it seems an eternity before I reach the principal's office of the Afrikaans high school. His bevy of secretaries, all white women, have been expecting me and jump to attention. The office is beautiful with dark paneled wood and historic figures and trophies in critical places. The greeting is firm and warm. This principal represents a quality of Afrikaners that the culture respects—straight talking—and I enjoy these terms of engagement.

Within minutes, the principal rails against what in subsequent visits proves to be his major grievance with the country: *die Engelse* (the English). He shows undisguised contempt for the English and before long takes me on a historical *tour de force* of the struggles of Afrikaners at the hands of these brutal handmaidens of the Queen. He reserves a special disgust for those Afrikaners who send their children to English schools, a growing phenomenon among the Afrikaans middle classes who see the imperial language as having much greater utility in the commercial world after Apartheid and as a ticket for mobility outside the country. *"Vir die hanskhakies, het ek geen tyd"* (For the hanskhakies I have no time). What on earth is a hanskhakie? I ask myself, careful not to interrupt him in full swing against these traitors to culture, language, and history. It is not a common word, hanskhakie, and my literary Afrikaans friends have only a vague idea of its meaning. But the older Afrikaners volunteer a meaning that was at once profound, from a richness-of-literature perspective, and at the same time clearly offensive as a way of labeling people and their choices. The khakies (pronounced "car keys") referred to the khaki color of the uniforms of the British soldiers during the South African War, and the hans, derived from *hans lammertjie* (little lamb), made reference to little lambs that were helpless or dependent for nutrition (milk) on help from others as a result of having lost their mother in some tragedy. These traitors or deserters who sold out to English schools were nothing less than lame lambs clothed in the garments of the old enemy seeking sustenance and recognition from the enemy.

The Afrikaans character of the school preoccupies this principal. It is a haven from colonial English and a place where Afrikaner culture, language, traditions, and independence will be fiercely protected. In planning my first visit, I make the huge mistake of writing a letter of introduction to this principal in English, simply because this was the fastest way to communicate in a busy day. I am called to the university principal's office to be told that the school principal has raged against receiving this letter in English; the university administration is fortunately sympathetic to my plight, having themselves come under fire from the same man for the *verengelsing* (Anglicization) of this historically Afrikaans university.

This does not stop the school principal from his crusade, and so I am surprised one day to find an appointment for him and his colleague, the principal of the other major Afrikaans high school in the area, in my office. They arrive, formally dressed and looking very serious. My attempts at some initial humor go nowhere, and they stare me down. They hear that there is English on my campus; this is a serious problem for them since UP is an Afrikaans university that for years has served Afrikaans schools. Parents pay money for their children to be taught in Afrikaans, and are not in favor of the use of English. I listen to the attack thinly veiled as a complaint, and then I speak up.

"Now listen here," I tell the two serious-looking men in Afrikaans, "this is a South African university and not an Afrikaans university, and the sooner you get used to the idea, the better." They sit back in shock. I tell them that my faculty will take in more and more black students, and this means flexibility on the language policy, which the university supports. I assure them that the majority of classes are still conducted in Afrikaans, because most students came from Afrikaans homes, and that most of my undergraduate lecturers are retained precisely for this reason. There is therefore no anti-Afrikaans sentiment in my leadership of the faculty, but at the same time the deracialization of the university is a national priority and this means that non-Afrikaans-speakers must be accommodated.

The situation is tense, and my firm response is measured. After all, I have led this transformation sensitively, careful to be as inclusive as possible and respectful of the traditional inhabitants of this space. I have made the effort to find a scholarship for one of the white girls at a neighboring Afrikaans girls' school and ensured that white students were included in the scholarship grants where there is financial need.

At the same time, the university needs to take seriously the charge that it is an all-white public institution that privileges a few on the basis of race. With that confidence, I challenge the two principals to transform their schools because this is where the fundamental challenges of changing our society lie. It is clear to me that they are not interested in my shining the light of inquiry on their schools. What I find mildly irritating about these principals is that their schools have produced the smallest number of student teachers of the Afrikaans high schools, and in some years no students at all. Yet they are the ones coming to complain about the loss of dominance of Afrikaans in a teacher education school—a loss that is clearly overstated.

After these principals leave, I understand why Afrikaans high schools are such difficult terrain for teaching children to live and learn together. This is the phase during which language pressures are more harshly felt at high schools than in most of the Afrikaans primary schools. Black students are knocking on the doors of these high schools, recognizing that a sound academic training at this level improves their chances of entering university. Principals are under pressure to open these institutions, but in the middle-class Afrikaans high schools they still have the numbers to ward off, for the time being, the demand for racial integration. Accordingly, they can retain for the moment a rigid language policy. It is also during admission to high school where middle-class parents, in this case white Afrikaans parents, begin to decide whether to choose an English school and broaden the options of their children or confine their children within all-white, all-Afrikaans high schools. High schools, moreover, are the place where young people begin to become aware of partners from the opposite sex, and where sometimes intense emotional relationships are formed. These two Afrikaner principals know the stakes and want not only to ensure language exclusiveness (and thereby racial segregation) in their schools but to retain this political sense into the university as well. As we part, I make clear that history is against their kind of conservative thinking, to which one principal responds, "History will have to take care of itself; this is what we want now."

What is important in the story of the high school principals is their influential role as leaders of young people. In hierarchically organized Afrikaans schools (and universities), the leader plays a stronger determining role than is the case in more democratic institutions. The principal sets the tone, opens or closes social spaces, directs the thinking of teachers, and conveys the essential knowledge of the past to receptive minds. This reproductive role of the principal in education is strong in such environments, and to be sure the young Afrikaner adolescents will learn historical prejudices toward the English, inherit negativism toward black people, and receive apocalyptic views about post-Apartheid society. The leader in the Afrikaans community is invested with enormous stature and authority and, in the context of my thesis, stands as a key figure in the transmission of knowledge.

What views of society do these education leaders convey? One of the clearest insights into this question comes when I am invited to address a convention of Afrikaans high school principals in Pretoria. Before I speak, there is the conventional Bible reading and prayer. The Bible reading is from one of the saddest books of Holy writ, Lamentations. The chosen verses bemoan the terrible fate of God's people on earth, the Jews, and what hardships they had to bear. The prayer follows. It exaggerates every conceivable problem in the new South Africa: violence, falling educational standards, problems of discipline, irresponsible parents, and a government that needs prayer and awakening to the many ills of society.

By the time I am due to speak, I am thoroughly depressed and tell them so. I cannot believe we are living in the same country, and I share this sentiment. It is clear that in the regular churchlike ceremonies of these schools, the discourses that occupy worship must be terribly depressing, and the children probably come away with knowledge of a crumbling society going to the dogs. There is no sense of hope in this kind of leadership talk, no sense of developmental challenges to be faced, no expression of citizen commitment to change, and no anticipation of great things to come. These are discourses of defeat. I now see the link between the fatalism of my male university students and the prayers and preaching of their elders.

### Inside the Classroom

Behind the classroom door, the Afrikaner child is exposed to an intense, disciplined, and well-managed educational environment that few South African children experience. Every minute is accounted for. Teachers are highly disciplined and work as a team. Timetables are sacred and the workday is efficiently managed. Portfolios are well delineated among teachers, leaders, managers, administrators, and support staff. Teachers in these schools do not walk, and they certainly do not walk slowly; there is something called a *drafstappie*, a trot, as teachers move between classes or on their way to the principal's office or a parent appointment.

A high premium in the classrooms is placed on orderliness. Writing is neat and tidy, something carried into adult writing as students enter university and beyond. Learner scripts are read closely and learning outcomes observed and measured. Assessment is frequent, with all work due and delivered on time. Discipline is enforced. This kind of predictability and orderliness is light years removed from ordinary township schools or from many of the English-medium schools.

No teachers in the Afrikaans schools simply work in the classroom. They are responsible for any number of supporting activities that together make up the whole educational experience of their charges. Coaching rugby or netball or athletics is a common task; preparing students for drama and musical evenings is central; meetings with parents are frequent and scheduled in advance. The teacher's duties in an Afrikaans school mean that a full day and often weekends are included in the commitments of the educator.

These are the kinds of orderliness, predictability, commitment, and wholeness of the educational experience that make teaching such an attractive profession for many young Afrikaners. They tell frequently of playing with dolls as children and lining them up for a lesson in the backyard, imitating the teacher in school. This affection for education lies deep in the history of Afrikaners, *onderwys* (education) being seen historically as an essential means for working their way out of poverty and despair.

There is a curriculum downside to this otherwise wonderful and positive experience of Afrikaner children. Despite the attractiveness of the structure within which education unfolds, the content of what is taught and the knowledge that is absorbed is far from neutral in this sealed environment. A teacher I am observing in an Afrikaans primary school begins her lesson by telling students about the differences between whites, coloreds, Africans, and Indians. She means well, wanting to demonstrate that there are differences that must be respected. Without knowing it, however, she plays into the racism on which Apartheid ideology is established. Coloreds live in Mitchells Plain (a colored residential area in Cape Town), she instructs; *"en waar bly ons?"* (And where do we live?). The children respond by naming Pretoria suburbs in which they reside. For the teacher, whites live in white areas and coloreds live in colored areas and so on. "And where do the Africans live?" she continues, and I find it hard to conceal my distress.

This is not very different from the dramatic incident in *Skin*, the 2007 film of the Sandra Laing story in which a young girl, born to white Afrikaner parents, is forcibly removed from her white school and pushed away by her white father in ways that tear at the emotions of her mother and every viewer of this unbelievably sad story. Sandra Laing's skin turned darker as she grew older, and her hair curled too much. The school could not tolerate this difference, and like thousands of other children she was ejected from the school and the community. A moving incident in the documentary is a teacher holding up animal hair to her primary school class comparing the Bushmen (*die Boesmans* to whites). *"Hoe lyk hulle hare? Hulle hare is nie soos ons s'n nie"* (What does their hair look like? Their hair is not like our hair).[25]

"Why," persists an American anthropologist visiting Pretoria, "do you not teach your students about their differences?" The visitor insists that teaching differences is critical to ensure the ethnic self-concept of children. I offer: "We feel uncomfortable as South Africans talking about how people differ since that is all we did for decades in a country that made a fetish out of racial and cultural differences." But she presses: "You should teach about differences; it's important." The two Afrikaner women in the audience nod firm approval. I cannot understand this unusual insistence, especially in a foreign country that she clearly knows little about. "How," I ask with some irritation, "do you teach about difference in a country that has never had a national conversation about sameness?"

For the first time I have the experience of leading a discussion where whatever I say is completely unheard. Yet this is the problem for white Afrikaner children: the only thing they know is differences centered on racial purity and racial exclusiveness. Even though race is no longer expressed crudely among Afrikaners, it is claimed as difference through more polite references to culture, language, and group identity. It is one of the immovable essences of white Afrikaner identity, an identity impervious to claims about the social construction of race.

It is of course not simply what is taught (the official curriculum) that conveys knowledge of the past, the present, and the future. It is also the informal, unintended teaching (the hidden curriculum) that conveys, some argue, even more powerful knowledge than that taught explicitly. In all-white schools, students take as normative the racial exclusion of others and the cultural homogeneity of the classroom. They associate whiteness with this kind of orderliness and predictability, and blackness with disorder and chaos. As one white principal put it, "I once thought that bringing blacks into the school, the taxis and the soccer, would be something we could not control."[26] With all-white teachers and all-white leaders, students associate authority and knowledge with whiteness. Students learn, moreover, the comforts and security of sameness, of organizing their social lives around those who speak the same language and are covered by the same skin.

For students to gain knowledge of racial sameness and exclusion not only intellectually but also emotionally, it is not enough to learn separately; it is critical that what is different is held up as foreign, as existing in another space and time. Returning to the teacher I am observing teaching about difference, I note that she sends out one of the primary children to fetch Johanna, an old woman who has been placed "on call" for the lesson. Johanna is brought in by one of the children; they pepper the old woman with questions that in content and approach would have been completely unacceptable if this same woman had been white:

*Johanna, waar woon jy?* (Johanna, where do you live?)
*Johanna, wat eet julle mense?* (Johanna, what do you people eat?)
*Johanna, hoe kom jy werk toe?* (Johanna, how do you come to work?)
*Johanna, watter klere dra julle?* (Johanna, what clothes do you wear?)
*Johanna, gaan julle kerk toe?* (Johanna, do you people go to church?)
*Johanna het jy kinders?* (Johanna, do you have children?)

It is difficult to explain the racial disrespect underlying this form of address by nine- and ten-year-old white children. *Jy* in Afrikaans does not simply mean "you"; it is in this context a casual term, almost dismissive, with lesser value than its other translation, *u*, which conveys respect and esteem, especially when addressing adults or people unknown to the speaker. If the person is known as well as older, as with Johanna the cleaner, then Tannie (Aunt) would preface the name Johanna. As I sit through this exchange, I find the tension inside me pulling in three directions: to intervene and correct these children for their obvious disrespect, to not embarrass the teacher in front of her class, and to simply observe and record this direct example of what happens inside racially ordered and exclusive classrooms in the new South Africa.

So by extending this ideology of sameness from family to church to primary school and to high school, the student learns lessons of association: stay with your own. There is constant reassurance that flows from this kind of social and racial exclusivity, bonds that not only yield *togetherness on the inside* of this homogeneous cultural existence but also offer *security from the outside* forces of diversity and difference. During observations of young white Afrikaner student teachers, I find ample evidence for the sociological claim that schools reflect racial ideologies from the broader society and are themselves race-making institutions.[27]

This is what makes it so difficult for white Afrikaans students to "mix" (as they often put it) with those who are different: black students, white English students, international students, gay and lesbian students, and any identity that challenges this constructed sameness within which they live most of their lives as children, as adolescents, and for many as working adults. The longer white students remain inside these cultural and linguistic enclaves, the more difficult it becomes to lead a normal, open, and integrated life in the broader society.

Beyond what students learn through the official curriculum and the hidden curriculum about race and difference that shapes their knowledge of the past, it is also what they never learn but that has significant social and educational consequences—the null curriculum.[28] Locked into these white spaces, students never learn an African language from other indigenous South African communities; they do not learn about the struggles of black people for self-determination; they fail to gain knowledge about international social movements for change such as civil rights movements in the USA, or anticolonial struggles in Latin America, or about the great African intellectuals and their literature. This Afrikaner-centric curriculum, even though it doubtless advances (partial) knowledge of this white ethnic group, cuts out *knowledges* of others beyond stereotype and subjection.

White students in this context also fail to learn about models of democratic thinking and practice beyond authoritarian modes of relating to others. They do not see and cannot imagine authority figures that in schools and society are black and women because of the absent but influential curriculum. The great theories and theorists of democracy are absent from their knowledge, with consequential effects. They cannot grapple with knowledge that is not positive without generating uncertainty and confusion.

Knowledge constitutes the most fundamental of struggles over the past. When the range and substance of knowledge is limited, even into the university years, then the possibility of curriculum renewal is extremely limited. What students learn more than anything is that knowledge is neutral, scientific, instrumental, mechanical, problem-solving, discoverable through fixed laws, measurable, certain, and racially distinctive. This is the epistemological bedrock of school and social knowledge that frames the young white child's knowledge of the past, present, and future. In this process of acquisition, white schools play a crucial role.

If the school curriculum in all three dimensions of knowledge (official, hidden, and null) is the main transmission line for knowledge of the past, then changing the curriculum constitutes a major site of struggle over transformation. Yet this is very difficult in white Afrikaans schools, as the government found out in the decade following the transition to majority rule. Initially, the curriculum was left alone after a largely symbolic attempt to "cleanse" the Apartheid syllabuses of the most outrageous racism and sexism; the problem was that the Afrikaner government had already done such cleansing in the years running up to the end of white rule. Nevertheless, the political posturing behind such an announcement carried considerable advantage during the years of early transition.[29]

By the time the energetic second minister of education[30] was appointed, he announced sweeping plans to bring a more radical view of knowledge of the past and knowledge of other cultures into the mainstream curriculum. What he could not foresee was a campaign across the country that brought together white and black conservatives to resist what they saw as a liberal curriculum containing relativist knowledge about race, culture, politics, and history.[31] A number of Afrikaner families swelled the ranks of those retreating into home schooling and independent *volkseie skole* (schools reserved for the Volk, in this case the white Afrikaner "nation" or "people"). The public resistance was so well coordinated through the major media, flooded by letters from the public, that the government went quiet on its dramatic plans for curriculum renewal and resorted to a largely hands-off approach to breaking this vital transmission line for second-generation knowledge.

The consequence of this curriculum abandonment by the post-Apartheid government is that the issue of critical content has not been resolved. Schools and teachers are left with a broad outcomes-based curriculum and associated texts that specify the kinds of values, skills, and knowledge that should be pursued. It is largely left to the teachers to "fill" the learning experience with their selected content, provided that what is learned in some way reflects back on the stated outcomes. In a democratic society in which there is social consensus on the goals of education and shared values about history and community, there are no serious curriculum dilemmas. But in a divided community with a history of white supremacy and black subjugation, this hands-off approach to curriculum does little more than ensure separate transmission of divided knowledge streams to black and white students.

## Conclusion

The literature on intergenerationality speaks at one end of the spectrum to transmission of *traumatic knowledge* and at the other end to transmission of *defensive knowledge*. By the former I mean painful and disturbing knowledge (with its attendant memories and emotions) carried over from one generation to the next and its negative effects on the emotional, psychic, spiritual, and psychological constitution of the receivers. By the latter I mean the knowledge of a painful past asserted by minorities or less powerful groups to defend themselves and their children against the continuing power of dominant majorities.

The literature on the transmission of traumatic knowledge favors in volume and empathy the victims of all kinds of experiences from sexual and physical abuse to the horrors of the Holocaust; the small but growing attention to transmission of such knowledge among perpetrators reveals a knowledge of silence with parents holding back information about their roles and functions under National Socialism.

The literature on transmission of defensive knowledge, on the other hand, favors almost exclusively the parents and children of marginalized minorities such as African Americans and Chicanos in the USA. In a review of the literature on the mechanisms through which parents transmit knowledge about race, values, and perspectives to their children, Diane Hughes and her colleagues identify four clusters of messages so transferred.[32]

*Cultural socialization* refers to transmission of knowledge about racial or ethnic history, promotion of cultural customs and traditions, and advancement of racial and ethnic pride. In this respect, "promoting cultural knowledge is one of the first things parents mention"[33] when asked about ethnic-racial socialization among their children.

*Preparation for bias* refers to the efforts of parents to build awareness of discrimination among their children and prepare them to cope in a prejudiced world.

*Promotion of mistrust* refers to communication of wariness and distrust in interracial interactions. It has to do with social messages about other race groups and warnings to be cautious and restrained in relation to others.

*Egalitarianism* refers to messages about equality and about becoming part of the mainstream culture rather than separating and distinguishing oneself on the basis of race.

Within this literature are correspondences with the transmission experiences of white Afrikaner children. Some of the more salient knowledge claims are extracted for comparison:

> Parents for whom race is a central social identity (high centrality) and with favorable views of their ethnic-racial group (high private regard) may be especially likely to transmit messages about group pride to their children.

> Most studies have found that cultural socialization facilitates children's knowledge about their ethnic-racial group and their favorable in-group attitudes.

> Boys are more likely than girls to receive messages regarding racial barriers.

> Findings suggest that ethnic-racial socialization increases as children age.

But there is a problem. None of this U.S.-based literature deals with knowledge and transmission among whites who held political power and then lost it, and about such whites as a minority within a black majority context. Whites generally in such a context have lost exclusive political power, but they still enjoy relative social and economic power even as such advantage is increasingly subject to competition and erosion under a black government.

Transmission of knowledge therefore reflects defeat and asserts loss. Here assertion of racial pride and identity is a defense of racial separateness lodged within a history of white supremacy. It would be a mistake to read stories of racial pride as simply a shield against the new power of a black majority culture without reference to the ideologies of racial separateness and racial superiority. This is what makes the problem of knowledge and transmission a more complex political subject than is available in the existing literature written from the perspective of those who were without formal power and who remain without it. This requires a new set of ethnographic studies within schools and families to gain a deeper sense of the politics of the transmission of knowledge within white communities and their changing institutions in post-Apartheid South Africa. This study on white Afrikaner children, their knowledge, and its transmission and reception barely scratches the surface.

# 4    Bitter Knowledge

But what if one discovers evil in what one has lost?[1]

Was Apartheid the product of some horrific shortcomings in Afrikaner culture? How do we live with the fact that all the words used to humiliate, all the orders given to kill, belonged to the language of my heart?[2]

IT IS THE ONLY UNIVERSITY in South Africa where Nelson Mandela was forced off campus.[3] This was in 1991, three years before the country's first democratic general election. Mandela had hardly been on a University of Pretoria stage for ten minutes when an elderly white-haired man walked slowly toward and onto the same stage of this open-air amphitheatre. The head of campus security claims he thought it was a professor who wanted to address the rowdy right-wing students in the crowd of more than six thousand young people; for this reason, he did not intervene. By this time an estimated one-quarter of the gathered students had created havoc. They shouted racist interjections at the person introducing Mandela; they burned an ANC flag shouting *"brand vlag brand, brand vlag brand"* (burn flag burn, burn flag burn); and when asked by the master of ceremonies to stand and sing the liberation anthem, *Nkosi Sikelel' iAfrika*, they turned their backs toward the stage and sang the Apartheid anthem, *Die Stem van Suid-Afrika*. To the side of the raucous right-wingers a disheartened group of mainly black students stood in competition, singing the liberation anthem.

Meanwhile, Mandela's bodyguards, who at first were uncertain of what to do with the old white man, realize the potential for trouble and stand in his way. The white students use this as a cue to rush onto the stage, and fists fly between the bodyguards and students representing Mandela, and the right-wing students now on the stage. Mandela appears briefly, smiling bravely, and is then whisked off campus, not having been able to deliver his prepared speech recognizing the cultural and language commitments of Afrikaners even as he made the case for a more inclusive democracy. Right-wing student bodies on campus and political organizations off campus used the incident to declare what dangers lay ahead if South Africa continued on its path toward majority rule.

The university appeared upset, apologized to Mandela and the ANC, and promised action against the culprits. Four months later, UP declared that no action would be taken against the students involved. Since then, every time an ANC leader attempted to come onto campus, there was fierce resistance from the right-wing white students.[4] In the meantime, it was found that the old man was Hendrik Claassens, who, 33 years earlier in 1958, had interrupted a meeting of a Pretoria study group where Chief Albert Luthuli—then the ANC president—was to address the group. He jumped onto the stage, declaring that "a kaffir[5] is not allowed to address white people," and punched the Nobel laureate in the face.[6]

The 1991 incident was led by students whose childhood was formed during the last years of Apartheid, and who came into the new South Africa with the racial knowledge but without the racial power of the past. Since then, UP continued to be one of the major sites for confrontation of knowledge of the past, the present, and the future. For almost a century, this large institution had trained the white Afrikaner community, advanced the Afrikaans language, and promoted the racial knowledge of the Apartheid state. Ordinary Afrikaners had expectations that some of this would continue, that Afrikaans would remain the dominant medium of instruction if not the only one. Their children expected to take up residence in the same tradition-soaked *koshuise* (university residences) as their parents and grandparents. The Afrikaans community also expected that the proud symbols of a racial past—the university choir, the ox wagon at the center of the university emblem, the institutional flag—would continue to enjoy prominence in identifying the institution.

What the presence of Mandela on the campus of UP did was to threaten the secure knowledge with which these children had grown up and of which they learned so reliably in those closed circles of influence through parents, teachers, coaches, peers, and dominees. The secure knowledge of the state and its institutions, UP among them, painted Mandela as the enemy, his organization (the ANC) as terrorist, and his world-view as Communist. It was something Nelson Mandela understood perfectly; witness his accommodating but assertive speech, which he prepared but could not deliver on that day:

I am pleased to have this opportunity to speak at the University of Pretoria. I am aware that this feeling may not be shared by all members of this university and there are undoubtedly many who will not welcome my presence. I think this hostility and fear is not directed at me personally but at what I represent as a leader of the ANC—an organization that *many have been told* threatens everything that you value [emphasis added].[7]

Mandela would then have continued by appealing to their own sense of history as Afrikaners:

Whites are living on a volcano. They are deluded if they think they can continue to live as they have on the backs of Black South Africans. Surely you, the Afrikaner, who fought for your freedom from British imperialism, would lose all respect for the African people and the Blacks in general if we just meekly accepted the denial of our rights?

It was a masterful speech that was conciliatory, with parts written in Afrikaans, and at the same time assertive about what the liberation movement stood for as a body that sought to remedy injustice on a racially inclusive platform.

Of course these elevated political ideals mattered little to the students at the time. If Mandela came onto this campus, black students would surely follow, and everything would be lost. When white students therefore ejected from their campus the president of the ANC, the man who shortly thereafter would become the first president of a democratic

South Africa, they were rejecting the threat of the new knowledge and the new clientele he represented. In a very direct way, the transmission line for secure knowledge was being challenged, and for many this was the first time.

## UP: Epicenter of White Student Resistance to Change

No other university campus in South Africa experienced a more sustained resistance to change in the post-Apartheid period than UP. All South African campuses experience disruption from time to time, but there was something special and intense about what happened at Pretoria. Here the resistance was not so much about escalation in student fees or exclusion of academically weak students, even though this dimension of complaint did become a reality once a black campus was incorporated into UP. What dominated the campus politics of Pretoria was resistance to transformation of the institution.[8] As individual events come and go, the frequency and intensity of these single incidents are not apparent, especially in a culture where a high premium is placed on subduing these events to save face to the outside (*"die beeld na buite"*; our image on the outside). But in a comprehensive analysis of reported student protests defined here as *political action against change*, this research discovered an astonishing number of critical incidents of resistance and disruption led by white students (see Table 4.1).

It should be said, parenthetically, that white student protest was a furious part of the institutional landscape, especially during the rising tide of Afrikaner nationalism in the first half of the previous century. One of the first recorded student protests was the burning of the Union Jack in 1919 by one "Duke" Erlank at the *Kollege* residence of UP. Students from the university were also part of a group that dragged French lecturer H. P. Lamont from his home in Arcadia Street, Pretoria, to Church Square in the center of the city to tar and feather him for insulting Afrikaners in his book *War, Wine and Women*—a novel written under the pseudonym of Wilfred Saint-Maude.[9] Students were unashamedly aligned with the neo-Nazi group the *Ossewa-Brandwag* (Ox wagon fire watch) during the war years, leading outsiders to describe UP as "a hotbed of nationalism" and "the breeding grounds for anti-Semitism and Nazism."[10]

**Table 4.1** Sample of white student protests against transformation at the University of Pretoria, 1990–2007

| Date | Issue | Source |
|---|---|---|
| 8/10/1990 | President de Klerk's speech at UP is disrupted by chanting and singing of a group of right-wing students opposed to negotiations with the ANC; the students are led by the son of a Conservative Party MP | The Star p. 1 |
| 9/30/1990 | UP students protest the "Communist" presence on campus, referring to the ANC's Thabo Mbeki | Sunday Times p. 22 |
| 10/17/1990 | Right-wing students disrupt a campus address by Dr. Gerrit Viljoen, a cabinet minister; burn the ANC flag | Beeld p. 2 |
| 1/22/1991 | Conservative Party students plan to protest racially open hostels by "educating" students about the dangers | Citizen p. 17 |
| 4/30/1991 | Nelson Mandela is prevented from speaking on campus; he is rushed to safety as ANC flags are burnt and the Apartheid anthem is sung | Sowetan p. 3 |
| 5/14/1991 | The National Socialist Party is behind the distribution of threatening pamphlets which read, "the price paid by traitors is death," and which include the contact information of four conservative students | Pretoria News p. 3 |
| 5/22/1991 | UP bans march by progressive students, the South African National Students' Congress (Sansco), and Students for a Democratic Society (SDS), claiming fears of right-wing student backlash | Pretoria News p. 3 |
| 7/18/1991 | Right-wingers are suspected in an attack on a hostel housing black students; three teargas canisters are fired into this UP residence; black students live in fear | Star p. 2 |
| 10/25/1991 | The newly formed organization *Aksie Volkseie Weermag* (AVW) (Action Our People's Army) plans to refuse to do national service, claiming that the New South Africa was forced upon the Afrikaner *Volk* | Sowetan p. 4 |
| 11/17/1991 | Large Swastika on graffiti wall at Tuks "is the work of a Nazi cell"; about twenty students are actively involved; the group is linked to the racist "Church of the Creator," which moved from America to South Africa | Rapport p. 6 |
| 1/31/1992 | Afrikaner students establish white "communes" in the first five houses purchased by right-wing organizations in the immediate neighborhood of UP; the hostels are "for Afrikaners only" | Beeld p. 4 |
| 3/10/1993 | Address by the ANC's Carl Niehaus at UP is continuously disrupted by right-wingers | Beeld p. 2 |
| 9/23/1993 | The university capitulates to right-wing white students by canceling a meeting which was to have been addressed by ANC deputy president Walter Sisulu | The Star p. 5 |
| 2/14/1994 | Right-wing students join Rag procession to collect money for a white charity | The Citizen p. 8 |
| 3/11/1994 | UP students disrupt a National Party meeting where Cabinet Minister Roelf Meyer speaks; students sing, shout slogans, storm the stage | Beeld p. 3 |

| Date | Event | Source |
|---|---|---|
| 4/28/1995 | *Aksie Red Tuks* (Action Save Tuks) is launched "because of the threat to the Afrikaner identity of the university" | Afrikaner p. 5 |
| 9/13/1995 | White students armed with steel pipes clash with striking black workers; students claim to be "protecting their campus" | Beeld p. 1 |
| 7/28/1999 | Freedom Front students propose racially segregated hostels with "cultural corridors" to separate the races | Pretoria News p. 4 |
| 5/4/2000 | Two white first-year law students are arrested for defacing the new coat of arms at the Union Buildings | Pretoria News p. 3 |
| 9/3/2000 | Right-wing (Freedom Front) students are accused of using racist posters and pamphlets in Student Representative Council (SRC) election campaign | City Press p. 5 |
| 10/19/2001 | Afrikaans veterinary science students threaten court action for being required to do their exams and orals in English | Impak p. 12 |
| 7/31/2002 | Students disrupt an address by deputy education minister Mosibudi Mangena; one of the students demands that Mangena speak Afrikaans | The Star p. 3 |
| 7/19/2005 | *Solidariteit-Jeug* (Youth Solidarity) gate-crash a meeting of the vice-rector and the SRC to protest the marginalization of Afrikaans | Beeld p. 6 |
| 4/17/2005 | Tuks students complain about the cessation of Christian prayers in order to respect religious diversity on campus | Sunday Times p. 6 |
| 5/20/2005 | Tuks students past and present march against the proposed name change for Pretoria, reasoning that if Pretoria is changed to Tshwane there is a chance that the name of the university will also have to change | Citizen p. 3 |
| 9/29/2005 | SRC representatives from all five historically Afrikaans universities mobilize for the retention of Afrikaans | Beeld p. 19 |
| 7/22/2005 | The SRC and its FF+ (Freedom Front Plus) majority reject a management proposal for a more representative student council | Business Day p. 5 |
| 8/19/2005 | Students march to Administration building to deliver a memorandum complaining about the marginalization of Afrikaans | Business Day p. 6 |
| 10/14/2005 | Students march to the Union Buildings to hand over a petition for the retention of Afrikaans in schools and universities | Beeld p. 6 |
| 10/7/2006 | White students paint their faces black and hand a memorandum to the President's office to demand their official classification as "African," given that labor laws favor African students | Witness p. 11 |
| 7/31/2006 | White students protest at the welcoming meeting for first-year students with a banner which reads "Rector you have my money, where is my Afrikaans?" to applause from the audience | Frontnuus p. 10 |
| 11/23/2006 | White UP students welcome tourists at the airport by handing out parcels of beetroot and garlic with a letter warning tourists about crime, HIV, and racial discrimination in South Africa | Pretoria News p. 3 |
| 1/8/2007 | The spokesman for Tuks Solidarity Youth says he will consult the UN Human Rights Commission about how universities like UP are discriminating against white students | Star p. 6 |
| 2/22/2007 | White right-wing students hold a vanilla cup cake sale where race determines the price of the confectionery. For white, Indian, and colored students the cakes are five rands each, while black students pay only two rands. Students with ANC membership receive theirs free, but have to put money into a "corruption" box. | Pretoria News p. 4 |

Since the 1990s, UP was constantly in the news as a result of the politics of white student resistance to anything that threatened to disrupt the social and cultural traditions of this historically Afrikaner and Afrikaans university. The scope of political protests ranged from attacks on the last white politicians from the Apartheid era coming to defend the government's decision to negotiate with the black liberation movements, to attacks on ANC politicians coming to present their case for change and assuage the fears of the Afrikaners, to outright racist posters and events intended to provoke and humiliate black students and staff and pour public scorn on the policies of the new government and the feeble attempts of the university to implement them, to muscular parades meant to intimidate black students who dared to protest on the main campus.

Of all the causes around which student protest was mobilized, the perceived loss of status for the Afrikaans language recurred most frequently. This was the perfect foil for the more race-minded students since the language cause relieved them of the need to name the more obvious problem: black students encroaching in larger and larger numbers on this white campus. Behind this rallying cry of Afrikaans, the right-wing student bodies could quite easily mobilize the mainstream Afrikaner students for whom the issue was more narrowly a concern about the loss of language and cultural identity.

One senate meeting after another would revisit the language policy of the university, and endless meetings of the senior administration (the executive and the deans) would devote hours of anguished and sometimes very emotional deliberations on the subject of Afrikaans. None of these meetings could ever reach a definite and settled decision on the place of Afrikaans at the university for the simple reason that within the upper reaches of the institution some of the senior Afrikaner administrators were themselves caught up in intense personal soul searching as fellow inheritors of the language. These were men whose parents were great Afrikaans *voorstaanders* (supporters), whose great-grandparents were prominent in the establishment of Afrikaans culture and power, and whose families, generations back, suffered through the South African War. These senior men in one sense understood the external demands for change from the government; in another sense, they were also products of Afrikaner nationalism. However enlightened and even pragmatic their politics might be, it was a conscience weighed down by an emotional knowledge of the past.

As leaders of the university changed, so did the emphasis in language policy. To the entrepreneurial vice-chancellor who hired me, Afrikaans had to respond to the changing politics of the time. "So what is our language policy?" I once asked him. "It depends on when you ask me," he quipped. To his successor, a man who once resisted the possible loss of the ox wagon from the UP emblem, the issues were deeply personal and emotional. I still recall his inaugural address as the new vice-chancellor to an audience that included international visitors, foreign embassy representatives, and the elite of the new black ruling class. Addressing them in English, he suddenly shifted to Afrikaans: "*En ek verstaan my plig teenoor Afrikaans*" (and I understand my duty toward Afrikaans). There are 11 official languages; he expressed a duty toward one of them.

Unsurprisingly, the students picked up on this ambivalence in language policy and made protests against the loss of Afrikaans central to the resistance against transformation at UP. It was a protest that would also drive white student politics at other Afrikaans universities, most notably the University of Stellenbosch and to a lesser extent the universities of the Free State and Potchefstroom, the latter having merged with a black university to become the University of the North West. At Stellenbosch the Afrikaans debate also involved the major elements of the university, including the Convocation (alumni) and the Institutional Forum (a statutory body representing all university stakeholders). There, senior academics and alumni headed the protest against the expanded use of English in undergraduate teaching, a move seen as the beginning of the end for Afrikaans. It was this language fury that eventually cost this university's open-minded and accommodating vice-chancellor his job.[11]

The racial and language demographic shifts at UP threatened Afrikaans much more imminently than in the relatively semirural small town of Stellenbosch, where most of the residents, black and white, were Afrikaans speakers. UP was in the wrong place for this kind of language protection. Situated in the shadow of the Union Buildings, the seat of a black nationalist government, a protectionist language policy was simply not going to be tolerated. Moreover, the university was engulfed by a growing cosmopolitanism in a city whose suburbs were dominated by embassies and whose new clientele consisted of the black elite from all parts of the country whose government jobs brought them, and their children, to the capital.

In this context, situated in a thriving metropolis of Gauteng province, surrounded by the large black provinces of Limpopo and Mpumalanga, and within calling distance of growing numbers of non-Afrikaans schools, UP was destined to change quickly, at least as far as its student demographics were concerned. Within a short period, black students constituted about 45 percent of the residential student body and more than 65 percent of total enrollment. Even more rapidly, the Afrikaans base started to erode as the majority of students now preferred their instruction in English; this included black students, English-speaking white students, and, significantly, those Afrikaans mother-tongue speakers who saw economic advantage and geographic mobility in the choice of English. In other words, language pressures were beginning to be felt among Afrikaans speakers in general, and especially among those right-wing students who made political links among Afrikaans, culture, and the loss of power.

The policy of the university declares a 50–50 application of English and Afrikaans in the classroom, with both languages enjoying the same rights and exposure in teaching, research, and administration. In practice, this is impossible because of the huge costs of duplication not only of materials but also of academic teachers. It wastes valuable administrative time, especially in an institutional context where it is clear that everybody understands English but fewer and fewer campus dwellers understand Afrikaans. The 50–50 policy therefore represents little more than a political holding pattern against the mounting criticism of dishonesty in institutional communications—the preaching of a dual language policy but increasingly the practice of an English-only teaching policy.

The verbal challenge of the Afrikaans students is seldom launched in direct racial terms, even though the symbolism is unmistakably racist in its terms of confrontation. But race, even to white students, represents distasteful terms for objection; naming race is an unnecessary tactic when culture and language can be invoked instead. A common expression of this nonetheless racial challenge is in terms of money.

The Afrikaans students would make the point that they or their parents pay for their studies, and that they pay for Afrikaans tuition. This is a loaded proposition.

If this were simply a language problem, it could be resolved with relative ease. At heart, though, it is a political problem, and one that is argued with increasing aggression by the second generation as more and more students choose English, and more and more academic staff—those hired from the outside—are unable to teach in Afrikaans. The aggression takes on nasty forms, like the popular Afrikaans T-shirt: *"praat Afrikaans of hou jou bek!"* (speak Afrikaans or shut up). It becomes especially offensive when the annual student election period comes around. It is a season, literally, when my stomach churns on the separate education campus, for election posters everywhere will proclaim the most offensive and racist messages to a generally receptive white student body.

UP is the only institution that, until recently, still organized its student body to correspond to external political parties; and so the ANC, the Pan Africanist Congress (PAC), the Democratic Alliance (DA), and Freedom Front Plus (FF+) enjoyed prominence, especially when a new student leadership had to be elected once a year. With few exceptions, the major parties attracted students on a racial basis—only white students in the FF+ and mainly black students in the ANC—so that the contests among parties were, inevitably, racially charged events that constantly threatened race relations on the campus.

The Student Representative Council (SRC) is a prized institution within UP. The student leaders take considerable pride in their role; they are dressed in formal clothing sporting the university colors. It is a dress code and culture that in many ways continues from what happens in schools with the old prefect system. It is also a dress code that alienates black students and student leaders because of its cost. The SRC has its own building and budgets, and it plays a key role in organizing cultural and social events on behalf of the student body, including the traditional Rag (raising monies for charity), in which huge floats move slowly through Pretoria and beautiful Rag queen finalists compete to be the chosen one.

The SRC has little power to influence or reverse university decisions (these are children who must listen to their elders), but they have come

to be a hugely disruptive force, especially since the 1990s. This has especially been the case after Apartheid since every year the election is
overwhelmingly won by the Afrikaner FF+, a conservative white organization of the student body. Every year, with each election, the victory
of this right-wing student organization is held up in the media to signal
the lack of transformation at UP, long stereotyped by the non-Afrikaans
universities as a politically backward institution stuck in an Apartheid
past. The regular landslide victories of the FF+ may seem anomalous
given the size of the black student enrollment, but the explanation is to
be found in the low number of black students bothering to vote.

The student FF+ body certainly did not act alone, finding material
and political support from its senior organization outside of campus: the
FF+ party, which has only marginal representation in the South African
Parliament. Every time there was opposition to the work of the FF+
student organization on campus, its elders would put the university administration under pressure to allow this elected body to fulfill its mandate to the students; after all, this was democracy at work. If blacks win
on the outside and whites must respect the outcome, then when whites
win on the inside everybody must respect that outcome.

To their credit, the university authorities (though not with one voice)
have sought to limit the considerable damage done to the public image
of an institution eager to demonstrate openness to the politicians on the
hill (the Union Buildings) and the people on the ground (the growing
internal constituency of black staff and students). A process was started to reorganize student politics on a nonparty basis. This attempt to
transform student organizations has had limited success, for it could
not collapse conservative white student opinion despite some gains in
bringing limited numbers of black students into the leadership structures. What the FF+ did demonstrate, however, was that there was still
a strong racially organized opinion among white students on the campus
that could be rallied around a number of themes: aggressive protection
of the Afrikaans language, preservation of the culture and traditions of
the university, the threat of black students to education quality, and loss
of Afrikaner identity on campus.

The annual elections, though, were not the only rallying calls for white
student protests at UP. These young white men, in the main, saw them-

selves as the physical as well as the symbolic protectors of Afrikaner culture and identity, the heritage that they saw being eroded on their turf.

There was an intense confrontation when black student protests from the small black campus of Mamelodi to the east of Pretoria spilled over onto the largely white main campus. The black students felt they were being treated as second-class citizens of this formerly white university, and they wanted to bring that message onto the main campus. Suddenly, out of nowhere appeared marching columns of young Afrikaner male students, dressed in quasi-military uniforms, determined to block the black students from disrupting "their" campus. The symbolism was unmistaken: white, racist, conservative, and aggressive reminders of a recent past. The white students marched to the Administration building, singing the Apartheid national anthem; some white secretaries and administrators from the balconies joined in the singing. The racial lines were drawn, more than ten years after Apartheid was legally ended.

It would be tempting to dismiss these protestors as a handful of misguided right-wingers working under the influence of and manipulated by adults on the outside. To some extent, this might be true. But it would be misleading to think that the values, concerns, anger, and aggression of white Afrikaner students were limited to this group of activists. Over and over again, I would see this smoldering anger and anxiety in the individual and collective lives of my own students on the Education campus.

## Living Together

It would happen at the beginning of every year, more intensely in one or more of the young men's residences on campus. There would occasionally be physical confrontations, but more often it was pushing and shoving, arguments and debates, about living together. What the direct confrontations often concealed were the daily snubs and provocations black and white students encountered on first contact. At least one of the residences remains all black, and this was conveniently placed off-campus. At least one residence was all-white, and the authorities are at pains to claim it is not an official university residence and indicate this by denying access to institutional resources for a student house with the unwelcoming, if not provocative, name of *Huis Voortrekker* (Voortrekker House).

The head of one of the oldest white male residences, one drenched in Afrikaner male traditions, could take it no more and asked me to workshop the white men so they could overcome the historical knowledge of exclusion and white pride represented so powerfully in the symbols, values, traditions, and practices of this residence, *Kollegetehuis* (College House). I insisted that this discussion should take place with both black and white students, but because the racial tensions were so high, facilitative meetings would initially take place with students separated by race. So for several evenings I would meet with groups of students from this house over pizzas and Coke and talk for hours about their experiences in a Tukkies residence.

What happened next scared me, for I had no idea at the time how deeply hostile, alienating, and racist the culture of the residences was, especially in relation to non-Afrikaner students. The first surprise was that the black students and the English-speaking white students came together, clearly having formed a community based on the bonds of common experience at the hands of the white male Afrikaner students. And they talked. For black students, entering the residences was a horrific experience. They knew immediately from the white boys that they were not welcome in this space, and they saw the reason as race. One recalled: "When I first arrived at the residence, I asked nicely: 'Where do I go?' They just stared at me, with such feelings of hostility. I did not expect the students to have such hostile racial feelings."

Another shared the same experience: "It keeps getting worse. When they're in a group, you feel it, and you know the message is 'You're black, you're not supposed to be here, and this is not your place.'"

For another black student, this did not fit his high school experience because in that integrated institution his experiences with white English-speaking children were very different:

At school the whites were okay. But here they look at you strange. One student nicked me with his car, and I knew what he was saying . . . "stay out of the way." When you're black, the whites are hostile to you but blacks are welcoming to you.

The white English-speaking students then spoke up, and they were especially confused coming from long-integrated English high schools where they had forged friendships with black students in the classroom and on the sports fields. But the Afrikaner students gave them the same hostile treatment; "it's worse for us," said one of the English students.

The emotional toll of this alienating and hostile experience shows in how students recall residence life:

You have to walk a thin line here. I feel unwanted in my own place. But you struggle to get used to it, that sarcastic smile in the lift [elevator]. I am a proud UP student, but I am not a proud Tukkie. It is as if the Afrikaans students just tolerate us, like they are saying, "You are here, and we can do nothing about it." There was a time when even I became racist because of how we were treated. Sometimes you feel so angry, you just want to bomb the whole place.

By this time I was obviously very interested in the experiences and responses of the white Afrikaner students to these riveting accounts of black and white English-speaking students. I was also careful, despite the obvious and strong emotional resonances that I felt as a black person and an outsider myself with these experiences, not to judge or prejudge what the Afrikaans students were going to say.

To my surprise, the Afrikaans students also wanted to speak, and to have their say about how they saw black students (the English white students were invisible in their stories). I conducted these interview-discussion sessions in Afrikaans, and this made emotional and language connections that clearly facilitated speaking from their side of the large table.

The Afrikaans students complained that black students were not "student orientated" on the main campus ("like on the Education campus"), and that they were "rebellious." Said one: "They go out of their way to provoke us whites by wearing their caps in the dining hall." The black students, they insisted, were *"sluipers"* (foot-draggers): they do nothing for the koshuis (residence).

I then discovered that at the time there were two sets of living arrangements, a "white house" and a "black house." There were also two clubhouses, one for kwaito, black music, and one for rock, white music.

There were two television sets, and each student group would raise the volume louder and louder to drown out the other. But the black students, complained this group, were always uncooperative:

It is always the white house that has to compromise, not the black house. Black guys do not come to house meetings, it is their way of protesting; they work behind your back (agterbaks). Because of them, the two clubhouses were made one; we had no say in the matter.

The white students were clearly concerned that the university's residence management was about to collapse these two living spaces into one, and that it was doing so in a heavy-handed manner without consulting the Afrikaans students. "Don't take everything of ours away," they pleaded; "we understand the need for *regstelling* (affirmative action), but why take bursaries away from white students?" The students claimed to support transformation, but "the goalposts keep shifting," they said.

I want to stay here of course. But let's create history together. Do not force change on us. I hate affirmative action, even though it might be necessary to a small extent [tot 'n mate]. But the way it is implemented misses the mark. There is no communication. They [the university management] must talk to us and not sit in their ivory towers.

What followed was a number of stories about perceived discrimination, including one about the Boer War generals. There were apparently a number of symbols and statues of Afrikaner pride within and outside the entrance to this old residence, including Boer War generals; but the students were adamant:

The Boer War generals were not about Apartheid; they led the struggle against imperialism. We want the English to be angry when they see this [die Engelse moet kwaad wees]. Die kanon [a cannon, at the entrance] is a neutral symbol, it is not about discrimination.

I mentioned that the white English students might feel offended or targeted by this kind of aggression about a war that took place more than a hundred years ago; there was no response from the Afrikaans students. Most of all, these Afrikaans students did not want to lose the culture and traditions of Kollege, this famed koshuis in which their fathers and grandfathers had lived and that carried with it powerful memories of past bondmanship, friendships, camaraderie, and character. Said an older student:

Kollege made me what I am. It gave me my identity and made me a man. It gave me confidence [*selfvertroue*] and friends that I will keep to my dying day. Kollege is a community, and that is why I hate sluipers. Here we learn social skills, respect, and pride. If you take this away, what do you replace it with?

What struck me was the caution with which Afrikaans students framed their responses to black students, even making ambivalent concessions that perhaps some kind of affirmative action might be necessary, as much as they hated it. But with the English white students, there was no such concession on the part of the Afrikaans students. As I listened to these students I remember calling in the head of the SRC, a huge fellow with unashamed right-wing leanings and heavily involved in FF+ politics on the outside of the university. The week before the white Afrikaans students had celebrated the Battle of Majuba,[12] where the Boers beat the English in battle. In the process, they had painted provocative words against English and the English-speaking community on one of the university walls. I told him that as dean of the Faculty of Education, I was disgusted with his actions and his leadership since this kind of behavior was insulting to my white English-speaking students. Then, to my surprise, he leaned over and sought what he thought was a completely reasonable search for empathy from my side of the table: *"maar Professor, ons het mos die Engelse se gatte geskop op Majuba!"* (But Professor, surely we kicked the English arses at Majuba!). I asked him to leave my office.

To understand this distance between black and white students living together, I accepted a subsequent invitation to speak to all the boys at this koshuis one night, an engagement that would continue in subsequent years. What I saw there that evening was unbelievable. In front of a crowded hall of male residents of this koshuis stood about six senior Afrikaner boys, feet astride, talking to their audience of young men, white, black, and English, fresh out of high school and sitting on the floor in front of them. The koshuis leaders spoke to them in staccato tones giving the house rules and specific orders for behavior. Disturbingly, the speeches from the lead boys were only in Afrikaans, instantly alienating about half of the boys on the floor, many of whom did not understand a word of the language; the fact is, the lead boys knew this.

The boys on the floor were ordered to stand to attention, answer questions in unison, and from time to time be blatantly insulted by the pack of leaders while one strutted across the stage smoking a cigarette dangling from the side of his mouth. I stood at the back in horror. This part-orientation and part-intimidation was how boys in this koshuis had been inducted into the culture for many decades. As happened to their fathers and grandfathers, these stocky Afrikaner boys were going to make sure that the new recruits had the same experience, whether they understood it or not.

At that first encounter with koshuis culture, I understood the damage that comes with the intergenerational transfer of coarse and unreflective knowledge, and the capacity of such knowledge for inflaming young people for whom these traditions suggest cultural insensitivity at best and outright racial provocation at worst.

When my turn came to speak, I first chastised one of the lead boys for smoking in my presence—something that would not be tolerated in his culture, I reminded him, when adults were around. Like a schoolboy, he instantly snuffed out the cigarette with an apology. I then turned to the boys on the floor and told them in very clear terms not to accept this quasi-military introduction to my university. The purpose of a university, I told them, was to produce open-minded thinkers, independent thought, and encouragement for dissent. The next time they are treated like military recruits for the army, I said, they should walk out.

The main leader of the pack, standing to my side, was bristling with anger. I made the talk longer than usual and spoke about the good traditions from the past in the koshuise, which we should respect and keep, and the bad traditions (such as *ontgroening*, literally to un-green a student, or initiation), which should be discarded. It was their duty, I told the leaders, to bring in new traditions representing all the students and keep old traditions that everyone could respect. Even as I said this, I realized that this elaborate act of induction by these Afrikaner boys was as much an introduction to the koshuis as it was a statement of defiance against the university management for forcing integration of their treasured space.

It is difficult, even as an outsider, not to feel the white students' sense of loss set against the knowledge of past glories handed down to them by their fathers. This sense of empathy evaporates quickly when the harsh racism and aggression shine through the epidermis so easily. Still, the inability of the university leadership to take students through a difficult transition has made this a hardship for both sides, especially those for whom the institution was not originally intended.

If dealing with received knowledge wrapped in the traditions of a koshuis is so difficult when students live together, how does this dilemma represent itself in the university classroom when students learn together?

## Learning Together

The racial demographics of the student body changed very quickly after the 1990s, when black students were first allowed into UP. Black students were "marching to Pretoria," screeched a headline in a major Sunday paper, a reference to a popular folk song that had also taken on political meanings in the black struggle against Apartheid.[13] Much more slowly, and against the backdrop of considerable resistance, the number of black academic staff also started to increase. What had not changed at all was the political content of received knowledge represented in the institutional curriculum. The curriculum was never the subject of critical review inside UP, outside of the regulatory requirements to package curricula in line with new qualification frameworks and an outcomes-based curriculum design. The regulatory demands were formatting requirements, a set of technical specifications for how knowledge should be presented for purposes of the national registration and accreditation of degrees. What was taught, how it was taught, and to whom it was taught remained, for the most part, an institutional matter.

When I assumed the deanship I realized that once the basics of staff and student transformation had settled, it would be important to take on the teacher education curriculum, which was still steeped in Apartheid's education philosophy, something called Fundamental Pedagogics[14] and imbued with content that every now and again would be revealed to contain offensive and outdated materials.

One of the innovations I proposed to some of the undergraduate lecturers is that they should take the students on a bus on the same day to two rival monuments representing two very different struggles; I would find the resources for this excursion, but it was important not to teach about difficult issues through textbooks in a classroom. The first visit was to the Voortrekker Monument in Pretoria, representing the struggles of Afrikaner nationalism to achieve racial power in another century. The second trip was to the Apartheid Museum near Soweto, representing the struggle of African nationalism for a democratic society. I then proposed that the lecturers bring these students back to campus and open discussion on what they saw, felt, and experienced during these visits.

On returning from the Apartheid Museum, one of the white Afrikaner girls stood up and, with express support from other white students in her group, said: "It was all well and good taking us to the Apartheid Museum; now tell me, when will they build a museum for all the whites who died in farm murders in South Africa after 1994?" For even the most experienced college lecturer, this was an exceptionally difficult question. The lecturer in this case was white, herself a progressive Afrikaner for whom this challenge was exactly the kind of outcome she had worked toward. But now that the question was posed, the answers were not so obvious.

Understanding what lies beneath the student's question is crucial before and in any teaching response. This young white student, fresh from the Apartheid Museum, had just experienced a massive rupturing of intimate knowledge about a glorious past of Afrikaner struggle and conquest during which her tribe ruled over South Africa for much of the past century and gave this southern tip of a dark continent the triad of Christianity, culture, and civilization that made this place so different from other Third World countries to the north. This is the knowledge she held dear. The emotional turmoil in this young woman's experience of the Apartheid Museum does not express itself as empathy and shame but as anger and rage; *she has just discovered evil in what she had lost.*

There are few teacher education colleges that prepare teacher educators for this kind of complexity. A rational response by a teacher would be to spend time with the data, the statistics on crime, and show the student and her supportive white peers that in fact many more black people died after Apartheid as a result of violent crime than did white citizens. By this reasoning, her inference that whites were somehow targeted or sacrificed to crime under a black government would not hold up in the light of the evidence. But this is not what the young white woman wanted to hear; she probably knew these "facts" anyway. The rational response, a temptation for any teacher, is not a very constructive one in these circumstances.

A political answer would also not achieve much, especially one that responded in anger. It would be tempting to set her straight, to point out that she had missed the entire point about the Apartheid Museum, and that she needed to acknowledge the painful history of others in the same way that she would expect black people to respect the symbolism of the Voortrekker Monument. A political answer would take the response into discussions about white accountability and that she needed to at least recognize, if not take responsibility for, what her parents' generation did to black people. Neither a rational response nor political chastisement would evoke the kind of reaction that connected with the pain and the confusion of the white student. To craft a meaningful response is to first understand the speaker.

What happened to this student was in part a function of personal knowledge disrupted and in part a result of a poorly constructed nationalist museum. By the time she had walked through the Apartheid Museum she came away with a powerful narrative that affirmed her everyday experiences: that blacks had taken over the control of meaning and the access to power in both material and symbolic terms. As she emerged from the museum, she saw a simple and simplistic story of white as evil and black as good. There is no recognition of Afrikaner struggles against an earlier poverty or confinement to concentration camps by the British, or even of white comrades who took sides with blacks against Apartheid's evils. Like all nationalist museums, this one celebrated a particular brand of nationalism, black nationalism, in which this young woman could not see herself and her people except in the disturbing mirror of white as evil. In the process, the indirect knowledge that had shaped her childhood and adolescence and secured her foundations into adulthood was now abruptly disturbed. She was angry.

## Lazing Together

As indicated earlier, the idea with the first-year lunches was to signal to students very early on in their four-year program that the faculty leadership appreciated and encouraged common learning spaces and that we would try to model them in many ways, including eating together. I must say that for me these were sometimes very difficult sessions. The white and the black students would, predictably, sit next to one another by race and the major challenge was how to conduct this meeting. The first challenge was language. I had to consciously balance the amount of time I spoke in English with the time taken to speak in Afrikaans, so that both groups felt this institutional space belonged to all of them equally. I had to measure the religious climate in the room and make sure to check whether there were any Muslim or Jewish students. If there were none, I would ask one of the students to pray and bless the food; black students would pray in English, white students in Afrikaans. The prayer was the one binding factor since most of the students, black and white, claimed Christian faith.

I would use these opportunities to conduct my own informal surveys of tolerance. Most times, especially with the women students, it worked fairly well but at other times it was nerve-racking. The ten students would be asked to take two minutes each to introduce themselves, declare why they had decided to become teachers, and share an anecdote about their families and their first few weeks on campus. The white Afrikaner students would speak in Afrikaans, and I would cast my eye around the room to watch the reaction of black students, especially those from KwaZulu Natal or the Eastern Cape or the south of Gauteng, who were not familiar with Afrikaans. One or two black students would express irritation, roll their eyes, or just stare out the window as the Afrikaans rolled on. When it was the turn of the black students to speak, they would always express themselves in English and here the Afrikaner boys would show body language that expressed profound irritation. None of this boiled over in large part because I was in the room and I made it clear by my use of the languages that everyone had the right and the opportunity to speak in his or her own language. But it was sometimes tense.

During these informal times, which I call lazing together, I noticed a distinct gender difference in the ways students responded across the color line. The male students were loud and aggressive, especially the white Afrikaans students, and made sure that they occupied the space in my small dining hall. They physically and socially crowded out the other male students, and were obviously much more comfortable in this space even though initially as nervous as others because this was the dean's den. There was no communication from white students to black students, and vice versa. The white male students would only speak to one another, across the table, in loud voices; the black male students would whisper to the black students next to them, and I would have to call on them to speak to the group.

The white girls, on the other hand would, from time to time ask questions of the black girls after the latter introduced themselves. Where does your brother go to school? What does your mother do? What is your major? Similarly, the black girls would ask the white girls questions following their introductions. In other words, there was much more of a chance of cross-table and cross-racial interactions during lunch with young women than with young men. As the year progressed, I would find that the girls had become friends in some cases, and in one memorable lunch sitting the white girls were learning an African language from the black girls, and the black girls claimed to be learning Afrikaans from their white friends.

It was clear to me that the kind of warmness of exchange within the relatively safe environment of the dean's den would translate with considerable difficulty into the public spaces where students spend their times relaxing. In twelve years of deanship at two universities in South Africa, I found that the social patterns of students' social lives were segregated by race and ethnicity even though they shared the same university campus.

One of my favorite pastimes was to walk around the UP campus around lunch time to talk with and engage students, and also to observe patterns of social assembly. These patterns have remained stubbornly predictable fourteen years after the end of Apartheid. African students have their marked space on the campus, gathering in groups on the lawn in the same areas day after day. Afrikaner students have their spaces on the grass, as if someone had circled these areas for communal assembly. Colored students, without exception, assemble in much smaller groups but unmistakably have their familiar areas of congregation. Indian student groups are also unyielding to integration, at Pretoria especially, and with a trained eye it is easy to see from the dress of the young people concerned that Muslim students hang out separately from other students in the Indian community. And even though there might be one or two students of color in the white English circles of students, their spaces too are marked by the same language and ethnic affiliations. It is not that these groups were so clearly marked by color that puzzled me; it was that they hardly changed over three or four years of study, into the years of graduate school, and into adult and family life.

If there is one thing therefore that can be said about schools and universities in South Africa, it is that they are legally desegregated but socially segregated spaces. One reason for these stubborn patterns of racial association is that at the level of teachers and leaders, the same trends are to be observed; in other words, there is no adult modeling of alternative ways of being together among those deemed to be different.

So whether it was the university cafeteria during lunch breaks, the open lawns throughout the day, the library reading rooms, the computer laboratories, the seminar rooms, the large lecture venues, the music and arts displays on campus, the off-campus eating and drinking facilities— in each and every one of these social spaces, students are segregated by race. Nowhere is this more firmly defended than among the white Afrikaans students.

I complained about this in order to gauge their reasoning during one of my undergraduate teaching sessions. Their explanations: "But our cultures are different"; "We are more comfortable with our own kind"; "We have the same language"; "This is how we were brought up"; "Nobody should force us to be together; that would be as bad as Apartheid"; and "Why is this a problem? It's natural for people to be with their own."

What was striking in these responses was that nobody named race as the reason for such social choices; the more polite reason was "culture." Everybody described the situation as natural and normal; some pushed back against a perceived insistence on integration; most believed that there were real differences between people to explain their patterns of association. I kept pushing, and then one of the more interesting lecturer-student exchanges took place between myself and a young Afrikaner woman student. It went like this:

**Student**: *Maar ons kulture verskil* (But our cultures are different).

**Professor**: *How verskil jou kultuur van myne?* (But how does your culture differ from mine?)

**Student**: *Ons praat Afrikaans* (We speak Afrikaans).

**Professor**: *Maar ek praat dan nou met jou in Afrikaans* (But I am speaking to you in Afrikaans right now).

**Student**: *Wel, maar ons is NG kerkgangers* (But we are Dutch Reformed churchgoers).

**Professor**: *My ma was nogals ook NG* (My mother was actually also Dutch Reformed).

**Student**: *Maar ons braai* (But we barbeque).

**Professor**: *Jy praat dan met 'n vleisvreter* (You are talking to a meat-eater).

It was a silly exchange, from my side, and I felt bad afterwards about engaging at this level with a first-year student. But what the exchange did do for me was to indicate how incredibly difficult it would be to teach about the social and indeed political construct of race, its ideological and material motivations, and its changing and tentative character in history and society everywhere. It is hard to teach against "innate" understandings of race secured in the minds and hearts of white students from a very young age. It could also explain the stubborn patterns of racial segregation observed in the everyday lives and associations of white and black students alike. It might too conceal a greater peril for the race-obsessed: what if the "innocence" of social integration leads to something much more serious?

## Loving Together

As the years moved on since Apartheid, black students were the first to begin making shifts in attitude and disposition toward white students. This is something I often told black students when they complained about perceived racism in the acts of white students or even white faculty. It was clear to me that if there was going to be any alteration in these rigid social spaces and racial attitudes, the first steps would have to come from black students and faculty. A demographic minority suddenly relegated to a political minority and increasingly fearful of becoming an economic minority was not going to initiate acts of racial reconciliation; that much was clear. But what I did not expect was the directness of this challenge to me as dean from black first-year students.

Just before I stood down as dean and resigned from UP in 2007, I held my final lunch with the ten designated first-year students. For the first time, those organizing the logistics for the dean's lunch made a mistake; instead of sending five white and five black students, ten black students showed up. Initially I was disappointed, for the purpose of these events was to encourage integration by modeling these ideals early on through the planned lunches. But having ten black students was an unforeseen blessing, for these bright and articulate young people said things they would probably not have volunteered if white students had been in the room.

After the formalities were over, I opened the discussion as usual with the question about how they were experiencing the education campus of the university and what we could do as the leadership of the Faculty of Education to strengthen the quality of those experiences as undergraduate students. Immediately to my left sat a strikingly beautiful young woman, her hair in braids. She spoke clearly.

You know professor, we really enjoy being here, and we must thank you for everything you and your staff have done for us as first-year students. But you know, where we live in Res [residences], it's so artificial; I would really like to date some of those white boys.

I nearly fell off my chair in shock. Date white boys? I was expecting the usual concerns about enough parking spaces for students, the unlit areas of campus that needed lights, limited access to the Internet, the restricted library hours, the odd lecturer who is unfriendly, and other familiar student complaints. But dating white boys was completely unexpected. I was still stuttering, and unsure what to say, when a handsome young man to my right, brightly bald, chirped in: "Prof, I agree with Thandi. I would really like to date some of the white girls on campus."

This was too much for my black consciousness state-of-mind, and I remember saying to myself: "Damn, the goal of the national democratic revolution was not to date white folk!" But I dared not utter this sentiment. As an experienced teacher stumped for a response, I again played for time. "Well," I said to the now eagerly awaiting audience of ten young black adults, "tell me more."

As the students spoke during that lunch time, I cringed at the clear but gentle criticism coming from my black students. As university leaders, we had created the architecture for change and integration on the education campus, they said, but in reality the black and white students continued to live separate lives. What was natural among college students, the act of dating, took on severe and rigid racialized forms. When dancing was organized between two or more koshuise, it was white students going with white students, and by language. The students, though physically together in the formal arrangements, lived light years apart. If there was one act of social interaction that was never discussed, but in which the lines were firmly drawn, it was on this matter of dating.

It took me some time during this extended period of listening, on my part, to realize that this criticism had little to do with dating per se and everything to do with the artificiality of social relations between black and white students. What would come completely naturally to young people, the act of dating, was the one firm line that nobody would cross on this race-divided campus. Nowhere was this racial distancing between girls and boys more acute than at the former Afrikaans universities.

When I travel on one or another seminar or conference assignment to the English-speaking white universities, I would without fail notice interracial dating; though by no means widespread and common on the English campuses, it nevertheless existed and without the head-turning effects this would have on the Afrikaans campuses. There are, of course, historical reasons for this phenomenon, the barriers to love between black and white students, and indeed between Afrikaans-speaking and English-speaking white students. But for "the rage against alterity" to turn manic in white society, it is at the suggestion of loving together. No knowledge has been more forcefully transmitted from parents to children before and after Apartheid than the knowledge of racial and ethnic purity that must be maintained at all costs. Something about race and sex drives white South Africans into a state of madness.

It was J. M. Coetzee who posed the question, "Where do [race-mixing] obsessions come from, and how do they spread themselves through the social body?"[15] He framed this critical question about transmission of obsessive knowledge in relation to a UP professor, one Geoffrey Cronje, who was arguably the foremost academic protagonist of race purity thinking and "a seminal contributor to the theory of Apartheid."[16] It is by reading this account of how racial ideas, and in particular the absolute obsession with race mixing, were entrenched and transmitted within Afrikaner thinking that one begins to understand why white Afrikaans students (and staff) recoil so viscerally when faced with the possibility of "mixing" with other groups. It is an attitude that comes from fixed knowledge about race, which has changed little from one century to the next.

In fact, there is a long tradition of research that shows the continuity of conservative attitudes among white university students over successive periods of political change in South Africa. This line of inquiry can be traced to the work of Orpen and his colleagues[17] in the 1970s through the surveys of Duckitt[18] and also Heaven[19] in the 1980s, to the research of Booysen[20] and Gagiano[21] in the 1990s, and stretching into contemporary studies.[22] It is crucial, however, not to see these beliefs as floating free of ideological interest, a point well argued by Furnham in his study of "just world beliefs" among white South African university students:

One of the most robust findings from the just world literature is that these beliefs function to help people cope with disturbing or threatening events (rape, poverty, racism) and that, if these events are shared, people develop a consensual view of the "reality" of the situation. Furthermore, because these beliefs actually succeed in reducing or preventing threat, *they are retained and socialized into succeeding generations* [emphasis added].[23]

This consistency in racial attitudes, it has been argued, reflects the closed and intact transmission line along which knowledge has been transferred from one generation of children to the next. Yet for the second generation, this knowledge received was further and further removed from direct experiences of an Apartheid past. The second generation remains therefore the receptacle for indirect knowledge from parents and other adults who actually lived through, benefited from, and contributed to the Apartheid terror. It was argued that the interlocking influences of family, church, school, peers, sports, and university created an environment close to hermetically sealed that kept the transmission line relatively uninterrupted and provided children with secure and intimate knowledge of how things were and how they ought to remain. Thus:

The typical Afrikaner will go to an Afrikaans school, live in a suburb where other Afrikaners are well represented, attend the service of one of the family of Afrikaans churches, rely on an Afrikaans language newspaper for political information, go to one of the six Afrikaans universities . . . and work for the state or for a firm with an Afrikaans ambience.[24]

What gave these sealed and interlocking environments their social, economic, and political legitimacy was

a formidable battery of laws, regulations, proclamations and judicial interpretations that prescribe behavior in a vast array of potentially inter-racial situations such as wedding, bedding, dining, entertaining, learning, praying, playing, defecating, voting, resisting, fighting, working; that is the medley of actions and activities that constitute a person's life.[25]

The argument pursued in this chapter was that with the legal termination of Apartheid in the early 1990s, and the coming to power of a black government in 1994, this transmission line was more and more vulnerable to rupture. There was no longer the legitimating canopy of Apartheid laws and regulations. There was no longer a state media that provided partial knowledge and ideological justification for the racial order. And there were no longer exclusively white universities, the point of first rupture for most white Afrikaner students, given the still sealed and insular nature of knowledge transmitted within schools, family, peer groups, and the church. As Nigel Crook predicted:

Such a strategy of transmission may endure with some success in a closed system; but it is an insufficient strategy to ensure the perpetuation of richness and power in a society that has once been opened to external challenge or suffered a permanent exogenous shock.[26]

What one would expect, therefore, if this analysis holds, is that the traditional Afrikaans university would become the terrain for playing out the politics of loss and change.

Conclusion

In this chapter, we found a number of major disruptive strategies.

First, white Afrikaner students sought to defend the status, symbols, spaces, and privileges that "their" campus offered in the face of the institutional changes that granted access to black students. To Afrikaner students, black students and English whites were outsiders coming in; the place was not intended for them. As outsiders coming in, they had to come in on the terms of the original habitants: the Afrikaners. They had to accept not only the rituals, symbols, and ceremonies of Afrikanerdom but also the leadership and instruction of Afrikaners. Afrikaners had built this campus; they had mobilized the resources to build these monuments to ethnic pride; and they had established over many years of struggle the institutional culture and character of the university. To the boldest among them, the Afrikaner student (and less boldly their ethnic administrators), these arrangements were to be accepted and adopted, not changed. Since there was no institutional leadership or clear policies or consistent plans to spell out the terms of racial integration in formerly white universities such as UP, a political gap was left into which young Afrikaners stepped to reassert their power, privilege, and identity in the face of loss.

Second, in defending symbolic spaces and material privileges, white students found themselves in confrontation and contestation with the university authorities, the most explosive and indeed handy vehicle for leading such contests being and remaining the Afrikaans language. Their protests were not targeted at the black government but at the white adults, fellow Afrikaners, those who should know better and whom they regarded as the last defense against the losses that came with integration. When the university authorities did not respond with the necessary empathy and affirmation of their cause, white students became confrontational and defaced buildings, provoked black students, and disrupted university ceremonies.

Third, such defensive action by white Afrikaner students led also to confrontation with the new residents, black and English-speaking white students. By treating black and English students with contempt, conservative Afrikaans students were venting their anger on the outsiders, the newcomers, the foreign. Whether the spaces in question were the dining halls, the residences, the classroom, or open campus grounds, white students would make sure that the messages sent declared they were not welcome. In many interviews, black and English students spoke of low-level intimidation and dismissal at the hands of white Afrikaans students. It is no coincidence that in these myriad small confrontations the male Afrikaner students exercised and led these actions. The gendered nature of confrontation is of course an artifact of the patriarchal character of Afrikaner society and of the aggressive militarism that defined Afrikaner nationalist politics for more than a century.

Fourth, defensive action led to confrontation with the new knowledge that white Afrikaans students were encountering for the first time. The instant that secure knowledge is threatened, as in the case of the students returning from the Apartheid Museum, there is disruption and disorientation. The first reaction is not empathy and understanding, let alone any outward sign of guilt or remorse. With the shock of disruption comes anger and distress expressed in coarse and uncomfortable ways. When the white woman student asks about white suffering on returning from the Apartheid Museum, we have here a powerful but underexplored phenomenon, what Eva Hoffman calls "the clash of martyrological memories."[27] If black students raise their indirect knowledge of the past in such spaces, white students raise their own, and it takes extraordinary teaching and leadership to navigate these treacherous waters where martyrological memories clash.[28]

Fifth, though the physical sharing of space was legally and politically inevitable, white students, and to a lesser extent black students, kept the social barriers firmly intact when it came to living, learning, lazing, and loving together. What such social separation did was to further entrench suspicion, fear, and stereotype, and sometimes lead to outright physical confrontation between white and black students.

One reason the transformation strategies at the university failed is that they dealt with the consequences of the disruption of secure knowledge rather than with the problem of received knowledge in the first place. This would require patient engagement with white students as they came to realize, for the first time, that the knowledge securely transmitted to them before they came to university was not as simple, pure, and innocent as given. Worse, some had to come to the terrible realization that the past was not as innocent as they believed. "But what if one discovers evil in what one has lost," asks Robert Jay Lifton with a sobering conclusion, "and by implication in oneself?"[29]

Knowledge received of others continues to define the spatial relationships among students on university campuses long after Apartheid. In an insightful collection of research essays, Tredoux and his colleagues (2005) examine race, isolation, and interaction in everyday life in South African educational institutions using the contact hypothesis of social psychology.[30] Throughout this recent collection, it is clear that racial separation continues to define relationships between students even when sharing the same space. One study examined patterns of racial segregation in university dining halls and still found "high levels of informal segregation and that the segregation manifests itself as a specific spatial configuration."[31] Another study in the collection, also at a white university, observed patterns of seating over time in public spaces on the campus. Once again, it was found that such patterns of association are rigidly marked by race, and that even appearances of integration are in fact segregative in terms of how, where, and with whom students occupy space.[32] This story of physical integration and social segregation continues to run through the current research about black and white relations on university campuses after Apartheid.[33] These racial patterns of association were certainly not restricted to white and black students; they find their mirror image among those employed by the university and who call themselves colleagues.

# 5    Kollegas! (Colleagues!)

Against this knowing, stands the silence.[1]

Yet what of the rage that continues unabated in the Afrikaner breastbone? Why are these people so tall of stature, big of build and fair in appearance so angry and tormented?[2]

NOTHING DISTURBED ME more emotionally during my time at UP than what happened one Saturday morning. I was walking with my 13-year-old daughter through a shopping center when I spotted a white colleague walking in the opposite direction. I brightened up, moved slightly in her direction, and greeted heartily in Afrikaans: "Good morning Michelle!"[3] She refused to make eye contact, looking down and moving along at a steady pace. This must be a mistake, I thought. Perhaps she did not hear or see me. I tugged my daughter further in her direction and raised my voice, this time greeting even more loudly. She looked at me quickly, quickened her step, and moved determinedly ahead without greeting. "I don't think she knows you," said my daughter. "But she does," I insisted to myself. At this point I felt racial distress, anger, and confusion at the same time. Just the day before we had been part of a long meeting; as a senior administrator, she took the minutes but also contributed some technical information. That *was* Michelle.

This simple act of not recognizing me, a colleague, was for some reason more devastating than a spoken rejection. How could people work together so closely in one public place, the administration buildings of the university, and yet pretend nothing happened in another public space outside the university? What was more hurtful was that my daughter witnessed the incident. I saw Michelle a few days after that, back inside the university campus; I noticed her blush. I said nothing. She resigned shortly afterwards.

For a long time I harbored the possibility that it might not have been Michelle. But then it happened again, with another colleague. At least now I was half-ready, as the emotional preparedness was in place against this kind of racial insult. Since Michelle, I had also learned how to turn hurtful puzzles into intriguing theory. This time it was a woman colleague from my own campus. She looked straight at me as she stood in line with her partner at the movies while my family moved in the same direction. She did not look away but before I moved to greet I remembered Michelle and decided that I would not greet or recognize first. I told her manager about this experience, he raised it with her, and she denied that such a meeting ever took place.

## Official Spaces

It has since become clear that the occupation of common employment space between white and black colleagues is, for many whites, an arrangement whose social and interpersonal rules do not extend outside of the campus. Like students, white and black colleagues are forced to function together in the same campus space, which until recently was reserved for whites—in this case, Afrikaners. But the lines for social interaction are strictly occupational.

What is confusing, though, is the intensity of the on-campus interactions: laughter, respect, common projects, joint seminars, and even co-publishing between white and black colleagues who also attend conferences and defend budgets together. There is no sense of animosity and no indication of racial ill-will. So from the point of view of academic work, there is no sense of problems in terms of race relations and race recognition.

It is true that, even on campus, white and black colleagues seldom share social spaces outside joint academic and administrative work. In the cafeteria, the coffee room, and offices, white and black colleagues sit separately from one another. Family stories, gossip, complaints, and other intimate concerns are generally shared within the racial group.

Such segregation is of course never complete, for there are individual white and black colleagues who step over these artificial boundaries. But who are they? They are often white colleagues who were themselves harshly treated within, and rejected by, the inner circle of Afrikanerdom in the past. One such person was a colleague who lived through the devastation that came with his being suspected of having what he called "colored blood"; it includes those who happened to come from a home in which one of the parents was English and who had to bear the brunt of Afrikaner prejudice as a result; there were also individuals who had rebelled since youth against the narrow strictures of Afrikaner culture and found themselves outcasts from the Volk. They were no more than a handful in a collegial staff of more than one hundred academics and administrators, mainly Afrikaners.

## Circumscribed Knowledge

Within these constraints, collegial discourses are regulated by unspoken rules, and this becomes evident as one enters this white Afrikaans world. The most important rule governing faculty discourse within the common space is never to talk about the past. This is difficult, especially because working together produces the kind of intimacy and knowledge that at the very least makes one curious about colleagues' historical and political past. Time and time again I discovered that, even in warm conversation, the moment the discussion turned toward the past, the shutters came down. And they came down abruptly.

This does not mean complete denial of intimate conversation, but such talk—where it happens—is limited to information about the routine of family lives, such as children's rugby games, husband's new job, family's new car, and renovations at home. Small talk of this kind flourishes. It is talk about common experiences that all staff share in one way or another. Most of all, it is nonthreatening. Everyday talk and official talk are cordial, kind, and generous for the most part.

When white Afrikaans colleagues did speak of the past, it was about a tranquil rural upbringing, stern but warm parents, family laughter around an open fire, memorable sporting events, great teachers who inspired, moving Afrikaans poetry. The stories about the past, when on offer, were stories about cohesion and community, order and stability, peace and harmony. Where these narratives drifted into discussion about black people, it was always about happy and contented black workers who were part of the family. There was no Apartheid, racism, inequality, poverty, civil conflict, state brutality, murder, or torture in any of the stories—only consensus, cohesion, and contentment.

What makes an open conversation about other stories so difficult in situations like this is that the institutional culture is steeped in what is called beleefdheid, an Afrikaans word that translates imperfectly as politeness. More than that, it is an arranged politeness, an exaggerated sense of courteousness. This does not mean vicious attacks on persons could not and do not take place outside the spaces that insist on beleefdheid, as in formal meetings. What beleefdheid demands, moreover, is absence of rancor and minimalization of conflict in communal talk.[4]

There is a painful abnormality to this situation among most of one's colleagues. It is especially difficult for black academics and administrators coming into such silent and polite settings, for Apartheid was the dominant experience of our lives during the very recent past. You want to talk, not for purposes of accusation but simply out of a deep and unfulfilled desire to know. Knowing about the other side, the perpetrators, what happened, resolves something deep inside the emotional and psychological lives of the victims. It is the kind of knowing that black people who lost loved ones during the Apartheid years demonstrated so powerfully at the Truth and Reconciliation Commission and after (*I know my child is no more, but I need to know what happened, how did she die, did she say anything, who did it, and why?*). It is a knowledge that goes some way to putting the spirit at rest. But this environment does not allow such knowledge. The silence is (the) knowledge.

### Angry Knowledge

An exception to these pained silences among most whites on campus was the outspoken aggression of some white Afrikaner men. These were invariably persons in senior positions who harbored an unresolved anger about their historical past. They were prepared to speak, forcefully and uninvited, and they would make their point for the specific attention of black colleagues.

The most direct instance of my experience with this type of confrontation was with the formal leader of the institution. On at least three occasions, he was at pains to point out to me the meaning of the middle letter in his set of initials, "I." It was apparently common in his family to carry down the "I" from one generation to the next. The letter stood for "Irene," a well-known place in Pretoria that was the site of a concentration camp where the Boers suffered during their humiliation in the war against the British. It would be mentioned suddenly, and out of the context of the conversation, but always for my edification. I was of course eager to listen, in part out of intellectual curiosity and in part because of the rare opportunity to talk about the past. But this intervention was short and sharp, and it did not invite dialogue about the Apartheid past. Here was a powerful case of white martyrological memory raised to make a point, and silencing the possibility of raising black memory of an intertwined past.

Others in leadership would not fail to tell similar stories of the Afrikaners' struggle for self-determination, and within these accounts their treatment as children at the hands of the English would come up over and over again. "I heard the English mother say to her child not to play with me because Afrikaners were dirty" or "Shut up, no Afrikaans in this class."[5] These are clearly painful stories, mixing indirect knowledge from parents with direct knowledge of maltreatment at the hands of the English. Not once in these accounts, however, will there be mention of what happened to English South Africans when the Afrikaner National Party stormed to power in 1948; how English jobs were lost, promotions denied, and Afrikaners privileged through one of the most successful programs of affirmative action on the African continent. In other words, this was and remains an insular story divorced from other stories of oppression at the hands of the perpetual victims, the Afrikaners.

At least these men tell their stories. There is another kind of telling that expresses intense anger when black colleagues make claims on resources or spaces or symbols or history. It seldom bursts out into the open, but when it does it is angry and intense. A colleague could not understand why as dean I questioned his membership in the *Afrikaner*

*Broederbond* (Afrikaner Brotherhood),[6] that secret society of Afrikaner men that excluded women and blacks alike and that provided the intellectual ideas for, and the political muscle behind, Apartheid. He was seething, insisting that the (new) Constitution gave him freedom of association. Further, this secret society had reinvented itself as the Afrikaner Bond; anyone could a become member, and its meetings were now a matter of open record. I tried to explain to him that this hated society lay at the roots of black oppression, and that his association with the Bond made it difficult for me to trust him in a position of senior leadership of the faculty. It was an angry confrontation, and one that was difficult for me since I saw him then and now as a friend, someone whom I could see was really struggling with this disruptive knowledge that I had shared and that, from his experience, simply did not carry the same meaning. As my friend struggled with this disruptive knowledge, it really pained me. I learned that he took this home, where it became a point of tension. At one point he resigned from the Bond, which must have been an incredibly difficult situation. What frightened me, initially, was the fierceness of his response. What concerned me later was the depth of his turmoil. What drew me toward him was his intellectual honesty, his willingness to grapple with disruption. He was making the transition from painful knowledge to open concession that there was a possible problem.

Others came into their relationships with black colleagues with the need to confess.

## Confessional Knowledge

One of my more enriching experiences was the opportunity to regularly engage three or four colleagues—never more than that—for whom talking about the terrible past came more readily. Mainly women, this minority within the Afrikaner community welcomed opportunities to talk about history, politics, and memory. They would come to my office and, whatever the problem of immediate concern—a disciplinary matter with a student or a curriculum conundrum in the undergraduate program—we would find the time to talk about the past. I valued these opportunities to gain insight from my colleagues about the architectonics of knowledge at UP, its history, meanings, purposes, and design. I wanted to know the simple and complex codes for behavior, their roots and their meanings. It was to this group that I turned whenever something happened that required cultural translation. Without them, this book would not have been possible, and my tenure as dean would have been unbearable.

They spoke openly and remorsefully, and even as they engaged this new knowledge they wanted to know more. "Was Apartheid like the Holocaust?" asked one. It was a question I never got around to answering. The mere fact that such a painful question with a potentially catastrophic answer could even be posed demonstrates the sincerity as well as the readiness of these colleagues to confront their own knowledge in relation to other people's knowledge. It was their pained but engaging response to disruptive knowledge that gave me the confidence to continue and instilled the hope that it might be possible to move toward a common knowledge and a shared future among my Afrikaner colleagues.

It was clear to me that colleagues in this group had unusual biographies—possibly including a personal or family experience of exclusion by the patriarchs of Apartheid,[7] or a critical incident that raised initial doubts about the certainty of received knowledge. When one of these colleagues travels to Paris on a student exchange program, she lands in the home of a French couple who tell her that Apartheid is slavery. Eager to serve as ambassador for her country at the height of the Apartheid years, she hears for the first time that she might be representing an evil system. This event becomes a turning point that leads to a grappling with disruptive knowledge in ways that lay the foundation for interracial engagement.

The break with the secluded world of Afrikaner society and the exposure to the international community had two effects among my colleagues, and indeed among their predecessors. Throughout the twentieth century, a segment of the Afrikaner elite would find study opportunities abroad, mainly in Europe and especially in Germany and the Netherlands. One effect was to return as scholars with hardened racial attitudes, often taking social theory from Europe and adapting and distorting these ideas to advance Apartheid.[8] Another effect was to open up academic minds to the more liberal social attitudes of Europe and begin questioning the segregationist logic that found its political expression in Apartheid.[9]

## Unguarded Knowledge

The process of change from secure to disruptive and new knowledge is complex. Understandings are incomplete, emotions fragile, identities fractured. Language struggles to keep up with new social and intellectual arrangements. The languages and beliefs of colleagues are "caught between the old and the new."[10]

One of the semiamusing moments that captured such dilemmas was an evening to which I was invited by a colleague to open and welcome to the university the members of the public who would come to listen to the children's choir she directed. This choir enjoyed an affiliation with UP and produced singing of very high quality under her capable baton as the *dirigent* (conductor). I was handed the program for the evening in advance, and the arrangements were set for me to open the event at 7:05 that Saturday evening; her family would also be attending.

I was delayed for some reason and reached the event a few minutes late; I was quite embarrassed since in this particular culture things start on time. Everything went well and I delivered the welcome and the necessary apology. But my colleague made sure I received notice of her concerns, with these words: "Professor, my family already thinks black people are incompetent and irresponsible, and I have tried so hard to convince them otherwise; and now you come late and they won't believe me because you proved them right."

I say "semiamusing" because on the one hand I found this quite funny. The fact that arriving a few minutes late becomes the basis for making firm racial judgments about people is so obviously ridiculous that I simply laughed at what she was saying. I was also relieved that she could even utter such revealing insights about her bigoted family, something that whites in a university environment are much better at concealing in a beleefdheid culture. On the other hand, this was offensive to human dignity and required reprimand.

But I did not, in this case, challenge the prejudice, because in my colleague's mind she saw herself as a bridge builder between two racial communities, however clumsily her talking about it came through. The temptation to judge, therefore, must be tempered by an understanding of how complex such a sudden transition from a recent Apartheid past is for white Afrikaners, long secluded in a fixed knowledge about how others think and behave.

This unguarded knowledge, learned in another period and transmitted into the new, can nevertheless be as disarming as it is embarrassing. The first time it happened I just could not believe that such unguarded comments could be made. I had been dean for several weeks and because of my research and teaching background in comparative and international education a senior Afrikaner colleague asked me whether I would address her undergraduate class on curriculum as a transnational phenomenon. I suspected that she might have realized I had not yet been exposed to white students at UP and that this would be an ideal way to introduce me.

As I do routinely, I prepared my lecture as meticulously as possible, conscious of the audience and their limited knowledge of the subject, and the need to move slowly through some tricky concepts. I walked into the class and could not believe my eyes: an all-white, almost all-Afrikaans class of students in a packed theatre. Some of the other Afrikaans lecturers also came to listen. I was, as with all my teaching, very excited about what I was going to do with the students and how I would model ways of teaching for these future educators. All those plans fell flat, however. As my Afrikaner colleague stepped forward to introduce me, I suddenly became aware of the students staring; for most of them this was going to be their first lecture by a black person. Even so, I relished the opportunity to demonstrate good, authoritative teaching. Then she said it:

Well, it is my pleasure to introduce our new dean, Professor Jansen. Now when we see a black man, we think of affirmative action. But I can assure you he is not an affirmative action candidate. He has his Ph.D. from Stanford and he has published a lot.

Whatever else she said, I cannot remember. I caught my breath in shock. Until that point I had decidedly not thought of myself as an affirmative action candidate, either here at Pretoria or anywhere else in the world. But now it was out there, and whether those white students thought about it or not the suspicion hung in the air. I forgot my lecture completely, with blurred notes in front of me. I tried my best to concentrate, and probably delivered a reasonable lecture, for they applauded. But I was emotionally off balance. How could my colleague do this? If she harbored such thoughts, what on earth were my other colleagues thinking who would not even have contemplated, at that stage, inviting me into their classroom?

As I reflected on what happened, I realized once again that this was unguarded knowledge carried in the consciousness from a recent past, a knowledge that framed the way colleagues, and indeed any other white South Africans, saw black people, irrespective of their accomplishments. My colleague did not mean to be hurtful; quite the opposite. But she did not realize that even in the negative framing of the black speaker, the dean, knowledge was no longer reserved and concealed. It was out there in the classroom.

### Controlling Knowledge

But knowledge of others need not be revealed in such an embarrassing and clumsy way as in the case of the director of the children's choir. More often in former white universities, knowledge plays a very different and unexpressed role, that of controlling knowledge. Though the number of black colleagues and students might ebb and flow, such transformative trends are not unaffected by, or unrelated to, controlling knowledge. How does this work? I will draw on examples from personal experience.

Consider the application or nomination of a formidable black scholar to take a position at UP. The person has an impressive *curriculum vitae* and is the subject of recruitment interest from several other universities. The excited head of department X in faculty Y makes the nomination. At this point a number of controlling processes can move into gear to prevent this appointment. First, a dean might conclude that the person does not fit the disciplinary interests of the faculty, and a less guarded senior colleague might make the point that "the standards" represented in the CV do not match the quality department X or faculty Y demands of its scholars.

Even if the nomination passes the test at the faculty level, there are complex processes at the level of the senior administration that could effectively block this appointment. The chief of finance might make the argument that department X is "oversubscribed"[11] and therefore cannot "carry" an additional staff member. The head of finance might get away with this if his senior colleagues, the principal or vice-principal of the university, do not override him. His seniors might not share the same enthusiasm for the appointment, and they might not be willing to use their knowledge of the system to find ways of bringing in this black scholar. In wealthy UP, this of course raises questions not so much about whether the resources are available as whether senior colleagues in administration are prepared to create the opportunities for such a colleague to come in.

In a second example, a dean decides that in a largely white student body every effort must be made to recruit black students from mainly black schools to attend this former white university. After lengthy recruitment drives and generation of external funds to contribute to such diversification of the student body, black high school graduates begin to show up at the gates of the university. However, as their numbers grow, it is necessary for the university administration to contribute to their tuition and residence costs since these students are, in the main, very poor. But central administration does not approve of this growth in black student numbers, which could in time effectively decrease the number of white students. It is not necessary to make straightforward racial arguments in this case; it is sufficient to argue that the quality of the incoming students is not as high as that of white students ("Why should exceptions be made?"). It could further be argued that the academic records of the black students do not meet the historical requirements for admission to the residence; or that central finances are insufficient and that it will not be able to sustain these students over a four-year period of study; or that the students lack crucial registration documentation (such as parental income statements)[12] for their cases to proceed.

The central administration, in this case, is presenting a concrete wall of resistance that is extremely difficult to penetrate because the knowledge on which such decisions are based is not openly available for scrutiny. More seriously, the knowledge of how to create alternatives within this maze of bureaucratic procedure is withheld, and in this way the rules ensure continuity rather than change in the racial character of student admissions.

I am certainly *not* suggesting that there is some conscious and deliberate planning about how to keep out or control black student numbers.

The point is rather that the processes managing and controlling student admissions and faculty appointments are governed by insular knowledge retained in the hands of administrators who can make such changes easy or difficult depending on what is at stake. How universities (for example) use knowledge to control and exercise power has not enjoyed sustained attention in organizational theory and research;[13] especially missing are detailed ethnographic accounts of the organization and management of knowledge, and how it is given and withheld in the inner workings of a university. A fertile territory for inquiry is "the hidden ways in which senior managers use power behind the scenes to further their positions by shaping legitimacy, values, technology, and information."[14]

Here knowledge is power, and "the struggle for power within an organization [influences] the design, implementation and ongoing management of a knowledge management system while at the same time the knowledge management system will influence the struggle for power."[15]

Such administrative knowledge was not created overnight; nor is it simply the invention of a single bureaucrat or tyrannical leader. This is knowledge long established in the organization—"cultural knowledge," as Sonja Sackmann[16] might call it—and retained within the collective mind of the university. Of course, such uses of knowledge for political means in organizations are not novel. What is pertinent in this case is that the knowledge is racially distributed and racially owned, for the important decision makers at the head of the organization are still white, even as black faces begin to appear within these levels of appointment. White universities now have black vice-chancellors (university presidents) but, as is routinely observed by black commentators, the key authorities over knowledge in human resources, finance, admissions, academic appointments, and staff advancement are still largely white.

I believe the most important impediment to the racial transformation of academic staff appointments at universities such as Pretoria is that the control over knowledge of processes, resources, and space is still largely in white hands. Knowledge is control.

This kind of controlling knowledge is, in some respects, impervious to collegial challenge. All it needs to do is block access to resources, frustrate efforts to deracialize staffing, or withhold approval of routine decisions.

One of the more impressive things that strike an outsider to UP is the sophistication of the knowledge management infrastructure, rivaling anything similar in the best universities in the world. There are data on everything, from personnel details to daily budget flow minutiae to demographic information on students.

For example, a bizarre event during my time in the institution was the display to the senate of institutionwide data to show that UP was still the first choice for most Afrikaans-speaking students, that these Afrikaans-speaking students had the best high school grades, and the highest pass and progression rates once admitted. Why would a university leader take something as trivial as the race and language of a particular group, his group, to make such specific ethnic claims? What was the context for this largely irrelevant information? Where was the sensitivity to the fact that the most privileged students performed relative to their class status, and that such information by direct inference was in fact offensive to black students and faculty who remain on the margins of institutional life? It would clearly be as gratuitous to single out white English-speaking students for such acclaim, or, for that matter, international students.

I stood up in that packed senate meeting and asked these questions and, as usual, they were met with silence; there was no answer. Would it not make sense to ask better questions about the changes in the language preferences of students, or the changing demographics of the student body and the implications for language policy, or the number of all-white academic departments despite a longstanding institutional policy on staffing equity? Such questions are not acceptable or entertained for discussion because they begin to unsettle the foundations of power and control attached to administrative knowledge.

Critical theory has yet to come to terms with this problem of knowledge and control within universities and how they operate to maintain ideological power and racial privilege at historically white institutions.

## Divine Knowledge

To understand the rage against alterity among Apartheid's progenitors, it is important to come to terms with the fact that the antiblack venom of white Afrikaners extended in equal measure to Muslims, Jews,

Hindus, and any other group whose God was deemed to be not only different but a threat to the dominance of Afrikaner Calvinism in its various guises on and around the campus. In this respect, it is important to realize that the Afrikaner church and the Afrikaner university exist in symbiotic relationship to each other; in fact, historically there was little operational and ideological distinction between the church, the university, and the state.[17]

The university, through its Faculty of Theology, trains successive generations of Afrikaner dominees. The Dutch Reformed Church, in turn, becomes the employment agency for absorbing the graduate dominees. In the process, the transmission of Apartheid's divine knowledge moves smoothly and securely between the university and the church, alert to disruption. "Would the Faculty of Theology consider incorporating a Center for Islamic Studies as part of our transformation?" I asked at a strategic planning session of UP deans and senior administrators. I could feel the room go cold. "Yes," said the dean of theology falteringly, knowing full well that such an action, even if he believed in it, would terminate the funding he received from the former establishment church to fulfill its historical role in the production of dominees and the reproduction of divine knowledge.

As one committed to faith, and raised as an evangelical Christian, this remains for me a bizarre feature of Afrikanerdom: that a deeply devout people could for centuries not see any contradiction between the love of God and the hatred of man. In the Afrikaner churches, this received knowledge of a chosen people "planted" by God in Southern Africa to advance culture, Christ, and civilization remains to this day, consciously or otherwise, an underlying belief commitment even though it is rarely expressed in such terms.[18] This knowledge was transmitted down the years in pure form and in a sphere, the church, that remains largely untouched by demands for racial integration. In any rural area of South Africa, the two-race church organization remains firmly in place: the colored church on one side of town and the Afrikaner church on the other.

Out of curiosity, I attended the Afrikaner church in a small town called McGregor in the Cape Province shortly after 1994, remaining in my seat as the church members filed out; at that stage I wanted to know whether the euphoria among political elites about a social "miracle" and the emergence of Archbishop Tutu's "rainbow people of God" was reflected in the Dutch Reformed Church. As the all-white church members filed out of the church, they looked right past me, not a single one greeting.

It was to be expected, though, that divine knowledge, as understood by the Afrikaner, would inevitably face challenge and dissent as the university and the community within which it was embedded responded to the broader shifts in the political domain.

One such challenge came when a small group of Muslim undergraduate students asked whether they could have a room in which to pray. I was aware that the university had made ample provision for Afrikaner students to receive spiritual counseling and prayer rooms throughout the campus. On fixed days of the week dominees from the surrounding churches would come to designated rooms on campus and work with students for the purpose of spiritual development; at one stage at least six rooms were set aside for this purpose on the Education campus alone.

I could as dean have assigned a room on the Education campus for the Muslim students with little need to consult anyone, except for my immediate colleagues, but this was an opportunity to advance transformation and raise the issue of multifaith prayer rooms more broadly and especially on the main campus. I therefore sent the request to the central administration, asking that, as was done for the Christian students, we set aside rooms for Muslim students to pray. The long wait told me there was something amiss and this request had clearly not been heard before; in other words, the otherwise efficient system of administration did not know how to deal with this abnormal request.

Eventually the response came: "It cannot be done," "There is a problem with space demands on campus," and "The administration is really sorry that the Muslim students cannot be accommodated." When this kind of message comes through to a middle-level black leader in a white university, it discourages, but it also charges the spirit forcefully. But when it happens again and again, the discouragement deepens and it becomes harder and harder to push against the formidable strength of white institutional authority; it becomes harder, in other words, to stay in Meyerson's boat. Eventually, it becomes a case of "one fight too many."

Clearly this was not a case of enough space. Any leader in the central administration with even the remotest sense of the transformation project would recognize this was not about physical space but about social inclusion and institutional recognition. It was, moreover, a request that asked whether the institutional sense of generosity that holds amply for white Christian students could be extended to those of another faith. But this was not to happen. I would obviously not tell my Muslim students, small in number to begin with, that my fellow Christian colleagues on the main campus told them, effectively, to get lost.

I did what I was forced to do so often for the sake of the broader transformation ideals that brought me to this white university. I used the power available to me and allocated the students a space directly opposite my office, so they could feel protected and sense the importance I attached to their presence by having them share my floor. In doing so, I realized that pushing my power to the limit, and sometimes over it, could result in the institution calling my bluff on the hidden rules of white knowledge and white authority. This was a risky business, but I kept telling myself that the cause of social justice was greater than such institutional small-mindedness.

The Muslim students collected the key from my secretary, and we set about emptying, cleaning, and preparing the room for student prayers. It was one of our commitments that gave me deep joy and helped play down the intolerance that governed the campus.

Later, a right-wing American evangelist was brought onto the campus to talk about "The End of Islam." The post-September 11 environment, which had infuriated South African Muslims, made the timing of this event particularly provocative.[19] Predictably, the broader Muslim community around Pretoria was outraged, and the minority Muslim students alarmed and fearful at the same time. The university leadership shielded itself behind "free speech" and made no outright condemnation of this act of religious intolerance.

I was furious and used my monthly newspaper column in the Afrikaans daily to berate Afrikaners for their intolerance;[20] until then, my approach in the column was to raise difficult issues directly but with a soft hand, using humor and the advantage of being nonpartisan with respect to the government's reforms in education. More than anything else I did, the column earned an audience of Afrikaners. This time I asked my fellow citizens if they would have demonstrated the same false calm if a Muslim preacher had come onto their campus proclaiming "The End of Christianity." A middle-aged Afrikaner came up to me in the streets and said: *"ek kon sien prof was kwaad vir ons"* (I could see professor was angry with us).

Muslims bring out the worst in South African Christians, and Afrikaner believers are no exception. It is not only the threat of color that provokes the rage (as with other black people); it is the additional threat of creed. I often heard my colleagues making disparaging remarks about "Asians" in the medical school and their disproportionate representation in the health sciences. It is a powerful stereotype of Muslim and Hindu South Africans that they are obsessed with becoming doctors, a profession that holds particularly high status in this community. The Muslim students stand out, therefore, in a white Afrikaans university, and because they succeed they draw this rage unto themselves.

In this struggle to open up the institutional culture to greater tolerance and inclusion with respect to divine knowledge, there was a serious stumbling block. The opening of all major university ceremonies was conducted through prayer and the reading of Christian scriptures. At a strictly personal level, I obviously found this meaningful and connecting to my private sense of Christian faith. As a public leader in a public university, however, I found such a practice offensive. I had spent significant time hiring colleagues to UP from all over the world, black and white, Jewish and Muslim, atheist and faith-committed. I had recruited them with the message that the university was committed to inclusion and transformation, and that even though things were far from perfect their presence would contribute significantly to erosion of the perception of a monolithic and racialized institutional culture. Now, these same colleagues had to be subjected at every public event to, effectively, a Christian service. When I first arrived, even the senate meetings were opened in prayer and Bible reading; this fell away despite some protest, but graduation ceremonies, formal addresses by the vice-chancellor, and welcoming and closing ceremonies still continued as Christian displays.

And so, at the annual *Bosberaad*[21] of senior managers, just ahead of the opening of the academic year, I again raised my objections and said that this time I was not prepared to stay on the stage with my colleagues if they continued to impose prayer and scripture on a diverse audience. There was a subdued response this time, but nothing substantial enough to indicate a change of practice. To my surprise, the ceremonies then started to change. First, ministers of religion from Christian traditions—not only the Dutch Reformed—were now invited to lead the ceremonies. Then the Dutch Reformed minister would pray in another African language as well as Afrikaans. Finally, the decision was to invite people to a moment of silence in which they could essentially spend the quiet time in a meditative moment. This transition did not always happen as linearly as indicated, but at least there was an attempt by colleagues to grapple with how to change from a narrow expression of faith to something broader and more inclusive. Still, there were no Muslim or Hindu or Jewish voices in this mix of worship styles. With the small number of non-Christian students and faculty, this battle was not going to be resolved easily.

## Hierarchical Knowledge

The UP's hierarchical organization epitomizes the view that "when power is highly centralized, control over important resources and decisions is concentrated in the higher ranks of the organization."[22]

In the hands of a strong and dedicated leader, committed to the transformation ideals of the new country, such singular authority can steer fundamental change at a considerable pace without much opposition. In the hands of a weak and insecure leader, transformation can grind to a halt.

### Example One: Overruling the Senate Executive

A meeting of the 20-member senate executive (consisting of deans, vice-principals, and directors) makes a decision unanimously about policy X. At this meeting, the usual chair, the principal (vice-chancellor) is absent. Though decisions of the senate executive are usually passed by the full senate automatically and by consensus, the principal is back in the chair at the next meeting of the full senate. When the item on policy X appears, the principal tells the senate he disagrees with the senate executive's decision. With one exception, the full senate—all 20 executive members—accept the leader's decision. I query from the floor the fact that one man can overturn a full senate executive decision. The chair then turns the issue to the floor for a vote, but I withdraw my objection, explaining that the vote will serve no purpose other than to confirm the one-man decision.

There are very few universities anywhere in the world, including South Africa, where this would be allowed to happen.

*Example Two: UP Management Culture*
You do not have to be at UP long before you start hearing repeated stories about the university's management culture. There would be the story of the member of staff who posed half-naked in a local magazine, and how he was called to the vice-chancellor's office not for a discussion but to tell him that his job was already terminated and his career a thing of the past. Or the women who were berated in public for the length of their skirts. Or the sharp-tongued put-down by the chair of a member of the senate who dared to speak. Or the student who opened the door of the lecture room for the teacher and was then barred from entering by the same professor on the grounds that he was now late. The ostensible purpose of these stories might be to invoke humor, but the underlying goal is to convey, especially to newcomers, a historical sense of "how things are done around here." The stories are powerful; they remain in the back of your mind, for this knowledge has a purpose.

In discussing the political functions of narrative in organizations, Dennis Mumby makes an astute observation:

Contrary to most research on organizational symbolism, narratives do not simply *inform* the organization members about the values, practices, and traditions to which their organization is committed. Rather, they help to *constitute* the organizational consciousness of social actors by articulating and embodying a particular reality, and subordinating or devaluing other modes of "organization rationality" [*emphases in the original*].[23]

A striking feature of this well-ordered culture is that middle management is technically competent and delivers on tight schedules, fixed budgets, and firm performance outcomes. If the entire senior management were to collapse, the management would continue to tick over irrespective of what happens at other levels. The lawns will be perfectly groomed, the salaries will be paid on time, the trash will be nowhere to be seen, the libraries will be stocked with the latest literature, the budgets will be monitored for overspending, and the entire system will be under middle management surveillance able, at the proverbial push-of-a-button, to give information on any staff member or any cost center or any student. If, hypothetically, every member of the staff resigned at the same time, there would be sufficient funds to cover the retirement bill. It is this well-polished exterior that often gives the outsider the impression that the institution is without problems.

*Example Three: Managing a Potential Financial Crisis*
A few years ago, UP received, at the last minute, a notice from the government that its subsidy would be cut by a few million rands. This caused serious alarm within the ranks of management. The loss of subsidy, which applied across the higher education system, could in the case of UP be easily remedied by applying replacement funds from its considerable reserves. But this is not how things are done. Budgets are planned well in advance of an academic year; processes run from departments to faculties to senior management with rhythmic precision; approvals are made at every step along the way; and the minutiae around student enrollments for each faculty are pinned down and costed early in the previous year.

To receive such late notice caused deep consternation within senior management. Once management recovered from the initial shock, amazed at how the government could function in this haphazard and unplanned manner, the university's machinery kicked into gear. A new management plan was devised, revised targets were set for each dean and director to meet, scores of cut-back sessions were arranged, and not a single dissenting voice was heard up and down the management hierarchy. Everyone pulled together, new staff plans were put on hold, contracts were terminated, and operational costs were dramatically reduced. In a short period of time, management managed itself out of a crisis with great skill. But what will remain etched on the institutional memory was the lack of predictability in government funding and planning; this, for a university culture that prides itself on order and predictability, is very hard to grasp.

This example is of management in crisis. But the normal, everyday managerial processes function very differently. They are ordered, calm, predictable, managed, and in a technical sense competent at senior and middle management levels. They are oriented toward stability and consensus, and they achieve this state of equilibrium on the basis of a stakeholder response that is trusting and fearful of management at the same time. Underlying the managerial order and politeness is a system that retaliates against those who dare to challenge this ordered authority, with all of the final decision making invested in the man at the top. A paternalistic management culture is therefore reinforced by retaliatory management instincts. Democratic structures exist as a matter of compliance with governmental regulation, but they are ignored for the most part when it comes to decision making. Such an ordered management culture comes at the expense of deep commitments to social justice and material restitution. But you would not notice, because the exterior of the place is perfectly groomed. It remains an ordering in which men, and especially women, know their place.

### Gendered Knowledge

What these dual citizens of two worlds, before and after Apartheid, bring into the university is also a gendered and sexualized knowledge of the past. The arrangements for male-female relationships were laid down early as rigid observations in domestic life that found religious justification in the Dutch Reformed Church and social confirmation in public discourses about women. As the weaker vessel, the woman subordinated herself to the man and served him as the head of the household. This does not mean that the woman is or was without power in the relationship, but it does mean that she knows her place in this patriarchal world of the Afrikaner.[24]

To understand the extremity of this gendered relationship, it is once again useful to observe actual practices. At the beginning of my term at UP, I had to lead the decisions on which of the college lecturers to retain following the forced incorporation of the nearby white College of Education into the university's Faculty of Education. An impressive and talented Afrikaner woman was not selected, and she made an appointment to see me. To my surprise, her beefy husband showed up as well. To my even greater surprise, he did all the talking. His body language and verbal representation were emphatic. She sat down but he paced around my office, the only one standing. He wanted me to know that he had legal opinion and that he would challenge this ridiculous decision not to appoint his wife. I was alert to this provocation, the bullying, and it was hard not to interpret racial intimidation in his aggression toward me.

But what intrigued me even more was this bizarre scene. A highly educated woman, holding a doctorate in her discipline, sits quietly in a seat in my office in a discussion about her job and career, while her husband paces up and down half-threatening what he could and would do if his wife were not appointed. I had never seen anything like this in the black community. Accomplished black women do not bring their men to discuss professional disputes, especially in a university context. Whatever irritations I might have had at that point about race and racism, here my intrigue focused on the gendered ordering of representation.

In this swirl of racial and gendered emotions in my office, I had no choice but to confront the man. "First of all, why are you here? This is business between your wife and my office." This stunned him, and for the first time the wife spoke: "I asked him to come." I told him to sit down and stay quiet, and that he was welcome to listen to the conversation, and at the end I would call on him if he had anything to say. If this were not acceptable, he would have to wait outside. The man was deflated, perhaps even stunned, by being told, possibly for the first time by a black person, what the terms of his participation would be.

This knowledge of place among women is a continuing burden in race and gender relations that weighs down the struggle for transformation. Yet it must be named to be rendered impotent, for it is the silent and unchallenged operation of patriarchy, its normality of posture and its taken-for-grantedness, that make change so difficult. Clearly there have been glacial shifts in Afrikaner culture as white women continue the slow march toward freedom. Divorce is more common, and white women have been included in the range of senior occupational categories that favor them as designated groups in terms of South Africa's employment equity provisions. But because white women do better than black citizens in employment appointments, their privilege of race has been questioned by black politicians concerned about the more stubborn racial inequalities in job advancement deep into the transition from Apartheid.

Gendered knowledge becomes sexualized knowledge in the relationship between black men and white women in the university context.[25] If there is any more poisonous knowledge transmitted in the minds and hearts of these dual citizens of a white past and present, it is the implicit warning of racial mixing. White South Africans can tolerate, to some extent, the "innocent mixing" of black and white where the possibility of sexual relations is remote. But that most vivid image of racial fanaticism—black men and white women—remains a powerful knowledge in the memories of white South Africans. It was, after all, the singular obsession of white nationalists under Apartheid who went well beyond the Prohibition of Mixed Marriages Act to install an Immorality Act that forbade sex between white and black. It was through white women that the purity of the race was threatened by rapacious black sexuality,[26] that enduring colonial obsession during and beyond Empire.

It should not therefore be a surprise that one of the more interesting challenges as a black male dean would come through the relationship with white women. There are clearly patterns of interaction that reflect such knowledge that derives from white history, religion, and society.

In the inevitable meetings with white women colleagues, I felt a racial distancing. Men—black and white—would sit close to you; women would choose the furthest available seat from where you were sitting. I have tested this proposition often enough to find it to be true. The patterns of conversation are equally revealing. When the business side of the conversation ends, or before it begins, casual conversation always evokes the husband first, not the children or their grandparents or any other members of the family. In casual conversation the evocation of the husband has an important social role: it is to create the barrier or the bordering line that separates white woman from black man. Even the slightest hint of a compliment, such as "congratulations on your promotion" is too threatening and often evokes the immediate response "I called my husband as soon as I heard" or "my husband says he is so happy." Often white women colleagues would come with another colleague rather than alone, even though the matter at hand had little if anything to do with the other colleague.

In the course of time, this racial distancing between white women and the black dean would ease for some white women as they became comfortable with the collegial relationship and, as already indicated, overcame the sexual stereotyping of black men that formed part of the knowledge inheritance of white South Africans.

## Conclusion

What makes colleagues such a fascinating link in the transmission of knowledge is that they represent the generation having *direct* experience of living in both worlds. They have knowledge of good (the democratic order) and evil (the Apartheid order). Unlike their students, they were actually *there*. These colleagues have to reconcile ways of thinking and behaving under white rule with ways of thinking and behaving in a newly open society. Even as institutional norms keep pulling them toward the past, unprecedented changes in the broader society require an orientation toward the future. Whereas before the collegial environment and the colleagues who populated it were of one racial and language community, suddenly there were new colleagues and a changing environment that redefined relationships, changed language practice, and required new modes of social interaction. Knowledge that once was firmly encoded in the traditional curriculum is now up for grabs. The rules for advancement, understood simply and consistently over many decades, suddenly required (at least in Education) much more stringent academic standards of performance. Whereas institutional authority was long settled as white and male, suddenly new kinds of authority figures—women and black—begin to lead within this changing environment.

White colleagues have to live with the knowledge of what happened under Apartheid, what it did to them, and their role within the maintenance of the Apartheid system. This is inescapable knowledge; they were there in the schools, churches, families, and peer groups that constituted the racial order. They were the products of transmission as children and adolescents growing up under the Apartheid regime; and they were the parents who in turn transmitted this secure knowledge to their own children in the home, and because they were often school teachers, to young people in all-white state schools. They were the ones who sang *Die Stem*, attended the cultural camps and the veldskole, imbibed the indoctrination, and carried out the orders of the racist state—whether it was the little things that sustained the privilege of white life or the big things in the violent oppression of black people. The men served under compulsory military conscription and fought against black people in defense of the white state. The women maintained the homes within which the men and the children received reassuring knowledge of their glorious past and anxious knowledge of the threatening Other.

With the end of Apartheid, these same colleagues now stumbled into the new democratic order. There was no reorientation program or political resocialization process. The teachers who transmitted Apartheid knowledge were suddenly in the same classrooms and the same meeting spaces as the racially other colleagues. Given the knowledge framework within which colleagues operated, it was clear that this transition would be extremely difficult. The adjustment that white colleagues would have to make was not only physical accommodation of new colleagues, new students, and a new curriculum; it was also an emotional, psychological, and social adjustment to pressing demands for change.

# 6     Knowledge in the Blood

> I knew. From the age of 14, I knew. And the Afrikaners around
> me knew. . . . I was determined to know.[1]

> When we look back on what we have done, or not done, we realize
> that it is the knowledge in the blood that has impelled us.[2]

T HE SELF-ASSURED Western consultant who stepped
off a plane in a Third World country he knew lit-
tle about avoided asking his hosts for a briefing, demanding instead a
simple set of documents with the rationale: *Show me your curriculum and
I'll tell you who is in power.* With this well-told story in mind, I knew
that disturbing the institutional curriculum was tantamount to touching power. None of my graduate courses in curriculum theory had prepared me as leader for what turned out to be the most difficult task in
the transformation of UP and, in particular, its Faculty of Education.
What was codified in the curriculum was not simply information in the
text; it was, I would soon discover, knowledge in the blood.

For the original author of the term, the Irish poet Macdara Woods,
*knowledge in the blood* is:

The sum total of what we learn (or have to learn—from experience), of love,
disappointment, age, loss, and how this knowledge can both make the necessary ongoing human reaffirmation of life and hope possible and at the same
time hinder it. . . . It is almost as though we are carrying psychological
antibodies inside us. The knowledge in the blood, however it got there, is as
ingrained as a disease—although at the same time it can be truly benign. In

this sense the knowledge (which we have been gathering since childhood, as well as having it handed down from before) can be—even at its best—as pitilessly indifferent, as ultimately powerful, and as random in why it propels us in any particular direction, as a microbe.[3]

In this vein, knowledge in the blood for me means knowledge embedded in the emotional, psychic, spiritual, social, economic, political, and psychological lives of a community. Such is the knowledge transmitted faithfully to the second generation of Afrikaner students. It is not, therefore, knowledge that simply dissipates like the morning mist under the pressing sunshine of a new regime of truth; if it were, then curriculum change would be a relatively straightforward matter.[4] Knowledge in the blood is habitual, a knowledge that has long been routinized in how the second generation see the world and themselves, and how they understand others. It is emphatic knowledge that does not tolerate ambiguity; this dead certainty was long given its authority by a political and theological order that authorized such knowledge as singular, sanctified, and sure. But it is also a defensive knowledge that reacts against and resists rival knowledge, for this inherited truth was conceived and delivered in the face of enemies—the English imperialists, the barbarous blacks, the atheistic Communists—all of them.

This does not mean that knowledge in the blood cannot change its outer coating and mimic in style and language what is ordered by the new state. Nor does it mean that through the transfusion of new knowledge the authority of received knowledge cannot be overcome. For this reason, knowledge in the blood is used here both as an assertion and a question. As an assertion, the phrase draws attention to deeply rooted knowledge that is hard to change; as a question, knowledge in the blood is itself subject to alteration.[5]

Even so, knowledge in the blood is not easily changed. Afrikaners, in what I shall later call *conditional pragmatism*, will more energetically than most revise and realign curricula to fit the exacting demands of officialdom and seek to demonstrate responsiveness to the new authorities. But it would be a serious mistake to read bureaucratic responsiveness to the formal demands of reconstruction as altering deep-rooted assumptions and beliefs about history, identity, knowledge, and change: the curriculum is, at base, an institutional subject.

## Curriculum as Institution

What does it mean to speak about curriculum as an institution?[6] It means regarding the curriculum not only as a text inscribed in the course syllabus for a particular qualification but an understanding of knowledge encoded in the dominant beliefs, values, and behaviors deeply embedded in all aspects of institutional life. Knowledge therefore becomes both what is formally designated for learning, such as in the course syllabus, and what are widely understood within the institution to be acceptable forms of knowledge and recognized ways of knowing that distinguish one university type (such as the Afrikaans universities) from others. To be sure, the course syllabus is an expression of the curriculum as an institution, but it is only one such manifestation of the regnant knowledge dispersed throughout the ceremonies, symbols, rituals, rules, regulations, discourses, and countless other cultural transactions within the common sense of, in this case, the public university.

If, therefore, an institution is "a socially embedded idea defined by well-known structures,"[7] then the university curriculum is this idea expressed in multiple ways that include but go beyond modes of teaching, learning, and assessing within a particular institutional context. It encapsulates what most workers within that institutional setting understand to be the character, content, and boundaries of knowledge that are part of being in that place, the university. It extends to include the understanding by institution dwellers of the particular link between knowledge and authority, about who possesses knowledge to act on and against others, and who are positioned simply as the recipients of authoritative knowledge.

This is what Amnon Karmon, in reference to the institutional organization of knowledge, calls *the epistemic environment*, where

the institutional level contains within it not only messages regarding ways of relating to learned knowledge, but also powerful messages regarding the very nature of knowledge itself. . . . This term [an epistemic environment] refers to a comprehensive system of epistemic messages that are conveyed through practices and organizational patterns [with] a message that provides us with ideas about the nature of knowledge itself.[8]

Learning this institutional knowledge can therefore lead to a specific qualification if the curriculum is understood to be the achievement of learning outcomes by those who choose (and indeed qualify) to pursue a particular course of study. But learning in an institutional perspective is more than an accumulation of modules and credit hours that signal attainment of specific kinds of knowledge; it is also learning the concealed knowledges of an institution—what counts as knowledge in the everyday operations of, in this case, the Afrikaans university; the penalties and strictures that come with moving outside this institutionally legitimated knowledge; and the benefits and advantages that result from "slotting in" to these dominant knowledge forms without breaking the historical resonances that cement relations between (in this case, white) staff, students, parents, and community.

The curriculum in this view is therefore both tangible (course outlines) and intangible (discursive patterns), but throughout it is "a shaping force"[9] in the lives of those who teach, learn, administer, manage, and lead within the institution. It is the knowledge the administrative clerk learns about who not to offend in an institution, about which rules to follow and which ones she can ignore, about the written and unwritten rules, and about how to navigate this embedded script without harm to oneself or one's career. It is the knowledge the young academic learns about what kinds of postures and positions can advance a career and which behaviors can inhibit promotion or even end a career; such knowledge goes way beyond what is written in the administrative guide to promotion, for it includes the unspoken but obtainable knowledge about how to advance academically within the peculiarities of the institution. Without access to such embedded knowledge, the newcomer is often exposed and disciplined, while the old hands can negotiate these hidden rules of behavior almost instinctively. In all these examples, the curriculum as embedded knowledge, values, and beliefs cements the operational crevices of the institution, controlling and constraining the behavior of campus citizens.

By rendering the curriculum as an institutional subject, it is possible to distinguish one institution from the next in comparing, in this case, the curriculum of different kinds of South African universities.[10] UP and the University of Cape Town (UCT) are among the top three universities in South Africa and are regularly listed among the top 500 universities in the world. Both universities boast impressive facilities, world-class scholars, and a high level of research productivity. Yet these two institutions are light years away from each other in terms of the curriculum as an institutional category; in fact, they might as well be in different national contexts. The open knowledge system of the historically English UCT and the closed knowledge system of the historically Afrikaans UP, both established more than 100 years ago, have in time inscribed very different contours, content, and expressions of knowledge in the two institutions, so that successfully navigating the curriculum (as defined here) in one institution could spell disaster for a young career in the other. Thus, for example, although UCT regularly has openly hostile debates about access[11] and fierce contestations over the institutional curriculum that make riveting reading in the local press, this never happens in the closed knowledge system of UP.[12]

Both institutions were shaped by Apartheid, both are subject to the same regulatory policies and measurement matrices from external agencies such as the government, and yet even a cursory reading of the quality assurance reports of the two institutions by the same body (the Higher Education Quality Committee of the Council for Higher Education) would reveal the contrasting inscriptions of knowledge within these two universities.[13] Knowledge—its character, substance, and ambitions—therefore takes on opposing forms in these two institutions.

What this means for curriculum change is that it is much more difficult in a place like UP to challenge the very deep assumptions, beliefs, and values that hold institutional knowledge in place. It is not so difficult to change the exoskeleton of the institutional curriculum, the kinds of alterations that could impress external agencies such as the government and signal alignment with bureaucratic expectations. But it is infinitely more difficult to crack the endoskeleton of the curriculum, the hard surface that holds in place deep understandings, norms, and commitments that over a century have come to represent settled knowledge within the institution.[14] Here it is important to distinguish the practices of individual innovators or outsiders coming into an institution whose work might very well exist inside of, or even challenge, institutional knowledge. As UP slowly opened up its staffing to those from outside its immediate community—white Afrikaans-speaking academics—it brought in black deans, black professors, and also English-speaking and progressive Afrikaners whose knowledge formation and consciousness were the result of advanced training outside the ambit of traditional Afrikaans universities.

But these individuals were, for the most part, too few in number and too limited in influence inside a large and complex organization to erode at its center what counted as institutional knowledge; even as they pushed for curriculum change, their efforts were overwhelmed by the inertia of embedded knowledge. Nowhere was the institutional character of knowledge more profoundly expressed than in an official university curriculum called *Ubuntu*.

## Ubuntu Introduced

Few words evoke more social confusion in South Africa than the term *Ubuntu*. A Zulu word translated commonly as "humanity toward others," Ubuntu has had many uses. It has been the subject of a crass commercialism selling books and merchandise that markets "humanity" for profit in post-Apartheid society.[15] Ubuntu was once mobilized for political purposes by the conservative Inkatha cultural movement and later political party behind its Zulu-based ethnic ideals.[16] And Ubuntu has also been invoked by religious leaders such as Desmond Tutu in an appeal to a broader African spirituality that recognizes our common humanity against criminal behavior and selfish individualism.[17] Its troubled history notwithstanding, Ubuntu is often naïvely attached without much reflection to any product as a way of signaling acceptance of the new South Africa and alignment with its democratic values. Such was the case with a UP undergraduate curriculum called Ubuntu.

How Ubuntu (the curriculum) evaded my early attention is not clear, but in the sweeping reforms of five years of curriculum change at both undergraduate and graduate levels it had not surfaced on the modular-based curriculum radar screen. One reason might be that it was "owned" by the Faculty of Humanities though nevertheless prescribed as a short but intensive one-semester module required of all Education students in the Faculty of Education. Students could therefore not obtain their teaching degrees without taking and passing Ubuntu.

It would probably still have avoided my scrutiny as dean were it not for the fact that more and more of the students admitted to Education were no longer only from the white Afrikaner schools. New students coming in did their school education at black and English-speaking white schools, where there was a greater sensitivity and well-honed criticality toward anything that suggested racism or patriarchy or classism. When one of these nontraditional UP students handed me the Ubuntu course outline, I at first denied that such a course was even possible within my Faculty; I would have known about it, I told the bemused student.

Now, as the two academics from the Faculty of Humanities sat in front of me in my dean's office, they looked terrified. They were the authors of the Ubuntu module. They represented the face of political correctness, a young black academic and a senior white Afrikaner professor. How could they be so wrong, this picture of interracial partnership? The reason they looked terrified was because of what I had required them to read while sitting in my office:

This course runs contrary to the basic commitments of curriculum transformation in the Faculty of Education, and works in ignorance of theoretical advances in studies on race, culture, identity, and education over the past 25 years. It resurrects a conception of African culture that is primitive, inferior, monolithic, stable, and essential in its assumptions about black people. It works within an Apartheid paradigm of what constitutes culture and ethnicity, neatly reinforcing myths about migration and settlement that no serious historian would defend. It presents a uniformly naïve understanding of Ubuntu, ignoring its multiple and contested meanings within recent South African history, including its specific mobilization under Zulu nationalism to promote an ethnic separateness for narrow political ends. This romanticized representation of Ubuntu might be the subject of crass commercialism in the world of business tourism but it cannot be defended in any serious scholarly context. It exaggerates difference to the point of absurdity, and reinvents white people around full or qualified concepts of "Euro-ness." By sharply juxtaposing African and European culture, all the worst excesses of Apartheid's construction of racial identity are not only resurrected but are also reinforced in the minds of unsuspecting students [South Africa has "cultural groups"]. It is clear that this course was conjured up in an attempt to introduce white

Pretoria students to African culture in the once insular social and institutional contexts of UP. It was in all likelihood well-meaning, despite the commitment of error and the misrepresentation of people. The audience alone suggests that this course has no relevance after 12 years of democracy given the growing numbers of not-white students and non-South African students in institutions such as Tukkies. Even so, the concept of the African in the curriculum outline is presented as one persona—that is, completely ignoring the many ways of being African within both urban and rural areas; hence impossible terms such as "the African culture"! Disturbingly, there are derogatory stereotypes of Africans littered throughout the materials, made worse only by holding up "Europeans" (presumably white South Africans) as the superior culture which should, among other things, correct such behavior by teaching Africans table manners . . . ! Further, the promotion of Ubuntu as representing contemporary practice is so incredibly out of whack with empirical reality—such as one of the highest crime rates in the world—that it begs the question as to the knowledge claims surrounding this concept. Yet the demise of Ubuntu within South African society, if taken seriously, would have to take account of colonialism and Apartheid, racism and the migrant labor system, forced evictions, and the criminalization of black people (e.g. the hated pass law system)—and on, and on. None of this is dealt with in this partial account of Ubuntu, thereby denying students access to the social context within which such terms emerged, were contested, started to change, and became marginal to mainstream society. By locking Ubuntu into these rural ideals which might never have existed, all sorts of myths and unrealities are sustained. So, for example, with the un-interrogated notion of the extended family in contexts where child-headed households are becoming widespread and AIDS has decimated any traditional concept of family, Ubuntu cannot account for change in the countryside and in the cities. This course cannot therefore be the focus of a modern/postmodern curriculum formed at the intersection of powerful global, continental, regional, and national crosscurrents in teacher education.

My two colleagues were clearly stunned, but what happened next placed *me* in the position of disbelief. "Well," said the senior professor, "we hear you and that's no problem; you are the client, and you are not happy with what we did, so we will simply revise it so that you, as client, are satisfied."[18] Everything I had just said in the angrily worded page of criticism went completely over his head; the deep ideological dilemmas represented in the curriculum were not going to be discussed; the clear indictment of racism would not be challenged. This was a market-related problem: Humanities was the service provider and Education was the client. Like a faulty computer disk about which the client complained, this curriculum computer chip would simply be replaced.

They did not fail to remind me, however, that this curriculum endeavor had won an institutionwide award for "innovation." The white professor half-chided me that his black woman colleague understood black culture, and this reflected her "authentic" expression of what happened in the black community. They told me as well about student evaluations showing that students (in this case, white students) really enjoyed exposure to black culture through Ubuntu. But since I was the client, they would simply change the content accordingly. "I don't think you understand a word I wrote," I told my colleagues, and asked them to leave.

## Embedded Knowledge Across the University Curriculum

I decided to raise the matter with the dean of humanities; somewhat predictably, she saw little problem with Ubuntu and was more concerned that, by withdrawing this curriculum offering from her Faculty, the Faculty would lose critical funding in an academic unit that was constantly under threat because of the *oorvoorsiening* (oversupply) of academic staff in relation to income generated through courses and degrees. In this Faculty, expensive but low-enrollment subjects such as African languages (under which Ubuntu was registered), music, and drama resulted in a slow stream of income as South African students shifted their attention to economics and accounting subjects at Pretoria and everywhere else. To the dean of humanities, the offensive knowledge contained in Ubuntu was of little concern; what mattered was financial survival, or what the institution called *viability*.

Beginning to feel that perhaps I was mad, and everybody else around me normal, I took my concerns to my senior colleagues in the university administration to whom the deans reported. Their reaction was mixed, but even among those who recognized the offensive material there was little energy or interest to act on this matter and take on institutional power on this sensitive matter. By this time my concerns had little to do with Ubuntu in the Faculty of Education but with the need to review the institutional curriculum as a whole. This was one of the most difficult times for me; I could not restrict change to the Education campus given what I now knew about the university curriculum more broadly. Curriculum review was an urgent matter for the entire university, and I felt that it was important to interrupt this unexamined knowledge that continued to prepare another generation of white and now black students for the new South Africa.

The problem with embedded knowledge is that it is not out there; it is not easily read off the outer coating of a public curriculum. It is the claims, silences, and assumptions about knowledge concealed in the belief and value systems of those who teach and learn; concealed behind the classroom door, they influence and direct the substance of what counts as the actual knowledge transactions among participants in the learning process. Teachers might, in an authoritarian and hierarchical culture, appear to be following the new curriculum script, but this does not translate into transformative knowledge in the classroom, and the students know this. Changing curriculum without changing the curriculum makers is especially difficult under conditions of a sudden and radical social transformation. Changing a curriculum too far ahead of the teachers—those who make the curriculum come alive in the classroom—might please the politicians and bureaucrats concerned with impressing new knowledge on their subjects, but it is unlikely to rearrange the epistemological order of things in the classroom. What the teachers of the new university curriculum were struggling with was knowledge in the blood.

This is the difficulty of conducting an analysis of the institutional curriculum. Its outer features would reflect the noticeable changes in the organizational technologies demanded from a new national qualifications framework. The curriculum is presented in the form of "exit-level" learning outcomes; each learning outcome is stated in a demonstrable action form; the achievement of specified outcomes is measured against what is called assessment criteria; and the combination of learning outcomes, following established rules of combination, makes up a qualification. The Afrikaans universities such as UP are told often by the government and the qualifications authority that they are most responsive to the organizational rules that must be followed in this elaborate architecture. What they are not told is that nothing in the content, nature, and purposes of knowledge has changed at all behind the walls of this organizational complexity called the university.

Knowledge in the institutional curriculum of UP is fixed, certain, positive, controllable, linear, and predictable. Scientific knowledge matters much more than human knowledge because the laws of science, in this view of truth, eliminate uncertainty and rule out ideology. It follows therefore that science, engineering, and technology enjoy much more institutional funding and political support than do the humanities, education, and commerce—the latter group regarded as constituted by a less certain and controllable knowledge than the natural sciences. Accordingly, it is no coincidence that the humanities are weakest at the Afrikaans universities and the sciences are strongest. This does not mean that "science" carried the pretense of control and neutrality during the Apartheid years; it was during this time that science was deployed in the services of the racist state, and it is one of the untold stories of "truth and reconciliation" that the laboratories of the Afrikaans universities have not yet laid bare their role in providing the knowledge base for justifying and upholding Apartheid as ideology and as practice.[19]

We now know that volkekunde (anthropology) yielded anthropological knowledge about the "Bushmen" that would enable their deployment as trackers for the Apartheid military machinery in places such as what was then South West Africa (now Namibia). We know that psychology provided so-called scientific studies of black behavior that would justify racial segregation and the hierarchy of races. We know that education theory, under the guise of fundamental pedagogics, linked teaching to Christian National Education, which gave divine justification to the racial ordering of schools and society under the pretense of what was called "a science of education."[20] We know that botanists at Pretoria named one of their species after the vicious military unit Koevoet—literally crowbar—in gratitude for funding received from the Department of Defense for their research.[21] We know also that UP sociologists constructed the social theory that justified separation and made these ideological commitments available to a nationalist regime.[22]

## Inside Ubuntu

At first glance, AFT 253 (the administrative classification of the Ubuntu module) comes across as a reasonable effort to introduce students to multicultural education and what it calls "tolerance" for other cultures. But on closer inspection, it represents the intact knowledge of Apartheid under the guise of teaching students respect for others. The first hints of trouble lie in what Ubuntu regards as worthwhile knowledge to be assessed: at the front end the assessment criteria indicate students will be judged on the basis of "ordering and presentation" as well as "appearance" and "punctuality." Here, writ large, is something I found over and over again among my students: an obsession with neatness and order in presentation, the systematic nature of organizing writing, the colorful pens used to illustrate composition, the near obsession with what things look like. This is not a trivial point, for what their socialization in school and society values is how things look from the outside rather than the substance of what is submitted for examination. Order trumps truth; appearance matters more than content; style conquers substance.

There is a deep psychological and epistemological grounding that generates this orientation toward knowledge, one that requires further study.[23] But in the end, what remain above close intellectual and social scrutiny are the qualities of argument, the value of positions taken, the originality of ideas put forward, the risk pursued in analysis, the courage of interpretation. Order enables control over knowledge and over students, and it structures what is allowed and disallowed in this tightly managed environment. This is what Louise Brenner in her excellent study on the transmission of knowledge in Muslim schools calls *controlling knowledge*—"the conviction that social behavior could be controlled through the knowledge transmitted in school"; but the term also suggests that "some knowledges are imbued with determining attributes of which individuals may not be consciously aware."[24]

With such control through order comes the management exercised over knowledge through appeal to the logic of science. Thus asks Ubuntu in one of its assessment criteria for students' work: "Is the process [followed] scientific?" On a subject as value-laden as Ubuntu, "the scientific process" nevertheless enables knowledge and control.[25]

But if patterns of knowledge that continue to constrain the institutional curriculum were limited to such subtle manifestations of ideologies of order, hierarchy, control, and scientism, it would in many cases not be noticed by those concerned with curriculum analysis. However, once such knowledge breaks through in more visible claims about race, identity, and culture, then analytical and political attention is forced on the subject. To illustrate, a number of samples of the curriculum will be drawn for discussion of the broader politics of knowledge signaled within each selection.

Consider the scenario from a subheading in Ubuntu called "Getting to Know Other Cultures":

Two school teachers went into a restaurant and ordered two baby chickens. The waiter set the table and completed bringing two silver bowls with lemon floating on top of the water. The two teachers looked at each other and without trying to find out from the waiter what the water was for, drank the water.

You see, in the African culture, you only wash your hands before sitting down at the table and you'll wash your hands again after eating. They did not know that in the Western culture you can hold your chicken with your fingers and wash your fingers in the silver bowl. I am sure that they struggled with the knife and fork trying to eat the baby chickens.

The only way these teachers could have known, was if someone from the Western culture who knew about table manners, could have taught them.

This scenario is read by every white education student at UP and every UP student who chooses Ubuntu as a module of choice. It is precisely the kind of racism that reinforces what white students bring into the university: a set of stereotypes consistent with their own socialization. By casting whites as "Western" the story secures the notion among Afrikaners that they are non-Africans separated culturally, behaviorally, and racially from black South Africans. The portrayal of black people in the twenty-first century as backward and primitive diners out of touch with the basics of kitchen utensils and the modalities of restaurant dining fits perfectly with years of racist indoctrination visited on white youth. By both depicting blacks as unsophisticated and at the same time placing the power of civilization in white hands, this curriculum is unlikely to disturb received knowledge but rather to secure it. It is almost too easy to grant this kind of curriculum the respect of analysis, but it is central to my argument that just below the external changes of the institutional curriculum to conform with new regulatory demands lies an as yet undisturbed set of assumptions about race, knowledge, and identity in the former Afrikaans institutions.

Under another section, called "Finding Ubuntu in Myself," white students are treated to a picture of black people fighting among themselves:

It was not only White South Africans who used to call Black South Africans names—Black South Africans also called other ethnic groups names. Even today there is ethnic undermining. The Zulus call the Sotho's "iZilwane"—things, the Sotho's calls the Zulu's "Mapono"—the naked ones—does not make sense because all the Black groups disliked wearing clothes. That is why today South Africans refer to other Black people from other African countries as the "KKK's" (not the Kluck Klack Klan of America) that is the code or abbreviation that I discovered this Sunday at a flea market because one lady who is a "KKK" thought I am a "KKK" from Gabon. Then a black South African lady who overheard her, said to me: "We were also sure that you're a 'KKK' meaning Kwere Kwere, a sound imitating expression meaning an ununderstandable cacophonic language."

Holding aside, for the moment, the very poor quality of the content and the language usage, especially for a university-level course, it is important to again witness what is being taught to white students through a now clearly personal account in the guise of a cultural story about black people. Blacks, like whites, act in demeaning ways toward each other. Blacks prefer a primitive way of life, eschewing clothing. Blacks in South Africa not only despise one another, but they also despise blacks from other countries. Here the rationale for the continuation of white rule constantly expressed by Apartheid politicians finds perfect resonance: whites are responsible for black people not annihilating each other because of their inherent tribal differences. Once again, the curriculum fits comfortably into the ideological apparatus that defines the historical knowledge about black people held by and transmitted through white South Africans to their children.

The examples shared throughout the curriculum text are so outlandish that it is doubtful whether even the most bigoted white South African would accept claims such as the recollection by a black lecturer:

As Black South Africans, our parents always told us that we are not supposed to fall in love with any Black person from Rhodesia—now Zimbabwe—because the people from there were cannibals. If you got married there, you will never be seen alive again.

It is truly stupefying that such an experience of intense prejudice of one person could be made the experience of "Black South Africans." It is even more distressing that for children coming in from white communities, this is the kind of knowledge that they receive about black people *after* Apartheid. And the chosen transmitter for this racist knowledge is a black woman.

One of the few times that I lost patience with this embedded knowledge of others was in a sequence of exchanges with colleagues at another Afrikaans university, this time in the Free State province. I had conducted training there in research leadership and on scholarly publications. I invited colleagues who attended the publications workshop to submit abstracts and draft manuscripts electronically so that postworkshop conversation and feedback on their emerging work could continue. Following a very positive and productive set of workshops, a young Afrikaner woman academic submitted the following abstract for comment:

*Is it necessary to create new computer icons for Black South African users of MS Office packages?*

Some authors propagate a Cultural User Interface that is intuitive to a particular culture because different cultures sometimes interpret things like colors and metaphors differently. The culture of most black South Africans is very different from the culture of Americans, who created the MS Office packages. Therefore, alternative computer icons were investigated to determine whether it could be better understandable by black South African computer users.

Black South Africans without a computer background, as well as black and white computer literate students, completed a questionnaire that contained icons from the MS computer program as well as alternative icons.

With the exception of one command, the black South Africans without a computer background chose an alternative icon as their first choice. It is deducted [sic] from the questionnaires that black computer literature students memorize the standard icons and do not have a problem using it.

If people are allowed some time to master the necessary skills, it might not be necessary to design new interfaces for black South African computer users.

I suppose I was tired. I had so much to deal with on my own campus with this embrace of essentialist knowledge of black people that it was just so difficult again, in another place, to engage young colleagues on this matter. Once again the intentions were positive, if paternalistic, and for this colleague it was an important observation: that cultural/racial difference should not be an obstacle to learning—simply give blacks more time learning necessary skills. My response was less than tactful:

This entire research project is on shaky grounds: any assumptions of essentialism that gives blackness certain features and predictable or different behaviors from other human beings will bring you very strong criticism, if not the "R" word, if you were ever to present this in intelligent company. I would urge you to drop this line of thinking altogether.

To my initial surprise, the young Afrikaner woman did not reply; from the email string I found that she had referred my comments to a man, the senior colleague in her department at the Free State institution, and the one who apparently led this research project. I was mildly irritated by this familiar display of the white male coming to the defense of the innocent female, but I found his response intriguing. True to the rules of beleefdheid, he started by praising me for the quality of the workshops and the positive responses of his colleagues, especially the young woman. But he wanted to engage me in an *opbouende* (constructive) manner and let me know that they had received criticism on this topic before but that they had also published from this research program. Then he said this:

As starting point I wish to make it clear that we are not racist at all nor do we want to be read in this way. In fact, the motto for research in our department is "IT for all." Our central focus is to make IT more accessible for people with less training and exposure to technology. As such we do work on the connecting points of office packages ("Office suites") and must of necessity determine the unique needs of users in this milieu. We regard the new South Africa on the one hand as an opportunity for research and on the other hand as an opportunity to do social upliftment work. We examine culture as indicator, but as you surely know, culture does not have one definition. That is why we also look at language and make a distinction between African languages and European languages. . . . THEREFORE we use black and white as indicators. We do not try to place people in boxes or to stereotype them, BUT in the Free State is it surely so that in 90 percent of the cases Black = socially less privileged and White = socially privileged. . . . We would not, to use your words, "drop this line of thinking altogether." This would mean than we would have to regard four years of building and publications as having no value whatsoever.

I use this extended quotation from the email exchange to point to several important markers of embedded knowledge. The first is that the narrative of whites uplifting blacks once again points to a neglected dimension of Apartheid in scholarly work: that hand-in-hand with the racial oppression of black people went the missionary objective of whites uplifting those described as less fortunate, that is, the blacks. The problem with such knowledge of black people is that it does not ascribe this state of "less fortunate" status to white oppression; it is, rather, a natural state to which the white Christian has the responsibility for civilization and upliftment. It is with this same reasoning in the post-1994 period that Afrikaners speak of black people as *agtergeblewe* (left behind) as a voluntary state of being, not as a result of a purposeful and deliberate system of discrimination. Nevertheless, what the Free State colleagues here draw attention to is a responsiveness to those left behind, a reaching out to "all," and doing so in the name of the white race lifting the black race from its unfortunate state.

In my next response, I simply declared that it was not possible for me to continue the discussion since my arguments were clearly not understood and because their ideas about race were "ingrained" within Afrikaner belief systems that led them to "believe deeply in race." My colleague responded with disgust: "Don't you think you have been a little brainwashed by the injustices of the old dispensation and therefore you over-react? Is it possible that you as a brown man inherently and unconsciously think in precisely the opposite ways from what you accuse us as whites?"

## The Problem of Change

The black person at a white university is a knowledge bearer of the institutional curriculum in one of two ways. First of all, there are black people, however small the number, who were trained within the Apartheid knowledge of the Afrikaner institutions during the crucial period of the early 1990s, that is, after UP opened its doors to black people but before the advent of democracy in 1994. This small group of black people included those hired by Afrikaners from within their own ranks. These were blacks who could be trusted, who bore the ideological and epistemological birthmarks of their trainers, who accepted the white supremacist knowledge of superior and inferior cultures, and who achieved their degrees and their junior-level posts within white universities precisely because they "fit in" and "fit the profile" that white people held of black citizens.

Who better to keep disseminating offensive knowledge about black people than black juniors themselves, like the lecturer in the Ubuntu tale? Of course, the junior black lecturer works under the supervision of the senior white professor, and so while the curriculum gains legitimacy within the university because of the white professorial authority it gains credibility among white students because it is represented by the "authentic" voice of the black lecturer. This is another aspect of the knowledge-power nexus after Apartheid that requires much more sustained analysis of the institutional curriculum than I intend here.

For these colleagues, the junior black persons trained within the Apartheid academy, curriculum change is especially difficult. With my colleagues in Education there was a rigid knowledge of race and ethnicity as biological and cultural givens, not as social and political constructions, and this made it very difficult—especially in the context of the social sciences—to begin training or reorienting colleagues in a broader theoretical understanding of received knowledge. Knowledge for these colleagues was positive and accumulated on the basis of scientific principles, not constructed, tentative, and changing as a consequence of human endeavor. Even when there was an intellectual understanding of such a new orientation toward knowledge, it was very difficult to change toward ways of thinking and seeing that required a more tentative understanding of knowledge and authority.

This often led to considerable frustration on the part of black junior colleagues, as was evident in the response by the Ubuntu lecturer to criticism of her module:

I don't understand what they mean when they said "that it is primitive." When they say it's primitive, it's inferior. I didn't understand, because I felt even if they say that it is inferior let them say what is inferior so that I can improve. . . . So I found myself frustrated and not knowing what to do. You see so it's really disheartening if somebody criticizes you, but they don't say that this is how you should do it. Criticism is good, because that is how one grows but if you are criticized, but there is no answer to the criticism.[26]

Once the initial disorientation has been felt, and the sting of criticism experienced, black and white colleagues from the previous knowledge regime would often (though not always) express this sentiment with various degrees of anxiety or indignation: "So, you convince me that I am wrong; now how do I get out of this? Show me how to access this new knowledge. Train me in the new methods of research. Where can I go, and what can I do to apprise myself of this different thinking?" These are hard questions, and it is extremely difficult for such colleagues to change, especially for those who are older or coming toward the end of their careers. Decades of socialization in race essentialist thinking and in epistemological fundamentalism do not yield easily to what is, in the end, knowledge in the blood. It is as hard for black academics to change as it is for white academics, and it was with this frustration in mind that I sent an SOS to ten colleagues around the world who worked on the problem of educational change; this is what went forth, the two examples constructed from real personae with whom I worked and interacted in the Faculty of Education:

When practitioners are presented with new knowledge that demands a change of behavior, they adopt, adapt, or avoid such knowledge; such responses are well documented in the change literature. What is less well understood is why persons might resist new knowledge especially when what is new is justified as rational, evidence-based, and holding promises of improvement.

What teachers, for example, resist is not always based simply on cognitive dissonance, a conflict between the existing knowledge constructs and beliefs of the practitioner and that proposed in new knowledge. It often resides at a much deeper level of disassociation—what I wish to call emotional knowledge.

Consider teacher Mary who for more than 30 years has taught Grade 1 reading using phonics; her success with this methodology has built her confidence and self-esteem; attracted awards and acknowledgments from peers and parents; and given her a profound sense of fulfillment that her ways of teaching reading are both effective and efficacious for the children entrusted to her care. Along comes a new methodology for teaching reading, and Mary struggles to change, even though she is even persuaded intellectually to "give the new thing a try." Her knowledge of how to teach reading is not simply committed to the mind; it is encased in the heart, part of an emotional attachment to what it means to teach reading and to learn reading. In other words, what we have here is emotional knowledge of the subject.

Consider teacher Max who has taught South African history to Grade 11 students for more than 25 years. As a white South African, reared in the political vortex of the Apartheid years, Max came to understand deeply that the history of white settlement was one of triumph over adversity, of civilization over backwardness, of Calvinist faith against atheistic Communism, of freedom against tyranny. He has lost male members of the family in the border wars, and he has witnessed the struggles of his parents against white poverty and their gradual rise, through the discipline of hard work, to a comfortable though not extravagant middle class lifestyle. Then 1994 happens, and a new history is to be taught with very different victor narratives to the ones he has come to believe, and through which he has come to order his choices in the world. For him, the teaching of history is emotional knowledge, even though he accepts, in the mind, the inevitability of a new official knowledge.

The standard intervention of governments to change teaching behavior is training. The assumption is that teachers, when faced with the logic and appeal of an innovation or reform, will make the shift toward the new knowledge. But what if the behavior to be changed is not simply a cognitive one, in which intellectual persuasion or political coercion are the means for securing compliance? What if the barrier is emotional knowledge?

Such knowledge is not amenable to training; changing the mind is in fact not the problem. It is perfectly possible for Mary and Max to find the intellectual arguments for change reasonable, even appealing, and yet remain emotionally committed to their beliefs about reading or history. They might even give the appearance of change in their statements of teaching (e.g. course out-lines), but remain emotionally committed to a very different understanding of reading and history. This emotional dissonance between official knowledge and personal knowledge invariably shows up in what they choose to teach, how they teach it, and with what levels of commitment.

In this regard it is important to state that emotional knowledge is not emotional intelligence, that ability to perceive and express emotion, to express feelings that advance learning, and to regulate personal emotions in the face of conflict. In fact, Mary and Max might find it very difficult to articulate or express what exactly it is that underpins their beliefs and emotions; they might even wish to demonstrate their ability to change, their acceptance of the new knowledge. Emotional knowledge is therefore not knowledge of emotions, the latter being the subject of considerable research and conjecture. Does the literature on educational change have anything to say to, or about, emotional knowledge?

Perhaps not surprisingly, none of my international colleagues came back with any concrete suggestions from the literature on educational change because this was new terrain. In these examples, the politics of emotional knowledge takes the literature beyond what it is comfortable with: first-order knowledge claims that emotions play a crucial role in decision making about everyday things and especially in the context of educational judgments. What the literature, as it stands, does not grapple with is power, and especially racial configurations of power and how this plays out in a transition where power changes hands from a white minority to a black majority. Politics, in this otherwise sensitive literature on emotions, had not yet emerged as an intellectual meeting place between human emotions and racial power. This was the heart of the curriculum dilemma with which I was struggling in a conservative institution where there was little support for, and even less understanding of, the harsh terrain of transformation on the knowledge front.

I have since come to a few tentative conclusions about the problem of curriculum change where the focus is transmitted knowledge and where the agents of change and continuity are real humans caught in the middle of a radical transition from long-established racial rule toward a nonracial democracy.

The first conclusion is that changing what people believe deeply about race, identity, and knowledge is much, much more difficult than changing from, say, traditional mathematics to new mathematics. Both are difficult to accomplish, but emotionally held beliefs are attached to the soul in ways that are different where the subject of change is a new set of instructional technologies. There is no literature on such complexity, and the problems of changing emotional knowledge will require much more research and theory than has been possible for this text.

The second conclusion is that for some actors within a human endeavor such as schooling, change is simply too difficult. This is clearly not a training problem, for the nature of the dilemmas faced by teacher Max is so deep and complex that no amount of training would be able to dislodge at an emotional level what Max believes, even though intellectual consent to the change project can be achieved. It might even be unethical to demand that Max change under the terms of the new regime, for whole belief systems and indeed a personal sense of worthiness are now up for grabs; this position clearly requires further ethical and philosophical thought.

The third conclusion is that for this kind of change to even start, the in-house black (and white) academics must be balanced in staffing plans by a completely new incoming stream of black (and white) academics from outside the resident social and epistemological world, and they must work closely together over a long period of time learning the new languages and discourses of humanness and change beyond racial essences and knowledge fixedness. This is perhaps the most profound argument for transformation of racialized patterns of staffing in formerly white universities: the challenge of transforming received knowledge.

The fourth conclusion is that such change makes severe demands on the second kind of black academic in a place such as Pretoria, those coming from the outside. These are the black scholars who know differently and who are schooled in "structures of thought" perceived to be threatening to resident knowledge. They do not respect authority as much as they respect ideas. They respond better to leadership persuasion than to leadership edict. They are more perverse in their reading lists than in the one true knowledge—scientific determinism—that dominates Afrikaans universities. They are more comfortable with open relationships across race and gender than the long-term residents are. They experience tremendous frustration with the randomness with which power is wielded. They feel excluded from dominant cultural representations of knowledge and power. They feel they have to make basic arguments about simple things, and this sometimes generates extreme feelings about marginality. And then they are tempted to leave, or not to come in the first place.[27] It is this strangeness of knowledge that keeps outsiders marginal.

The fifth conclusion is that leadership matters in changing the institutional curriculum. Hierarchy works well when the senior leadership has democratic instincts and is able to advance change at a pace that would not be tolerated in universities more accustomed to a broader participatory ethos. Hierarchy, however, can also damn transformation if senior leadership seeks to conserve and protect the racial status quo and insists on investing all authority within itself. In the latter case, strategy and position, though suggesting change, can constrain it. For example, consider the university leader who decided to have white Afrikaner colleagues lead workshops on diversity on the Pretoria campus! I repeatedly raised objections, arguing that you could not ask those who were shaped by, and benefited from, social and institutional racism to be the same persons leading its undoing. Or in the memorable words of Audrey Lorde, "The Master's tools can never dismantle the Master's house."[28] Given the hierarchy, those objections fell on deaf ears, but at least the claim could be made that "diversity" was receiving attention.

## What Ubuntu Says About the Institutional Curriculum

The curriculum analysis has pointed to three concerns revealed in the Ubuntu module: the commonsense of racial essences, knowledge scientism, and identity hierarchies. Ubuntu reinforces the notion that there are races and that race is real, given, and fixed, and therefore that racial differences should be the starting point for student understanding. This essentialist understanding of race was the foundation on which Apartheid established its legitimacy, especially among white people, and it was the notion of unbridgeable divides based on color that justified the rigidities of social segregation. From this understanding, the most extreme forms of repression could be visited on any of those who rebelled against Apartheid, white or black. Ubuntu therefore resonated perfectly with incoming white student understandings that they received in family, church, and cultural or peer groups en route to university.

It is also important to note in the curriculum text the easy exchange between culture and race. *Race* remains a sensitive word in post-1994 South Africa, though Ubuntu is less reserved about this kind of language. Still, cultural essences on how blacks behave substitute for racial essences about who blacks are. In the Ubuntu narrative, *all* blacks—rural, urban, educated, illiterate—are implicated in the allegedly aberrant behavior. A single observation is a racially universal observation, and again this is the kind of racist logic that fits comfortably within the race-essential understandings of white South Africans.

That such knowledge of race—and everything else—is founded on a scientific understanding of human behavior is another important foundational plank of the institutional curriculum. Knowledge, as indicated earlier, is fixed, certain, predictable, and knowable. Science so conceived removes ideology and politics from the conversation and reasonable people would therefore accept the status quo as given by higher (that is, scientific) authority. Knowledge in this understanding both imposes control over reality and is itself controlled by the rules of science. The word *wetenskaplik* (scientific) is therefore extended beyond the natural sciences to every subject of study, from political science (called political studies or politics in other universities) to pedagogical sciences (called educational studies in other institutions)[29] and even to history.[30]

It is not only that knowledge is fixed and races are given, but there is a distinct hierarchy among human beings, with whites higher on the plane of civilization and blacks lower in everything as indicated in their cultural practices. On the one hand Ubuntu, in essentializing black behavior, desires whites to understand these lower behaviors (this is the crux of the multicultural education endeavor in the curriculum) rather than condemn such lifestyles and choices. On the other hand, Ubuntu requires those higher on the plane of civilization to reach down, educate, and uplift blacks so that they can come to a common and therefore white understanding of appropriate behavior. This theme runs throughout the Ubuntu curriculum, with more than a hint of encouraging white amusement as these extreme stories of black aberration are handed down to incoming white students.

Ubuntu's problem is not that it peddles this offensive knowledge on a university campus; the dilemma of this curriculum is that it makes explicit what is often concealed in white understandings of the Other and what is less evident in the knowledge, values, and beliefs that underpin the supposedly neutral scientific knowledge presented across the institutional disciplines. To understand how Ubuntu is received as "normal" within the institutional curriculum, a question must be posed. How did this curriculum pass approval at the level of the department, the faculty, and ultimately the senate of the university as a whole? Furthermore, how did this curriculum—reviewed closely by a universitywide innovation committee—actually win an institutional award for innovation? The answer is simple: it resonates deeply with white understandings in this Afrikaans university about what counts as legitimate knowledge of other people.

## Changing Curriculum

I realized early on that changing the institutional curriculum was always going to be incomplete. Even as dean in an authority-driven university, I did not have the energy or power to ensure that a completely new knowledge would sweep teaching, learning, and assessment within the broad teacher education curriculum across two schools, seven academic departments, five faculty centers, and any number of curriculum and research committees. The more than 500 modules made it almost impossible to scrutinize each learning unit to determine the extent to which it shifted the deeper understandings of race, knowledge, and identity toward a more open, tentative, and democratic knowledge of school and society. We decided on a number of strategies to support curriculum renewal within Education.

The first was to conduct departmental and program reviews of the organizational units and the curriculum using external experts from other South African universities and with associates from leading international universities. Predictably, the reports came in pointing to the conservative nature of faculty knowledge, the distance of our curriculum from mainstream thinking in the disciplines, the anachronistic naming of some of our departments (such as teacher *training*), and the narrow and instrumental character of teacher education knowledge at the expense of theoretical understanding. We used these reports to steer discussions within schools and departments about the need for change, and we even made operational lists of "things that needed to be done" to change the curriculum.

The second strategy was to appoint to headships persons from outside the Afrikaans universities, but this in turn was balanced with younger resident faculty who showed an understanding of the larger change project and who were willing to accept the imperative of knowledge transformation on which we deliberated. The theory was that with the right school and departmental leadership the knowledge base of teacher education could be interrogated and academics within a unit could be inspired and led to change their values, knowledge, and beliefs. Regular and intensive workshops and meetings were held with these unit leaders to develop a coherent and shared understanding of what we wanted to achieve with curriculum change.

The third strategy was to change the inherited names of schools and departments as far as possible. Thus "psychopedagogics" became educational psychology, "sociopedagogics" became sociology of education, and "department of didactics" became curriculum studies. The School of Educational Studies reflected in its new name the academic character of the faculty rather than its "teacher training" designation, which reduced the intellectual endeavors of teaching to little more than training; another school called Teacher Training was then established (for reasons discussed later).

The fourth strategy was to change the criteria according to which intellectual work was assessed. New and elaborate schemata changed the faculty promotion rating scales in favor of intellectual depth, creativity, and originality (literally these words) rather than simply production of a large number of publication units. The evaluation of especially doctoral dissertations required a new set of performance standards that included contributions to new knowledge and innovation in theory and method; and the community of scholars involved (or required to be involved by faculty regulation) in the "moderation" of student examinations was to be drawn from a more cosmopolitan crew of national and international academics. The logic here was that by changing what was valued at the level of terminal outcomes or performance criteria, there would be a backwash effect onto knowledge and curriculum in the classroom.

There is little doubt that the combination of these strategies started to erode certain and fixed knowledge, and that as the standards of knowledge changed new kinds of faculty and new kinds of academic work started to be noticed, appearing for evaluation. The university administration, to be fair, acknowledged and even admired these qualitative shifts in the academic culture of Education, and some even commented that we might be too "strict" in what we required of academic quality and performance. But such attempts to change the deep structures of knowledge with their encasing beliefs and values cannot of course happen simply by changing what is valued.

### The Tensions Between Deep Change and Mandated Change

In the meantime, though, this attempt to revise the institutional curriculum at the level of the Faculty had to compete with an even more compelling (from the perspective of the university administration) change project: to align the individual faculty curricula with the formats and standards of the South African Qualifications Authority (SAQA). This largely technical exercise did little for knowledge transformation, even though the idea of placing all qualifications on a national framework expressed more idealistic ambitions for curriculum transformation. The energies of every academic were clearly devoted to this curriculum alignment exercise; it was easier to do, it did not question underlying belief systems, it did not disturb received knowledge, and it came with senior management instruction, die opdrag (the command) that pushed aside any other kinds of political and intellectual efforts to interrogate concealed knowledges.

In the midst of these efforts to change deeply the knowledge base of teaching came yet another overarching administrative command system, called *quality assurance*. Once again, hundreds of faculty hours would be diverted into preparing documentation for the new Quality Assurance review of a statutory body called the Council on Higher Education, which, through its Higher Education Quality Committee (HEQC), made final judgments about the approval or closing down of funded programs. The significance of attaining accreditation, without which no programs could be offered, held severe repercussions for institutional reputation and faculty funding. Once again the energies of the staff were pushed toward compliance with external regulation, with considerable pressure, of course, from central administration.

The point of this discussion is that energetic pursuit of curriculum change seeking social justice and corrective knowledge is severely impeded when it happens in overarching social contexts where a new government places added regulatory frameworks over universities that demand and win the attention of academics and administrators within them. It is therefore not only the difficulty of changing a micro environment (one faculty, Education) within a macro-institutional context that is so difficult; it is the added dimension of state regulatory changes that further complicate the process of transformation within an academic unit such as a Faculty of Education. The academics concerned feel the burden of what they experience as one wave of change after another; they feel tired and frustrated trying to read the new rules of the game. The problem is that there are multiple and competing rules for change, and under such pressure white (and indeed black) academics tend to lean toward those change forces coming from the higher authority and holding the greater threat to academic standing and employment security.

Here then is the complex of curriculum change during periods of dramatic social transition. Changes happen simultaneously at multiple levels: the department, the faculty, the university, and the society. Each level of change has its own script and its own academic and ideological demands. Some demands are intellectual, and others are bureaucratic; some seek compliance with set rules, and others seek changes in beliefs and behaviors; some threaten personal and institutional penalties, and others remain mainly exhortatory in nature; for some reforms the guidelines for change are relatively straightforward and technical, while for others the change demands are more political and personal. When this happens, academics find it easier to work with the technical and the regulatory than with the more troublesome matters that demand personal and emotional changes in understanding and commitment.

Beyond Ubuntu, smaller and less dramatic changes in the curriculum knowledge and ideologies were hard to shift. It was difficult to convince a colleague that a course on family and sex education was little more than an attempt to persuade black students (the main if not exclusive audience) about the dangers of sexual liaison and the problem of HIV/AIDS; and that sexual correction and promotion of a particular version of Christian living was not the goal of a university curriculum. It was hard to persuade my colleagues teaching about school discipline that it was important to go beyond teaching techniques of keeping children under control, and to bring in Michel Foucault and others to grapple with the meanings of punishment and its institutionalization under years of Apartheid. It was especially difficult to convince colleagues about the contested standards of knowledge and the multiplicity of ways of knowing beyond the quantitative worlds of experimental science.

## Conclusion

The supreme test of change proclaimed in new academic policies, pursued through a broad array of training programs and engineered through the bringing in of new academics from outside the political and epistemological worlds of the Afrikaans university, was, of course, what happened inside classrooms. Away from the foreboding offices of leadership and at some distance from the surveillance schemes of the new government bureaucracy, what did the curriculum-in-practice actually look like? There were three responses from the resident academics on how they expressed the curriculum in practice.

It must be remembered that this new knowledge was deeply disturbing and in some ways quite foreign to resident knowledge. Moreover, this new knowledge was disempowering, for it was often experienced by the resident academic as a message holding that everything they thought was true was not. Suddenly there were crises of confidence in what colleagues knew; some saw immediately that their doctoral degree was of little value in this swirl of change that came into Education.

The first response was to engage and make sense of this new curricular knowledge. These respondents were generally younger colleagues who either recognized the weaknesses of their received knowledge or saw the practical and personal interests that could be served by adapting as soon as possible to the new curricular demands. Sometimes this eagerness was reflected in a new language spoken, but it often did not manifest itself in a new practice expressed in the classroom. I reviewed syllabuses and gave feedback on revised curricula; we organized countless seminars and writing review sessions during which colleagues could gently access the new discourses and find ways of translating the new curriculum into practice. For many of these colleagues, this engagement led to a higher level of productivity, appearances in a broader range of scholarly journals, and eventually awards and recognition in South Africa and abroad.

Gradually, the writing and the teaching of colleagues became more flexible, new reading lists were engaged in some depth, and the epistemological character of their beliefs started to show up as deep understanding of the new knowledge. This process of transformation is of course never complete, and every now and again there is evidence of the old, but at least for this group of younger scholars (not necessarily in age but in terms of recent entrance to the academy) there was a reawakening that was expressed in terms of intense joy as they recognized, for the first time, the constrictions and the constructions of knowledge within which they had been bound.

The second response was outright rejection of the new curriculum, but never directly. The institutional culture did not allow direct confrontation with authority; the way to do this was to feign allegiance to the new knowledge but to continue in practice with the resident knowledge. I did not believe such responses to the new curriculum orientation were deliberate attempts to undermine the new knowledge; it was simply too difficult and too risky to even begin to open up to these new demands. These respondents were often older colleagues, often very gracious persons, but for whom the changes had come too late in their careers to hold any personal benefits. Moreover, the changes were so radical in ambition that it would expose the limitations of existing knowledge. Such colleagues simply stood back and continued what they were doing, quietly hoping that there would be no external or internal pressure that forced change.

As dean I did not intervene. How does one coerce change that academics simply do not believe in? What kind of change results from compulsion? Again, is it ethical to demand change when it flies in the face of what people feel competent to do? Is a university not a place in which all kinds of knowledge—unless clearly offensive—should be tolerated? Fortunately this was a very small group.

The third response to the new curriculum orientation was the most difficult for me to deal with from the point of view of leadership. These respondents were a small group of colleagues who wanted to engage the new curriculum knowledge but found the task very difficult. They would attend all the seminars and workshops, and they would frequently set one-on-one meetings to make sense of the content and direction of what was required, but they were simply not able to make the transition. There were several reasons for this dilemma. One was their poor intellectual grounding in the undergraduate and initial postgraduate training that simply did not prepare them for this level of teaching and inquiry; a second and related reason was that they should never have been appointed to university positions in the first place. This sounds harsh, but it reflects a reality that came with a number of structural reforms in the post-1994 university environment: the forced incorporation of college-level personnel into universities.

It is important for the education change literature to come to terms with this reality rather than succumb to the eternal optimism of Western change writings—everyone can change. The restrictive labor relations regime of the new South Africa protects workers in ways that make it very difficult to prove and act on incompetence. Furthermore, in the racially sensitive political environment of transition, it would be very difficult to deal with this dilemma. More important, how does one release academics who through no fault of their own—but as a result of the harsh consequences of history—find themselves marginalized and disempowered under new social and intellectual demands? How, in such a context, does one release those who do everything to demonstrate enthusiasm for the new curriculum and the project of change, even though they cannot change?

# 7    Mending Broken Lines

The recognition of "likeness" in the face of different and dissonant knowledge paralyses rather than liberates imagination.[1]

T HE YOUNG WOMAN must have been sitting on the couch outside my office for some time. By her nervous manner so early in the morning, about 7:15, I sense that this is not likely to be another routine meeting between the dean and an undergraduate student. She holds her bag and a book tightly to her chest, and when I appear from the elevator across from my office door she leaps to her feet in attention. *"Goeie môre,"* I venture, guessing that like most of the undergraduates she is Afrikaans-speaking but, if not, she will greet in English to softly correct me and of course the conversation will proceed in her language. This simple gesture, a greeting, can be such a sensitive matter at UP. With white residents in the city itself, depending on the language of initiation, I am constantly aware of this potential dilemma. When I am not sure, I will greet in both languages in rapid succession, *Goeie môre* / Good morning, and leave it to the student to lead the language of conversation. With African students, I might even add *Dumela* (Sotho; Tswana) or *Thobela* (Sepedi) or *Sawubona* (Zulu)— not that I can go much beyond this first word of greeting in some of South Africa's 11 official languages—but it makes a difference to students to be recognized in what they regard as their own language. The language of greeting, the initiation of conversation, still carries enormous emotional and political meaning for white and black alike in this language-sensitive environment.

"Goeie môre, Dekaan" (Good morning, Dean), says the student, and asks if she can see me. "Well it depends," I remind her of the rule, "whether you are a first-year student." Allowing first-year students to see me without an appointment drew applause from the parents and communicated early on to the students that they are highly regarded in this new place. It always provokes some degree of humored appreciation when they are told at the annual welcoming ceremony that the university vice-chancellor, on the other hand, needs an appointment. My visitor makes it clear that she is a first-year student and I invite her in. She again sits on the edge of the seat opposite me, and it is clear that small talk is not working; so, after making her coffee, I ask what the problem is. The young woman becomes very earnest and says:

Dean, I notice all the things that you and your leadership team do for students, especially us first-years, and last night I was thinking and thought I should come and say thank you, and ask you whether I could pray for you.

I remember catching my breath and being completely silenced by this rare and dramatic request to pray for someone she hardly knows. I must have been in this state of shock for a moment too long, for she interrupts: "May I?" I respond quickly: "But of course, my child, you can pray for me; in fact, I would really appreciate it; thank you so much." She bows her head, takes my hand, and prays that God might protect me, give me wisdom, and bless me for my leadership of the Faculty and the students. The knob in my throat is unbearable, and I burst into tears. *How on earth is this possible?* I ask myself for weeks and months and even years afterwards. Why would a first-year white girl come all that way to pray for a black dean with such genuine concern and compassion? How is it possible that in those early years after Apartheid (this is 2003) a young white woman can rise above the racial devastation that plagued the land and do something so profoundly humane?

To understand why such an event is unlikely requires understanding of the closed circuits of ideological transmission that shaped white Afrikaner children in South Africa. For this young woman to travel the short physical distance from the women's residence to my campus office, she has, in fact, to travel a much greater emotional, cultural, and political distance. In the first place, she has to cover the racial distance that separates a white student from a black dean. Race had separated us for centuries, and race still defined both in the university and in the broader society predictable patterns of association between white and black citizens.

In the second place, she has to cover the gendered distance that separates men from women in this highly patriarchal institution. A woman asking to pray for a man overturns the tables of the patriarchal order in both our Christian traditions (evangelical and Dutch Reformed), where men lead as priests and women sit in silence and support. This action of the young woman calls for a lot of ground to be covered. And then she has to cover the authority distance that socially sets the dean's office at some elevation from that of staff and students.

Race, patriarchy, and authority combine to make this an unusual journey for this young Afrikaner girl, and it marks the first of many events in which my white students start to chip away at the suspicion, the reticence, and the moral certainties that I carry as a black South African in relation to my white compatriots.[2]

## In Tension

What were "the things we did" that inspired this student to walk such a distance? Once we surveyed the emotional, cultural, and political landscape of this all-white university, I recognized that the challenge facing us as a Faculty of Education was as complex as it was clear: how to do reparation and reconciliation at the same time. It was a formulation that resonated with my own understanding of social and educational change: that it was unnecessary and in fact would be disastrous to choose between the options of redress or reunion. But I was also aware that this approach found its compelling echo in the broader terms of social transition, one represented in the incomparable example of Nelson Mandela. In other words, the process I was to lead within the institution would find its political corollary within the surrounding society, and this knowledge gave me courage and direction.

The task of redress within the Faculty of Education[3] had to embrace all five components of educational change.

First, we needed to change the complexion of *leadership* so that what students witnessed was an observable example of the kinds of values we wanted to inspire and embed in this conservative, white environment.

Second, it was a nonnegotiable commitment that the *academic and administrative staff* had to be diversified; those who taught our students and those with whom they made first contact, the secretaries and administrators, would be those who could relate to them, speak their language, and give them a sense of connection to the institution. (In our research, we would later call this "at-homeness."[4])

Third, the *curriculum* had to change, for without challenging and changing received knowledge there could be no transformation.[5] Being taught by black scholars in integrated lecture theatres would mean very little if Apartheid knowledge—its philosophical orientation, its epistemological foundations, and its social commitments—were not uprooted. These were the ambitious goals we set early on in the change agenda.

Fourth, the *institutional culture* had to change, at least as it expressed and represented itself within and on the Education campus.[6] The fact that we had a dedicated campus made this task much easier than if we were simply another building lost in the sprawling expanse of the main campus.

Fifth, the complexion of the all-white *undergraduate student body* had to change, not only because we simply could not continue the business of preparing teachers only for white schools (the chosen destiny of almost all white preservice teachers) but also because it was important that the white students live and learn with and from black students, and the other way round.

The task of reconciliation, even as we pursued the project of restitution, was no less important and constituted perhaps an even more daunting task. This task of reconciliation I understood to mean retaining the best and most affirming elements of the institutional heritage even as the redundant, the anachronistic, and the offensive were ejected. White Afrikaners in this environment needed to "feel" that whatever was happening in the name of transformation was not vengeful, threatening, and disrespectful of who they were; this I understood not simply as a scheming move of strategy but as a moral and spiritual commitment to fellow human beings, the common occupiers of the same emotional space. At the very least, this meant allowing ample and continued space for practicing and recognizing the Afrikaans language. It meant colleagues would need to know that appointment, promotion, and advancement were not restricted to those who previously lacked access to these privileges in public universities such as UP. It would require sensitivity to campus memorials and monuments. It would mean communicating with parents in their language and with a clear sense that this was still "their" university even though the space was now rightly shared by other South Africans.

I relished the challenge of doing both—reconciliation and redress—but knew it was going to be difficult to keep these two commitments of our leadership in tension.[7] My new and incoming black colleagues needed to believe they had made the right choice; coming to UP is a questionable destination for many black and the more liberal white English-speaking academics who had their intellectual upbringing in contrasting institutional cultures. My resident white colleagues, on the other hand, needed to believe they were part of the picture, that their dreams and ambitions could be fulfilled at the same time as those of the newcomers, and that their cultural and social goods were still recognizable and appreciated.

## Changing Staff

The first thing we did was launch an international search for the best black (but also white) South African scholars in education and convince them to join UP. I was aware of the familiar argument that "there are no good black academics out there" as the prime reason for explaining the *status quo* not just at Pretoria but also at the other former white universities. Even where promising black academics could be found, I would often hear, "They don't apply." I traveled to leading universities in North America and Europe, determined to find black South Africans who were in the terminal stage of their doctoral studies and regarded by their academic mentors as holding promise of becoming fine scholars. It helped to have international networks I had built in my earlier academic life, and this made it possible to ask friends and colleagues to act as lookouts to alert me to promising black academics. Unsurprisingly, there were many, and I had the choice of speaking to and luring the best of the emerging young scholars to consider academic appointments at Pretoria.

I also traveled inside South Africa seeking out excellent black and white academics who had differing social and especially intellectual backgrounds, and who could help to transform the foundations that held educational knowledge captive at UP, in teacher education as well as the many other fields represented in Faculty programs such as education policy studies, assessment, curriculum, and education law. Every time, I faced the same questions from potential recruits. Is Pretoria still so conservative? Do they speak only Afrikaans? Will I be able to have my own voice? How do they deal with outsiders? The history and politics of Pretoria were formidable obstacles to attracting (and indeed retaining) promising and leading scholars in education.[8]

But new appointments come at a price, and it was going to be far too slow a process to wait for senior white colleagues to retire and then fill their posts with black scholars. I was musing over this problem of having enough open positions when the university vice-chancellor who hired me cornered me after a meeting and said, "You are not moving fast enough; make me some firm proposals for new staffing and we will find the money." This is what I needed to hear, and it came just at the right time. I had come from a black university where deans were socialized into "deficit thinking" all the time—how to manage resources simply to stay afloat on the annual budget. I was therefore naturally conservative when it came to Faculty funds and staff appointments. Those simple words changed everything.

The first plan was to deal with the academics who were about three to five years from retirement. These were all men, and I was astounded how they had come to attain seniority without a shred of evidence in their CVs that they had ever written a single article of substance in any learned journal. I kept asking myself how colleagues who were constantly complaining in public about "standards" and the threat posed to them by blacks coming in could themselves have such limited standards. Again it became clear that these men were the beneficiaries of affirmative action. One application of this rampant affirmative action program was the Afrikaans university, where men were favored above women in senior appointments and especially those who demonstrated loyalty to the secret society of white men, the Afrikaner Broederbond, and its ideals.

These men had an uneasy relationship with me. More than the women, they had great difficulty accepting the authority of a black dean, and for good reason. Just a few years earlier, they and their sons had gone to battle on the country's borders against black people fighting for democracy. At home, they lived out the beliefs of white supremacy in their relationships with black people. Suddenly, the man occupying the dean's office was everything they were told to hate, despise, and rule over. I had more than a hint that this was a problem for the men, so I saw them individually and informed them that I was here to stay and would like to offer them the choice of leaving. Most of those approached accepted the terms of early retirement. This opened up a number of positions.

There was another opportunity to expand the black staffing numbers. When the minister of education required incorporation of colleges into universities, the UP Faculty of Education was asked to incorporate the white Afrikaans college with which it had historical relationships such as moderating the examinations of the college as it prepared primary (elementary) school teachers. The incorporation became a three-way battle among the college leadership, the university leadership, and the new dean of education; this was also the first time I felt the power of the Afrikaner brotherhood in action and my marginality in the process of college incorporation. Here was my first major test of transformation within UP culture.

The university leadership was represented by the senior vice-principal and the college leadership by its rector. I reported to the vice-principal, and I made it clear to him I was not going to appoint all the college lecturers. One reason was that complete staff absorption would significantly set back the process of faculty transformation I had undertaken so far, since most of these colleagues were simply not trained to step up to the challenges of university scholarship, and almost all of them were white.[9] The second reason was that by choosing only those with the most academic promise, I would be able to expand the appointment of black scholars and those white scholars with more diverse intellectual backgrounds.

It seemed as if I had convinced my vice-principal, but every time I had a meeting with him the college leaders were waiting to go in or were coming out of his office. Initially I did not attach any meaning to this, until I found that even though the vice-principal would agree with me in one meeting, it would be very difficult to persuade him by the next meeting. He was clearly under pressure from the college leaders to take all the college staff into the Faculty of Education. I needed to fight back, so one day I went into the vice-principal's office and made it clear to him that I was not prepared to take all staff; that the academic project would suffer if I were forced into this position; and that critical opportunities for staff equity would be forever lost. He went quiet for some time, looked up, and said: "I agree with you; this is an academic question, and we must respect your judgment as dean. We also need to support you on the equity question."

I was surprised by his firm position on this matter, one from which he would not again back down. But what happened next was even more unexpected. He started to tell me about his upbringing as an Afrikaner with roots in the conservative church establishment and his own outsider status as a professor from the even more conservative University of Potchefstroom. He told me about how intact his own socialization into Afrikanerdom was, and how the transmission narrative was undisturbed as he left for graduate studies at a prestigious university in the Netherlands, one of many Afrikaners who even in the period after the Second World War found a receptive if not always uncritical acceptance into Dutch and Belgian universities. Unlike some of his predecessors who went to Dutch universities and fortified their racism in elaborate theories of white supremacy, the vice-principal spoke of how he was challenged by democratic thinking and by the open society, how he started to learn from prominent black South Africans who studied at the same university, and how the ruptured transmission line challenged his understandings of race and equality. He came back so changed that he eventually joined the local branch of the African National Congress. I remember my pen falling from my hand at this shocking news. Here, in front of my eyes, I had just witnessed one of the most powerful stories of personal transformation in the heart of conservative Pretoria. His honesty and commitment to principle were something I would respect in this vice-principal throughout our relationship. I suddenly found an ally in pushing forward the task of staff transformation.

But why would the remaining white staff even trust the new black leadership to act in their best interests? Why would white colleagues not expect retaliation at worst, or marginalization at best, as the inevitable changes favored those left behind and excluded from access to these privileged white institutions? These were questions that occupied my mind from the beginning. I needed to find some way of signaling to white staff that they were part of the plan for transformation. One decision, more than any other, resolved this potential problem of trust. As it turned out, the problem shared by all white academics and the few (at that point) black academics was that their scholarship was either nonexistent or embryonic, and most had only a master's degree or a recent Ph.D.

We designed what became known as the Young Scholars Development Program (YSDP), which would take 20 of the young academics, black and white, and offer each of them a year of study with a leading scholar in their field in the United States or Europe. When I made this announcement, someone burst out laughing; others too thought this was a joke. "We have to apply for leave simply to go to Johannesburg," said one, "and you're telling us to leave the country for a year?" I scanned the faces in the room and it was clear that few believed this was a serious scheme. There was a problem, though. Through the long years of the academic boycott and the isolation of Afrikaans universities and their scholars, there was very little knowledge of what was happening in the broader world of higher education and very few known networks established in this Faculty and among young scholars in particular.

The main academic connections were with sympathizers in the erstwhile homelands, principally the Netherlands and Belgium, and one or two links to American universities as a result of some entrepreneurship from an individual. But by and large, the only academics known to these young scholars were fellow Afrikaners at the other Afrikaans universities in Bloemfontein, Johannesburg, and Port Elizabeth.[10] An intimate network of links between scholars at these universities, sometimes their former and indebted students, had created incestuous academic and social relationships in which assessment of dissertations, moderation of examinations, doctoral orals, manuscript reviews for journals, and conference planning were all retained within this closed circle of Afrikaner friends and colleagues, with one result: a serious decline in quality and a frightening monotony of thought.

So when I asked these young scholars who the top two or three leaders were in their field—such as educational psychology or education policy studies or teacher education—they simply did not know. The next few months were taken up with making these connections, and eventually all the young scholars were paired with leading persons in their fields. They left for universities that included Stanford, Harvard, Yale, Sussex, and Manitoba. Their initial visits would be to the largest education research conference in the world, the American Educational Research Association (AERA) Conference, held that year in Seattle, Washington; after this event the young scholars would go to their respective universities to begin the process of becoming serious academics and researchers through exposure to a broader network of scholarship.

This plan caused chaos in the ranks of the administration of the university. An anxious administrator called to say this could not happen because most of the staff did not have enough leave to make up for a year away from campus. Another asked who would teach their classes during this extended absence. Others pointed to the setting of a precedent that could come back to haunt the new dean. It helped, at this crucial juncture, to have supportive leadership at the head of the institution. I also understood that the role of leadership was to make the administration support the overarching academic goal of creating a world-class faculty from the raw material given to me: young, insular, inexperienced, and conservative colleagues who were almost certainly destined to reproduce the intellectual mediocrity of their forebears if there were not a radical rupture in their scholarly experience. As I surveyed this academic mediocrity in arguably the wealthiest university on the continent of Africa, I again asked myself how whites had managed to fool black people for so long with the myth that they had academic standards.

YSDP won credibility for the Faculty leadership as a serious investor in young scholarly talent. It convinced new academics that investment in development of young scholars would not be based on color. It indicated the level of scholarship required in order for the Faculty to operate within the international academic environment. It opened up an entirely new world of scholarly thinking and academic partnership to emerging scholars on an international plane. And it shifted emotional and political allegiances in favor of the new intellectual project and its leadership. YSDP ruptured the political lines of academic knowledge that shaped the incipient scholarship of these new academics. It also started the process of mending the social lines of disengaged knowledge that could have kept a new black leader at some distance from the resident white followers. The university did a survey of the faculties and departments involved to examine the leadership and followership climate; the Faculty of Education led by a huge margin.

But training academics in overseas universities was costly and had to be combined with professional development at home. Once again the Faculty did something that was seldom done in university contexts: we launched an intensive program of research development for all academic staff, with at one stage daily research training workshops enabling in particular the staff inherited from the college to learn the basics of research and publication and, in the process, to work toward achieving a higher degree. From across the country, this was one of the most ambitious research development programs ever, covering topics from qualitative data analysis to publishing tips on academic writing to mixed methods research to "preparing for the professoriate" and "writing your first scholarly book." Every year the publication rate increased, staff gained advanced degrees, and in the course of time three or more serious academic texts were produced annually through local and later international publishing houses. For this massive investment, staff were held accountable; once a year the young academics had to publicly present progress reports on their productivity as scholars—an event during which they received direct and intense feedback on what they had done (or had not done).

For all these activities, the immediate goal might have been to improve the research profile and academic standing of the Faculty of Education at Pretoria as well as in the country and abroad. But underlying all these initiatives was the broader ambition of building new allegiances among black and white staff focused on the academic project as a common desire rather than on ties of race or ethnicity that, for almost a century, had defined identities and careers at UP for those inside and outside the gates.

## Changing Students

If the transformation of the Faculty depended on changing the perceptions and orientations of the undergraduate students, it would have to happen early in their time with us. A number of interlocking plans were designed for this purpose. First, through a welcoming ceremony the students (and their parents) were told about the distinctive character of the campus, the special rules that applied to and favored them, how the facilities were organized to benefit them, and how the staff and the curriculum were designed to specifically advance their learning and living experience on the Education campus. Without exception, this announcement brought students and parents into the fold, with expressions of gratitude for the special welcome and the unusual attentiveness to first-year students.

Important in this opening ceremony was representation of the faculty and the students. Students and their parents would immediately see integrated leadership on the elevated podium, black and white, both among the faculty and among the students. This was the first signal of what to expect. Doing this in a way that made language and cultural connections to the students and their parents signaled both racial change and cultural continuity. Most of the ceremony was conducted in Afrikaans, and key administrative and marketing items on the program were delivered largely in Afrikaans.

The sense of personal connection to the students was very important, and the announcement that they had access without appointment to the dean's office was met with applause from the floor but a raised eyebrow from my secretary. This was unusual for students and for their parents, and it made a considerable difference, right from the start, in their positive attitude toward their new campus. I spent some time during this welcoming talk making sure that the students, through their parents, understood that this was a homecoming for many whose parents had also come into a place rich with memories and traditions.

When students heard they were invited to weekly lunches with the dean, it immediately opened otherwise suspicious minds and hearts. They looked forward to this arrangement, so unusual for any university and especially for UP. The first-year lunches opened the door to lasting emotional and social connections with the students. I also invited and accompanied the students to other social events, and here the rugby at the famed Loftus Versfeld stadium was very popular. From time to time, and when our box was available, I would invite some of the first-year students there. This became another way of enjoying their company and, more important, extending their connection to the Education campus and its leaders.

I realized it was crucial to be involved in their learning as well, so once a week I would enter their classrooms and lecture halls, and occasionally engage them. My colleagues took advantage of my being present, and I soon found myself invited to do guest lectures; the most enterprising of my staff would regularly bring students after a field trip to present their work to the dean. I was delighted to find that some of my co-leaders did the same, becoming involved in student life inside and outside the classroom, and before long the campus gained nicknames for its informal style as a resort for learning.[11]

As I moved along the campus during one of those warm Pretoria days, I saw two Indian students standing under a tree. "Good afternoon," I greeted them and asked how they were enjoying the Education campus. "Much better than the main campus," they volunteered. "Why do you say that?" I asked. "Oh, too many Indians!" The humor signaled an important shift. Of all the minority groups on campus, the Indian students were the most cliquish, tending to stick very close together physically inside and outside the classroom. What these students were beginning to appreciate was the value of the diversity around them, the richness of a many-cultured campus. This was encouraging, but it took some time.

It was important in this institutional environment that combined a college of education culture and a university research culture not to lose the undergraduate students in the campuswide pressure to increase research productivity and academic publications. This meant attending the cultural events and sporting challenges of the students. It also meant redirecting the students into joint campus ventures. A white soccer team, composed mainly of English-speaking male students from the surrounding English schools, was eager to gain my support. I was delighted by this initiative, since part of the transformation was to extend the cultural suite of sporting events beyond rugby. We put some money into the soccer team, and shortly afterward a group of black students came saying they too had decided to establish a soccer team. I would give them money, I promised, if they joined up with the white soccer players to give the Education campus a single competitive team.

We needed to steer the students by example toward the goals of social integration that we had set for all our students.

Being involved in the range of social and residential activities of the students, as guest and participant, brought about some enduring friendships with parents and students alike. I started to visit students' homes, observed them during teaching practice, watched them perform in the rugby finals, and sponsored them for wrestling, judo, and tennis. When a white student wins the *Jool* (Rag, or festival) competition, the impressive young woman comes to tea, and the photographs are displayed in the hallways. When a white high school student with ten distinctions in her "matric" year nevertheless decides to study teaching, she too is invited for tea. Few academic leaders would regard these kinds of activities as necessary within a university context; but here it was an important way of demonstrating racial inclusion and recognition.

One such decision drew a positive response from the broader public. The Afrikaans Sunday newspaper *Rapport* decided to launch a bursary (scholarship) fund to support student teachers. This was yet another example of the deep commitment of the Afrikaner community to teaching, the kind of initiative that would never be undertaken by any other racial or ethnic group in South Africa. I knew deep down that this was intended mainly for white Afrikaans students, and sure enough, members of this group were almost exclusively the recipients of bursaries. But it also represented a tremendous opportunity to demonstrate to the white public that the black leadership of the Faculty would make this investment in their children. In a pervasive white public discourse of loss and defeat, and the perception that black leaders in the political and business domain had largely abandoned their children, such a symbolic move was an important signal to my Afrikaner students and their families that on the Education campus their children would be included. True, most of our bursary funds in the undergraduate program and the special resources raised outside went to black students, so this broader message of inclusion to the outside as well as inside the Faculty was important. So I invited the editor and his senior people to receive Faculty and personal donations to the bursary fund, and the mandatory photograph of the handover appeared in *Rapport*.

The problem with South Africa before and after Apartheid is that we insist on collapsing race and economics into the same face; whites are rich and privileged, blacks are poor and underserved. This may be true of blunt averages as a national measure of social status, but it conceals the thousands and thousands of poor whites and the struggling classes among them who barely make it. Apartheid was as much a racial system of oppression as it was a capitalist system of exploitation; among the victors, the nationalists want us to believe only the former, and the Marxists only the latter. But it was both, and the second event to render me silent was a visit by another student and her father.

The picture before me already suggests that this is an unusual visit. A young girl in her first year of study, neatly dressed, sitting upright with a tentatively bright smile on her face. Next to her, her father with a half-dirty shirt missing two or three buttons, and shoes that had seen some years. "Welcome," I begin, "how can I serve you?" Then the impossible happens. The man starts to shiver, and with a broken voice tells me he has a confession to make. I lean forward, move my chair closer to him, and tell him to take his time. "My daughter has been attending your classes illegally," he struggles to say. "I know it is wrong, but I could not bear to keep her away from university because teaching has been her passion all her life. The truth is, I do not have money to pay her fees." Once again I am emotionally moved by the plight of this parent as I see him struggling to articulate what must be doubly painful: owning up to financial struggles in the presence of your child with such obvious eagerness to learn, and acknowledging economic vulnerability in the presence of a black man with the authority to redress his situation. I look at him and as I turn to his daughter I just cannot avoid the tears running down my face, for as I see this poor father I see my own. Here Clendinnen's "recognition of likeness" (1999) can draw only a compassionate response.

I softly admonish the father for not coming sooner, and ask why he doubts that we will not try to find the resources to fulfill his daughter's dream of becoming a teacher. I send them to the Student Administration, and my resourceful colleagues find a bursary to cover her expenses. What transpires in my office that morning carries social significance well beyond the otherwise ordinary case of a student in financial need. A white father and a black dean have just overcome Clendinnen's "different and dissonant knowledge[s]" (1999) to mend the tattered lines that separated us. Both of us need to come into that space in which we acknowledge a human problem, and the white parent takes the first step. As I watch his daughter leave the room, a bounce in her step, I wonder if she realizes how she has changed me without saying a word.

## Changing Institutional Cultures

The knowledge of an Afrikaner past as well as an Afrikaner present is ubiquitously posted throughout UP. It is represented in the architecture of the campus, including the tallest of buildings dwarfing incomers through the gate, the Arts Building.[12] It is given in the names of buildings such as *Rautenbach* or *Merensky*, or student newspapers such as *Perdeby* or campus museums such as *Von Tilburg* and *Van Wouw*. It is fixed in the university flag and the *wapen* (coat of arms or, literally, weapon) still carrying an ox wagon as symbol of what was once called the Voortrekker university. It confronts you in the almost all-white elite choir, the Tuks Camerata, with its white conductors and its emphatically white / European repertoire; it is a curious phenomenon, hearing so many Italian classics in an African country. It is hard not to share Daniel Herwitz's perceptive conclusion that this bold assertion of white culture is a means for "sustaining oneself as an adjunct of European culture" where institutional display of this kind functions "as a badge of identity (European rather than 'native') . . . the refusal of the project of remaking one's culture in a way that reflects essentially new conditions of existence."[13]

It reminds you in the simple fact that almost every piece of signage is in Afrikaans, and where the English appears as well it is at the bottom; there is no sign of any other African language in sight. It overwhelms you when attending a senate meeting, a body representing the senior professors of the university, and in a sea of white faces you suddenly become aware of your blackness.

It catches the consciousness of every residential student who must decide whether to enter residences with names like *Taaibos* or *Boekenhout* in the case of men or *Katjiepiering* or *Magrietjie* in the case of women. It weighs down on you as to whose voice carries in those crucial decision-making bodies, from the SRC to the senate to the Institutional Forum to the University Council; it is, over and over again, white voices that count and that can advance or restrain transformation. It makes its mark on you as you enter the large meeting room of council, where the wall is covered with every white male Afrikaner vice-chancellor and every white male chancellor and every white chairperson of council—until the recent appointment of an Afrikaner woman in the chair position.

A black student or faculty member stepping into this institutional culture immediately feels lost, an outsider or even an intruder. A white student, on the other hand, feels instantly at home. It is under this institutional canopy that the struggle for change is pursued and within which black and white inhabitants of the campus must work and learn together. On assuming the deanship, I saw clearly that the terrain of institutional culture, not only in the artifacts but also in the behavior of people, had to change; but how to do this in a way that kept the twin ambitions of conciliation and correction on the same track?

The first time I felt the power of institutional culture was as I walked along the short corridor to take up my new post. On each side hung the heads of stern-looking patriarchs: the white male Afrikaner deans of education who had gone before. These were Broederbond luminaries, the recognizable authors (such as Landman, van der Stoep, Nel, and others) of influential *pedagogiek* (pedagogy, education) textbooks that became the standard material for Christian Nationalist indoctrination and that were widely prescribed for anyone wanting to become a teacher in South Africa. I remember feeling their disapproving eyes following me through the double door into my suite, and deciding there and then that they would be buried. If *I* felt uncomfortable with these hanging heads, what must a black student or faculty member or visiting outsider think? To my considerable surprise, nobody challenged this quick decision, although I am sure it must have evoked some discussion among my colleagues.

Shortly thereafter, we moved from this main campus to the campus of the former white teachers' college about ten minutes' drive away, and there too the campus architecture, names, signage, statues, portraits, and human relations were saturated with an Afrikaner past carried through into a very visible present. The first decision was to change things in a way that signaled a broader community of service, and so we worked on bringing in new symbols, the most prominent being the work of a township artist showing carved wooden figures in human embrace; additional works were commissioned to reflect this broader vision of inclusion and acceptance.

The second decision was to retain those things that held deep emotional meanings for my Afrikaner students and staff, the most prominent being the huge monument of an Afrikaner Boer War heroine (Natie du Toit) who provided care and sustenance to the soldiers and children fighting in that vicious conflict. But misreading my intentions, someone from the main campus had decided to uproot this statue from its prominent place right in the middle of the student administration. I reversed the decision, and we retained the statue commemorating a Boer hero. Sadly, some white students from the main campus, in one of their right-wing fits, published a photograph of this statue on the Education campus during one election period to show that the commemorative figure still stood there because they had fought for the retention of Afrikaner symbols. At that moment I had a fleeting temptation, I must admit, to retire the monument.

What confused my black colleagues and several visitors was why I would keep a smaller statue that represented the quintessential philosophy of Christian National Education (CNE): a tall woman bending over a small child and taking its hand in an act of teaching. This was the "leading the child to adulthood" metaphor of Afrikaner education, a position heavily criticized by progressive scholars for its insistence that the child was nothing but an incomplete adult, one whose social and academic aspirations were coupled directly to the educator. This child of CNE knew nothing morally or intellectually or emotionally other than through the person of the adult who teaches and in so doing becomes the parent. The critical instincts of outside scholars saw this imagery for what it was. I was insistent that by removing this symbolism we would also lose the opportunity for dialogue and critique of what went before; by taking everything away, we remove the chance to challenge received knowledge and negotiate new meanings in an institutional culture that was far too silent about a terrible past.

So what we were left with in the symbolic architecture of the Education campus was a rich and planned mix of old and new, change and continuity, fresh images signaling political redirection, and old images demanding intellectual engagement.

Among the more difficult decisions was changing the college ethos that sat within this broader culture of Afrikaner dominance on the campus. This meant changing the schoollike arrangements for seating (colleges were bound administratively and pedagogically to schools), for example, by changing the school desks and replacing them with seminar tables. It required revising the book collections of the college library away from their pedestrian focus on "teaching methods" and parochial house magazines to serious scholarly journals and new collections of handbooks and research materials. It meant transforming little language translation rooms and woodworking shops into prominent centers for advanced and international research in university disciplines. It meant extending library hours and creating student parking spaces. It meant changing the notion of students as children from high school behaving as relatives of the lecturers to independent adults responsible for their own learning, who had to be taken seriously on their own terms.

Human relations was the most difficult thing to change in a rigid, authority-driven, top-down institutional culture. No matter how hard I tried, white colleagues insisted on calling me "Professor." Sometimes this took a funny turn, as in confused white students whose traditional way of greeting older adults was being challenged by this transition. An older person, especially in the college education context, was called "Oom," a term of course that did not normally apply to black people. Here was a black man, an adult, and a dean in charge. A tall first-year Afrikaner male student enters my office and asks for clarity:

| | |
|---|---|
| *Meneer, hoe moet ek vir meneer sê?* | Sir, how must I greet you, sir? |
| *My vriende noem my Jonathan, andere noem my professor, en soms Dekaan; maar ek sal verkies as jy my Jonathan noem.* | My friends call me Jonathan, others call me professor, and some call me dean, but I would prefer if you called me Jonathan. |
| *Nee maar goed, Oom Dekaan.* | Okay then, Uncle Dean. |

I laughed with him. That was the day I decided not to push the issue on simple things. He means to be respectful, and the new context has thrown the rules of greeting into disarray as he is caught between race and authority on a former white campus. If this deep sense of respect for adults engendered in their children by Afrikaner parents can be extended to all of humanity, then perhaps it is not a bad idea in a broader culture where such respect and trust have broken down.

With my colleagues, it was different. Our ability to work together would depend on a respect based on formal authority rather than on grounds of professional behavior and academic achievement, and most important, on recognition of a common humanity. But the knowledge that established the rules of relationships preceded my colleagues even as it shaped them; it is deeply entrenched within the institutional culture over a long century. Such orientations do not, to coin a defensive phrase, "change overnight." Yet something had to be done, and what happened next carried considerable risk on a number of fronts. But I felt spiritually compelled to do it.

Toward the end of the academic year, in late December, I asked my secretary to set 30-minute appointments with five selected members of staff: a woman Afrikaner professor, a black man who was the *bode* (or messenger, carrying mail between campuses), a white Afrikaner secretary, and two others. The group was deliberately diverse by race, socioeconomic status, and gender, but all were, nominally at least, Christian. They were terrified, some calling the office to find out from my secretary why they were being summoned to see the dean; in the institutional culture, a call from the dean's office could only spell trouble. But my secretary had no idea.

On the appointed day I brought along a basin, five towels, and five bars of soap and placed these on the floor of my office, with water added to the large basin. I asked a senior Afrikaner woman from the Student Administration, one respected by all, to join me for these meetings. She would sit quietly and observe, but I felt her presence would be important, especially for my female colleagues when they arrived. She was a devout Christian, and when I explained what was going to happen she silently nodded her head. "When our previous dean left so suddenly, the women in my section prayed that God send us the right dean," she said. "I now know he answered our prayers."

One by one my colleagues came in, the first being the white Afrikaner woman. She was a tough, unsmiling computer education professor who had seen her share of troubles. As she strode into my office, her first words were "Dekaan, wat het ek verkeerd gedoen?" (Dean, what did I do wrong?). "Nothing," I answered, "please take a seat." By this time she had seen the contraption on the floor and I sensed Christian recognition of the symbolism.

I then said this, which was repeated to every one of the five members of staff:

I have told you before that I regard myself as a servant leader, and that my only purpose in this job is to serve you, and I have been thinking of a way in which to demonstrate that sense of service to you, my colleague.

Even as I said these words, which I had rehearsed without difficulty, it suddenly struck me how odd this was. I resented my father working as a servant to white women in Cape Town during the early part of his working life, bent over on the floor with a bucket serving the English madam. I continued, noticing the growing unease reflected in the body language of my colleague:

So, if the greatest teacher who ever walked the face of the earth could wash his disciples' feet, who am I, not to at least ask you, whether I could wash your feet in gratitude for who you are and in service to you as colleague?

I will never forget what happened next. She leaped to her feet and in a firm voice said, "Jy maak seker 'n grap!" (You must be joking!). I assured her I was not, and she sat down quietly as I waited for a response. At this stage I thought this whole idea was ridiculous and started to have some doubts. Eventually she responded: "I would be honored."

So I rolled up my sleeves, knelt before her, and washed and dried her feet. Tears flowed freely. A few days later she wrote me a long and moving email. No man had shown her such respect before, and no leader had ever done something like this. She now understood, she said, what our leadership was trying to accomplish.

This symbolic act would have had no meaning in my previous university, where most of my colleagues were Hindu or Muslim; and it would be dismissed in an English university with all kinds of caustic response. But in this context it was understood for what was intended: to demonstrate through a spiritual act a sense of servant leadership. The story leaked to the media and became the subject of much discussion in churches and workshops on leadership. From that day onward, and as the story spread through campus, I began to feel a small but important difference in how my colleagues related to me. Several changed to a first-name basis, including the colleague mentioned here, and I knew that another thread in a broken line was being mended, slowly but surely, and as unfamiliar knowledge confronted the familiar and the routine.

## Changing Leadership

Given the hierarchical and historical character of leadership in Afrikaner institutions and particularly UP, the composition of the leadership of the Faculty of Education had to communicate our new values and commitments. The natural path for young Afrikaner men to enter and accelerate through the system into formal leadership positions was so well established that some of my younger male colleagues were really confused when the passage was hindered because of a common appeal to the same standards for black women and of course white male colleagues as well. This caused severe distress for some, and even though they did not mention this directly, it was clear that promises made under one regime of leadership no longer held the same exchange value under another kind of leadership. What to do about this?

Because of the deep respect for authority in Afrikaner culture, the choice of leadership would be a powerful set of signals about transformation, and it had to reflect our twin commitments to reparation and reconciliation. To break the weight of patriarchy, I decided that the two school chairs, in effect deputy deans, would have to include an Afrikaner woman of stature and potential and one who was young enough to grow into the new culture and unfamiliar knowledge of social justice that we were trying to instill among staff and students. The choice of a woman would signal to the undergraduate class—more than 80 percent female—that we took the value commitment of gender representation seriously, and it would indicate to women faculty that there was no longer a ceiling to gender advancement. The fact that she was an Afrikaner would send a signal to staff within the university that we wanted to include and affirm the traditional inhabitants of the university, and it would strengthen my hand as dean in the external communications with alumni and Afrikaans schools through her leadership. In fact, at one stage both school chairs were women. Nothing would more disrupt received knowledge about who was appropriate to lead than the power-ful symbolism that such an appointment would convey.

I decided that the second school chair had to be a black person, and here a wonderful opportunity presented itself when we were able to hire a Nigerian chemistry education professor who was also an outstanding leader in his field. Here two prejudices were dealt with simultaneously: the white prejudice against black leadership and the black prejudice against immigrants from another African country. The fact that my new school chair was a devout Catholic was not lost on the institutional audience, challenging an inherited bigotry that included in Afrikaner-dom not only *die swart gevaar* (the Black menace) and *die rooi gevaar* (the Red or Communist menace) but also *die Roomse gevaar* (the Roman or Catholic menace).

This was the key academic leadership team, and fortunately it worked together very well; there was healthy respect for one another and broad commitment to the same goals. It was a joy to observe how my white students responded to the black school chair, whose warm personality and competence in chemistry drew many in the largely white, Afri-kaans undergraduate class for which he was responsible toward him as a leader. To observe the love and affection he received from these stu-dents both in the classroom and in informal social gatherings, such as the ubiquitous *braai* (barbeque), would amaze me. How utterly unlikely such a change in social relations between white conservative students and a black professor-leader should be in the immediate years after Apartheid! It was also satisfying to see the other school chair, the young white Afrikaner woman, rise to the challenge of leadership and gain the respect of all her colleagues for her sensitivity, depth, and competence as an academic leader.

The same kind of thought went into the choice of heads of depart-ments, and suddenly there were three women among the seven leaders at this level. From being an all-male and all-white educational enterprise, the new leadership team suddenly reflected the ideals of racial diversity, gender affirmation, and internationalism. Even as they led, three of the departmental leaders from the former college were encouraged to complete their Ph.Ds. and were later required to do so as a condition for renewal of their headship. It was crucial that the symbolic representation of the new leadership be accompanied by the academic substance required to lead with authority and confidence; once again, there would be no compromise between social diversity and academic standing.

But leadership tied up in the dean, or even in school chairs and department heads, would simply reinforce the notion of top-down leadership issuing orders rather than a more democratic form of authority. In this respect, I found the body of knowledge on distributed leadership to be of enormous value, despite the shortcomings of this emotionally and politically anemic literature.[14] In a large faculty distributed over an extensive campus, it was important that the ideals of this knowledge transformation be represented in many leadership circles and personae. Program committees and special commissions had their own team leaders, and great care was taken to ensure that the key committees such as curriculum and research were led by academics who already shared a broader understanding of knowledge, curriculum, and change.

One of the more difficult challenges of bringing into prominence leaders who shared the broader intellectual knowledge and political orientation that the traditional leaders—in this case the senior white Afrikaner men and, in one or two cases, women—did not possess was that it was read by the traditionalists as displacement. Such intellectual work, which they could simply not perform as leaders in the new environment, was now taken by scholars at a lower rank of formal appointment but who clearly had a broader knowledge orientation, a more extensive network of international linkages, a more cosmopolitan array of journals in which they published, and a greater fluency with the language and the terms of educational change in the organization. Yet the traditional leaders held the professorial positions, while the younger scholars led much of the academic leadership work. The young scholars were sometimes frustrated that they were carrying a load that would ordinarily fall on the shoulders of the senior professors; the senior professors were frustrated that they could not confer, and worse, were not asked to provide, such leadership.

It took hard work to keep the senior professors on board. One mechanism for doing this was to allocate the important task of *administrative leadership* to the traditional professor colleagues while handing the crucial task of *intellectual leadership* to the younger colleagues and those professors hired from the broader university community. Whenever a traditional professor refused to make this distinction, I had no choice but to insist on this division of labor. At stake was the broader transformation of the Faculty, of teacher education, of the university, and of the country.

Here once again, I was confronted not with hostility but with an immense sadness. These senior white male (and a minority of women) colleagues were, without exception, hard-working, dedicated colleagues who gave me every support I required to be effective in my work as dean. One of these colleagues ran into my office one day, after a seminar in which younger black colleagues led the theoretical discussion, and said:

Whatever you do, do not tell me again that black people were disadvantaged. When I listen to our black colleagues lead the discussions, they had exposure to new theoretical ideas and inventions in methodology to which we simply did not, or were not allowed to, have exposure. Yes we might have had the resources, but this meant nothing since we were isolated and out of touch with what was happening in the rest of the world.

In various ways, I heard this lament often, and it was true. Black colleagues had a broader repertoire of theories and methods, a more fluent language, and a more worldly sense of the intellectual landscape within which ideas were born. Over and over I saw this in seminars, in published papers, in conference reports, and in book proposals. To impose simple terms such as *disadvantage* on this reality did not make any sense. What is seldom said in these rare but intense concessions is how the stereotype and the myth are challenged and dispelled before their very eyes, and how the received knowledge white colleagues had of the capabilities of black colleagues was painfully confronted and irreversibly overturned. Since then I too have often wondered, in this context: Who really was intellectually and emotionally more disadvantaged under Apartheid, white South Africans or black?

When black scholars provide leadership in the intellectual domain, one of the more powerful rationales for social and academic integration is reinforced; it is not, simply, that integration benefits black staff and students by granting access to white resources gained through oppressive means. It is that integration begins to transform white staff and students as they are confronted with undeniable knowledge of (and through) those deemed by way of inherited knowledge to be less.

## Second Steps

With these changes under way in the racial and gender representation of staff and students, in the content and purposes of the curriculum, in the character and complexion of leadership, and in the resident institutional culture, the knowledge boundaries that separated white and black campus dwellers started to soften. Slowly, students like the one at the start of this chapter began to bring their knowledge into the open, sometimes in an aggressive manner, and sometimes in a conciliatory advance.

So too with staff. One moving incident came through an email communication from a colleague who eventually opened up on hearing how the political head of police during the 1980s, Adriaan Vlok, had confessed to his role in the attempted murder of church minister and anti-Apartheid activist Frank Chikane, who was now head of the presidency in the new South Africa. She wrote:

What makes me different from Vlok? I also knew and did not know that I knew. . . . I accepted that the black domestic worker could only eat mixed-fruit jam in our house; that her children did not need the education that I got; that the Communists were hiding behind black takeover, Coca-Cola and butter-flies on denims.

One accepts the system dished up for you provided it makes you feel safe and privileges you. And you do not ask too many questions: "There are people at the top who know what they're doing, my child. . . ." Only when you begin to feel the pain yourself and something bad happens to someone you know, then you begin to rethink. . . . But I did not know anyone, and especially did not know their pain because artificial separation ensured that there were no opportunities to discover each other. And such separation was enforced through fear, for association could quickly bring the security police on your track.

Rising up against the system was appropriate for the rebels and the art-ists and those rich people who were exposed overseas to other anthropolo-gies. . . . This is my rationalization: they lied to us. The system deceived me. Forgive me, because I did not know what I was doing. The fact that there were people like Oom Bey[15] or Amanda Strydom or whoever else, those I idolize [and] they free me from who I am. Because how else must I cope with my unbearable whiteness of being?[16]

There are all kinds of social messages contained within this powerful communication between a white Afrikaner woman academic and a black male dean within this historically Afrikaans university. The closed circles of transmission that shaped her consciousness are confirmed as she demonstrates that Apartheid was not simply a matter of keeping people apart; it was a system designed to shield children from other kinds of knowledge: the knowledge of other people, their pain, and their struggles. Moving with the singular story through her life, everything seemed to fit into place even down to the most ordinary observations, such as the choice of jams (jellies) for the domestic worker.

What keeps her in this knowledge frame is not only the received knowledge from her mother and the reassurance that others know better but also the veiled threat that to depart from the storyline as given is to be disciplined. She is, however, conscious of her own choices, not simply a victim of authority and circumstance, and consequently she points to the rewards of security and privilege that come with not seeking to know more. At this point she comes to the recognition of another knowledge and is then able to make the complex moves that enable her to seek forgiveness.

This kind of openness, the move toward recognition and the quest for forgiveness, does not happen easily. For some it takes an entire lifetime, and for others it mercifully comes sooner. But it happens only if the conditions are set in a context that invites such engagement. It comes with trust of the other not to rush to judgment or expose or demean. And this I believe is what our leadership was able to establish: an emotional, psychological, and social community that enabled *toenadering* (coming together) for dialogue, disclosure, and embrace.

We do know something about the *embracing knowledge* that socializes white Afrikaans youth into separatist and racist behavior through myriad positive and affirming lessons about their own kind. What we do not have, however, are fine-grained studies of the problem of *disciplining knowledge*, the sometimes soft and sometimes harsh hand that keeps white children and youths from straying from received authority. It is a discipline that refers them elsewhere, to a higher authority that knows better and in whom they should trust; it is the discipline that carries the threat of recrimination for those who stray. But it is also the discipline that comes through a rich mixture of body language and verbal reprimand that together signal approval and disapproval of specific social acts.

A male Afrikaner colleague recalls his mother's glaring look when she was told he was seen fraternizing with an English-speaking white girl. It is the disciplining that prohibits young children from doing what young children do naturally: play with any child irrespective of race or language. It is the disciplining that keeps students from asking questions about what they initially witness as unfair or unequal and learn quickly to swallow their words. It is the disciplining that teaches them the differential modes of communication with a white adult and a black adult. And it teaches them the consequences of what happens if they dare cross the line to the other side.

Those who condemn the second generation for their racial attitudes have little idea about how those attitudes are formed in this combination of discipline and embrace. Every year I would encounter at least one heartfelt story from a black student and a white student who had found love together. They know this is something I admire and applaud as a completely natural consequence of what happens when people interact with one another on the basis of a common humanity, rather than in response to racial essences that trap their emotions and constrict their thoughts. The white student's anxiety was expressed in this (paraphrased) way:

I love Thabo, and I know he is the guy for me. Please do not tell anyone about us. We are taking you into our confidence. The problem is that if my Dad finds out, he will kill me. He has not told me specifically about dating black guys, but I just know he will disapprove strongly. If we go all the way, and ignore my parents, I will be thrown out of my home and will lose all my family; my parents will disown me, I just know that. What, professor, do you advise us to do?

It is difficult to explain the depth of emotional stress that I experience when I encounter such tragedy. Here the bare bones of human wholeness (in the loving students) and human tragedy (in the disapproving parents) are revealed at the same time. In these repeated stories, two knowledges clash: the knowledge of the past and the knowledge of the future. As a leader, what do you say? Fortunately, by the time I got to Pretoria I had as academic leader and university teacher encountered similar difficulties among South African undergraduate students who defied boundaries—Muslim and Hindu students, African and Indian students, Muslim and Christian students—at another university.

The natural response is to want to encourage the students, to tell them to follow their hearts, to hail them as the necessary generation that will need to break the madness of segregation and the persistence of bigotry. At the same time, such a response must alert students to the very real consequences of isolation and dispossession, an often unbearable loss for any human being and especially for those coming from closed cultures where the affection and endearment of loved ones mean so much to their sense of community, purpose, and direction in life. In the end, I found that the only meaningful role for leadership was to affirm the courageous actions of young people and outline the positive and negative consequences of their decisions. In the end, however, it is their decision.

## Conclusion

In the context of the broader transformation of the Faculty of Education, UP, and South Africa itself, these stories are not insignificant and begin to point the way to normalcy and healing, the mending of broken lines, the reconciliation of rival knowledges. Though such changes are agonizingly slow, they offer hope and promise in institutional contexts where the imposing knowledge of the past is present everywhere but slowly challenged, and eroded.

My colleague who asked for forgiveness and who carried the burden of what she called "the unbearable whiteness of being" wanted me to see her connection to the words of a song of the progressive Afrikaans singer Amanda Strydom. Her song captures so powerfully the confrontation between the knowledge of the past and the future, and the disciplinary knowledge of parents conveyed here through maternal redirection of emotions and paternal signaling of disapproval; watch how Amanda (and my colleague) encounter the confrontation with the knowledge of

Hector Petersen, the first child to fall when he was shot and killed at the commencement of the Soweto Uprising in 1976. On this occasion black school students marched to resist the extension of Apartheid control in the curriculum through the Afrikaans language:

Hector P (Soweto 1976)[17]

*Ek was neëntien jaar oud toe Hector gesterf het*
I was nineteen years old when Hector died

*Hy was dertien jaar oud met 'n koeël deur sy lyf.*
He was thirteen years old with a bullet through his body

*Dit was koud in ons voorhuis op die sestiende Junie*
It was cold in our sitting room on the sixteenth of June

*En die wind het geruk aan die vlag by die hek*
And the wind tugged on the flag at the gate

*En my pa het gesê "draai tog jou serp om"*
And my father said "please put on your scarf"

*Uit die sitkamer voor ons nuwe TV*
From the lounge in front of our new TV

*En dis toe wat ek sien hoe jy val langs jou suster*
And it was then that I saw how you fell alongside your sister

*En my ma sê "kom eet: die bobotie word koud"*
And my mother said "come and eat: the *bobotie* [spicy minced meat dish] is getting cold"

*Ek was neëntien jaar oud toe ek sien wat hier aangaan*
I was nineteen years old when I saw what was happening here

*Hy was dertien jaar oud en het lankal geweet*
He was thirteen years old and had known for a long time

*En my pa skud sy kop vir Soweto se kinders*
And my father shook his head at Soweto's children

*Wat mars teen die taal wat hy jare lank praat*
Who marched against the language he spoke for years

| | |
|---|---|
| *Ek was neëntien jaar oud en Hector* | I was nineteen years old and Hector |
| *skaars dertien* | barely thirteen |
| *Ek was veilig verskans teen die* | I was safely protected from the |
| *skreeuende waarheid* | burning truth |
| *In die naam van die Heer en die* | In the name of the Lord and the |
| *swakheid van vaders* | weakness of fathers |
| *Wat niks aan die sirkus van waarheid* | Who would do nothing to the |
| *wou doen* | mockery of truth |

# 8    Meet the Parents

> The past is not dead; it is not even past. We cut ourselves
> off from it; we pretend to be strangers.[1]

I T WAS CLEARLY AN AMBUSH. I had suggested in my
monthly column in a national newspaper[2] that one of
the reasons for a recent spate of violent public acts by white Afrikaner
boys might be their feelings of rejection by the new black government
from a meaningful role and a productive future within post-Apartheid
society.[3] I challenged the new civil service in particular for hiring only
black bureaucrats and ignoring young white men for whom a role in the
public sector was something they and their parents saw as a position
of high esteem and an opportunity for service. I had seen this before, I
noted, when I encountered in the Education residences of UP smartly
dressed young Afrikaner men in training for the post-Apartheid military[4]; I quizzed them about working for and in a black government. For
these young white men, the job was less ideological and more a tradition
of service that their fathers and grandfathers had embraced under the
old government. It mattered little to them that this was Nelson Mandela's government.

I made the further point that the civil service was not an appropriate arena for application of affirmative action since government bureaucracies were always places in which most black people found jobs
administering Apartheid in ethnically defined urban bureaucracies and
in the rural "homelands." By sending a signal that young white men too
could make careers, as did their parents, in this sphere of occupational

life, the government would get more and more white South Africans to embrace the new democracy. I concluded with sad stories of how many of my white Afrikaner male students confided to me their sense of loss and exclusion from such occupational opportunities.

A prominent Afrikaner from the education sector called me and asked if he could use our campus to bring together people from the community to listen and respond to my positions on the role of white youth after Apartheid. It sounded like an innocent proposal, and I agreed to participate and make the facilities available. At the back of my mind, I thought there would be at least some positive responses to the main argument that we need not keep young white men out of employment even as we advanced the necessary project of black empowerment. What happened next, though, was a coordinated attack by a hand-picked group of very conservative, some outright racist, Afrikaner men who made sure I understood a few things.

The first thing I needed to understand was that these were their children, and I had no right to speak for and make proposals about their children. The second thing I should know is that Afrikaners do not need handouts from black people, and that they would create their own employment, thank you very much. The third thing for me to know was that they did not want to return to lives of faceless bureaucrats serving the state but were quite capable of working for themselves. My advice was not needed.

What struck me was not the difference of opinion, but the stridency of argument, the emotional intensity of the response, the political attack on my person. This meeting was clearly dominated by right-wingers who transformed what I thought was going to be a public seminar into a heckling match with myself the main speaker. It was a mess, and completely out of tune and tenor with any meetings I ever had with the Afrikaner community. I was in shock, and what made it worse was that I was trying to communicate in Afrikaans when the strongest emotions and the language fluency I had available were in English; in retrospect, the constraints on my speech that night were probably a good thing.

Bizarrely, some ethnic chauvinists from the "colored" community also showed up and, motivated by the same essentialist thinking as the Afrikaner speakers, ranted on about my focus on Africans and Afrikaners—

"what about those who were 'not white enough' under Apartheid and 'not black enough' under the new government?" Here was a lethal cocktail of ethnic chauvinism, anti-African sentiment, and antigovernment rebellion in one room. All of this targeted me, the black dean, who stood in leadership of an Afrikaans university and who dared to speak up for the inclusion of young Afrikaner men. It was left to a particularly smooth right-wing politician, the son of an archconservative white politician, and leader of the FF+ political party, to make an unexpected point: "You know," he told the audience, "ordinary Afrikaners in my rural constituency will agree with Professor Jansen."

It took me some time to understand what had happened in that meeting with Afrikaner adults claiming to represent my white students. In follow-up meetings with individuals and with my colleagues who attended, it was clear that the fact that a black man spoke up for white youth had really riled these Afrikaners. Worse, the notion that young white men should be absorbed into a black government that their parents did not care that much about to begin with, and to take a place in its civil service, was to add the insult of aid to the injury of loss after power changed hands. They were still smarting from the collapse of white supremacy and white power, and the fact that they were now being told—by one who exemplified the taking over of white space and white authority—that their sons should be accommodated in the new regime was a bridge too far. It unleashed venom.

What Afrikaner adults feared most—apart from "cultural obliteration"[5]—was a return to the economic desperation of almost a hundred years ago. It still jars, the time of the poor whites, humiliated in battle with the English and emerging as an economic underclass in the early part of the previous century. Now the real prospect of a slide back into such a state loomed large under the new black government.

Afrikaners felt they had worked themselves out of poverty and, through ethnic self-determination, raised the Volk to an unrivaled class position among African nations. They did not need black help then, and they did not need black assistance now. It was a racial slap in the face to take away their power and then invite white boys through the back door, as they saw it, to eat the crumbs falling from the table of the freshly anointed black masters. As it turned out, not a single one of the men present in this intense quasi-political meeting was a parent of a current student of mine; they simply assumed to speak for them.

It also turned out that the worst of the right-wing white adults showed up that day, and though there were clearly more moderate men in the audience, including some of my colleagues, they remained silent through the ambush on the black dean who wrote what he thought was a conciliatory newspaper column.

### Initiating Embrace

It was to be expected that parents would be the ones most concerned about their children, the second generation, and what would happen to them inside the educational institutions of the new South Africa. The children would be released from all-white high schools and all-white family circles, and indeed all-white churches, to step into their first integrated experiences, the public university after Apartheid. They wanted their children to be trained—in this case, as teachers in South African schools—and they would expect the historically Afrikaans university to continue to provide this service as it had done faithfully in earlier decades.

Yet they realized, of course, that the political terrain had changed, and therefore they came into the university environment with a heightened sense of awareness and sensitivity to any corresponding institutional changes that might have an impact on their children's education. Would their language still be the medium for carrying teacher education? Would their children still receive a rigorous program of teacher training? Would the curriculum respect the values of the community that enabled Afrikaners to emerge from poverty? These were the questions the parents would ask me at each Open Day, as they and their children prepared to make decisions about study choices.

The first public event to test such questions would be the day first-year students were welcomed to the UP Education campus. The student head of the men's residence, Sipho Ngobeni,[6] stepped up to the lectern to welcome the new class of mainly white Afrikaner boys who would be living under his authority. I confess, I was nervous and my emotions were with Sipho, wanting him to do well. But I could not be sure, for as I looked down on the crowded hall all I saw were white men and women, looking very serious. I felt I could read their thoughts: "What is this? A black boy in charge of a student residence at UP? How could this be?" Yet this exceptional young man was highly respected by the white boys, who had elected him as their leader. But would the parents know this? How would they take to both a black dean and a black student residence head on this still overwhelmingly white campus?

Looking regal in his residence uniform, blue blazer and tie, well-pressed pants and shirt, Sipho spoke into the microphone, his dean's heart in his throat. "Good morning parents," he said. "I am here to tell you that I will make a gentleman out of your son." Instantly, thunderous applause broke out among the large assembly of white parents, and I nearly fell off my chair.

What was this? Why would such a simple and emphatic statement of authority by a black student about what he will do with white students so impress the parents? Why would the white parents respond positively to the "gentleman" bit, a term associated with the English, the cultural enemy?

Needless to say, I was greatly relieved—not just because of Sipho's acceptance by the white parents, but because it was now easier for me to speak next. Although I spoke to parents mainly in Afrikaans, I was conscious of the need to include English in my welcome as there was a growing number of black and English-speaking white parents. The mainly Afrikaans-speaking audience warmed to my Afrikaans. As I was often to find, Afrikaners appreciate a black person speaking or trying to speak what they regard as their language, even though they are usually less tolerant of white speakers who are grammatically clumsy with Afrikaans. Without fail, someone in the audience would come to me afterward and commend my Afrikaans. Though I enjoyed the compliment, I knew my language usage was much less fluent than I was told.

I also knew these parents wanted reassurance that their children would be accepted in this changing environment and that their education would be of a high standard. The man who hired me, the charismatic vice-chancellor who had since left the university, once addressed this audience of Education while I listened backstage. When I complimented him on the things he said, he gave me invaluable advice. "Remember," he said, "all they want to know is that their girls will be safe, their language will be spoken, and their teachers will be well trained."

I told the audience about our plan to put student teachers in schools for much longer than before, so that they could learn in practice how to become better teachers. I told them that, given the crises in our schools, we planned to increase the standards of teacher training. I told them about the elaborate security arrangements on campus as well as the improvements in the physical infrastructure to make this former college[7] a safe and enjoyable university campus experience for their children. And I told them how things would change, how first-year students would be able to see the dean without appointment, that parents were free to call me, and that by the time they left after four years their children would have had an unforgettable experience helping them make a lasting impression as a new generation of teachers in South Africa's schools. Sustained applause.

While delivering this message, I was always conscious of the fact that the parents were keenly watching the on-stage behavior of colleagues. They noticed how easily and joyfully black and white senior staff interacted on stage. They noted that one of my school chairs was a black man speaking in English, and the other an Afrikaner woman addressing them in Afrikaans. They saw me as dean hugging the white and black student leaders on the stage, making it clear that a relationship had been forged long before this event. In other words, parents saw change, and they saw an inclusive practice of change, in which their people, their language, and their traditions were still visible and respected.

There was every indication during the speeches of the first black student leader and the first black dean, that white Afrikaner parents were not unaffected by these dramatic changes and the new complexion of leadership.

## Conditional Pragmatism
In response to the kind of change and continuity witnessed on stage, the exemplary leadership of the student leader, and our attempts to signal a warm, safe, and inclusive education campus, white Afrikaner parents adopted what I call a *conditional pragmatism*. It is true that Afrikaners are pragmatic, and that they have a history of adapting to

adverse circumstances as an ethnic minority in Africa. Sometimes this pragmatism was expressed as withdrawal under conditions of defeat.[8] At other times, it asserted itself through the racial logic of Apartheid, where pragmatic thinking still insisted on dividing South Africa into neat racial territories in which each group could determine its own affairs. For the most part, since 1994 this pragmatism has shone through in a gradual acceptance of the new order.

In the shame of defeat, not all Afrikaners fled South Africa. They adjusted awkwardly and sometimes shamelessly to changing conditions; in the language of a popular idiom, *" 'n Boer maak 'n plan"* (a Boer will make a plan). It was the pragmatic language of the pugnacious Apartheid hardliner P. W. Botha, who, as prime minister, urged whites at the end of the 1970s to "adapt or die"—even though he did not himself make the kind of adaptation that might have taken white South Africa much sooner into a workable political settlement.

It is a mistake, however, to read this kind of pragmatism as a disinterested, value-free, adapt-at-any-cost kind of politics. It is a conditional pragmatism in which loyalty and affection for the new state are based on firm preconditions. In terms of a black student and a black dean in a white university, this pragmatism could be illustrated as follows.

First, *"I respect you because of your authority."* Ordinary Afrikaners have a deep respect for authority, including governmental and educational authority. Leaders are deeply respected, and their word is taken seriously. For many this orientation has Biblical roots: "Every person is to be subject to the governing authorities. For there is no authority except from God, and those which exist are established by God."[9] It was also the principled leadership and authority of Nelson Mandela that drew white South Africans and even conservative Afrikaners to this son of royalty. The same people who put him in prison for three decades would embrace him without question. The smallest gesture of friendship or expression of decency among leaders is applauded, such as when Thabo Mbeki attends the funeral of the former white President Botha, a man despised by black South Africa. Bad behavior draws fiery criticism; principled leadership draws support.

Second, *"I connect with you because you share our values."* It is the commitment to producing "gentlemen" or the promise to "improve the quality of teacher training" that enables Afrikaners to rise above the crudity of racial thinking and identify with the leader, black or white. "Jy praat so in ons kraal"[10] (you talk in our kraal—in ways we can understand), said the Afrikaner check-out clerk at the local shopping center when she found out I was the author of a monthly column in an Afrikaans newspaper, *Beeld*.[11] Common values, or at least the perception of shared commitments, draw respect from Afrikaners for credible black leaders. This too is an act of pragmatism. The universities are going to change no matter what whites do, so ordinary Afrikaner families gradually begin to look at ways of expressing themselves within this inescapable reality. One way of doing this is to search for common values.

Third, *"I applaud you for using our language."* The emotional connection that Afrikaners make between themselves and other people on the basis of language cannot be overstated. The speaker is listened to differently when he speaks English. Together with the other elements that constitute conditional pragmatism, speaking the language strengthens the depth and the quality of engagement between Afrikaner and non-Afrikaner, and it may lead to a positive and productive relationship.[12]

Fourth, *"I am grateful that you do not impose the past on me."* Afrikaners, like all white South Africans, are hypersensitive to anything reminding them of South Africa's horrific past and their role in it. To be able to sustain a discussion with, or win over, this group, it is important not to harass Afrikaners with historical knowledge. What the student leader does is point forward and to the future: What positive outcomes can you expect from your sons as they graduate? It is the kind of optimistic message that Afrikaner parents can relate to, and that can win their support. If direct confrontation with historical knowledge is not possible, it has to be represented in other ways, but not through leadership bitterness or by giving a sense of "now it's your turn to suffer."

Fifth, *"I therefore commit my children to you to teach them well."* Once white Afrikaner parents have a sense of a leadership commitment to the basic values of discipline, authority, decency, training, and respect, they are again prepared to rise above racial bigotry and act pragmatically. This means communicating the coincidence of interests, and reinforcing shared commitment in the choices of teacher educators, schools, and curriculum. It means understanding the idiom of teaching that is familiar and reassuring to the parents. When a review committee said we should change the name of one of our schools from Teacher Training to Preservice or Initial Education, I understood the arguments but I also knew that the words *onderwyser-opleiding* (teacher training) carried a strength of purpose that a name change would dilute in the minds of Afrikaner parents; so we did not change, although we still referred to Teacher Education in the General Programs.

Sixth, *"I remain with you because I sense myself among you."* Again, the Afrikaans language, still prominent in part because of the large group of Afrikaans-speaking students, carries a welcoming and identifying signature that immediately consoles the nationalistic spirit. The fact that white Afrikaners are included in the leadership and the teaching staff again conveys a sense of identification with the past and makes the changes more palatable. This sense of identification with leaders such as Sipho Ngobeni also makes it possible for whites to continue coming into this changing space. Little things, too, all help, such as the ways of greeting, the warmth of reception, the follow-up on promises, the open door, the speed of response, and even a simple thing such as standing up to greet a visitor.

Seventh, *"I will open myself to you as much as you open yourself to me."* The risk of opening up to other people is real for Afrikaner parents. For many, there is fear of condemnation and for some the burden of shame. It is not clear where opening up will lead and whether such attempt at conversation will simply close down discussion or evoke bitter retaliation. In each of the stories in this book, there is an opening up of the possibility for dialogue.

Such dialogue can lead to an uncomfortable realization for those of us who firmly believed that Afrikaners were racial *idioglots*[13] who persecuted black people simply because they were black. At times in the long struggle against Apartheid, great frustration would often feed the belief that the illogical and violent attachment of Afrikaners to race rested simply on the crudity of racism. Herman Giliomee was of course right: racism was not an inherent trait among Afrikaners, or any other human grouping for that matter. Racial rule was a means toward ethnic mobilization. Where Giliomee fails, though, is when he downplays the actual racism[14] that drove such ethnic ambitions and their devastating consequences for black people and white people as well.

A conditional pragmatism does not, however, mean lifting all the barriers to social interaction; it is conditional, also, in its embrace of the Other. These same parents would resist any intimate social relations with black leaders or parents, and some would disown their children if, for example, a black lover was brought home. Many—though certainly not all—Afrikaner parents would frown on and discourage a black-white friendship, especially if it became known in their white neighborhood and among their white friends. Teaching and leading their children on the university campus is one thing; sharing homes, lives, and loves is another.

### The Sins and the Shames of the Fathers

I had just completed my first welcoming ceremony as dean to the first-year class of student teachers on the Education campus. I returned to my office in a rush before a planned departure for an executive meeting on the main campus of the university. As I passed my secretary's office into my own, I saw a man standing over her in a demanding pose; I sensed her discomfort. "What is wrong?" I asked of my efficient and caring secretary, who was always very conscious of a diary that I tended to overload, of the constant demands to see the dean, and of course of my next meeting. Reluctantly, she told me that this man was very angry and wanted to see me despite hearing that I was on my way to another meeting. Something told me not to rush off without intervening in what appeared to be an intimidating man hovering over the desk of my soft-spoken secretary. After asking the secretary to apologize for my possible late arrival for the meeting on the main campus, I took the man into my office and closed the door. I was going to put him in his place.

He refused to sit down, now hovering over my desk even angrier than I had seen him in my secretary's space. *"Ek verkies om te staan"* (I prefer to stand), he insisted, and that was the last straw. I rose from my chair, pointed my finger at him, and said: "Now listen here, you, this is my office, and in my office, I tell you what to do. So sit down or get out of here." It was a measured, self-secured, and pointed message—righteous anger, I would tell myself later. To my surprise, he shrank and sat down. Then something completely unexpected happened.

The middle-aged white man burst into tears and, sobbing on the chair only three feet away from me, began to tell me a heart-rending story of his rural upbringing and his racial attitudes. At the height of his lament, he said this:

Dean, when I came through the gates of the campus this morning, I must confess, I was a racist. I am a farmer from Vereeniging, and I grew up hating people like you, let me be honest. I still hate black people, it's just how I am and what I was taught. But when I listened to you speak to us first-year parents this morning, and the way you made my daughter feel welcome on your campus, I realized how wrong I was. I am still struggling with all of these things, but I wanted to tell you that I am sorry for what I believe, and thank you for accepting us and for making my daughter feel so good about being here.

It is difficult to make the emotional shifts from anger to empathy in such a short time, but I suddenly understood what his earlier aggression was about. Here was a man battling his own conscience, building up the courage to tell a black man, for the first time, about his racism and being told there was no time for a meeting. This difficult but compelling impulse—to tell—which he needed to do there and then, for it might not come again, propelled him into my office, and he needed to get this off his chest. To tell the story before breaking down, the mask of aggression was the only way he knew in which to come forward.

Since that day, I would often ask myself the same question: What lies behind the aggression of the fathers, this tendency among white men toward spontaneous combustion when challenged or when facing a new and awkward situation? Was it simply a learned racism, the expression of white supremacy, the white male defense ego at work? I have no doubt that somewhere in this complexity lies also a troubled soul, deep shame, and unresolved guilt. Aggression is often a mask for something else, as I saw time and time again in my white male parents.

This was not the only parent to be stirred by our welcoming ceremonies. As I made my way through the crowd, greeting parents and welcoming their children in Afrikaans, there was a slightly uncomfortable but always warm response by the parents. They genuinely appreciated the after-speech and less formal conversations. Even in these encounters, I was still nervous in those early years, not sure what kind of confrontation would spring a surprise attack on this black dean.

After one of these welcoming ceremonies, I had a sense of trepidation as I become aware of a truck following me as I made my way along a narrow road on the Education campus toward my car. I glanced up and, sure enough, there was a white man driving, his sullen and nervous-looking wife looking straight ahead, and their clearly excited daughter sitting high in the back seat of the double-cab truck. My walk stiffened, expecting the worse, and preparing what to say. Slowly the driver wound down his window. By this time the truck was level with me. I stopped walking, the truck braked, and I moved to the open window.

Excuse me, Professor. My name is Jan du Toit[15] and this is my daughter. She will be your first-year student. I listened to your welcoming speech today, and it really touched me. I am a rural Afrikaner, and you know, we grew up raw and conservative with very firm views of black people; but we farmers also say things like it is. And so I just wanted to tell you: we are proud of you as our dean.

As I reached out to shake his hand, we both had tears. I thanked him for his words and his openness, and I promised I would do my best to make his daughter feel at home and become the best teacher she could be. I looked toward the back of the car, welcomed the daughter, and ended by greeting the wife, who now wore a nervous smile.

These unexpected turns in black-white meetings of this kind tend to play with the emotions. As a black person growing up under Apartheid, you measure your emotions with white people, and from bitter experience you learn to brace yourself for the negative in defensive maneuvers that will soften the pain of rejection and humiliation. These defensive instincts are to some extent still with me. Yet when the embrace happens, the emotional apparatus is completely unprepared, even if the cognitive apparatus accepts this unfamiliar posture of the white man.

What was happening to white parents in these cases was the confrontation of intimate knowledge with new knowledge through the leadership of black people. The knowledge that white parents bring into this campus situation is directly challenged by how leaders lead. It is an emotional experience, this confrontation between the knowledge inherited from parents and grandparents and the knowledge now experienced through contact with other human beings who were long deemed not only different but threatening to white culture and identity.

Like their children, white parents stumble into the unfamiliar knowledge of a new reality, and what tumbles out, under the right conditions, is the confessional, the owning up to wrong thoughts and hurtful practices, and even the willingness to embrace. What happens to black leaders is surprise and disorientation at the unexpected responses of white parents. For a black leader, the presumed predictability of white behavior is shattered; so this new knowledge of white parents also begins to change as it grapples with an unexpected experience. In short, this is a two-way process that transforms both white and black in contact. But this does not happen without the conditions first being set for such encounters.

## Changing Parents

What became clear in our work with white Afrikaner parents was that the notion of parents as racial ideologues was clearly wrong. Parents were also pragmatic with respect to the changing economic terms of the new political terrain. For many parents Afrikaans and Afrikaans culture were still strongly held ethnic assets, but even these assets were subject to pragmatic considerations. Initially, I would hear regularly from parents about the threat to Afrikaans when we started to introduce more and more English classes in response to the growth in number of black and English-speaking white students. Since the Afrikaans students were in the majority, these were mainly separate classes, but where numbers were very small the economics of running a Faculty required that some classes offer dual-medium instruction.

This was never a perfect arrangement because of any number of complexities. Sometimes the Afrikaans-speaking lecturer could not speak English very well, and the non-Afrikaans-speaking students resented this. Often the English-speaking lecturer could not speak Afrikaans at all, or very little, and it was the Afrikaans students who were resentful. Sometimes a bilingually competent Afrikaans- or English-speaking lecturer would spend too much time in one language or the other, either out of habit or because of some other practical consideration ("all the students understand English anyway"). What both Afrikaans- and English-preference students all resented was the time lost as the lecturer diverted in-class time to speaking in the other language, for they would then be wasting time.

It was an attempt at making things work in a university that had by this time adopted two languages for teaching and administration. The sheer practicalities of the situation meant English was becoming dominant, sparking protests led by white right-wing students for whom the loss of Afrikaans and its culturally attendant practices was unacceptable. A few deans, like the pragmatic dean of engineering, himself an Afrikaner, made it clear that in his discipline the insistence on Afrikaans teaching at higher levels was simply disadvantaging white students in the broader economy. He and some black deans, including me, were now labeled by right-wingers as *"vyande van Afrikaans"* (enemies of Afrikaans) in graffiti and posters placed on public display. I felt aggrieved by this, given our attempts not only to make ample instructional provision for Afrikaans but to speak and advance the language in everyday communication.

Two considerations were important to me in the language arrangements. I wanted to make sure all students were comfortable with the instructional language inside the classroom, and also, even if it were affordable, I really did not want de facto racial segregation on the campus, this time adjudicated on the basis of language. I wanted students to learn together, but the language barrier was proving to be a major challenge to the ideal. I knew this would not convince parents; they would sense social engineering, which would be distasteful to white parents. What they wanted, I thought, was cultural affirmation (Afrikaans) and competent teaching (the subject matter). Not uncommonly, though, some white parents would cite the language problem when their children were not doing well in academic performance.

One such incident followed the appointment of a brilliant young physics education specialist who taught the undergraduate class of preservice teachers. I knew her appointment as a black physicist was crucial in adding yet another layer of disruptive knowledge to the social encounters of white students. The young scholar taught in a family of disciplines, including mathematics, that the founding fathers of Afrikaner nationalism did not regard as "useful" knowledge for the native to acquire since it created unrealistic expectations for "him" in the occupational world.[16]

The appointment was especially important because schools and universities, when they do appoint black teachers, tend to hire those who teach the "native" languages such as Zulu or Xhosa, which they were presumably better equipped to handle. Physics, on the other hand, was a discipline in which only a handful of black scientists could be found during or after Apartheid, and almost no black women. I worked hard to secure this appointment for all these complex reasons.

The young physics educator was also an outstanding teacher, and she soon won accolades from black and white students in equal measure. I breathed a sigh of relief that my white students could rise above the confrontation with skin color and appreciate outstanding teaching in a difficult subject. "The best teacher I have ever had in physics," a young Afrikaner student confided. Things were going well until an Afrikaner parent called to complain. For a while in this extended telephone conversation I had difficulty in getting to the bottom of the parent's distress. She kept saying that the physics educator was teaching in English, and this made it difficult for her daughter to do well in the subject. There were three reasons I doubted this to be the cause, even as I listened patiently to her repeated description of the problem.

First, every other white Afrikaans-speaking student had waxed lyrical about their new physics teacher, so I knew that language was unlikely to be the reason for her daughter's poor showing in the subject. Second, physics, like mathematics, is highly dependent on language-neutral symbols for instruction, and many second-language English students find this to be a relief rather than an obstacle because they can follow the teaching nonetheless. Third, it was the end-of-year examinations, and I knew from experience that this was usually the time when parents called to find some reason for underperformance other than the simple fact that their children were not well enough prepared. After about a half-hour of listening and probing, I said simply: "Now Mrs. X, please level with me; tell me what the real reason is you are calling." The answer was precious: "OK, I'll tell you what the reason is—you're forcing my daughter to think!" For many college students the step up to university-level physics teaching proved to be intellectually more demanding than anything they had encountered before. This was not the first or only time that Afrikaans would be incited as a shield to fight battles over other things.

## Changing Contexts

In the course of time, however, the language issue largely subsided on the Education campus as a matter of protest among students. A more pragmatic set of concerns became noticeable among the white parents: they wanted their children to become more comfortable and fluent in English. A significant percentage of their children would leave the country to teach—mainly in the United Kingdom—soon after obtaining their education degree. They would form part of a growing contingent of South African teachers who contribute the largest share of professional educators from the Commonwealth nations to the teaching force in the United Kingdom, with Australia a distant second.[17] But being the children of Afrikaner parents, most of these graduates eventually returned home to teach in South Africa, with many of them establishing their own preschool centers for teaching young children. Undoubtedly, English had market value for this new and mobile global class of knowledge workers, and in the process a more flexible attitude had developed among the parents toward English, even if warm cultural attachments to domestic language and culture still remained in place.[18] For some, this flexibility toward English was part of an escape-ticket logic, especially for those parents who feared their children might be completely marginalized in the post-Apartheid economy; facility in the language of the Boer War enemy would enable relocation within another Anglophone setting.

This kind of thinking had also permeated the main campus of the university because the language preference of most of the students was decidedly English, and this majority was possible only because of a shift in the language orientation of those who came from Afrikaner homes. Situated in one of the most cosmopolitan cities in Africa, at the crossroads of many international cultural flows, UP will inevitably move toward becoming an English-medium university. Within another decade, there will be very little Afrikaans at this erstwhile bastion of Afrikaner nationalism; this will not be possible without a shift in the attitudes toward language among Afrikaans speakers themselves.

## Committed Parents

In no other racial or ethnic community are parents more involved in the educational future of their children than among Afrikaners. The in loco parentis principle is alive and well within Afrikaner families; that is, adults at school and university responsible for their children's education are still regarded as acting in the place of parents in teaching the children. Parents often show up with their children to discuss academic or social problems with the dean, the relevant head of department, or even the lecturer concerned. Parents do all the talking, except when they occasionally defer to the children with "*jy moet praat!*" (you must talk!).

But this concern is again centered on the depth, quality, and thoroughness of their children's education and the extent to which they will succeed in their studies and find jobs after graduation. I spent much of my time as dean reassuring parents that their children would not be abandoned in a post-Apartheid economy, even as I dreaded that my government had some leaders who in private and public would signal otherwise. But it was true that for those education graduates who remained in teaching, there was certainly no shortage of posts within the large white Afrikaans school community, which tended to hire and rehire white Afrikaans teachers—itself another challenge for transformation.

What was clear, though, is that pragmatic concerns preoccupied these highly committed parents around one question: Will my child be employed? I do not in a period of seven years recall an Afrikaner parent ever coming to challenge the content of the curriculum or the appropriateness of the pedagogy or the fairness of the assessment. Initial concerns were raised about the language of instruction, but again it is in relation to their children's chances of success (will instruction in English or dual-medium classes impede our children's learning?) rather than the continued socialization of their offspring in the cultural, ideological, and social knowledge of Apartheid.

### What Does This Mean?

How is it possible that white Afrikaner parents can change so quickly, at one moment being advocates and supporters of Apartheid and then suddenly becoming these pragmatic citizens of a new social order? How can belief systems, so strongly entrenched over decades, be traded so easily in the opportunism of the market? What happened to hardened racism and racial beliefs about black people? What makes the confessional possible among this minority within Afrikaner families? What are the possible consequences of this still pervasive silence about horrific knowledge within the scramble to adjust to the new order and obtain the most from it, at least for their children?

### From the Perspective of Political Identity

Courtney Jung takes on the broader question at play here in *Then I Was Black: South African Political Identities in Transition.*[19] Jung examines the political and politicized identities of three groups in South Africa: colored, Zulu, and Afrikaner. Using the period 1980–1995, the author argues that these identities shift and are malleable within changing social contexts. Identities are constructed, not innate, and they are responsive to change in society. So far so good. But what Jung is after are the processes by which *political identity* (taken as separate from, say, cultural identity) is constituted, by which actors, for which purposes, and with what consequences. Political identity is taken to mean "that part of identity which emerges as salient in the organized struggle for control over the allocation of resources and power residing in the state."[20] At different points in time, these political identities have varying rather than fixed meanings, suggesting possibilities for democratic change.

At the heart of Jung's position is her thesis that political identity is a function of the interaction of five variables: *political institutions* (those that organize political space), *mobilizing discourse* (the language used by politicians to rouse particular identities), *material conditions* (resource or class positions), *available ideology* (coherent ideas that legitimate power relations), and *organization* (networks invoked by political entrepreneurs that bind members of a group to one another). In addition, there is a dependent variable, *resonance*, the extent to which people or groups or individuals internalize the meanings that flow from the five variables. In two chapters discussing Afrikaners, Jung comes to the conclusion that "quick shifts in political identity are not surprising under conditions of considerable flux among the factors that interact to construct identity."[21] She asks why whites would support a democratic transition under the National Party of Apartheid, given fears of majority rule, and she correctly concludes that "their perception of the solution"[22] was very different from the actual endgame and would later lead to claims by some of being sold out by the "traitorous" leadership of the party.

There are several problems with Jung's analysis. First, by committing to fixed variables she ironically imposes a rigidity on the very phenomenon she describes as flexible; white behavior is much more complex than these five variables; the spiritual, religious, economic, and cultural self-interests are not irrelevant to political identity. Why these five variables are deemed significant, to the neglect of others, is therefore not clear. Second, by limiting the conception of political identity to "power residing in the state," the conclusion is agreeable; the state is in black hands. But power is much more dispersed and influential than what is organized or mobilized inside political parties or within the state, and this is where "political entrepreneurs" (not only on the right wing) have been very forceful in setting constraints to the pace and depth of reform in and beyond the period described. Third, by reading Afrikaner political behavior off survey results, complexity is completely underestimated; so, for example, to say that "Cape Afrikaners do not fear *swart gevaar* (the Black menace)" (p. 129), or that 73 percent of Afrikaans speakers from the upper middle class support school integration (p. 132) is to misrepresent the deep racial divisions and fears that continue to keep schools segregated nationally and predict voting patterns in the Cape. Fourth, by locating resistance to change only within right-wing Afrikaner political bodies is to misunderstand the powerful network of cultural and other nonpolitical organizations that shape governmental responses to Afrikaners and restrain more radical actions in the state.

It is simply wrong, therefore, to make dramatic claims that "among Afrikaners, attitudes toward Apartheid and exclusionary race-based politics changed significantly during the 1980s" (p. 130) or that the "Afrikaner appears for the most part to lack resources in the nascent politics of post-Apartheid South Africa" (p. 134). Furthermore, by overstating the distinctions between cultural identity and political identity, Jung cannot explain, for example, how cultural power became the new playground for ethnic politics in the post-1994 period. None of these criticisms detracts from a general point that Afrikaner identities are, like all identities, subject to change and increasingly dispersed within this ethnic group. But political and cultural identities are not like an overcoat that can be slipped off as easily as weather changes; they are a much more complex and constrained process in which change exists

alongside continuity, and the preparedness to change is not unconditional, divorced from self-interest, or without contradictions.

### From the Perspective of Historical Inquiry

In their deliberation on "the mending of broken memories" in postwar
Germany, Jarausch and Geyer ask the fundamental question regarding
change among German adults as they reflect on late responses to the
Holocaust: "How could such a fundamental reversal of attitudes toward
the past occur?"[23] This remains a crucial question not satisfactorily answered by either political studies or social psychology. What the authors
of *Shattered Past* do is to look more intensely at both the macro (societal)
level and the micro (school) level changes that enable such "reversal."

The first important observation in this historical account of human
change is that adult Germans for the most part did not change in the
first decades following the postwar period; "the majority of the population rather preferred to cover its own complicity with merciful silence."[24]
In other words, the perpetrators and beneficiaries of evil systems do *not*
change even in response to direct confrontation with horrific knowledge. As the Allied commanders forced German communities in some
areas to march through, observe, and absorb direct knowledge of bodies piled on one another, the pieces of tortured human skin destined to
become lampshades, and the stench of torture and death, a common response was to look away even as the most patriotic among them would
still deny these events.

The optimism of the new South African elite, buoyed by the exaggeration of Christian religious symbols (Damascus, Rainbows, People of
God), that whites, confronted with horrific knowledge through the tele-
vised sessions of the Truth and Reconciliation Commission (TRC), would
step forward, acknowledge their complicity in Apartheid, and change,
was clearly misplaced. The opposite happened. Whites went into deeper
denial; worse, many rounded their anger on the TRC with charges of
exaggeration, one-sidedness, and bias. For the authors of *Shattered Past*,
this is a historical response, to deny aggressively and withdraw behind
a veil of silence. In this respect, the German and South African experiences are similar, even though in both countries there were certainly
individuals of conscience (leftist intellectuals among the Germans and

among white South Africans, for example) who not only accepted this knowledge but urged those in their groups to do the same.

The second observation from this long view of change is that the "reversal of attitudes" is unlikely to come from the participating generation—that is, those directly involved in atrocities whether as known perpetrators or as complicit bystanders. It was "only when many perpetrators were starting to pass away in the 1960s and 1970s [that] critical approaches to the German past begin to make real headway with the populace."[25] However, not only the passage of time allowed a critical consciousness to emerge; there were also changes in the surrounding environment. Such changes include the growing and compelling writings of German authors critical of the past, the small political steps taken to create greater awareness and recognition of Jewish suffering, and the establishment of both legal and prosecutorial capacity within the German state for dealing with those who killed Jews. It was the accumulation of these various events that began to occupy public consciousness and that together made it possible for another response to Germany's horrific past—something that became easier with distance from the event. What must not be missed here is that such a reading does not imply a waiting voluntarism (let time pass and things will come right, people will come around). It also suggests agency in that inspired changes led by elites (political, literary, cultural), however small, began to have an impact on the minds and hearts of successive generations.

The third observation from a historical perspective is that the capacity for the perpetrators to change arose after the political elites recognized more than one pain and "the link between the suffering of victims and perpetrators" was established. What Germans were unable to do in the decades immediately following the Second World War was raise the vexed question of German suffering under Allied bombardment, the rape and destruction caused by the Russian army, and the loss of German soldiers, "which had become more painful because it had lost its overarching national purpose."[26] As a result, everyone clung to their "more favorable memories" of the past—even the notion that National Socialism was a good idea poorly carried out.

There are some powerful resonances here with the South African condition, the inability of the new elites to recognize more explicitly the horrific memories of Boer War concentration camps and how this knowledge contributed to the virulence of a rising Afrikaner nationalism, and the fear of receding into the conditions of poverty and shame that accompanied that earlier defeat. The atrocities of Apartheid are perhaps still too close at hand. Nevertheless, what Jarausch and Geyer refer to is not recognition simply of dual sufferings but of their connection as "causally related and inextricably intertwined," without the danger of sliding onto the quicksand of moral relativism.

The fourth observation is the crucial role of educational knowledge in this process of reorientation; it was "the hiring of a new cohort of critical history teachers [that] made the subject of the Third Reich a more central part of the curriculum, and the critical work of contemporary historians helped explode popular myths."[27] Note that this required new teachers and implied that those closest to the old history in classroom pedagogy and in social practice might not have been able to rise above the burden of direct knowledge of history and society so close to the Holocaust. There are valuable lessons here, for the understandable impulse to launch "teacher training" in a new history in postconflict societies fails to take account first of the cognitive constraints and second of the emotional loyalty to a fallen regime of truth. The burden resides with these teachers when they encounter "the transmission of individual recollections that do not always agree with what is officially represented as 'history.' "[28] It would take a generational shift among those who fought for a "more critical teaching in the schools [that would] create a virtual identification with strange victims."[29]

The fifth observation about how adults change recognizes the impossibility of bringing everyone (perpetrators, victims, and bystanders) into common knowledge. For these authors, "the conflicting stories . . . may never be brought into complete harmony since they represent widely different experiences that are interconnected only by the infliction of suffering."[30] It is not the giving up of the search for common knowledge that should be recognized; it is instead the futility of insisting on "complete harmony." It is also not a pedagogical retreat from seeking harmonization, but the use of contending stories in a way that "accepts its fundamental fragmentation but that also looks for points of intersection between different experiences."[31] These "points of intersection" represent the pedagogical quest, the search for what is common, and resting with the knowledge that insisting on the one great unifying story is not a prerequisite for nation building even though it might be the pipedream of the nationalist impulse.

### Conclusion

Reversal, however, carries severe consequences when it happens without an honest confrontation with the burden of past knowledge. A pragmatic reversal might be lauded for its practical reasoning and for human adaptability to new conditions, but as emotional, psychic, and spiritual beings humans do not turn without cost; in short, you can adapt and still, in a manner of speaking, die. Jarausch and Geyer observed:

In the long run, willful forgetting risked the creation of . . . a "second guilt" because it simply hid the skeletons in the closet. . . . Mounting evidence made even reluctant Germans realize that they could only live with their haunting memories if they related their personal fate to larger processes and accepted responsibility for those whom they hurt along the way.[32]

What these warnings imply is that a pedagogy for postconflict societies must account for these complexities and engage both concealed and confessional knowledge in ways that enable an authentic encounter not only with the past but with the actors within it.

# 9    Teaching to Disrupt

The challenge reside[s] in the old and recurrent tightrope walk:
how to adopt the knowledge of the victor without damaging
the soul.[1]

What kind of public memory culture emerges from [these] contests,
especially when popular recollections conflict with intellectual
efforts to impose critical versions for didactic purposes?[2]

O N   T H E   O C C A S I O N  of a keynote address to the American Educational Research Association,[3] I presented my research on how white South African principals came to engage with and recognize the burden of knowledge they carried into the present, and how such knowledge laid the foundation for their decisions to transform their formerly all-white Afrikaans schools into sites for the practice of social justice.[4] During question time, one of the most distinguished leftist scholars in the academy in the United States stood up and said, "I follow your work and I heard you today; my question is, whatever happened to critical theory?" I do not know if it was the flattery of having such an eminent scholar claiming to "follow" my work, or the sheer directness of the question, that had me mumbling something incoherent about there being many kinds of critical theory and that my theoretical work took its critical meaning from the context in which education was practiced. At the time, I was certainly not happy with the answer but I knew that the questioner was not alone among my progressive friends who wondered quietly whether this was *critical* theory after all.

I was raised as a graduate student on critical theory, and especially critical theories of education that went by variant names such as critical pedagogy or emancipatory education or border pedagogy. With another graduate student,[5] I devised and taught an innovative class on critical education during my graduate school years, and I brought to the Stanford University campus such luminaries as Henry Giroux, Patti Lather, and Peter McLaren. I read everything from the translated Paulo Freire texts on dialogical education[6] to the Marxist critiques of schooling by Michael Apple[7] and Jean Anyon,[8] to reproduction models of schooling held up in the classic text of Bowles and Gintis on *Schooling in Capitalist America*,[9] to the response of the resistance theorists (principally Giroux[10] and Paul Willis[11]) as well as feminist (Lather[12]) and race theorists (such as Cameron McCarthy[13]), who took on and refined the class-based critiques of education. As a high school teacher, I was especially fascinated by Ira Shor[14] and Marilyn Frankenstein[15] and Jesse Goodman,[16] who tried to bring practical meaning for activist educators to the arcane theoretical formulations of people such as Giroux. And I read everything I could lay my hands on about the anticolonial critiques of Third World schooling, such as Martin Carnoy's *Education as Cultural Imperialism*[17] and Julius Nyerere's richly imaginative alternatives in *Education for Self-Reliance*.[18] For someone coming out of the oppressive regime of Apartheid education, critical theory was almost an inevitable attraction to help understand and change not just racist pedagogy in South Africa but the entire oppressive system within which it anchored its logic.

Critical theory remains a crucial body of scholarship in education that offers a lens for understanding the role of schools in perpetuating and subverting the race, class, and gender interests of state and society. But critical theory, interpreted broadly,[19] is severely limited in postconflict situations for making sense of troubled knowledge and for transforming those who carry the burden of such knowledge on both sides of a divided community. Critical theory receives and constructs the world as divided between black and white, working and privileged classes, citizens and illegal immigrants, men and women, straight and queer, oppressors and oppressed; its dialogical pretenses notwithstanding, the world is taken as torn among rival groups.

Critical theory then takes sides, once this divided world is constructed in terms of these polarities. The goal of a critical education is liberation, to free the oppressed (those on the underside of history) from the shackles of their oppression, and to take on evil systems and resist the agents of exploitation. As one review put it, "The primary goal of critical pedagogy is to empower students to understand the links between knowledge, history, and power and to use this knowledge to resist hegemonic structures and dominant ideologies."[20] Or in a primer on the subject, critical pedagogy is "the concern with transforming oppressive relations of power in a variety of domains that lead to human oppression."[21]

The evangel of critical theory therefore enables us to see the world from the perspective of those denied human rights or economic access or racial justice. Though critical theory has moved beyond the incisive class analyses of the 1960s[22] into a more richly textured account of the *intersectionalist*[23] character of oppression, it remains a *pedagogy of the oppressed.*[24]

Of course, much of the intellectual labor that spawned critical theories of education came from within advanced capitalist societies, principally the United States, and this location in part explains the rather fixed terms of the debate—the oppressed classes struggling against the overwhelming power of an oppressive system.[25] Still, the focus of this critical literature is less on what to do with the racist or tribalist in the classroom and more to do with how to "empower" or give "voice" or lend "recognition" to those marginalized within school and society.[26] The often facile deployment of these categories, of course, tends to gloss over the complexities of power and inequality represented in the classroom, a point made elegantly in Ellsworth's famed critique of the limits of critical pedagogy.[27]

Yet it is not only that critical theory divides the world; in its more radical version the enemy is not a human Other but a capitalist system, oppressive processes, imposing ideologies, the neoliberal state. The task is to "face capital down,"[28] to challenge oppressive structures and destabilize regnant pedagogies and beliefs. Such a conception of the other side, without real human beings to encounter, engage, confront, and change, has little value for a postconflict pedagogy. This is not to deny the systemic and institutionalized character of oppression, but simply to lament the denial of what confronts teachers in schools and universities in the aftermath of genocide and conflict: real human beings. There is a different and more compelling question that confronts teachers within postconflict societies, one posed so poignantly by Freema Elbaz-Luwisch. It is, "How is education possible when there is a body in the middle of the room?"[29] Elbaz-Luwisch talks about the kind of pedagogy appropriate to contexts where Arab/Palestinian and Jewish students face one another in the same classroom. By extension, this is a question that applies equally to black and white children in the post-Apartheid classroom, Catholic and Protestant children in Northern Ireland, Hutu and Tutsi children in Rwanda.[30]

These are of course extreme examples, but inequality and prejudice exist everywhere, and what critical theory does is assume that a critical pedagogy can lead what is sometimes presented as a socially homogeneous group of teachers and students toward a common understanding of the nature of oppression and how to confront its systemic elements.[31] But classrooms are themselves deeply divided places where contending histories and rival lived experiences come embodied with indirect (and sometimes *direct*) knowledge into the same pedagogical space to create deeply complex challenges for teachers. Indeed, even within this space the divisions are not restricted to the student body. The teacher is implicated within the social and pedagogical narrative, not some empowered educator who has figured out the problems of an unequal world and stands to dispense this wisdom to receiving students. It is a point made by Gur-Ze'ev in criticizing the positive view held in critical theory of the position of the oppressed, "as if their self-evident knowledge is less false than that which their oppressors hold as valid."[32] The teachers are themselves carriers of troubled knowledge, and this has serious implications for critical education.

It follows therefore that it is not simply the master narratives of the official curriculum or the controlling ideologies of state examinations or the capitalist interests of the textbook industry that are at stake in the critical classroom; it is also the people there, the bodies in the classroom, who carry knowledge within themselves that must be engaged, interrupted, and transformed. Moreover, these bearers of received knowledge do not come with one story about the past, a common understanding of the present, and a shared vision of the future. It is divided knowledges *within* the classroom that constitute the starting point for a postconflict pedagogy.

Taking sides, as in critical theory, is therefore not a very productive stance in settings where "the clash of martyrological memories" confronts the teacher of the memory holders. The goal of a postconflict pedagogy under these circumstances is first to understand the emotional, psychological, and spiritual burden of indirect knowledge carried by all sides in the aftermath of conflict. The teacher takes a position, for sure, but in a way that creates a safe space within which the afflicted on all sides can speak openly and without fear of dismissal. Furthermore, even from positions in which the teacher is herself implicated—like the black teacher hearing white grievances about black people—there is at least an attempt to understand how such knowledge came about, what it does to white students, and then how that knowledge can be productively engaged.

The important point here is that in the rush to judgment and openly taking one side, critical theory dislodges the teacher from a compassionate involvement with the knowledge of the other side. Such positioning estranges the teacher from those who are arguably most in need of critical engagement with their troubled knowledge—and makes it impossible for constructive confrontation and transformation of this knowledge.

Again, by dividing the world neatly into rival camps—the oppressor and the oppressed—a self-righteous stance is assumed that absolves the teacher/liberator or the critical theorist from critically engaging their own place in the state of oppression. This position is certainly not to suggest a moral relativism that does not name and confront racism or tribalism or classism as destructive ideologies imposed by one group on another; but it does permit self-scrutiny and at least acknowledgment of one's own demons as critical educator, thereby opening up possibilities for personal transformation in the engaged classroom. Put bluntly, in any oppressive situation the moral world is a lot more complex than critical theory suggests.

Apartheid could not sustain itself without black collaboration, and the same Apartheid could not be overthrown without white solidarity. Black South African elites are as much part of the capitalist system of exploitation as are their white compatriots, while prejudice and bigotry are not restricted to white citizens. Again, the general dilemma of white racism and exploitation visited upon blacks historically is not being questioned here; it is simply the point that, within schools and society, critical theory often comes off as a position that floats above the moral, ideological, and political messiness of real classrooms—encasing itself in a language of "certainty, abstraction and universalism."[33]

## Critical Theory as Postconflict Pedagogy

Undoing oppression in dangerous and divided communities requires bringing together the perpetrators and the victims in the same dialogic space. This means there is diminished opportunity for such a dialogic encounter in segregated classrooms, for the presence and the passion of the Other enables the clash and engagement with conflicting and conflicted knowledges. The longer schools remain segregated—and in cases where schools become resegregated—the chances of creating opportunities for a postconflict pedagogy to take root are dramatically reduced.[34] This does not mean inventive teachers in same-race classrooms cannot and do not create such extracurricular moments of encounter with others, or that white teachers in black schools, for example, cannot provide such opportunities for cross-racial engagement through skillful teaching and exemplary leadership. But it does mean that intense and sustained opportunities for prolonged engagement among white and black students (in this case) are absent and the chances of separate knowledges being retained, with all the consequences of stereotype and racism, will remain. Moreover, separate education simply hardens the boundary lines that separate young people coming in from already divided communities.

With this in mind, what constitutes the *critical* in such a critical theory of education? More specifically, what are the critical elements of a postconflict pedagogy? I propose nine key elements emerging from the stories and experiences captured in this book.

### The Power of Indirect Knowledge

A critical theory of education as conceived in this study recognizes the power of indirect knowledge. Students come into the school or university classroom with powerful ideas and constructs about the past, present, and future. They carry knowledge of a past in which they did not live or which they did not experience, and yet it is a knowledge that has profound individual and social consequences for how they live, how they learn, and how they see. This knowledge is both cognitive and emotional, for what the second generation of children carry with them is strongly attached to their ethnic, cultural, religious, language, and even political identities. It does not matter that they were not "there"; they nevertheless behave as if they were, and this poses complex questions for the kind of critical pedagogy that needs to be deployed to reach and engage young children and adults.

It is not that these second-generation children carry knowledge of specific historical events. They probably do not "know" the detail of dates and commanders in the South African War, or the information about specific atrocities in encounters with English imperialists or Zulu warriors. What they carry with them is thematic knowledge, meaning knowledge of broad themes about conquest and humiliation, struggle and survival, suffering and resilience, poverty and recovery, black and white.[35] Although the more outrageous themes are no longer trumpeted in public spaces, the underlying ideological and emotional attachments remain more or less undisturbed.[36]

Because indirect knowledge is also emotional knowledge, it can be explosive in classroom situations in which teachers are unprepared to mediate such engagement. When such pedagogical explosions happen, from the side of white students, they involve both the teacher and the black students in the same space. Therefore to say that indirect knowledge is consequential is to imply that teacher preparation programs need to take account of this phenomenon in developing educators and that in-service programs must prepare teachers in practice for something they did not have to encounter before. Indirect knowledge has curricular implications; now the design of what is taught has to anticipate a new kind of knowledge—one that is not simply a reflection of knowledge built in a previous grade in, say, algebra, but knowledge gained in a broader spectrum of social institutions about, say, the struggle to establish the Afrikaans language.

Indirect knowledge is also partial knowledge. Of course, it needs to be remembered that all knowledge is partial and that the choice every school and teacher make about what to teach is not simply an intellectual decision about appealing knowledge or a planning decision about appropriate knowledge (say, for a particular grade level) but also a political decision about valued knowledge. This partiality, though, refers on the one hand to what white students do not learn in their choice of knowledge themes about the past and where there is little attempt to even consider the possibility of rival or alternative knowledge. On the other hand, the partiality refers to how the students learn what they do, the emotions and the outrage that accompany and surround thematic knowledge, and the ethnic ideals and racial ambitions such knowledge carries over to white children from one generation to the next and through, until recently, relatively closed networks of social institutions.

It is easier for teachers to recognize cognitive or intellectual knowledge as prior knowledge to be accounted for in designing, planning, and executing teaching. Every student teacher comes close to reciting the Ausubelian[37] dictum that the most important thing influencing learning is what the learner already knows. Yet it is much more difficult to convince educators that the same applies to social or political knowledge, and that attempts to chart the nature, origins, intensity, and meaning of indirectly received knowledge are as vital to the effectiveness of any kind of pedagogical intervention.

Any teacher who fails to recognize the existence and the influence of indirect knowledge, in, say, a history classroom or a language seminar, might as well be in a minefield. It is true, of course, that teachers have found nimble ways of navigating these minefields to circumvent any controversy or conflict by relaying official knowledge in very technical terms or doing so in all-white (or all-black) classrooms, or avoiding the conflict altogether. Such curricular or pedagogic aversion postpones deep-rooted problems, continues to extend the supremacist ideas of white children, leaves unresolved the burden of knowledge they carry, and denies the possibility of moving schools and community toward what Paul Gilroy calls a planetary humanism.[38]

### The Importance of Listening

The natural compulsion of any teacher is to tell, demonstrate authority, and impart knowledge. This is especially the case in authoritarian societies, and it explains the spectacular failure of Western pedagogies in Third World states because of its insistence on open, critical, and student-centered classrooms.[39] When students initiate a question, the familiar impulse of the educator is to anticipate and correct, respond and direct an answer toward the goals of the lesson. This representation of the teacher as the authority who knows all and who controls the classroom is routinely presumed in texts and manuals on classroom management and student discipline. It is especially the case that when controversial questions or difficult subjects emerge, the teacher is even more attentive to "managing" the classroom situation lest things get out of control.

Unfortunately, this is the direct opposite of what is required for a critical dialogue in divided societies, schools, and classrooms on subjects of history, identity, and power. What a postconflict pedagogy demands is a very different approach, where the teacher has to consciously position herself to listen; this will not come naturally, but without it there is no chance of any speaking and certainly no opportunity for listening. This kind of proposition implies a highly skilled teacher who is not only confident in the subject matter and comfortable with diverse students but who is competent to manage difficult thematic knowledge. In other words, the success of a postconflict pedagogy depends almost entirely on the qualities of those who teach.[40]

The problem with listening is that even well-intentioned teachers are emotionally drawn into student stories in ways that could put them off balance in critical dialogues of the kind required for cross-border engagements. In the outbursts of the white students returning from the Apartheid Museum, a black teacher will often feel offended and rush to give a moral corrective, or shut down unappreciative comment, or even accuse a student of racial indifference. A white teacher under attack for an action perceived by black students to be racist or taking sides could become defensive and find it difficult to listen to what students have to say. This is emotionally taxing work, yet the steady position of the teacher is crucial for critical dialogue.

Listening is obviously more than the physical act of receiving auditory stimuli that flow from student to teacher. It is, more correctly, a process of hearing. This means listening for the pain that lies behind a claim, the distress that is concealed in an angry outburst, the sense of loss that is protested in a strident posture. Listening in a postconflict pedagogy does not mean "anything goes" and that the recklessness of accusation is simply tolerated. Not at all. The teacher has a crucial role in setting an atmosphere that enables talking and listening to occur in the first place, and at crucial points to reprimand where talking randomly insults other students or the teacher herself. But hearing in this sense means delaying interruption, opening up expression, and understanding the claims and the silences, the body language, the verbal expression, the pain inside the voice.

Listening in a postconflict pedagogy is therefore an active rather than a passive event; but it is also attentive to being evenhanded in allowing all to speak in equal measure. This is difficult, for the teacher has to listen to and follow what is being said, while at the same time being conscious of who spoke, what was said, how it was said, and what was not said. The identity of the speaker matters, and giving voice to students in a tense and intense critical dialogue is about allowing expression while being conscious of one's own identity all the time. Listening is also important in terms of who does not speak at all; an observant teacher is listening for silences, for sulking, for anger, and for disappointment. This requires emotional attunement to the classroom as a whole and is another level of listening crucial for enabling and sustaining critical dialogue between white and black students. It is also critical knowledge for disrupting received knowledge.

### Disruption of Received Knowledge

Listening indicates respect, not agreement; it is an empathic attempt to understand, not an amoral attempt to condone. The indirect knowledge that students receive and carry should be directly challenged and critically engaged as a matter of social justice—for white students. This indirect knowledge that the second generation brings into learning and living spaces comes from closed circles of socialization that reinforce single messages about white superiority and black subordination. It essentializes and triumphalizes a white ethnic identity in opposition to rival identities—black, English, other—and in the process it assigns differential and hierarchical value to these subordinate identities. For these reasons alone, indirect knowledge should be made explicit, and its potential and real harm should be discussed openly.

The harm that white knowledge imposed on black children is well documented under and after Apartheid,[41] and the scars are still readily visible deep into the years of democracy. What is less obvious in the critical literature on schooling is what indirect knowledge does to the second generation of Apartheid's rulers. Their received knowledge renders white students incapable of competent cross-cultural communication; it limits their ability to gain freely from the richness of the intercultural experience; it has done as yet unmeasured harm to their racial psyches (masters one moment, equal citizens the next, and minority subjects forever in the new social order); it leaves them isolated and fearful within the new national arrangement, where, no matter what they do, whites are framed by the majority as racial suspects all the time; it deprives them of the skills, knowledge, and values to meaningfully access the changing and more cosmopolitan knowledge of the new regime; and it leaves them stunted in their social, moral, and emotional development in the same way Apartheid distorted their parents' sense of themselves within the human community—a distortion transmitted to the children. Why is it that nobody writes about this?[42]

It does not help that the post-Apartheid state produces official victims—those who deserve empathy, support, and resources and those who do not. Official victims do not include poor whites, even though socioeconomic status is a more equitable and sensible way of accounting for difference in a capitalist society that professes nonracialism. In the new narrative, official victims alone carry a burden from the past; white parents and their children do not. This is crucial, for the pain of white second-generation students shows that even though they were not directly involved in the atrocities, not being born at the time, they nevertheless inherit relative economic privilege as well as the pounding burden of guilty knowledge.

For these reasons alone, a postconflict pedagogy demands that the received knowledge of white students be engaged and interrupted. They, too, are victims of Apartheid, and their heroic stories of conquest and narratives of uniqueness must be disrupted in ways that achieve liberation for white students.

Such disruptive knowledge requires white students to be set in critical dialogue with black students; to observe examples of leadership and living that counter and confront their own logics of race and identity; and to engage the new knowledge presented (the Apartheid Museum, for example) through reexamination of the old knowledge given (the Voortrekker Monument, as the counterpoint example).

### The Significance of Pedagogic Dissonance

The value of pedagogic dissonance cannot be overstated. It is *pedagogic* because it is designed to teach, without the necessity of speaking, the contradictions inherent in a racially organized and racist worldview. Dissonance happens when, for example, a white student observes a black student outperforming him in mathematics, and when the evidence is irrefutable in this subject that white patriarchs singled out as "not for him, the Bantu,"[43] white doubt sets in and the process of disruption unfolds.

This was the case with Surgeon Xolo, a brilliant young black high school graduate who scored reasonable marks in his rural, black high school in mathematics. Sought out to come into the Faculty of Education and enjoy unfamiliar resources, he scored the highest marks in mathematics in all his education classes from the first to the fourth year of study, and he did this in the midst of almost all-white classes composed of students from well-endowed white schools with qualified teachers in mainly middle-class suburbs. At one of the many prize-giving ceremonies, this one for a team task, a white woman student in her acceptance speech tells the mainly white crowd, "I was only able to do this because of Surgeon." There is a massive pedagogic dissonance on display here, one that does not need a moralizing "see what happens when" lesson by teachers. It is simply there in a public and disruptive way; it is all the more powerful because it is not "taught" directly.

A single incident of pedagogic dissonance does not of course lead to personal change, but it can *begin* to erode sure knowledge. It is, however, the collection of dissonant events, spread over multiple school years, that eventually collapses the foundations of indirect knowledge. Dissonance happens when black school or university leaders step forward with acts of kindness and generosity toward their white staff. Seen from the other side, dissonance is unavoidable when a white woman undergraduate student comes into the office of a black male dean to hold his hand and bless him. Dissonance is imposed on a school or university campus when the institutional culture and the public curriculum includes and integrates multiple knowledges within a social justice framework.

The case for dissonance in a postconflict pedagogy is not, however, a simplistic concern for "overcoming resistance"[44] or "motivating the disinterested" among privileged students. It is, rather, a pedagogical commitment to locate, interrogate, and engage troubled knowledge within (in this case) white students in ways that permit disruption of received authority. Only in this way, through human engagement, can a broader inquiry into the ideological and structural foundations of racism proceed.

Even so, direct and unmediated confrontation with disruptive knowledge seldom works; it is more likely to fuel egotistical aggression, as we have seen. Taking the way white students live, and asking them to reflect on what they embrace (such as the process of coming to know the domestic servant as human and not only as servant), is more likely to begin to alter secure and intimate knowledge. For interruption of received knowledge to work, the white student must first be drawn into a trusting relationship, which will not be achieved if the new nationalists merely inscribe victor knowledge onto a new curriculum.

### Reframing Victors and Victims

When human beings from opposite sides of a divided community begin to honestly engage one another, they are often drawn toward the core of each other's humanity. In witnessing the weaknesses of others, we see their humanity reflected within our own. This is the story of Pumla Gobodo-Madikizela, when she interviews the icy Apartheid killer Eugene de Kock in his prison cell;[45] it is the story of Dan Bar-On who as survivor of the Holocaust interviews the children of the perpetrators;[46] it is the story of Nelson Mandela as he towers morally and emotionally over his captors and his accusers, leaving no doubt that a simple narrative of black victim and white victor or black victor and white victim cannot begin to capture this unexpected complexity of the human condition.

One of the reasons why we have made such little progress in resolving race and racism in society is that we set the accusatory stage, demanding that white teachers and students change their behavior in relation to black people. What we do not allow in this strident posture is an examination of how the white racist is himself scarred by and dehumanized through his own bigotry.[47] Nor do we spend time asking and inquiring how this damning belief system came about within the biography of the bigot. We certainly do not find it worth the time and effort to begin probing what lies behind such disgusting behavior for, if we did, we would be peering into a dark and uncomfortable pit where we are likely to see something of our own selves.

What is required is a pedagogical reciprocity in which both sides are prepared to move toward each other. Put simply, the white person has to move across the allegorical bridge toward the black person; the black person has to move in the direction of the white person. Critical theory demands the former; a postconflict pedagogy requires both. The quest for understanding therefore works both ways and is simply not possible when the daggers are drawn on all sides and the powerful refuse to talk to the other side; this is a recipe for war and annihilation.

In the classroom situation this is yet another example that conveys the complexity of teaching: How does a teacher even begin to create the pedagogical atmosphere in which the starting point is recognition of the humanity of the Other? It has to begin by insisting that both sides at least make the effort to listen empathically and therefore patiently to what the other has to say. It requires teaching that once the initial statement (or outburst) has been delivered, the speakers should be moved in the direction of talking about what lies behind the outward expression of a position. "What are you afraid of? Why do you feel so strongly about that? Where did you learn about this?" This kind of tactical questioning does not take what is first said at (in a manner of speaking) face value. It understands that often the outward expression masks pain, anxiety, and fearfulness. Even the most egotistical expression of racism conceals vulnerability that can and should be laid bare.

"What are you so angry about? Do you really think it is this? How did this make you feel? Has this happened to you before? Tell me about it." These are the kinds of questions I often ask my black colleagues and students when they complain about racism. These claims are often real, and it is devastating as a leader to witness the hurt of racial bigotry inflicted on your colleagues and students. It is important to acknowledge the racism and its effects, and it is especially important to embrace a colleague or student who has been the target of such violence.

But in a postconflict pedagogy, the teacher's intervention has to go beyond acknowledgment and embracing those hurt by such acts. A postconflict pedagogy requires that the target of racism be empowered to confront such behavior and do so from a position of strength. "What do you think can be done to change this behavior?" This is a startling question, because it places the agency back in the hands of the person insulted. It does not dwell on the hurt, and it does not feed a sense of defeat. Changing the storyline is vital, even as the pain of racist assault is acknowledged.

### Acknowledgment of Brokenness

The origins of brokenness come from the spiritual world of evangelical faith. It is the construct of brokenness, the idea that in our human state we are prone to failure and incompletion, and that as imperfect humans we constantly seek a higher order of living. Brokenness is the realization of imperfection, the spiritual state of recognizing one's humanness before the forgiving and loving power of God. But brokenness is more; it is the profound outward acknowledgment of inward struggle done in such a way as to invite communion with other people and with the divine.

This might be unfamiliar and even uncomfortable territory for some, but it is a powerful set of ideas for relating to other people in a divided school or university community. The aggression of the white grade ten girls (see Chapter 3) breaks down in the face of an acknowledgment of my personal struggles with white people given my own pain and my haunting memories. I do not need to tell this story. I could pretend it is all their dilemma, their burden, their history. I could extricate myself from the powerful moment offered by the grade ten questioner and place myself in the position of the didactic and moral authority, giving a neat set of instructions for coming to terms with the consequences of Apartheid.

In a postconflict pedagogy, therefore, the teacher and the leader are part of the classroom story. They are not distant and "objective" pedagogues floating above the emotional and political divides that separate those in the classroom. Teachers in this pedagogy not only bring in their own identities; they also carry their own knowledge of the past.

Such knowledge is out in the open and is shared as part of the process of making sense of how to live together in the shadow of a shared history and with the prospects of a common future.

Brokenness compels dialogue. The grade ten girls suddenly want to share their own stories and how they wrestle with parents and other significant adults in their lives, caught between an old knowledge that is faltering and a new knowledge that is compelling. They have questions about what happened and how it could have happened, and as they move forward to talk they risk both confiding in a (black) stranger and also breaking primordial bonds of loyalty with the (white) family. This is a significant moment in a postconflict pedagogical situation; it is the beginning of the end for the certainty conveyed thus far through indirect knowledge. It is possible only when and because white students witness the humanity of the other side through acknowledgment of brokenness.

Contrary to the logic of masculine thought, brokenness is not weakness. By contrast, brokenness reveals inner strength, the capacity to acknowledge not only human frailty but also human sameness. It is the paradox conveyed in Christian verse: "When I am weak, then I am strong." This sounds like a near-impossible task for a teacher trained to (and indeed, eager to) establish her authority in the classroom. Yet it is crucial to draw the students in and, more important, demonstrate what it means to live openly and honestly with one's own knowledge about and in relation to those in the classroom.

### The Importance of Hope

When the white grade ten girl asks the pertinent question "How?" (how do I move across the bridge toward those who look like the black men who almost killed me in a car hijacking?) she is not only posing a question about the mechanics or the methodology of change; she is expressing a desire for the future. In this context, "How?" is a hope question, a recognition that, in crossing, a better outcome may come from the togetherness.

A postconflict pedagogy is founded on hope. It does not get lost within a circularity of oppression talk where whites retell stories of "them" as being less and blacks retell stories of "us" as being harmed. It is strongly against any sense of victimhood, for this traps white and black in an endlessly downward spiral of defeat. This kind of critical pedagogy recognizes the power and the pain at play in school and society, and its effects on young people, and then it asks "How?"—how things could be better. It shifts martyrological memories toward seeing the possibility in others, and in ourselves. But this kind of sight (vision) is not possible if the characters in the divided setting are seen as essentially evil white racists, or as terminally disempowered black victims. Hope imagines, in a very real sense, a way out of the two quagmires, one black and one white. Hope starts by asking the same question within the pedagogical situation—"How do I move toward . . . ?"—in order to relocate to a safer and more secure place, with others.

Hope in a postconflict pedagogy is not some empty, air-headed, and aspirational quest of pedagogical Pollyannas detached from the hard ideological and material conditions that constrain and shape interracial relations. In this argument, hope recognizes and works through those conditions of oppression by recognizing the common bonds and bondage of white and black students and teachers in school and in the community. Hope requires recognition of racism and the privilege it bestows; hope demands that the consequences of white history and power be redressed. However, it cannot be taken on without the bonds of solidarity being first established between white and black, and this in turn cannot happen until the participants in the classroom and indeed in the community come to understand and confront themselves, and their disparate knowledges, in the historical and contemporary story.

Hope in this kind of pedagogy therefore begins with the quest for individual and collective understanding within the classroom. Under postconflict conditions, there can be no discourse of—or even desire for—hope unless and until human beings within the same living and learning spaces, students and teachers, achieve some amount of self-understanding, some measure of common humanity, and some degree of disrupted knowledge.

A postconflict pedagogy founded on hope once again requires intergenerational stories of victimhood to be disrupted. I believe that in addition to the structural faultlines that sustain divided communities there are repeated and well-worn stories of defeat transmitted from one generation to the next. In this regard, I distinguish stories that remind black children about their shared heritage of a colonial past or a slave history (which is crucial) from stories that conclude with a terminal ending of despair and distress. What destroys hope is that the story of the bondage of slavery is not always accompanied by a story of the bravery of the enslaved. One pedagogical story told by a black parent to the next generation might be to see Nelson Mandela as imprisoned for his beliefs by evil white captors; a complementary way of telling the story is to show how he imprisoned his white guards by the sheer force of his moral authority and his political cause. On its own, the first story leads to despair; the second story signals hope.

Hope in a postconflict pedagogy inside divided communities insists that the stories about oppressing and overcoming be mutually conceived and resolved. In other words, it is essential that students understand that from the beginning white resisters to slavery and colonialism were fighting on the side of the black cause. In Rwanda stories must be told of Hutu resisters who lost their lives as one of the most efficient genocides in history was visited on the Tutsi minority by their Hutu neighbors. Stories must be told of the Germans who stood by Jews, of the Afrikaners who stood by blacks, of the whites in the civil rights marches in the United States—all of whom faced the same ferocity of attack as those originally targeted for their race or ethnicity or religion. Embedded in such stories of solidarity are stories of hope. What students learn is that there is no genetic or social "essence" that predisposes any group of people toward hatred, or for that matter toward love.

### The Value of Demonstrative Leadership

For a postconflict pedagogy to gain any traction in divided and suspicious learning contexts, the critical key is the quality and depth of leadership. I take leadership to be less a formal position than a set of dispositions; not an allocated posting but the ability to influence the behavior of followers.[48] This leadership concept therefore accepts the notion of distributed leadership, and it also understands that such leadership can come from students, teachers, or principals within any educational setting.

It became repeatedly clear to me at UP that white students, staff, and parents had no reason to accept my authority beyond the formal designation of "dean of the Faculty." Indeed, in the first months of my appointment there was very little contact with white students. They walked right past me, heads dropping or staring straight ahead to avoid eye contact. They always seemed to be in a hurry when I was around, engaged in tight conversation with friends when I passed by. When I did initially introduce myself, there were cold stares, but out of sheer demands of Afrikaner decency they would mumble a greeting. I could not, at that time, sustain any conversation without making a fool of myself. For many, this was after all their first contact with a black person in authority of any kind, and I had more than a fair suspicion that the subject of my deanship must have come up at home and among peers.

Words, with teenagers, have very little meaning in a cynical world. Front pages of globalized media testify to a profound breakdown in leadership at all levels and across national borders. Young people know this. In postconflict situations where divides run deep, the credibility of leadership is more important than ever. Conventional leadership training focuses on and measures performance in terms of technical competence; this is not enough to bridge deep racial divisions in a community. A leader must have credibility to convince black and white students or black and white staff to even consider the possibility of crossing over.

Teachers and leaders (here, the same thing) are being watched more than they are being heard, for we know that what students remember and value is not the subject-matter content taught as much as the life led, the example set, the actions demonstrating value. In a racially divided community, it makes no sense for leaders to teach about multicultural education or espouse values of interracial community if their daily lives do not demonstrate the living out of such commitments. Do students see within the teacher a choice of close friends that goes against the grain of their own ethnic or religious origins? If not, no amount of professing in the classroom will have much meaning with youth. Do leaders speak out against injustices of any kind, but especially when they are committed by members of their own ethnic or religious or national groups? If not, they should not expect strong responsiveness to taught ideals within the student body. Do leaders demonstrate the same distress when their nation's children are killed as when the children of a self-designated "evil empire" are horrifically wounded or killed in battle?

The superficiality of common school plans that isolate compassion and consciousness within a global week or ethnic holiday or AIDS day, or even a black history month, is clearly wasting valuable curricular and pedagogical resources. Students do not respond, I have found, to empty symbolism or occasional bouts of consciousness; they are drawn toward personal involvement in their lives and daily, demonstrable commitment of what is worthwhile in the pursuit of social justice.

Students are surprised by lives and leaders who act against the grain of their own biography. Touching leadership in a postconflict pedagogy does the unexpected. It is the story of white principals integrating their formerly all-white Afrikaner schools by transforming the student body, the teaching staff, and the curriculum as well as the culture and ethos of the school in ways that embrace black citizens as part of the school community. It is the story of Sipho Ngobeni, the residence student head, as he welcomes white parents onto their historical campus in a way that embraces and includes the surprised parents. It is the story of the girl who comes to pray. When this happens, those who observe leadership come to respect it and wish to emulate it.

Such leadership against the grain can be a costly exercise. It risks losing friends and alienating family. It often draws criticism from those still comfortable within racial zones defined by their received knowledge. It means that invitations to homes and weddings dry up. This is a painful isolation that must not be underestimated in the life of the courageous leader. But leadership on principle draws in new friends and enlarges circles of friendship, eventually demanding the respect of those watching from a distance. Like any critical position, a postconflict pedagogy takes a stand on what is important and demonstrates in practice what is possible by leading upstream in divided schools and society.

### The Necessity of Establishing Risk-Accommodating Environments

White students do not rush into pedagogic spaces confessing guilt or acknowledging racism; nor do white parents suddenly own up to years of privilege at the expense of black citizens. Even when such compulsion is felt, it is extremely difficult for human beings to unburden themselves in private or public spaces. The most serious mistake of the Truth and Reconciliation Commission (TRC) in South Africa was the assumption that whites, given the platform, would stream forward to tell the truth about their complicity in and benefits from Apartheid. Chair of the TRC and Nobel Peace Laureate Archbishop Tutu was adamant that whites should use this invitation to speak the truth, and in the process advance reconciliation. This did not happen, because human beings do not willingly release painful memories, especially not on a public platform, that could draw the ire of black victims and impose the shame of association with Apartheid.

When I do such workshops on risk accommodation within the classroom, invariably a teacher or professor becomes adamant: there can be no reconciliation without truth. People need to acknowledge their racism and their privilege as a very first step, or there's nothing to talk about. This is a particularly Western way of thinking: "'fess up," as if this were an involuntary reflex to some central command. The explosion of talk shows in American public culture in which the most personal and bizarre behavior is displayed without restraint to live audiences strikes many in the Third World as disgusting. This is not the real world. Guilt and shame are more common responses to burdensome knowledge than the apparent reveling in extreme and obnoxious behavior.

Nevertheless, when I sense the adamant position that whites must simply step forward and acknowledge their racism, I ask a simple question: "Do any of you here have a memory of something so painful that you have not shared the memory with anyone, even those closest to you?" As the thud of this unexpected question takes hold in the room, I scan the faces of the participants as they struggle for a few seconds to process what was just asked. Slowly, most of the hands in the room go up, acknowledging that there is a knowledge of something known only to them that cannot be spoken.

Nothing demonstrates this point more powerfully than the acknowledgment of Günter Grass, after so many years, that he, the Nobel Laureate for literature, was actually a youthful member of Hitler's notorious Waffen-SS during the Second World War. For half a century, the author of *The Tin Drum* was the moral conscience of postwar Germany, urging his fellow citizens to own up to their terrible knowledge about the Holocaust and their role in that horrendous conflict. But he harbored secret knowledge such that "What I had accepted with the stupid pride of youth I wanted to conceal after the war out of a recurrent sense of shame."[49]

It is essential in a postconflict pedagogy that the teacher create the atmosphere, and structure the teaching-learning episodes so as to reduce the risk of speaking openly about direct and indirect knowledge. Students must be able to speak without feeling they will be judged or despised for what they say. They must know that in a divided classroom there will be an attempt to "hear them out," no matter if their ideas seem to be outrageous or even offensive. The students must be reassured through the example of the teacher-leader that the teacher-leader can be trusted with such personal and ethnic knowledge. What is true, in this example, for white students is of course true also for black students, especially when the latter group is a minority within the classroom. To repeat, this creation of a risk-accommodating environment does not mean that "anything goes" and that a student can spout offensive words about another group without consequences. Long before the pedagogic encounter, the atmosphere should have been set, the terms of engagement explained, the rules of dialogue shared. Such difficult dialogues can take place only if trust in the teacher-leader is already ensured through demonstration of an example of conciliation within and outside the classroom. The notion that "the lesson" starts in the classroom is misguided.

Nonetheless, such encounters remain risky. I used to speak about risk-removing classroom climates; it is clearly impossible. At best the teacher will work toward a risk-accommodating environment in which students, in taking risks, are assured they will be treated fairly and their positions given serious consideration. It is only when students trust the teacher-leader, however, that the ability to speak is made possible. It is also when such trust is established that the teacher can take what is said and steer the students in the divided classroom toward a dialogue that counters racism, sexism, and classism (among other things that divide), and demonstrate the harmfulness and the offensiveness of bigotry in school and society.

## Finally, Changing

I now find it possible to concede what I never thought possible. This is that the more I taught, led, and lived among my white students, the more I found myself loving them as my children and caring for them as my own. The more I witnessed their social awkwardness, their clumsiness with other people's language, their fear of what was foreign, and their anxiety and aggression, the more I wanted to embrace them. The more I came to know their troubled biographies, the more I understood how humans can become victims of indirect knowledge. The more I saw my white students struggle to come to terms with this completely new terrain of transition from racial rule to democracy, the more I wanted to help them traverse this difficult road.

I now know that my students sensed, as only they could, my own vulnerabilities. They knew this was new territory for me as well. I know they grasped how difficult it was for me to stride across a wide open quad to a circle of white students and try to gain access to their world and their conversations, and yet leave them with a word of hope and encouragement. They knew it was so difficult for me, because it was difficult for them. They knew I struggled with my own racial demons, just as they struggled with theirs. They saw my clumsiness on stage, my heart-stopping moments trying to translate both language and custom even as I sought to lead and inspire my charges. They sensed my anxiety when black and white students gathered around my table for lunch, and I so desperately wanted all of them to enjoy one another's languages, traditions, and beliefs. I come away from this experience of leading feeling that I was a direct beneficiary of a postconflict pedagogy, and that my most powerful teachers were my white students.

As the Afrikaner student moved across the ordered graduation stage before a huge audience to receive his degree after four years of study, he bowed in my direction and said loudly enough for some of my colleagues to hear: "*dankie prof vir wat u vir my gedoen het*" (Thank you, Professor, for what you have done for me). As the two immaculately dressed senior representatives of the Faculty invited me for coffee to show off their premises on the main campus where they had been elected onto the university's SRC, they made two moving speeches about the transformation of their lives under our leadership; one was a black girl from a rural fishing village, the other an Afrikaner boy from the big city, Pretoria.

And as the large collection of young people in the Jacaranda Children's Choir sang under the baton of the conductor, a dear Afrikaner colleague, I saw a dream come true after years of struggle. I had long argued for a diverse choir of black and white children; I had insisted on a more inclusive repertoire; I urged the use of other African languages besides English; I wanted the heavy European character of the music replaced by a more Africa-centered music, including Afrikaans. Now, after seven years, the choir would perform one more time before I left.

Across the stage come these elementary schoolchildren, black and white. On come the African drums and Afrikaner traditional dress. Songs in African languages enrich the beautiful score while black and white dance together under the leadership of senior girls of all colors. White and black children perform traditional Zulu dances even as both groups meld into each other to sing my all-time Afrikaans favorite about a *skilpad* (tortoise) crossing a busy road. On this night, I feel a dream coming true not only for the university and for my country but for all humanity. Here, in a dramatic and colorful moment, a newly liberating knowledge is slowly displacing the stubbornness of indirect knowledge. As the choir sing their South African songs, I recall the hopeful closing verse of a song Paul Robeson made famous at a school graduation more than sixty years ago:

Our country's strong, our country's young
And her greatest songs are still unsung.[50]

# Reference Matter

# Notes

Prologue

1. Harris 2007. The archives in politics (chapter 14): 249.

2. Taken from Paul's letter to the Philippians, chapter 3, verse 20, in the King James version of the scriptures.

3. District Six was the name of the large black residential area in the inner city of Cape Town that became one of the best-known sites targeted by the Apartheid regime for "forced removals" to make way for white residence and property development. The District Six Museum in Cape Town celebrates this memory of struggle and resistance.

4. Jansen 1990 is an account of how students influenced my personal transformation as a high school teacher.

5. The "divestment movement" was a massive social energizing of students across American university campuses; see Soule 1997.

6. Most of the black universities were established as separate ethnic institutions in 1959; the University of Durban Westville (UDW) was set aside for South Africans of Indian descent. UDW was also the only university, because of the anarchy on campus, where President Nelson Mandela had to call into being a Presidential Commission of Inquiry in 1997.

7. No South African writing can escape becoming entangled in Apartheid's distasteful system of racial classification, which distinguished whites (formerly called Europeans) from Indians (South Africans of Indian descent), coloreds (claimed to be "mixed race"), and Africans (ethnic Africans, presumably). These were political categories, of course, not firm classes of people, as was demonstrated by the annual reclassification of people across these "types," during the time of the Apartheid Parliament.

8. At least since 1934, black (and international) students had sought admission to UP, but through a steadfast racist policy of refusal this was resisted until the late 1980s. What is astounding, though, is the convoluted arguments made in defense of racial exclusion and the complex arrangements for partial accommodation through registration but not class attendance; in class but not residence; on campus but not in the library; in learning but not in sport. See the fascinating account titled *Die Universiteit van Pretoria en Anderskleuriges* (The UP and other races), in Spies and Heydenrych 1987: 399–406.

9. For historians such as P. G. Nel, the origins of UP were "purely cultural," the outcome of an ethnic search for consciousness, attachment, and pursuit of values; see Nel 1982.

10. Jansen 1991b, Prah 1999, and Dubow 2006; also B. M. Du Toit 1984. For the ideological tenor and intellectual ethos that shaped UP, see Nel 1982, a collection of professorial standpoints on the occasion of the 50th anniversary of the institution. For an unusually critical account of the role of professors at UP in shaping (and contesting) nationalist versions of history, see Mouton 2007.

11. Prime Minister J. G. Strijdom received a law degree from Pretoria, and he and his predecessor, D. F. Malan, were rewarded with honorary degrees from UP. Anton Rupert, who made his millions from tobacco, was probably the best-known UP businessman. Bettie Cilliers-Barnard (painting) and Anna Neethling-Pohl (theatre) were two well-known artistic graduates. Famous judges included Frikkie Eloff, Jan d'Oliviera, and Willem van der Merwe, alongside two judges who played a crucial role in the transition: Johan Kriegler (who as chair of the Independent Electoral Commission declared the first democratic elections "substantially free and fair") and Johan van der Westhuizen (who serves on the post-Apartheid Constitutional Court). Springbok rugby captains included Wynand Malan, Naas Botha, Joost van der Westhuizen, and Victor Matfield, although three others also carried the captain's band in single matches, namely, Rudolph Straeuli, Gary Botha, and Mahlatse "Chiliboy" Ralepelle.

12. In 1932 the UP Council decided that Afrikaans would be the only medium of instruction; only six decades later, in 1994, did UP once more allow instruction in English, alongside Afrikaans.

13. This symbolism was a potent marker of the institution, and for many years UP was affectionately called the Voortrekker University.

14. I use the word *Faculty* (upper case *F*) here to refer to a subunit of organization within the university, in the same way that Americans might refer to the School of Education, etc. In other words, Faculty here does not refer to academic staff or faculty (lower case *f*), as used in the North American context.

15. Van Zyl spoke openly about "market forces" as a key driver in the university's positioning strategy, one that included a shift toward English alongside Afrikaans as the medium of instruction. This position drew predictable fire from mainstream Afrikaners who believe the struggle for language is as much a struggle for cultural recognition once political power was lost. See http://www.vryeafrikaan.co.za/site/lees .php?id=46, accessed on March 20, 2008.

16. A more detailed account of my entrance experiences and subsequent passage through UP appears in Jansen 2005.

17. Jansen 2007a is about growing up "colored" in South Africa and the enduring impact of black consciousness on my political attitudes.

18. Among other personal writings on white Afrikaans schools striving for social justice, see Vandeyar and Jansen 2008, Jansen 2007b, and Jansen 2006a, the last of which appears in abbreviated form in *UCEA (University Council for Educational Administration) Review*, XLV (3): 1–4, Fall 2006.

19. Formed in 1918, the Afrikaner Broederbond (League of Afrikaner Brothers) grew increasingly political as a front for the advancement and defense of Afrikaner

cultural, economic, and political interests, becoming a major force in nationalist politics leading up to and since 1948. In 1993, it reconstituted itself as the Afrikaner Bond, nominally open to women and blacks for the first time.

20. Translated as the Afrikaans Language and Cultural Association, the ATKV was established in Cape Town in 1930 with its target group the illiterate and poor Afrikaners streaming into the cities without a strong sense of culture, language, and identity. For a brief historical account, see the ATKV website, www.atkv.org.za/content .cfm?ipkCategoryID=927, accessed on February 2, 2008.

21. In addition to splitting the Dutch Reformed Church into racial and ethnic churches under different names (one each for white Afrikaners, Indians, coloreds, and Africans), the DRC itself split over time into several white churches with varying degrees of theological and political conservatism.

22. Chapter 8 includes an extended discussion on the parents of the second generation of Afrikaner children.

23. *Baasskap* (the state of being the boss or master) conveys racial domination over black people.

24. Jansen 2007d is a collection in book form of most of these articles.

25. The senate is a body composed mainly of senior academics and is responsible for the academic mandate of a university; the council is a university's highest decision-making body, with responsibility for broad institutional policy, hiring and firing the vice-chancellor, approval of the annual budgets, and overall governance of the university.

26. For obvious reasons of confidentiality, I will not disclose the substance of any deliberations from council or senate meetings in this or any other text.

27. One of the more fascinating accounts I heard about how *transformation* became the term of choice for explaining the transition from Apartheid was that the ready alternatives *reform* and *revolution* were both tricky devices for naming the post-1994 period. There was no revolution, in any sense, but a negotiated settlement, and even though black politicians would from time to time invoke the word in appealing to radicalized constituencies, it was clearly disingenuous to name it such. There were a lot of reforms under the Apartheid government as it tried to stall the inevitable end of white rule; but it was precisely the distasteful nature of those efforts to secure black cooption on white terms that gave *reform* a bad name.

28. One of the more talked-about essays delivered to the university community after I had served as dean for a year was a paper called "Why Tukkies Cannot Develop Intellectuals"; see Jansen 2001. My thesis was that authoritarian and fearful cultures are inimical to the emergence of intellectuals and that this enduring legacy at UP stood in the way of developing and maintaining a rich and vibrant scholarly culture. *Tukkies* is the nickname by which UP is affectionately known, an Afrikanerization of its early embodiment, then English, as the Transvaal University College, or more correctly, Tucs or Tuccies.

29. D. M. Joubert. Uitbouing van die onderrigtaak van die universiteit (Extension of the training task of the university). In Nel 1982: 25–43 (40).

30. Throughout the world, Faculties or Schools of Education always enjoy lesser status in universities than the equivalent science and engineering faculties or schools; South Africa is no exception. When financial crises hit, Education and Humanities are always the first to feel the pinch of restructuring and closure.

31. My senior colleagues told me that the vice-chancellor at the time made it clear that with the appointment of the new dean they had one more chance to prove themselves or else incorporation into and under Humanities would proceed.

32. Colleges of education, of which there were more than 100 in South Africa, fell under provincial governments and offered two- and three-year diplomas, often to students with not enough credits to study teaching at faculties of education in the universities. A major national study had shown that, with notable exceptions, the colleges were of extremely poor quality and highly inefficient as the continuing and major source of supply of new teachers. This was one of the main reasons for the demise of most of the colleges. For a detailed study of incorporation (and mergers) in this period, see Jansen 2002.

33. Another dimension of the Apartheid scheme was that universities were linked to colleges of education representing the same racial or ethnic grouping. The university as the senior partner would approve certificates and moderate examinations set by the college, and even share teaching resources. With incorporation, therefore, it was common practice that in most cases the college was incorporated into the university with which it enjoyed this historical and racial partnership. Accordingly, NKP was to be incorporated into UP.

34. This dogma was called *fundamental pedagogics*, a conservative theory of education that for years underpinned Apartheid education. A perversion of Dutch phenomenology under the educational theorist Langeveld, fundamental pedagogics rendered education as a neutral science, framed authority in God and adults as given, and in this way furnished the educational justification for the Apartheid system.

35. There were two smaller incorporations before and after that of NKP into UP in 2001. The first was before my time, of individuals from two black colleges (Laudium, an Indian township in the west of Pretoria, and Soshanguve, an African township to the north of Pretoria). The second came later and affected the entire university, the incorporation of one of the black campuses of the now "unbundled" multicampus Vista University, once designed by Afrikaner nationalists to accommodate urban blacks in the major city centers of South Africa. UP incorporated the Mamelodi campus of Vista.

36. As part of the retraining of former college staff to become researchers, reflection and analysis of the incorporation experiences was turned into joint publication. See, for example, Becker et al. 2004 and Van der Westhuizen 2004.

37. I made a firm but private decision at the time that such a relocation would be far too traumatic for older Afrikaner women, who would face two bleak choices: resign with considerable risk of economic hardship for some, or accept redeployment by the province to an education district in a black township far from their homes. This was the first time I saw, up front, what trauma the changes of 1994 could wreak on vulnerable white colleagues. As a result, I retained several of the older white women colleagues on the faculty.

38. In South Africa, a professor is a senior appointment to which academics aspire as they move from lower levels of appointment; typically the promotion pathway is from junior lecturer to lecturer to senior lecturer to associate professor and then full professor.

39. A senior leader in the university told me this college, with its considerable space and formidable resources, was built in the hope that it would one day be able to seclude white Afrikaners in this privileged space in anticipation of a change of government. I am unable to verify this.

40. I completely underestimated the difficulties of the shift to English, though it should be said that this transition was easier for the few who had a more progressive and open understanding of changes in the country. But for many others, young and old, teaching in English was extraordinarily difficult.

41. White English students definitely do not have the attraction to teaching that is so widespread among Afrikaner students, suggesting a cultural link that needs exploration. It should be added, though, that the profession within this group has also become increasingly feminized, with the particularly strong affinity among Afrikaner women to teach in early childhood education yet another aspect of this phenomenon that requires study.

42. Meyerson 2003.

## Chapter 1

1. Fourie 2006. Her reference to "the single announcement" is to the famous speech in Parliament of the last white president of the Apartheid government, F. W. de Klerk, on February 2, 1990, when he released Nelson Mandela and unbanned the exiled liberation movements.

2. Psychiatrist Dr. Rosen (Christopher Plummer) to Alicia Nash (Jennifer Connelly), wife of the schizophrenic patient John Forbes Nash (Russell Crowe), in director Ron Howard's movie *A beautiful mind.*

3. John Carlin (2004), The Deadly March of the Chosen Ones, *New Statesman*; see www.newstatesman.com/200401050015, accessed January 11, 2008. Minnie Pretorius, a UP graduate, lost her husband and three sons to a prison sentence, convicted for being part of a *Boeremag* (Boer Force) that in 2002 attempted to overthrow the state through a series of bomb attacks that caused the death of a black woman.

4. I use the reference to *settler states* only to distinguish those classical European colonies that withdrew to their geographical centers after the collapse of colonial rule, from those in which large numbers of original, white settler descendants remained afterward, as in Kenya, Zimbabwe, and South Africa. I certainly do not mean to ascribe the term *settler* to contemporary white South Africans.

5. Brewer 1989.

6. Gann and Duignan 1991.

7. Cohen 1986.

8. [Rockefeller Foundation] 1978. This study was chaired by Franklin Thomas of the Ford Foundation and focused largely on South Africa even though the original mandate was Southern Africa more broadly.

9. The subtitle of Brewer's 1989 edited work.

10. The most evocative account of the transition comes from the pen of veteran journalist Alister Sparks in a trilogy of books; see Sparks 1991, 1996, and 2003. For another journalist account of transition, see Nyatsumba 1997. For an optimistic account of the transition, see Waldmeir 1997. For a highly personal and entertaining account,

see Van Zyl Slabbert 2006. For critical and left-wing accounts of the transition, see Alexander 2002, Marais 2001, Bond 2000, and Michie and Padayachee 1997. For more conventional scholarship on the events leading to transition, see Price 1991, Spitz 2000, and Howarth and Norval 1998. By far the most incisive and insightful assessment of the political transition literature in South Africa is Guelke 1999.

11. Few words were invoked with such regularity in popular protest and scholarly writing alike to pour scorn on the Apartheid state as a "pariah" (a social outcast) among nations.

12. These were meetings in which third parties sought to bring together the leaders of the Nationalist Party Government and the African National Congress.

13. Lieberfeld (2002) defines "track-two diplomacy" as talks "explicitly intended to further conflict resolution by improving understanding and relationships between groups, by humanizing adversary groups through face-to-face meetings, and by preparing the ground for official negotiations by exploring, in an unofficial and informal setting and without commitment, underlying issues and possible solutions": 356.

14. Ibid.: 355.

15. The 61 Afrikaans-speaking intellectuals who met a delegation of 17 ANC officials for three days in July 1987 in Dakar, Senegal, and in particular the white Afrikaners, were mercilessly attacked in the Afrikaans media and by the Nationalist Government itself. Yet shortly thereafter senior Afrikaner leaders held at least six meetings with senior ANC officials in England (late 1987 to 1990).

16. Malan (2006) is a self-serving account of the Apartheid military, devoid of reflection or even the hint of concession of the illegal and murderous activities of the defense force.

17. Levy (1999) is a measured assessment of the impact of sanctions on regime change.

18. The term *constructive engagement* was originally coined by Chester Crocker, who attracted the attention of the Reagan Administration, when he served as assistant secretary of state for African affairs. Constructive engagement became the policy of the Reagan Administration toward Southern Africa, a failed policy by recent, independent accounts. See Davies 2007.

19. Between 1990 and 1994 some 14,000 deaths and 22,000 injuries were recorded. See Ramphele 2008.

20. See the thesis of Guelke 1999 on the impact of violence on the negotiations.

21. The "sunset clauses" proposed by the ANC enabled continuation of negotiations by offering both literal commitments (such as a coalition government for five years) and symbolic commitments (such as limited intervention in school governance) to nervous whites and their outgoing nationalist government.

22. Literally, "a people's state" where in Afrikaans *Volk* (people) has deep historical, emotional, and mythological meanings linked to and binding the group called Afrikaners.

23. Van der Westhuizen (2007) is a recent account of white Afrikaner opinion and politics on the transition.

24. F. W. first announced his decision to quit the post-Apartheid unity government with his white-led National Party on May 9, 1996 (effective June 30, 1996); he

then personally resigned as head of the National Party in 1997, at which point he also retired from politics.

25. An interesting case was a white ANC parliamentarian, Jennifer Ferguson, who found that she could not support, as required, the ANC's Termination of Pregnancy Bill and left Parliament. See Geisler 2000.

26. Human Rights Day (March 21), the day of the Sharpeville Massacre in which blacks protesting the hated pass laws were shot by police, leaving 69 dead and 180 wounded in 1960; Freedom Day (April 27), the date of the first democratic and non-racial elections in 1994; Youth Day (June 16), the start of the 1976 Soweto Uprising, which led to hundreds of schoolchildren being killed and thousands more imprisoned or forced into exile; and National Women's Day (August 9), the day in 1956 on which women marched on Pretoria in protest against the pass laws.

27. In theory, teachers are appointed by the head of the education department in each province; in practice, schools are seldom challenged in the names they recommend for vacant positions. This practice is now being challenged by the government in an effort to bring greater racial equity in staff appointments among white schools. But the challenge will be difficult for both political and legal reasons, including the commitment in the Schools Act to give schools greater participatory powers in decisions that affect them. This reasoning was intended to wrest power from white authorities under Apartheid and place such decisions in the hands of black governing bodies; yet this very arrangement is now being invoked by white parent bodies to protect their right to appoint teachers.

28. Although this odd statement by an ANC leader might provoke not only white but also colored and Indian angst, this is long-established policy of the liberation movement, as confirmed on the website of the ruling party with the precise wording: "The main content of the NDR (national democratic revolution) is the liberation of Black people in general and Africans in particular. They are in the majority, and they constitute the overwhelmingly larger majority of the people" under the heading "Nation Formation and Nation Building. The National Question in South Africa"; see www.anc .org.za/ancdocs/discussion/nation.html, accessed on December 24, 2007.

29. Marris (1987) offered the initial conceptual frame for my thinking about how Afrikaners experienced democratic transition after Apartheid. The original publication was produced much earlier (1974) by Pantheon Books. Marris explores the meaning of loss and change in everyday life through studies of bereavement and the stages of recovery among those who lost loved ones.

30. Jenkins 2007.

31. An early reversal of this kind was the Constitutional Court's decision in *City Council of Pretoria v. Walker* (CCT 8/97), where a white man from "old Pretoria" complained of discrimination in paying his municipal bills on the grounds that he was treated differently in the payment demand from black residents in the surrounding townships of Mamelodi and Atteridgeville. The court ruled that aspects of his treatment by the municipality amounted to "unfair" and "indirect" discrimination against him.

32. Former Defense Minister Mosiuoa Lekota (now leader of the new Congress of the People opposition party) was one of those lone voices making this point at regular intervals, such as his "Time to Move Beyond Diversity" speech (Sapa, October 26, 2004, Johannesburg) and his address to the Parliamentary Portfolio Committee on

Defense, where he posed the stirring and unusual question, "When will we cease to be Africans, coloreds, Indians, and whites and merely South Africans? This is the question we must ask ourselves"; see http://news.bbc.co.uk/2/hi/Africa/3770143, accessed on December 24, 2007.

33. Giliomee 2003.

34. Giliomee 1995.

35. This expression is attributed to N. P. van Wyk Louw, recently by Hermann Giliomee in several papers and public addresses, including "Afrikaans as instrument vir versoening en ontwikkeling: 'n Bydrae tot 'n Taalberaad," Argief van Toesprake, August 4, 2004. Accessed on January 4, 2008 from www.fak.org.za/site/artikels_argief .php?id=64; and "The rise and possible demise of Afrikaans as a public language," University of Cape Town, Praesa Occasional Paper 14: 14.

36. This is the Taalmonument in a town called Paarl in the Western Cape Province. See Beningfield 2004.

37. See the reference to Giliomee in note 35.

38. Ibid.: 158.

39. Steyn 2004: 150.

40. On a motion from anti-Apartheid activist Allan Boesak, the World Alliance of Reformed Churches, meeting in Ottawa, Canada, in 1982, declared Apartheid a "heresy" and suspended the membership of the white Dutch Reformed Church of South Africa, insisting that readmission required repentance in terms of which the church had to declare Apartheid "wrong and sinful, not only in its effects and operations, but also in its fundamental nature." See website of the Alliance, www.warc.ch.

41. Chapter 2 of the 1996 Constitution is the Bill of Rights, which states clearly that "everyone has the right to receive education in the official language or languages of their choice in public educational institutions." Yet, as if anticipating the mobilization of language to protect privilege, the same Constitution makes this right subject to concerns about "equity, practicability and the redress of past discriminatory laws and practices."

42. The reason mother-tongue instruction does not enjoy support in classroom practice is reasoned calculations on the part of parents that social and economic advancement requires proficiency in English.

43. A case that attracted much political and policy attention involved Ermelo High School in Mpumalanga province; the white Afrikaans school turned to the Pretoria High Court in 2007 after being instructed by the provincial department of education to enroll 113 learners who required instruction in English (read: black students); see *Ermelo High School and Another v. The Head of Department Mpumalanga Department of Education and Eight Others*, Transvaal Provincial High Court of South Africa, Case 3062/2007, accessible through the website of Legalbrief Today. Another prominent court case was that of *Kimberley Girls' High School and Another v. Head of Department of Education, Northern Cape Province and Others* 2005 (5) SA 251 (NC) 2005 (5): 251; in this case, the school governing body short-listed only three white candidates, and not three candidates from disadvantaged groups whom the Department of Education deemed to be suitable and qualified candidates. The head of department (of Education) then declined to appoint one of the recommended candidates on the grounds that the

governing body "failed to consider its duties to promote affirmative action in the hiring process" (quote from case record). A third case of great interest at the time was *Head of Department, Department of Education, Limpopo Province v. Settlers Agricultural High School and Others* [2003] JOL 11774 (CC); here the school, located in rural Bela-Bela (formerly Warmbaths), challenged the appointment by the department of a black woman principal over a white man to whom they had assigned the job. A fourth case of significance was *Laerskool Middelburg en 'n Ander v. Departementshoof, Mpumalanga Departement van Onderwys en Andere* 2003 (4) SA 160, in which the Middelburg Primary School sought a court order to set aside a decision by the Department of Education in that province that the school function as a dual-medium facility, thereby providing access to 24 black (that is, non-Afrikaans-speaking) students.

44. Johnson 2007.

45. The first notice of this policy initiative to assert greater government control over teacher appointments came through the Education Laws Amendment Act of 2005.

46. It is not only outsiders who depict Afrikaners "monochromatically," as Goodwin and Schiff 1995 put it: 21. White English-speaking and black South Africans tend to do the same.

47. Davies, R. (2007) went so far as to argue that "it is moot whether an Afrikaner grouping exists in any formal sense": 357.

48. Verwoerd 2001.

49. Taking a long knife into Parliament, the parliamentary messenger Demitrio Tsafendas stabbed Verwoerd four times in the chest, killing him in the parliamentary chambers of the Apartheid state on September 6, 1966. Described as "mad" and confined to mental institutions for much of his life thereafter, Tsafendas, the stateless son of a Greek father and a Swazi mother, refuted in his very person the madness of Apartheid. For an excellent account of the man, see Van Woerden 2001.

50. The so-called tricameral parliament (1984–1994), with a House of Assembly for whites, was roundly dismissed by the majority of black South Africans since this last-ditch attempt of the minority government was seen as yet another way of keeping Africans out of central government and retaining white power within a sham arrangement where coloreds and Indians in any event had a very limited voice.

51. With permission from Sallas de Jager from the Album Klopjag, 2005.

52. Wearing the black sash of mourning, this group of middle-class white women were known for both silent anti-Apartheid protests on major city roads in South Africa as well as offering advice and counsel to desperate black workers navigating the dense Apartheid legislation on everything from pensions to pass laws (regulating black movement in urban areas); they also monitored and reported on police beatings, detentions, and torture of activists.

53. Started in 1983, the End Conscription Campaign gained much publicity as more and more refused to undertake the compulsory military service required of all white men.

54. See Wessels 1994. I will always treasure the call from Leon Wessels for us to meet urgently on the eve of the 30th anniversary of Steve Biko's death because of the shame he felt at the fact that, to this day, Afrikaners still have not acknowledged his murder; he was deeply troubled by this, especially because no Afrikaans newspaper carried a single article on the subject on the day in 2007 commemorating Biko's death.

55. Van der Westhuizen 2007: 307.

56. The arguments for consociational rule are well described and assessed by Guelke 1999.

57. Bloom 1998: 122.

58. This apt phrase comes from Fourie 2006. She sees a store of knowledge as functional "for the sake of the survival of the Afrikaner and the white race at the southern tip of dark Africa": 168.

59. For a mix of journalist reports and academic studies capturing these memories on which Afrikaner identity is built, see Villet 1982, Fisher 1969, Moodie 1975, and of course the classic Harrison 1981.

60. Brink 1998: 15.

61. The referendum of March 17, 1992, asked white voters to respond to one question: "Do you support continuation of the reform process which the State President began on February 2, 1990, and which is aimed at a new constitution through negotiation?" The turnout of 85.1 percent rendered a yes vote of 68.7 percent.

62. I am constantly puzzled by the soul-searching questions posed by defenders of the National Party who simply cannot understand how this reliable carrier of Apartheid ideology could collapse so emphatically. The answers circle around explanations of the weakness of political strategy and the timidity of political leadership rather than the bankruptcy of ideas on which the NP was built. See, for example, Aucamp and Swanepoel 2007.

63. For stirring accounts of the traumatic experiences and effects of that war on white soldiers, including the systems of indoctrination that compelled male participation, see Thompson 2006 and Holt 2007.

64. A string of analysts from diverse disciplines, including psychopathology, have sought to understand the trauma of transition on and among Afrikaners; see Korf and Malan 2002, Vestergaard 2001, and Fourie 2008.

65. Marris 1996: 126.

66. The analysis in the Afrikaans Sunday newspaper *Rapport* gives ample evidence of this persistent lament among the defeated.

67. With permission from Seans Else and Mozi Records, from the album DE LA REY by Bok van Blerk, 2006. Music by Johan Vorster. Lyrics by Sean Else, Johan Vorster, and Bok van Blerk.

68. Grobler 2007.

69. Perhaps the most poignant summary of this position was given in the epigraph to Ausubel 1978: "If I had to reduce all of educational psychology to just one principle, I would say this: The most important single factor influencing learning is what the learner already knows. Ascertain this and teach him accordingly."

## Chapter 2

1. Hoffman 2002: 291.

2. Hoffman 2004: 25.

3. Wineburg et al. 2007: 40–76.

4. Hoffman 2004 and 2005.

5. Danieli (ed.) 1998.

6. Hoffman 2004: 25.

7. Ibid.: 25.

8. Hellig 2003: 64–67.

9. Langer 2006: 82–96.

10. M. A. Simpson. The second bullet: Transgenerational impacts of the trauma of conflict within a South African and world context. In Danieli 1998.

11. Levi and Rothberg 2003: 441–443.

12. I am grateful to Tali Nates, director of the Johannesburg Holocaust Center, for helping me clarify this point: the experiences of suffering cannot be compared, but the effects of a cataclysmic event on those who come after can.

13. Ari Roth, Plays in Process, *Born guilty*, based on the book by Sichrovsky (1988), vol. 12 no. 3. Quotation from unnumbered page, Materials for the Play, Playwright's Notes, New York, Theatre Communications Group.

14. Schivelbusch 2003.

15. Perpetrator. Dictionary.com. WordNet 3.0. Princeton University Press; see http://dictionary.reference.com/browse/perpetrator, accessed 7 January 2008.

16. Perpetrator. Dictionary.com. *American heritage dictionary of the English language, fourth edition.* Houghton Mifflin, 2004; see http://dictionary.reference.com/browse/perpetrator, January 7, 2008.

17. Attributed to Theuns Dreyer, chairperson of the Reformed Church (Hervormde Kerk), in Kerk Kry Wind van Voor [Church faces uphill battle], *Rapport*, September 29, 2007 (reporter Carien Kruger).

18. This thinking described as a *belief system* is captured from summaries of Afrikaans newspaper articles, letters to the editor, and many public debates in which I participated; one of the most poignant expressions of this thinking appears in the transcript of a submission at the Johannesburg Children's Hearing of the Truth and Reconciliation Commission, Day 1, June 12, 1997, where Afrikaner youths were represented by leaders from the Junior Rapportryers, Chris van Eeden, Jannie du Plessis and Christo Uys; see www.doj.gov.za/trc/special/children/rapportr.htm, accessed October 19, 2007. The Rapportryers—the men who dispatched messages among commandos during the South African War—have continued since then as a cultural organization for men.

19. This is the repeated view of former Apartheid police minister Adriaan Vlok in three sets of interview-discussions with me during 2007.

20. The editor of the Afrikaans Sunday newspaper *Rapport* knows that he speaks for a large segment of his readership when he argues that "people are feeling more assertive than before. As if they want to say: we are fed-up with being singled out as the only scapegoat for all the evils of South Africa's racial past. Was it only white Afrikaners who benefited from Apartheid? Is our whole history sullied and compromised? Did we do only bad things? We feel we are constantly being delegitimized." From his article "Afrikaners: De la Rey rides again," *Financial Mail*, February 9, 2007.

21. *Gatvol* is a strong word not adequately conveyed by English phrases like "fed-up" or "had enough" or "full up to here."

22. For one of the more systematic treatments of this subject, see Thompson 1985. The Transvaal Education Department for whites understood the knowledge thesis quite

well in its justification of the history curriculum (called the syllabus): "In the teaching of history one seeks to attain several objectives. There is the knowledge which is imparted of one's own and of others, knowledge which leads to a better understanding . . . how God leads a nation to pious deeds, how character formation takes place and how a Divine plan with a nation is carried out" (quoted in Thompson 1985: 24).

23. Translated as Restructured or Reformed National Party.

24. Translated from the Afrikaans of Willem de Klerk (2000): 15. Among the traditional standpoints held within this community, Willem de Klerk (the brother of F. W.), includes these: the Afrikaner was planted by God at the southern tip of Africa to spread the light of the gospel and civilization on a dark continent; the Afrikaner is exclusively a white race and those who are not of pure white blood are excluded; the Afrikaner is Christian, but specifically Calvinist-Christian, and this is the test of selection as to who is part of the inner circle of Afrikaners; and the Afrikaner has elevated the cultures of his mother nations by giving a new image to the rich heritage of Dutch and Huguenot. These latent old racial ideas surface powerfully in the cross-section of detailed interviews conducted on the eve of democracy in South Africa, as reported in Goodwin and Schiff 1995.

25. An astonishing justification of Apartheid comes in the recent publication by an administrator of what was then the Transvaal; see Van Niekerk 2006.

26. Pillay 2005: 58.

27. For the full quote, see Giliomee 2003: 651.

28. Ibid.: 651.

29. See Gunnar Theissen. Between knowledge and ignorance: How white South Africans have dealt with the Apartheid past. Centre for the Study of Violence and Reconciliation, Cape Town, accessed from www.csvr.org.za/papers/papgtsum.htm on October 19, 2007.

30. Herf 1997.

31. Steinitz and Szonyi 1979.

32. Epstein 1979.

33. Hass 1990.

34. Fine 2001: 78–92.

35. Hoffman 2004.

36. For a sampling of literary and cinematic sources, see Berger and Berger 2001: 3. This is one of the few sources that bring the literatures on children of survivors and perpetrators into one volume.

37. Julie Goschalk. When children of Holocaust survivors meet children of Nazis. In Berger and Berger 2001: 336–343 (338).

38. Bar-On 1989: 9.

39. Sichrovsky 1988.

40. Fine 2001.

41. Posner 1991.

42. Heimannsberg and Schmidt 1993 (2001).

43. G. Hardtmann. Children of Nazis: A psychodynamic perspective. In Danieli 1998: 85–96.

44. Sereny 2000.

45. Epstein 1979.

46. Anna Rosmus. Troublemaker in a skirt. In Berger and Berger 2001: 270–288.

47. Barbara Rogers. Facing a wall of silence. In Berger and Berger 2001: 289–302.

48. Liesel Appel. Honor thy mother: Reflections on being the daughter of Nazis. In Berger and Berger 2001: 303–309.

49. Reichel 1989.

50. Goschalk 2001: 340.

51. Appel 2001: 303; see note 48.

52. Gordon Wheeler in his translator's introduction to Heimannsberg and Schmidt 2001: xviii.

53. Ibid.: xx.

54. Mitscherlich 1975: xix.

55. Ibid.: 23.

56. Stanley 2006: 14.

57. Ibid.: 19.

58. Hirsch 1977: 22.

59. This beautiful and apt term comes from Goodwin and Schiff 1995: 21.

60. See the next chapter for a fuller description of the main trends of thought and response among Afrikaners in relation to Apartheid.

61. In her foreword to Goodwin and Schiff 1995: 9.

62. Mitscherlich 1975: 25–26.

63. Lambley 1980: 198.

64. Auerhahn and Laub 1998: 37.

65. D. Kupelian, A. S. Kalayjian, and A. Kassabian. The Turkish genocide of the Armenians: Continuing effects on survivors and their families eight decades after massive trauma. In Danieli 1998: 197.

66. Starting in the 1830s, more than 12,000 Boers migrated from the Cape Colony to the northern and eastern parts of South Africa, in part because of their dissatisfaction with living conditions under the English colonial authorities.

67. The family is of course a historical concept. There are illuminating examples of a parallel family structure to that of the Afrikaners in the Armenian community, itself a subject of an unheralded atrocity when, under cover of the First World War, the Turks killed 1.5 million Armenians, mainly men, or more than 80 percent of the population. A tightly sealed family structure has evolved here in response to the perception of the external environment, a constant sense of persecution, and an unacknowledged history of the attempted extermination. "They had to share fundamental beliefs and values that would translate into cooperation regarding basic family survival and life. This expectation of family interdependence, cohesion, and primacy of the family group is the template survivors brought into the New World" (Kupelian et al. 1998: 197; see note 65). Is it possible that the peculiar and insular family structure of the Afrikaners is a direct response to that history of suffering at the hands of the English, where children in their thousands died in the concentration camps? Does this turning in on the ethnic family carry both protection and pathology, as studies on familicide and incest in Afrikaans families suggest? For pertinent references, see Du Toit 1990 and Russell 1997.

68. Dalhouse and Frideres 1996.

69. Booysen and Kotze 1985; Booysen 1989; and Booysen 1990.

70. See many sources on the role of the Afrikaner woman in the identity formation of her children and in the broader project of ethnic mobilization, including Brocklehurst 2006: especially 120–124; Walker 1990; Gaitskell and Unterhalter 1989; and Du Toct 1992.

71. Hoffman 2004: 99.

72. The Johannesburg Children's Hearing of the Truth and Reconciliation Commission, Day 1, June 12, 1997; see note 18.

73. See the excellent account of learning race in Ritterhouse 2006: 77.

74. Meiring 1975. This little-known but insightful paper, radical for its time and yet protective in its writing, sheds light on the role of the Dutch Reformed Church in advancing Afrikaner nationalism.

75. Once again, there are striking parallels in the role of the church among Armenian survivors of the Turkish genocide. There the church was central to linking Armenians "to their long and troubled past, their homeland, their language, their literature and their faith. It provided the Armenian-Americans with the centuries-long function of the church: the preservation of the culture from assimilation." Kupelian et al. 1998: 197; see note 65.

76. Among many sources tracing especially the link between rugby and nationalism, see, for example, Grundlingh 1994, Nauright 1996, Allen 2003.

77. A fascinating account of the invisibility of blacks in white school life inside Afrikaner educational institutions then still applies in many ways today in all-white Afrikaner schools; see De Villiers 1988: 364–366.

78. Vandeyar and Jansen 2008.

79. Explication of the principles of Christian National Education, in the wake of the 1948 Apartheid victory of the white nationalists, is captured in the still invaluable collection of historical documents and commentary by Rose and Tunmer 1975: 123; see also Paasche 2006.

80. Du Preez 1983 is still the best description of these master symbols.

81. For a recent discussion of the struggles against master symbols in new South African textbooks, see Engelbrecht 2004; see also McKinney 2005, who makes the important observation that even though racial symbols and representation were evident in the texts reviewed, "[they] presented almost no opportunities to raise or address issues of racism, sexism, poverty, disability and other forms of social exclusion in texts": xi.

82. King 1979: 488.

83. Jansen 2004a.

84. Gamede 2005.

85. The right-wing stridency of the home school movement is found in the Pestalozzi Trust, calling itself "the legal defense fund for home education"; see www .pestalozzi.org.

86. A detailed analysis of the politics of music and the reassertion and search for a new Afrikaner national identity comes through in the excellent paper by Bezuidenhout 2007.

87. Kitshoff 2007: 21.

88. Mitscherlich and Mitscherlich 1975: 25.

89. In making these points about the insular nature of ethnic socialization, I am not suggesting that youths trapped in these concentric layers of knowledge do not escape this racial grip and resist such authority, or that the ideals of Afrikaner social ambition are perfectly met in practice. No social system is watertight—even one as intense and exclusive as this; see Lange 2003.

90. Taken from Milchman and Rosenberg 2003.

91. Danieli 1998: 7.

92. Wineburg et al. 2007.

93. Auerhahn and Laub 1998.

94. Marris 1996: 11.

95. Hardtmann 1998 (see note 43): 87.

96. Levine 2006: 102.

97. Ibid.: 102.

98. Ibid.: 103.

99. Bar-On 1989: 327.

100. The Johannesburg Children's Hearing of the Truth and Reconciliation Commission, Day 1, June 12, 1997; see note 18.

## Chapter 3

1. Administrator of the Transvaal, quoted in Johnson 1982: 214.

2. Tomaselli 2006, especially chapter 9 (Evil Englishmen, pure Afrikaners and gender politics), and the review of Hans Rompel's Afrikaans cinema.

3. Hickson and Kriegler 1996.

4. Ibid.: 142.

5. Foster. The development of racial orientation in children: A review of South African research. In Burman and Reynolds 1986: 158–183.

6. This trilogy of sophisticated textbook analyses under Apartheid are Dean, Hartmann, and Katzen 1981; Auerbach 1965; and Du Preez 1983. To these I would add the very short but incisive analyses of textbooks by Thompson 1986: 51–68, and Witz 2003, especially the section Schooling the past: 52–70, which reviews textbooks from the 19th century through the 1940s.

7. Johnson 1982, especially the pages on education and socialization: 222–225.

8. Evans 1989: 283–297.

9. Ibid.: 283.

10. Ibid.

11. P. le Roux. Growing up an Afrikaner. In Burman and Reynolds 1986: 184–207.

12. Ibid.: 202.

13. S. Cohen 2001: 146.

14. H. Adam. 2003. Visions of the future during political transitions: Comparing Afrikaner and Israeli attitudes, *Social Text* 21(2): 95–100. Accessed on October 26, 2007 from http://eproxy.stanford.edu:2126/journals/social_text/v021.2adam.html.

15. Dawes and Finchilescu 2002: 156, and the almost identical publication by the same authors, Finchilescu and Dawes 1998.

16. This is one of the oldest Afrikaans schools where middle- and upper-middle-class elites send their children for training. Some of South Africa's leading white Afrikaner politicians, businessmen, and rugby stars came from this school; its cultural capital is enormous, and its physical size and infrastructure are very impressive for a public high school.

17. William E. Connolly, quoted in Kuus 2002: 93.

18. This title for the story does not appear in the Bible as such, but it is inserted by preachers in the margin of the biblical text as the name of the story.

19. The introduction to the Information Letter 2007/1 January 22, 2007, Die Voortrekkers, by H. L. Piet Strauss under the heading The Voortrekkers after 75 years (translated from Afrikaans).

20. Vandeyar and Jansen 2008.

21. Jansen 2006a.

22. A fascinating name; these small jam cakes with coconut are named after an Afrikaner prime minister called Hertzog, whose wife apparently made these tasty tidbits as her stock in trade.

23. *Koeksusters* in the north of the country are long, twisted, syrupy doughnuts associated with the Afrikaners, while in the south of the country, Cape Town, they are round and soft with a spicy Malay taste.

24. Evans 1989.

25. The film is directed by Anthony Fabian and is accessible on www.archive.org/details/skinscriptdev. See also Stone 2008.

26. Interview with the principal of Diversity High.

27. This is the point made convincingly and eloquently in Lewis 2003.

28. Eisner 1994 first described and defined aspects of the null curriculum: "It is my thesis that what schools do not teach may be as important as what they do teach. I argue this position because ignorance is not simply a neutral void; it has important effects on the kinds of options one is able to consider, the alternatives that one can examine, and the perspectives from which one can view a situation or problems": 97.

29. Jansen 1999.

30. This was Kader Asmal, who served as minister of education from 2000 to 2005 and whose term was characterized by a highly energetic campaign to radicalize the school curriculum, improve matriculation results through a strict regime of accountability in high school, and rationalize universities and colleges through strategies of closure (colleges of education being closed down), incorporation (colleges being taken over by universities, or the multicampus sites of Vista University being taken over by the major universities in the cities where the campus sites were located), and merger (universities combining to establish new entities).

31. Jansen 2004c.

32. Hughes et al. 2006.

33. Ibid.: 756.

Chapter 4

1. The words of Robert Jay Lifton in the preface to Mitscherlich and Mitscherlich 1975: vii.

2. Krog 1998: 238.

3. I have compiled the narrative on this remarkable incident from a thick collection of newspaper reports on the event as well as rare film footage obtained from the AP Archives in New York City. The UP Archives, under the leadership of Karen Harris, were particularly helpful with locating the newspaper reports, and Alet Rademeyer of *Beeld* helped locate some of the Afrikaans press reports. The media clippings studied are:

Tuks CP plan "warm welcome" for Mandela, *The Citizen*, April 29, 1991: 5.

Mandela Rumpus shows F W has misread Whites: Prof, *The Citizen*, May 1, 1991: 9.

Unconditional Tuks apology to Mandela over meeting, by Keith Abendroth, *The Citizen*, May 1, 1991: 3.

Mandela verjaag: vrees vir sy lewe in groot regse amok by Tukkies [Mandela chased away: fears for his life in large rightwing amok at Tukkies], by Mike van der Merwe, *Beeld*, April 30, 1991: 1.

Tukkies besluit regses moet Nelson om verskoning vra [Tuks decides rightwingers should make apology to Nelson], by Mike van der Merwe, *Beeld*, May 3, 1991: 2.

Varsity to punish those involved in disruption, *The Star*, May 1, 1991: 6.

Fists fly at Tuks as Mandela routed by rightwingers, *The Star*, April 30, 1991: 1.

Geen optrede oor Mandela [No action over Mandela], *Die Patriot*, August 2, 1991: 6.

4. When Thabo Mbeki visited UP, rightwing students again gathered to lambaste a senior ANC official, burning the ANC flag, singing traditional Afrikaans songs, and waving the *Vierkleur* flag of the old Transvaal Republic. When the rightwing students gathered behind the podium where Mbeki was speaking, he turned to greet each one of them. One student refused to shake his hand. A student leader then read a statement prepared by several rightwing groups: "The free Afrikaner at Tuks says you, Mr. Thabo Mbeki, are not welcome at Tuks. As a member of the South African Communist Party and an outspoken Communist, you have chosen to be an enemy of the Christian Afrikaner." Source: *Pretoria News*, September 27, 1990: 2 ("Mixed fortunes for Mbeki at Tuks").

5. The Arabic word *unbeliever*, but which had taken on a deeply offensive meaning within racist South Africa to mean something equivalent to the word *nigger* in the American context.

6. The source for this information is an article "Mandela rumpus shows F W has misread Whites: Prof," *The Citizen*, May 1, 1991: 9. The main informant for this recollection was Willem Kleynhans, a retired professor from the University of South Africa, who witnessed the 1958 attack on Chief Albert Luthuli.

7. From the University of Fort Hare Archival Collections, available at www.liberation.org.za/mandela_pretoria_university and accessed on October 29, 2007.

8. This study on the nature of post-Apartheid student unrest was commissioned by the Centre for Education Policy Development (CEPD) in Johannesburg. See Koen et al. 2006. Although this study offers rare insight into the differences in student protests between historically black and historically white universities, its failure to distinguish and theorize differences between the white English and white Afrikaner universities means that crucial interpretive power is lost in this comparative work.

Nonetheless, this report is correct in finding that protests against racial integration, especially in the residences, and language loss constitute the leading causes of revolt at white universities; this applies principally to the Afrikaans universities. A study still needs to be done that investigates historically the racial connections and racial tensions between the English and Afrikaans universities. Such tensions stretched far back in history and often led to direct confrontations, as when UP students attacked students from the University of the Witwatersrand (Wits) on August 14, 1968, when the Wits students marched on the Union Buildings in Pretoria to protest the racial exclusion by government of black academic appointments at English universities, the case at the time being the attempts to appoint the celebrated anthropologist Archie Mafeje at the University of Cape Town.

9. Saint-Maude 1931. In his exceptionally pedestrian novel, the author riles against Natives (niggers) and Boers alike, but spares special treatment for the latter. The Boer *predikants* (religious ministers) are "narrow-minded, intolerant, selfish, harsh, and un-spiritual"; the Boers were the target of a British mission "to civilize and educate them" since "the back-veld Boer bathes only for baptism, marriage and burial" and "has no notions about sanitation and often uses his bedroom as a latrine." Not only were the Voortrekkers "illiterate boors, surly and morose" but "their favourite pastime was be-getting children, both with their wives and their numerous black concubines." These "utterly degenerate" trekkers lived "worse than natives": 295–296. In the rising tide of Afrikaner nationalism at the time, Lamont did not stand a chance. He left the country shortly afterward, having been subjected also to a disciplinary tribunal of UP.

10. [University of Pretoria] 1960: 54 and 88.

11. C. Brink 2006.

12. Regarded as a decisive victory for the Boers, the defeat of the British forces on Majuba Hill in present-day KwaZulu Natal on February 27, 1881, led to the end of the first Anglo-Boer War; from it came the rallying cry "Remember Majuba."

13. Cornia Pretorius. Black students march to Pretoria, *Sunday Times*, March 28, 1999: 1 (lead story).

14. This all-pervasive Apartheid "philosophy" of education has been severely cri-tiqued for pseudo-scientific pretenses, latent justification of the racial order, negative position on the potential of children (not-yet-adult, an initial object), arcane and pre-tentious language, authoritarian posture, and claims to universal truth to the exclusion of other ways of knowing and believing in the field of education. See the collection of critical writings in Beard and Morrow 1981.

15. Coetzee 1991.

16. Ibid.: 1.

17. Orpen 1973; Nieuwoudt and Nel 1975.

18. Duckitt 1983.

19. Heaven 1984.

20. Booysen 1989 and 1990; Booysen and Kotze 1985.

21. Gagiano 1990.

22. Jansen 2005b and 2004c.

23. Furnham 1985: 365.

24. Gagiano 1990: 192.

25. Foster and Finchilescu 1986: 172.

26. Crook 1996: 3.

27. Hoffman 2004: 140–141.

28. One of the more impressive accounts of "the ways that contending memories clashed or intermingled in public memory" is found in Blight 2001. His account of the American Civil War is aptly titled "Race and Reunion: The Civil War in American Memory": 1.

29. See note 1.

30. Tredoux et al. 2005.

31. Schrieff et al. 2005: 433.

32. Tredoux et al. 2005.

33. See also Durrheim et al. 2004.

## Chapter 5

*Kollegas* is at once a binding word and a separating word. It is the English word "colleagues" and is often invoked in a meeting to signal common purpose and (the derivative) collegiality. Yet no word conceals more division and separation between white and black administrators and academics. Positions taken in meetings are, more often than not, taken on the basis of race; more important, after formal meetings there would instantly be private meetings, almost always on the basis of race, where what happened in the more organized setting would be decried or lamented. The word *kollegas* therefore binds by injunction and separates in practice

1. From the translator's introduction to Heimannesberg and Schmidt 2002: xviii.

2. Antoine van Gelder (2004), Afrikaner deep culture, accessed on January 17, 2008 from www.g7.org.za/Diep_Afrikaner_Kultuur.pdf. I am grateful to the author for engaging me on this fascinating piece of historical reflection on his family upbringing and the raging conflict within the Afrikaner soul.

3. I change her name here, reluctantly.

4. I discuss the concept of *beleefdheid* in Jansen 2005a.

5. The donkey board is a familiar image from this period, when Afrikaans students who spoke their home language were forced to carry a sign board around their necks that read "I am a donkey."

6. Founded in 1918 as *Jong Zuid-Afrika* (Young South Africa), it changed its name to the *Afrikaner Broederbond* (Afrikaner Brotherhood) in 1920; see note 19, Prologue. A secret society of Afrikaner men, the *Broederbond*, as it was called, served to advance white nationalist interests. It sought to remold itself in 1994 as the *Afrikanerbond*, open to all provided they served the advancement of Afrikaans and Afrikaner interests.

7. It was not uncommon among this small group of Afrikaners to hear stories about a father who refused membership of the *Broederbond*, and the social and economic consequences of not "playing ball" with this cultural-political elite.

8. Such distortion is well documented in the case of education in the doctoral work of Suransky-Dekker 1998.

9. Du Toit 1984: 626–627.

10. Borrowed from the title of McKinney 2007: 215–231.

11. Since South African universities are in large part funded on the basis of student heads, even under a new funding formula the appointment of academics within a department is often determined on the basis of enrolment. A department is therefore "oversubscribed" if the number of staff exceeds the ratio for the number of funded students registered for courses within that academic unit.

12. A seemingly simple task such as carrying and accessing financial documentation from one's parents is infinitely more difficult for poor and rural black children with illiterate, unemployed, or AIDS-deceased parents than for children of middle-class white parents. Yet the institutional processes resolutely insist on not making such distinctions, with often devastating consequences for black students. It is hard to explain to colleagues that *this* is the crux of institutionalized racism.

13. For an insightful collection around this topic, see Hardy 1995; Clegg and Palmer 1996; and Clegg et al. 2006.

14. Clegg et al. 2006: xviii.

15. Gordon and Grant 2005: 27.

16. The term comes from Sackmann 1991.

17. Du Toit 1984.

18. The fact that such knowledge is based on race mythologies is irrelevant to what people believe and how they behave; see Du Toit 1983.

19. See the report by Zelda Venter (2005) in the *Pretoria News*, Anti-Muslim Pamphlets at Tuks, July 19; see also the response by the sending organization, Frontline, on its website www.frontline.org.za/news/end_of_islam.htm, accessed on January 16, 2008.

20. See Christian intolerance, in Jansen 2007d: 63–65.

21. Literally, bush council, an Afrikaans word for breakaway workshops of the senior management; alternatively called *lekgotlas* or *indabas* in other South African languages.

22. From Harrison 1994: 101.

23. Taken from Dennis K. Mumby, The political functions of narrative in organizations. In Hardy 1995: 231.

24. For a thorough survey and critique of the *volksmoeder* discourse, see Du Toit 2003.

25. Allen 2002 is a sensitive portrayal of the subject of gendered fear. Here she argues that "the relationship [of white women] to race is complex. They reflect the fears of white people in a process of enormous political and cultural transition. Apartheid discourse at its height placed women in a position of being both superior to and threatened by an othered black male population . . . the threat was of a sexualized nature and was used to justify and reinforce racist segregation" (77).

26. Posel [undated], especially page 4. See also Chait 2000 and two broader pieces within which such obsession can be historically and ideologically located: Stoler 2002 and McClintock 1995.

Chapter 6

1. Thus opens the introductory chapter of Van der Westhuizen 2007. What the author does not do is to come to grips with "What does it mean to know?" in a totalitarian system where knowing itself is a managed, constrained, threatened, controlling, and legitimating process. What exactly is known? What are the structures of knowing? Why does knowing make perfect sense to so many under one regime and come to have a completely different meaning under another? How do some, like Van der Westhuizen, come to refuse subjection to such imposed knowledge when the majority did not? What is it in her social biography that explains her minority dissent in the face of the normalcy of everyday white Afrikaner knowledge? To suggest, as she does, that ordinary citizens knew that what they were doing to black people was wrong and simply kept on doing it anyway is to collapse all meaning that can be derived from the power of political socialization through the multiple agencies described in earlier chapters.

2. From email correspondence of December 20, 2007, with the Irish poet Macdara Woods, who used the phrase in a poem and as the title of a 2007 collection of his poems, *Knowledge in the blood: New and selected poems*, Dedalus Press (first published in 2000). I am grateful to Woods for responding to my inquiry about the meaning he assigned to the richly expressive title.

3. Ibid.

4. I have in various writings demonstrated how changing ideological regimes run ahead of embedded knowledge regimes in postcolonial curricula. See, for example, Jansen 1991b.

5. I am grateful to Sam Wineburg for making the point that *knowledge in the blood* carries in itself genetic and determinist overtones reminiscent of Nazi ideology; hence my acknowledgment here of the redemptive path open to those who carry such knowledge. Perhaps the invocation of the phrase, as assertion and question, is precisely the emancipatory point in a nationalistic context where blood features prominently in the social discourses of Afrikaner history. Such hematological mythology is concretized most clearly in the memories of *The battle of blood river*, the epic physical contest between Zulus and Voortrekkers. Blood, moreover, remains one of those "guiding metaphors of nationalism" everywhere; see Baruh and Popescu 2008.

6. This perspective on *curriculum as institution* is inspired by, though making significant elaborations on, the work of the leading theorist of curriculum on the subject, W. A. Reid, whose thinking is represented in, among other sources, Reid 1999, especially Part II: Curriculum as institution: 97–198; Reid 2006, especially chapter 2, The institutional character of curriculum: 3–18; and Reid 2004.

Reid describes and indeed reviews *curriculum as institution* as something that is socially pervasive, culturally contingent, and holding a national character. "Curriculum as institution" is an abstract idea, "something that is simply there" (Reid 2006: 19), apart from its expression in organizational structures and processes; yet it is habits and traditions as well as organizational arrangements. I am closer to one perspective he reviews that sees "curriculum as institution as about more than learning in the sense of achieving familiarity with facts and ideas . . . skills and competence" (Ibid.: 22), but rather as something shaped by historical values, ideals, and purposes (Reid 1999: 187).

When curriculum as institution functions in the day-to-day life of an institution, it is indeed in the form of "abstract categories that enter into the consciousness of the community at large" (Reid 2004: 92). Nevertheless, changing the curriculum has real consequences because "innovative courses threaten to sacrifice elements . . . which are definitive of the institutional categories" (Ibid.: 94) and because it represents "the possession of a community" (Reid 1999: 190).

7. Reid 2006: 20.

8. Karmon 2007. For this writer, institutional knowledge is not tucked away within the crevices of the institution but has real consequences, for this is knowledge conveyed to institution dwellers. "My claim is that every knowledge-oriented educational system creates a certain epistemic environment [which] determines this environment's dominant color [and] transmits to those within it a particular conception of knowledge": 622–623.

9. Reid 2004.

10. One of the first descriptive accounts of these institutional differences in how knowledge and culture are distinctively represented in the higher education institutions of South Africa is found in Cloete et al. 2006. For an earlier attempt at making these descriptive distinctions for UP, see Jansen 2001.

11. One such intense explosion of debate on the UCT campus was the reaction to one of its professors, David Benatar, who made the case against affirmative action in his inaugural address of April 11, 2007. His position and some of the reactions to it are all accessible through UCT's Monday Paper on the Web at www.news.uct.ac.za/mondaypaper/archives.

See these sources in the *Monday Paper*:

David Benatar. "Affirmative Action" not the way to tackle injustice, 26.05 April 23, 2007.

Martin Hall. The case for equity, 26.05 April 23, 2007.

Leslie London. Affirmative Action and the invisibility of white privilege, 26.08 June 4, 2007.

Zimitri Erasmus. Governing Whiteness! Now that cannot be allowed, 26.07 May 21, 2007.

12. A neat collection of these debates that centered in the late 1990s on the African studies curriculum appears in a special issue of the University of Cape Town journal *Social Dynamics* 24(2), called Critical Exchanges; see for example Jansen 1998.

13. The institutional audit reports are accessible as executive summaries for the two institutions, and others, from the website of the Council on Higher Education at www.che.ac.za.

14. The useful notions of endoskeleton and exoskeleton in relation to curriculum are attributed to the Stanford sociologist John Meyer in Reid 2004: 93.

15. Such as the works of Lovemore Mbigi on African management; see Mbigi 1997.

16. An excellent and rare analysis of the appropriation of the concept for ethnic purposes is in Mdluli 1987; see also D. Gordon 1991.

17. In Tutu 2004.

18. The language of clienthood had deliberately entered the managerial discourses at UP, showing up as keywords in strategic planning documents and even in the naming of its newest building at the time, the Client Services Centre.

19. Jansen (ed.) 1991a.

20. The Faculty of Education at UP was without question the leading producer of intellectual content that energized the Apartheid theory of education. This was fundamental pedagogics in all its guises. The leading texts of the day, purveyed throughout black colleges and Afrikaans universities, were written by deans and professors of this Faculty, including C. K. Oberholzer, W. A. Landman, Floors van der Stoep, P. G. Nel, and others. The sheer volume of writing on pedagogics was in some quarters referred to as the Pretoria School of Thought. See, for example, the review and well-established website of George Yonge, who translated these UP materials into English http://georgeyonge.net. Though professing a scientific and apolitical position in an education theory concerned only with "essences," the broader writings of these Broederbond members left no doubt about their adherence to and justification of Apartheid; in this regard, see Oberholzer 1959.

21. R. Gordon 1987.

22. It would not be surprising that many of the major Apartheid disciplinarians were in fact based at UP, such as professor of anthropology W.W.H. Eiselen and his student P. J. Coertze, who together trained most of Apartheid's anthropologists; professor of sociology Geof Cronje, who made elaborate sociological arguments for white domination; and professor of theology E. P. Groenewald, who invoked biblical interpretations to support Apartheid. Drawn from Du Toit 1984: 625–627.

23. I will not explore this potentially interesting line of inquiry here, but it seems to be that some conceptual traction could be provided through Foucault's distinctions between connaissance (the school knowledge transmitted to students in school), savoir (knowledge outside of school, deployed by those talking about school knowledge), and episteme ("a world-view, a slice of history common to all branches of knowledge, which imposes on each one the same norms and postulates, a general stage of *reason, a certain structure of thought that the men of a particular period cannot escape*" [my emphasis]); from Foucault 1986: 191.

24. Brenner 2001: 8.

25. This is the story Christie van der Westhuizen depicts so powerfully in Van der Westhuizen 2007 as she courageously wrote against the dominant narrative as a seventeen-year-old schoolgirl at Dr. E. G. Jansen High School in Boksburg and as a student at the Rand Afrikaans University in Johannesburg. She recalls the power of watchful authority, whether in the form of the Afrikaans teacher who edits down "provocative" thinking and warns of danger (page 1) or the university dean of students who threatens to expel her for daring to move outside the frame of acceptable knowledge of past heroes (page 6). In these rare but revealing snapshots of young Afrikaner lives under the strain of Apartheid lies a much more important story of knowledge, power, and curriculum under Afrikanerdom. The discipline of knowledge keeps potential rebels and critics in place through threat: the examinations will not tolerate dissent (the high school teacher) and your degree might not happen (the dean of students).

26. Taken from the text of an extended interview with Heidi Esakov, a master's

student in UP Faculty of Education, whose thesis is an analysis of the Ubuntu module at the university.

27. A powerful example of how "the institutional psyche" and the ordinariness of exclusion function at UP is found in a lecturer's letter explaining his resignation; see Tabensky 2004, My Life at the University of Pretoria: A story of two evils, Centre for Civil Society, University of KwaZulu Natal. Available at the website of the Centre, www.ukzn.ac.za/ccs.

28. Lorde 1984: 110–113 (the quotation is a chapter entry by the same name).

29. I did notice, however, the return of the entry "science" into educational discourses in the United States in part because of the need to assert the scientific basis for educational inquiry and in part because of the evidence-based movement (with its roots in the medical sciences) driven from some quarters, including the federal government.

30. For a fascinating and recent account of the scientific tradition in the history of the history department at UP, see Mouton 2007.

Chapter 7

1. Clendinnen 1999: 19.

2. In the burgeoning literature on white-black relations in schools and universities, I have yet to find sustained research on the relationship between white students and black faculty, which is surely a necessary inquiry in post-Apartheid society.

3. There are very few studies of change and transformation within academic departments and faculties of South African universities; a rare, insightful, and empathic historical study of the history department at UP is Louis A. Changuion's report, UP Departement Geskiedenis: Die Afrikaanse stem uit die noorde [UP History Department: The Afrikaans voice from the north], accessed on January 21, 2008 at http://academic.sun.ac.za/history/news/changuion_la.pdf.

4. The conceptual terrain for "at homeness" as an analytical framework for studying institutional cultures appears in a commissioned study; see Thaver 2006. The application of this framework to UP appears in a study by Wilna Venter-Mbabama 2006, A snapshot of institutional culture at the University of Pretoria: The perceptions and experiences of residential students, M.Ed. degree, minithesis, Faculty of Education, University of the Western Cape, November.

5. The curriculum analysis appears in Chapter 6 and will not be repeated here.

6. I was fortunate to lead a national study on the institutional cultures of several South African universities; these unpublished studies were done by Beverley Thaver (for the University of Cape Town), Sibusiso Chalufu (for the University of the Free State), Mankolo Mfusi (for Rhodes University), Saloshna Vandeyar (for the University of Stellenbosch), and Venitha Pillay (for UP).

7. I have written elsewhere about the balancing task of leadership at UP. The leadership task, as this chapter shows, required emotional and political balancing, all the time knowing when to assert and when to withdraw; developing expertise and advancing integration; demanding performance and creating capacity; affirming traditional collegial ties and expanding into new networks; broadening national interactions and drawing in international institutions; promoting racial affirmation and advancing gender equity; pushing for racial advancement and acting on class in-

equalities; changing others and being open to change oneself. See Jansen 2007b, 2007c, 2006a, 2006b, and 2005a.

8. For some sense of these obstacles, see Potgieter 2002.

9. This large incorporation was preceded by smaller processes of absorption of college staff from smaller colleges, so that a few of the staff were not white but Indian; see note 35, Prologue. The smaller incorporations into the larger white college did, however, also bring in white Afrikaner colleagues who were teaching in the black township colleges, so that the net number of white college teachers increased even further.

10. All but one of the Afrikaans universities have since 2000 merged with other universities or technikons or incorporated campuses of a multicampus institution.

11. The designation Groenkloof Aventura, after South Africa's string of Aventura holiday resorts, irritated some of my colleagues eager to ensure that the academic rigor and reputation of the Education or Groenkloof campus remained in sight.

12. Daniel Herwitz was certainly not the first to observe that the architecture of white Afrikaans universities where students found themselves was "dwarfed by [the] encircling structure and watched from every window" which serves to "secure identity among the white Afrikaans-speaking students." See Herwitz 2003: 149. In a similar vein, Saul Dubow observed the semicircular design of the campus buildings of the Rand Afrikaans University (now the University of Johannesburg) to be "suggestive of a concrete laager" carrying the overall message of the time that "knowledge was being politicized, institutionalized, and nationalized as never before." See Dubow 2006: 265–266.

13. Goosen 2005: 130.

14. Jansen 2006a is a specific critique of distributed leadership based on case research with South African principals.

15. Oom Bey was Beyers Naude, a prominent Afrikaner theologian who broke away from the Afrikaner political and theological establishment to become one of the leading anti-Apartheid voices in South Africa.

16. Translated from an Afrikaans email communication.

17. With permission from Amanda Strydom, from the album *Vrou by die Spieël*, 1996.

## Chapter 8

1. Wolf 1980.

2. The original piece appeared in English in the now-defunct daily *This Day* under the title "Revisit the Afrikaner Quota," October 15, 2003, saying "Ordinary black and white South Africans need a common occupational space to work and laugh together: an integrated civil service could provide the foundation. Many young Afrikaner males feel trapped and some act out their fear and frustration in the excesses being witnessed today": 14. The Afrikaans newspaper *Beeld* translated the essence of the story under the misleadingly phrased title "*Gee Afrikaanses werk om hulle uit die kwaad te hou: die geweld spruit uit ontmanning*" [Give the Afrikaners work to keep them out of trouble: the violence springs from emasculation] as reported by Jan-Jan Joubert, October 17, 2003: 5.

3. I was referring in particular to the case that became known as the Waterkloof Four, a group of high school boys from the elite Afrikaans public schools in the east of Pretoria who were charged with kicking a black man to death and a spate of aggressive incidents in and around the university suburb called Hatfield.

4. At this point the residences were shared with military personnel in training; these were not Education students.

5. I borrow the term from Gail Gerhart in her review of Giliomee's *The Afrikaners* (see Giliomee 2003), in which she observes the centrality of "cultural obliteration" to the author's historical account of the Afrikaners; see Gerhart 2003.

6. I have changed only his last name.

7. *College* in South Africa refers to a junior-level institution, a nondegree-awarding place of learning, different from a university, which awards degrees and does advanced research.

8. Danie Goosen makes the argument that "the alienation experienced by Afrikaners manifests itself in a withdrawal into private existence. In other words, a feeling of being left without any meaningful say in their own affairs translates into a collective farewell to public life"; see Goosen 2005.

9. From the *New American Standard Bible*, 1995, and from the Pauline letter to the Roman Church, Romans 13, verse 1.

10. *Kraal* of course is used here metaphorically—not indicating the traditional African kraal from which the chief ruled his tribe, but the location within which Afrikaners dwell and the common cultural beliefs and values that hold them together.

11. This and other pieces from my *Beeld* column appear in book form in Jansen 2007d.

12. I am deliberately avoiding being drawn at this stage into a debate on whose language Afrikaans is, for it is clearly not the exclusive preserve of Afrikaners either in its historical formation or its hybrid character.

13. *Idioglots*: stubborn and ignorant people without the capacity to see beyond their own rigidity of mind.

14. For Newell Stultz's review of *The Afrikaners: Biography of a people* (Giliomee 2003), see Stultz 2003.

15. Not his real name.

16. The person to whom this view is most often attributed was the Apartheid minister of native affairs and later prime minister, H. F. Verwoerd.

17. For a more detailed analysis of teacher migration with South Africa in focus, see De Villiers and Johnson 2007.

18. Globalization tendencies within Afrikanerdom are the subject of interesting recent scholarship that pits global identity against localized ethnic identity in the post-Apartheid period; see R. Davies 2007.

19. Jung 2000.

20. Ibid.: 9.

21. Ibid.: 133.

22. Ibid.: 131.

23. Jarausch and Geyer 2003: 339.

24. Ibid.

25. Ibid.: 334.

26. Ibid.: 131.

27. Ibid.: 334.

28. Ibid.: 319.

29. Ibid.: 339.

30. Ibid.: 340.

31. Ibid.: 340–341.

32. Ibid.: 339–340.

## Chapter 9

1. Schivelbusch 2003: 167. The writer's unit of analysis is the nation, and this quotation refers to the French dilemma in relation to Prussia in the 1870s, but I find the quotation (adapted from his original observation) to hold powerfully true for white South Africans and Afrikaners in particular: *how to adopt the knowledge of the victor without damaging the ethnic soul located within the newly imagined black nation.*

2. Jarausch and Geyer 2003: 320.

3. The invited lecture was titled "The Color of Change" and delivered on April 12, 2005, at the AERA Conference in Montreal, Canada.

4. This presentation was subsequently published; see Jansen 2007b.

5. That fellow Stanford student was Bruce Bryant King, who died tragically of AIDS in the same year; I write this chapter with this great friend in mind, and in his honor.

6. Principal among Freire's writings of course was *Pedagogy of the oppressed*; see Freire 2000.

7. At the time, his landmark contribution was *Ideology and curriculum* (see Apple 1979), in which he laid out his thesis of ideological, economic, and cultural reproduction in and through schooling.

8. Arguably one of her best-known and most-often reprinted contributions of the time was Anyon 1980.

9. Bowles and Gintis 1976. I was always fascinated by the fact that in the year Bowles and Gintis published their "correspondence thesis" (between education and work), students in South Africa were in revolt against Apartheid capitalism and racist schooling (1976), an event better explained in another major critical publication that followed; see Giroux 1983.

10. Giroux 1983.

11. Willis 1977.

12. What first drew attention to Patti Lather's impressive works was Lather 1986.

13. The inventive response of Cameron McCarthy to the work of his Ph.D. adviser Michael Apple's *Ideology and curriculum* (see Apple 1979) was his *Race and curriculum* (see McCarthy 1990).

14. The book that most impressed me at the time was Shor 1980.

15. She made an impact in mathematics education circles in South Africa, gaining attention through Frankenstein 1990.

16. Jesse Goodman's critical work on teacher education was influential in shifting my focus from student learning in science education to curriculum design; see Goodman 1986.

17. Carnoy 1974.

18. Nyerere 1967.

19. For a useful discussion of the narrow and broad meanings of critical theory, see the Stanford Encyclopedia of Philosophy entry on Critical Theory (first published on March 8, 2005), available on http://plato.stanford.edu/entries/critical-theory and accessed on January 26, 2008.

20. Hesford 1999: xxxvi.

21. Kincheloe 2005.

22. See the collection of recent works in Weiss et al. 2006.

23. The construct of *intersectionality* is now used widely in the social science literature; one of the more sustained analyses of its meaning is by S. V. Knudsen 2007, Intersectionality: A theoretical inspiration in the analysis of minority cultures and identities in textbooks, available on www.caen.iufm.fr/colloque_iartem/pdf/knudsen .pdf and accessed on January 26, 2008. In general, intersectionality means that social constructs such as race, gender, and social class do not operate separately but "intersect" in the identities and actions of individuals.

24. This of course is the title of Paulo Freire's influential *Pedagogy of the oppressed,* first published in Portuguese in 1968; see Freire 2000.

25. This point is made through very lucid examples in practice in Choules 2007. Choules juxtaposes the meanings of popular education in Latin America with critical pedagogy in the Western societies to demonstrate the absurdity of assuming homogeneous class relations within one classroom. The point is well made, but Choules's argument fails to recognize the very real class differentiation within, for example, the classrooms of the United States, where a popular mythology that everybody is "middle class" deters from an analysis of the working classes within such educational settings. In other words, the distinctions between popular education and critical pedagogy are too sharply made.

26. Two important criticisms of the conceptual and philosophical claims and assumptions of critical theory can be found in Maddock 1999 and Tubbs 1996.

27. Ellsworth 1989.

28. See the review of two books, one by and one on Peter McLaren, by Richard Kahn (2005); also McLaren 2006.

29. Elbaz-Luwisch 2004.

30. Davies 2004.

31. It is a point made by Gur-Ze'ev 1998 as well, noting the tendency of critical theory to assume a "weak, controlled, and marginalized collective" sharing a "common optimistic view of change."

32. Gur-Ze'ev 1998.

33. This point is made more than once in Lather 2001. See the summary of the article by the editor (Kathleen Weiler) on page 10 of the book for the direct quote. See also Lather 1998.

34. There is empirical substantiation for this point in the excellent study of integrated and nonintegrated Catholic and Protestant schools in Northern Ireland; see Byrne 1997.

35. As she digs into the personal history of Apartheid's most notorious killer, the

man called "Prime Evil" in the South African press, Pumla Gobodo-Madikizela un-
covers the operation of what she calls "constant themes" and "refrains" in Afrikaner
family and adult discourses that shaped Eugene de Kock's knowledge of past and future
enemies, and that motivated his deadly ambitions. See Gobodo-Madikizela 2003: 21.

36.  It is a point made somewhat bluntly in Da Cruz 2005.

37.  The educational psychologist David Ausubel; see Ausubel 1978.

38.  Gilroy 2000a and 2000b.

39.  Jansen 2005c.

40.  Few postconflict interventions have achieved such resonance among black and
white teachers as the listening that comes through hearing stories of the Other, as in
Facing the Past, a nongovernmental organization in South Africa; see Tibbits 2006.

41.  Two well-known sources are Burman and Reynolds 1986 and Barbarin and
Richter 2001. See also Straker 1992.

42.  Throughout the research for this book I would encounter only brief, often very
emotional, reflections by white children on incidents in the course of growing up that
had a lasting impact on their racial formation; there is, to my knowledge, no systematic
inquiry on this subject in educational contexts.

43.  Though the word *Bantu* strictly refers to a language group, it came to mean,
like so many other political words, something else—in this case, black Africans in South
Africa, as opposed to, say, white or colored or Indian South Africans.

44.  I am arguing here with McFalls and Cobb-Roberts 2001.

45.  Reflecting on her time writing the book in the United States, the author muses:
"Alone with this material, thousands of miles from the streets of Pretoria, I was afraid,
not of the memory of the evil schemes that were concocted in that city but of my own
empathy for De Kock"; see Gobodo-Madikizela 2003: 116.

46.  Bar-On 1989 and 1996.

47.  This is the recognition that Dan Bar-On comes to after years of research and
interviews with children of Nazi perpetrators: "When moving later into working with
parties in current conflicts, I had to learn to distinguish between the clear-cut definition of victim and victimizer in the case of the Holocaust, which is less clear a differentiation when addressing current conflicts." From a new introduction to *Legacy
of silence* in German, March 2003, available at www.bgu.ac.il/danbaron/Docs_Dan/
Introd-german.doc, accessed on January 28, 2008.

48.  I am grateful to Gene Carter, executive director of the Association for Supervision
and Curriculum Development, for sharing this conception of leadership with me.

49.  Taken from Maureen Isaacson's A brave and riveting confession, *Sunday Independent* in the section called *Sunday Dispatches*, July 15, 2007: 13, which appears in a
review of Grass's book *Peeling the onion*, published by Harvil Secker.

50.  From Jeffrey Mirel 2002: 150.

# References

Alexander, N. 2002. *An ordinary country: Issues in transition from Apartheid to democracy in South Africa.* New York, Berghahn Books.

Allen, D. 2003. Beating them at their own game: Rugby, the South African War and Afrikaner nationalism, 1899–1948. *International Journal of the History of Sport* 20(3): 37–57.

Allen, D. B. 2002. Race, crime and social exclusion: A qualitative study of white women's fear of crime in Johannesburg. *Urban Forum* 13(3): 53–79.

Anyon, J. 1980. Social class and the hidden curriculum of work. *Journal of Education* 162(1): 67–92.

Apple, M. 1979. *Ideology and curriculum.* New York, Routledge and Kegan Paul.

Aucamp, I., and J. Swanepoel. 2007. *Einde van 'n Groot Party: 'n Vrystaatse perspektief op die (N)NP* [End of a great party: A free state perspective on the (N)NP]. Allensnek (South Africa), Paarl.

Auerbach, F. E. 1965. *The Power of prejudice in South African education.* Cape Town and Amsterdam, Gothic.

Auerhahn, N. C., and E. Laub. 1998. Intergenerational memory of the Holocaust. In Y. Danieli (1998) *International handbook of multigenerational legacies of trauma.* New York and London, Plenum: 21–41.

Ausubel, D. 1978. *Educational psychology: A cognitive view.* New York, Holt Rinehart and Winston (second edition).

Barbarin, O. A., and L. Richter. 2001. *Mandela's children: Growing up in post-Apartheid South Africa.* New York, Routledge.

Bar-On, D. 1989. *Legacy of silence: Encounters with children of the Third Reich.* Cambridge, Mass., Harvard University Press.

———. 1996. Descendants of Nazi perpetrators: Seven years after the first interviews. *Journal of Humanistic Psychology* 36(1): 55–74.

Baruh, L., and M. Popescu. 2008. Guiding metaphors of nationalism: The Cyprus issue and the construction of Turkish national identity in online discussions. *Discourse and Communication* 2(1): 79–96.

Beard, P. G. N., and W. E. Morrow (eds.). 1981. *Problems of pedagogy.* Durban, Butterworth.

Becker, L., et al. 2004. The impact of incorporation on college lecturers. *Higher Education* 48(2): 153–172.

Beningfield, J. 2004. Native lands: Language, nation and landscape in the Taal Monument, Paarl. *Social Identities* 10(4): 509–526.

Berger, A. L., and N. Berger (eds.). 2001. *Second generation voices: Reflections by children of Holocaust survivors and perpetrators*. New York, Syracuse University Press.

Bezuidenhout, A. 2007. From voelvry to De la Rey: Popular music, Afrikaner nationalism and lost irony. Stellenbosch, University of Stellenbosch, Department of History seminar (September 5).

Blight, D. W. 2001. *Race and reunion: The Civil War in American memory*. Cambridge, Mass., Harvard University Press.

Bloom, L. 1998. *Identity and ethnic relations in Africa*. Aldershot, England, Ashgate.

Bond, P. 2000. *Elite transition: From Apartheid to neoliberalism in South Africa*. Pietermaritzburg, University of Natal Press.

Booysen, S. 1989. The legacy of ideological control: The Afrikaner youth's manipulated political consciousness. *Politikon* 16(1): 7–25.

———. 1990. Political change and the socialization of Afrikaans students: A case study. *South African Journal of Sociology* 21(4): 181–194.

———, and H. Kotze. 1985. The political socialization of isolation: A case study of Afrikaner student youth. *Politikon* 12(2): 23–46.

Bowles, S., and H. Gintis. 1976. *Schooling in capitalist America: Education reform and the contradictions of economic life*. New York, Basic Books.

Brenner, L. 2001. *Controlling knowledge: Religion, power and schooling in a West African Muslim society*. Bloomington, Indiana University Press.

Brewer, J. D. (ed.). 1989. *Can South Africa survive? Five minutes to midnight*. Basingstoke, Macmillan.

Brink, A. 1998. Interrogating silence: New possibilities faced by South African literature. In D. Attridge and R. Jolly (eds.), *Writing South Africa, literature, Apartheid and democracy, 1970–1995*. Cambridge, England, Cambridge University Press.

Brink, C. 2006. No lesser place. *The taaldebat* [language debate] *at Stellenbosch*. SUN Press.

Brocklehurst, H. 2006. *Who's afraid of children? Children, conflict and international relations*. Aldershot, England, Ashgate.

Burman, S., and P. Reynolds (eds.). 1986. *Growing up in a divided society: The Contexts of childhood in South Africa*. Johannesburg, Ravan Press.

Byrne, S. 1997. *Growing up in a divided society: The influence of conflict on Belfast schoolchildren*. Cranbury, N.J., Associated University Presses.

Carnoy, M. 1974. *Education as cultural imperialism*. New York, David McKay.

Chait, S. 2000. Mythology, magic realism and white writing after Apartheid. *Research in African Literatures* 31(2): 17–28.

Choules, K. 2007. Social change education: Context matters. *Adult Education Quarterly* 57(2): 159–176.

Clegg, S. R., D. Courpasson, and N. Phillips. 2006. *Power and organizations*. Thousand Oaks, Calif., Sage.

Clegg, S. R., and G. Palmer. 1996. *The politics of management knowledge*. London, Sage.

Clendinnen, I. 1999. *Reading the Holocaust.* Cambridge, England, Cambridge University Press.

Cloete, N., et al. (eds.). 2006. *Transformation of higher education: Global pressures and local realities.* Netherlands, Springer.

Coetzee, J. M. 1991. The mind of Apartheid: Geoffrey Cronje (1907–). *Social Dynamics* 17(1): 1–35.

Cohen, R. 1986. *Endgame in South Africa?* London, James Currey.

Cohen, S. 2001. *States of denial: Knowing about atrocities and suffering.* Oxford, Blackwell.

Crook, N. 1996. The control and expansion of knowledge. An introduction. In N. Crook (ed.), *The transmission of knowledge in South Asia: Essays on education, religion, history, and politics.* Delhi, Oxford University Press: 1–27.

Da Cruz, P. 2005. From Narrative to Severed Heads: The form and location of white supremacist history in textbooks of the Apartheid and post-Apartheid eras: A case study. M.Phil. (History of Education) thesis, School of Humanities, University of Cape Town.

Dalhouse, M., and J. M. Frideres. 1996. Intergenerational congruency: The role of the family in political attitudes of youth. *Journal of Family Issues* 17(2): 227–248.

Danieli, Y. (ed.). 1998. *International handbook of multigenerational legacies of trauma.* New York and London, Plenum.

Davies, J. E. 2007. *Constructive engagement? Chester Crocker and American policy in South Africa, Namibia and Angola, 1981–1988.* Oxford, James Currey.

Davies, L. 2004. *Education and conflict: Complexity and chaos.* New York, Routledge Falmer.

Davies, R. 2007. Rebuilding the future or revisiting the past? Post-Apartheid Afrikaner politics. *Review of African Political Economy* 34(112): 353–370.

Dawes, A., and G. Finchilescu. 2002. What's Changed? The racial orientations of South African adolescents during rapid political change. *Childhood* 9(2): 147–165.

Dean, E., P. Hartmann, and M. Katzen. 1981. *History in black and white: An analysis of South African school history textbooks.* Paris, UNESCO.

De Klerk, W. 2000. *Afrikaners, Kroes, Krass, Kordaat.* Pretoria, Human and Rousseau.

De Villiers, J. J. R., and R. D. Johnson (eds.). 2007. The political economy of teacher migration. *Perspectives in Education* 25(2), vii–xii.

De Villiers, M. 1988. *White tribe dreaming: Apartheid's bitter roots as witnessed by eight generations of an Afrikaner family.* New York, Viking Penguin.

Dubow, S. 2006. Apartheid science and the renationalization of knowledge. In S. Dubow (ed.), *A commonwealth of knowledge: Science, sensibility and white South Africa, 1820–2000.* Oxford, Oxford University Press: 247, 252–268.

Duckitt, J. 1983. Culture, class, personality and authoritarianism among white South Africans. *Journal of Social Psychology* 121: 191–199.

Du Preez, J. 1983. *Africana Afrikaner: Master symbols in South African textbooks.* Alberton (Johannesburg), Librarius.

Durrheim, K., K. Trotter, D. Manicom, and L. Piper. 2004. From exclusion to informal segregation: The limits to racial transformation at the University of Natal. *Social Dynamics* 30(1): 141–169.

Du Toct, M. 1992. Dangerous motherhood: Maternity care and the gendered construction of Afrikaner identity, 1904–1939. In V. Fildes, L. Marks, and H. Marland (eds.), *Women and children first: International and infant welfare, 1870–1945*. London, Routledge.

Du Toit, A. 1983. No chosen people: The myth of the Calvinist origins of Afrikaner nationalism and racial ideology. *American Historical Review* 88: 920–952.

Du Toit, B. M. 1984. Missionaries, anthropologists, and the policies of the Dutch Reformed Church. *Journal of Modern African Studies* 22(4): 617–632.

Du Toit, M. 2003. The domesticity of Afrikaner nationalism: Volksmoeders and the ACVV, 1904–1929. *Journal of Southern African Studies* 29(1): 155–176.

Du Toit, S. I. 1990. Family violence: Familicide. In B. McKendrick and W. Hoffman (eds.), *People and violence in South Africa*. Cape Town, Oxford University Press.

Eisner, E. W. 1994. *The Educational imagination: On design and evaluation of school programs*. New York, Macmillan (third edition).

Elbaz-Luwisch, F. 2004. How is education possible when there is a body in the middle of the room? *Curriculum Inquiry* 34(1): 9–27.

Ellsworth, E. 1989. Why doesn't this feel empowering? Working through the repressive myths of critical pedagogy. *Harvard Educational Review* 59(3): 297–324.

Engelbrecht, A. 2004. Who moved the textbook? A case study describing how ideological change in South Africa manifested itself in terms of racial representation in a transitional Afrikaans textbook series. M.Ed. thesis, Pretoria, University of Pretoria.

Epstein, H. 1979. *Children of the Holocaust: Conversations with sons and daughters of survivors*. New York, Putnam.

Evans, G. 1989. Classrooms of war: The militarization of white South African schooling. In J. Cock and L. Nathan (eds.), *Society at War: The militarization of South Africa*. New York, St. Martin's Press.

Finchilescu, G., and A. Dawes 1998. Catapulted into democracy: South African adolescents' sociopolitical orientations following rapid social change. *Journal of Social Issues* 54(3): 563–583.

Fine, E. 2001. Intergenerational memories: Hidden children and second generation. In J. K. Roth and E. Maxwell (eds.), *Remembering for the future: The Holocaust in an age of genocide*. New York, Palgrave: 78–92.

Fisher, J. 1969. *The Afrikaners*. London, Cassell.

Foster, D., and G. Finchilescu. 1986. Contact in a "non-contact" society. In M. Hewstone and R. Brown (eds.), *Contact and conflict in intergroup encounters*. Oxford, Blackwell: 119–136.

Foucault, M. 1986. *The archaeology of knowledge*. London, Tavistock (translated from the French by A. M. S. Smith).

Fourie, W. E. 2006. 'n Fenomenologiese interpretasie van Afrikaanse briefskrywers aan *Beeld* se persepsies van die sosio-politieke veranderinge in Suid-Afrika, 1990–2004 [A phenomenological interpretation of perceptions of those writing to *Beeld* newspaper about the socio-political changes in South Africa, 1990–2004]. M.A. thesis in communication sciences, University of South Africa (December).

———. 2008. Afrikaner identity in a post-Apartheid South Africa: The self in terms of the other. In A. Hadland, E. Louw, S. Sesanti, and H. Wasserman (eds.), *Power, politics and identity in South African media*. Pretoria, Human Sciences Research Council (HSRC): 239–289.

Frankenstein, M. 1990. *Relearning mathematics: A different third R radical maths*. London, Free Association Books.

Freire, P. 2000. *Pedagogy of the oppressed*. New York, Continuum (30th anniversary edition, translated by M. B. Ramos).

Furnham, A. 1985. Just world beliefs in an unjust society: A cross-cultural comparison. *European Journal of Social Psychology* 15: 363–366.

Gagiano, J. 1990. Ruling group cohesion. In H. Giliomee and J. Gagiano (eds.), *The elusive search for peace: South Africa, Israel and Northern Ireland*. Cape Town, Oxford University Press (in association with Idasa Contemporary South African Debates): 191–208.

Gaitskell, D., and E. Unterhalter. 1989. Mothers of the nation: A comparative analysis of nation, race and motherhood in Afrikaner nationalism and the ANC. In N. Yuval-Davis and F. Anthias (eds.), *Women and children first: International and infant welfare, 1870–1945*. London, Routledge.

Gamede, T. 2005. The biography of "Access" as an expression of human rights in South African education policies. Ph.D. dissertation, Faculty of Education, University of Pretoria.

Gann, L. H., and P. Duignan. 1991. *Hope for South Africa?* Stanford, Calif., Hoover Institution Press.

Geisler, G. 2000. Parliament is another terrain of struggle: Women, men and politics in South Africa. *Journal of Modern African Studies* 38(4): 605–630.

Gerhart, G. M. 2003. Review of *The Afrikaners: Biography of a people*. *Foreign Affairs*, November/December.

Giliomee, H. 1995. The growth of Afrikaner identity. In W. Beinart and S. Dubow (eds.), *Segregation and Apartheid in twentieth century South Africa*. New York, Routledge: 189–205.

———. 2003. *The Afrikaners: Biography of a people*. Charlottesville, University of Virginia Press.

Gilroy, P. 2000a. *Against race: Imagining political culture beyond the color line*. Cambridge, Mass., Harvard University Press.

———. 2000b. *Between camps: Nations, cultures and the allure of race*. London, Allen Lane.

Giroux, H. 1983. *Theory and resistance in education: A pedagogy for the opposition*. New York, Bergin and Garvey.

Gobodo-Madikizela, P. 2003. *A human being died that night: A South African story of forgiveness*. Boston, Houghton Mifflin.

Goodman, J. 1986. Teaching preservice teachers a critical approach to curriculum design: A descriptive account. *Curriculum Inquiry* 16(2): 179–201.

Goodwin, J., and B. Schiff. 1995. *Heart of whiteness: Afrikaners face black rule in the new South Africa*. New York, Scribner.

Goosen, D. 2005. The Afrikaners: Who are they? What is their future? Paper for the Harold Wolpe Memorial Seminar, April 6, 2005. Braamfontein, Johannesburg, Edge Institute.

Gordon, D. 1991. Inkatha and its use of the Zulu past. *History in Africa* 18: 113–126.

Gordon, R. 1987. Anthropology and Apartheid: The rise of military ethnology in South Africa. *Cultural Survival Quarterly* 11(4), 58–60 (December 31).

Gordon, R., and D. Grant. 2005. Knowledge management or management of knowledge. *Tamara: Journal of Critical Postmodern Organization Science* 3(2): 27–38.

Grobler, J. 2007. *Uitdaging en antwoord: 'n Vars perspektief op die evolusie van die Afrikaners.* [Challenge and response: A fresh perspective on the evolution of the Afrikaners]. Pretoria, Grourie Entrepreneurs.

Grundlingh, A. 1994. Playing for power? Rugby, Afrikaner nationalism and masculinity in South Africa, c. 1900–c. 1970, *International Journal of the History of Sport* 11(3): 408–430.

Guelke, A. 1999. *South Africa in transition: The misunderstood miracle.* New York and London, I. B. Tauris.

Gur-Ze'ev, I. 1998. Toward a non-repressive critical pedagogy. *Educational Theory* 48(4): 463–486.

Hardy, C. (ed.). 1995. *Power and politics in organizations.* London, Sage.

Harris, S. V. 2007. *Archives and justice: A South African perspective.* Chicago, Society of American Archivists.

Harrison, D. 1981. *The white tribe of Africa: South Africa in perspective.* Berkeley, University of California Press.

Harrison, M. A. 1994. *Diagnosing Organizations: Methods, models, and processes.* Thousand Oaks, Calif., Sage.

Hass, A. 1990. *In the shadow of the Holocaust: The second generation.* New York, Cornell University Press (second edition).

Heaven, P. 1984. Afrikaner patriotism today: The role of attitudes and personality. *Canadian Review of Studies in Nationalism* 11: 133–139.

Heimannsberg, B., and C. J. Schmidt. 2001. *The Collective silence: German identity and the legacy of shame.* (Translation of the 1993 German original by C. O. Harris and G. Wheeler). San Francisco, Jossey-Bass.

Hellig, J. 2003. *The Holocaust and antisemitism.* Oxford, Oneworld.

Herf, J. 1997. *Divided memory: The Nazi past in the two Germanys.* Cambridge, Mass., Harvard University Press.

Herwitz, D. 2003. *Race and reconciliation: Essays from the new South Africa.* Minneapolis, University of Minnesota Press.

Hesford, W. S. 1999. *Framing identities: Autobiography and the politics of pedagogy.* Minneapolis, University of Minnesota Press.

Heyns, C., and K. van Marle. 2005. *Disasters of peace: An exchange, November 2005.* Pretoria, Pretoria University Law Press, Center for Human Rights.

Hickson, J., and S. Kriegler. 1996. *Multicultural counseling in a divided and traumatized society: The meaning of childhood and adolescence in South Africa.* Westport, Conn., Greenwood Press.

Hirsch, M. 1997. *Family frames: Photography, narrative and postmemory.* Cambridge, Mass., Harvard University Press.

Hoffman, E. 2002. The balm of recognition: Rectifying wrongs through the generations. In N. Owen (ed.), *Human rights, human wrongs.* Oxford, England, Oxford University Press: 278–303.

———. 2004. *After such knowledge: Where memory of the Holocaust ends and history begins.* London, Secker and Warburg.

———. 2005. *After such knowledge: Memory, history, and the legacy of the Holocaust.* London, Secker and Warburg.

Holt, C. 2007. *At thy call we did not falter.* Cape Town, Zebra Press.

Howarth, D., and A. J. Norval (eds.). 1998. *South Africa in transition: New theoretical perspectives.* New York, St. Martin's Press.

Hughes, D., E. P. Smith, and H. C. Stevenson. 2006. Parents' ethnic-racial socialization practices: A review of research and directions for further study. *Development Psychology* 42(5): 747–770.

Jansen, J. D. 1990. In search of liberation pedagogy in South Africa. *Journal of Education* 172(2): 62–71.

———. (ed.). 1991a. *Knowledge and power in South Africa: Critical perspectives across the disciplines.* Johannesburg, Skotaville Press.

———. 1991b. The state and curriculum in the transition to socialism: The Zimbabwean experience. *Comparative Education Review* 35(1): 76–91.

———. 1998. "But our natives are different!" Race, knowledge and power in the academy. *Social Dynamics* 24(2): 106–116.

———. 1999. The school curriculum since Apartheid: Intersections of politics and policy in the South African transition. *Journal of Curriculum Studies* 31(1): 57–67.

———. 2001. Why Tukkies cannot develop intellectuals. Pretoria, University of Pretoria Innovation Lecture Series, May 11.

———. (ed.). 2002. *Mergers in higher education in South Africa.* Pretoria, University of South Africa Press.

———. 2004a. The politics of salvation and the school curriculum. *Verbum et Ecclesia* 25(2): 784–806.

———. 2004b. Race, education and democracy after 10 years. *Perspectives in Education* 22(4): 117–128.

———. 2004c. The regulation of teacher accountability and autonomy in South Africa. *Research Papers in Education* 19(1).

———. 2005a. Black dean: Race, reconciliation and the emotions of deanship. *Harvard Educational Review* 75(3): 306–326.

———. 2005b. When institutional cultures collide: Race, reconstruction and leadership in post-Apartheid South Africa. *New Zealand Journal of Educational Leadership* 20(1): 5–14.

———. 2005c. Why recitation persists: The relationship between authority and pedagogy in third world classrooms. In M. Beveridge, K. King, R. Palmer, and R. Wedgwood (eds.), *Reintegrating education, skills and work in Africa: Towards informal or knowledge economies? Towards autonomy or dependency in development?* Edinburgh, University of Edinburgh, Centre for African Studies: 105–136.

———. 2006a. Leading against the grain: The politics and emotions of leading for social justice in South Africa. *Leadership and Policy in Schools* 5: 37–51.

———. 2006b. Learning, living and leading in South Africa. In G. Gunnarsen, P. MacManus, M. Nielsen, and H. E. Stolten (eds.), *At the end of the rainbow? Identity and the welfare state in the new South Africa.* Copenhagen, Southern Africa Contact.

—————. 2007a. King James, Princess Alice and the case of the ironed hair: A tribute to Stephen Bantu Biko. In C. van Wyk (ed.), *We write what we like*. Johannesburg, Wits University Press: 123–134.

—————. 2007b. The leadership of transition: Correction, conciliation and change in South African education. *Journal of Educational Change* 8: 91–103.

—————. 2007c. Learning and leading in a globalized world: The lessons from South Africa. In T. Townsend and R. Bates (eds.), *Teacher education in times of change*. Netherlands, Springer.

—————. 2007d. *On second thoughts: Reflections on the South African transition*. Pretoria, Aktua Press.

Jarausch, K. J., and M. Geyer. 2003. *Shattered past: Reconstructing German histories*. Princeton, N.J., Princeton University Press.

Jenkins, E. 2007. *Falling into place: The story of modern South African place names*. Cape Town, David Philip.

Johnson, D. 2007. Building citizenship in fragmented societies: The challenges of de-racializing and integrating schools in post-Apartheid South Africa. *International Journal of Educational Development* 27(3): 306–317.

Johnson, W. R. 1982. Education: Keystone of Apartheid, *Anthropology and Education Quarterly* 13(3): 214–234.

Jung, C. 2000. *Then I was black: South African political identities in transition*. New Haven, Conn., Yale University Press.

Kahn, R. 2005. Reviews. *Learning for Democracy* 1(3): 85–88.

Karmon, A. 2007. Institutional organization of knowledge: The missing link in educational discourse. *Teachers College Record* 109(3): 603–634.

Kincheloe, J. L. 2005. *Critical Pedagogy Primer*. New York, Peter Lang.

King, E. 1979. An educational way ahead for South Africa? *International Review of Education* 25(4): 483–500.

Kitshoff, H. 2007. Claiming cultural festivals: Playing for power at the Klein Karoo Nasionale Kunste Fees (KKNK). Stellenbosch, University of Stellenbosch (unpublished paper).

Koen, C., M. Cele, and A. Libhaber. 2006. Student activism and student exclusions in South Africa. *International Journal for Educational Development* 26(4): 404–414.

Korf, L., and J. Malan. 2002. Threat to ethnic identity: The experience of white Afrikaans-speaking participants in post-Apartheid South Africa. *Journal of Social Psychology* 142(2): 149–170.

Kramer, R. L. 2000. Political paranoia in organizations: Antecedents and consequences. In S. B. Bacharach and E. J. Lawler (eds.), *Organizational politics*. Stamford, Conn., JAI Press: 47–88.

Krog, A. 1998. *Country of my skull*. Johannesburg, Random House.

Kuus, M. 2002. European integration in identity narratives in Estonia: A quest for security. *Journal of Peace Research* 39(1): 91–108.

Lambley, P. 1980. *The psychology of Apartheid*. Athens, University of Georgia Press.

Lange, L. 2003. *White, poor and angry: White working class families in Johannesburg*. Aldershot, England, Ashgate.

Langer, L. L. 2006. *Using and abusing the Holocaust.* Bloomington, Indiana University Press.

Lather, P. 1986. Research as praxis. *Harvard Educational Review* 56(3): 257–277.

———. 1998. Critical pedagogy and its complicities: A praxis of stuck places. *Educational Theory* 48(4): 487–497.

———. 2001. Ten years later, yet again: Critical pedagogy and its complicities. In K. Weiler (ed.), *Feminist engagements: Reading, resisting, and revisioning male theorists in education and cultural studies.* New York, Routledge: 183–195.

Levi, N., and M. Rothberg. 2003. Uniqueness, comparison and the politics of memory. In *The Holocaust: Theoretical readings.* New Brunswick, N.J., Rutgers University Press.

Levine, M. 2006. Writing anxiety: Christa Wolf's *Patterns of Childhood* and the throat of the witness. In *The belated witness: Literature, testimony, and the question of Holocaust survival.* Stanford, Calif., Stanford University Press.

Levy, I. 1999. Sanctions on South Africa: What did they do? Economic Growth Centre, Yale University. Discussion Paper 796 (February).

Lewis, A. 2003. *Race in the schoolyard: Negotiating the color line in classrooms and communities.* New Brunswick, N.J., Rutgers University Press.

Lieberfeld, D. 2002. Evaluating the contributions to track-two diplomacy to conflict termination in South Africa, 1984–1990. *Journal of Peace Research* 39(3): 355–372.

Lorde, A. 1984. *Sister outsider: Essays and speeches by Audrey Lorde.* Berkeley, Calif., Crossing Press.

Maddock, T. 1999. The nature and limits of critical theory in education. *Educational Philosophy and Theory* 31(1): 43–61.

Malan, M. 2006. *My life with the South African Defense Force.* Pretoria, Protea Books.

Marais, H. 2001. *South Africa: Limits to change. The political economy of transition.* Cape Town, University of Cape Town Press.

Marris, P. 1987. *Loss and change.* Reports of the Institute of Community Studies. New York, Routledge and Kegan Paul.

———. 1996. *The politics of uncertainty: Attachment in private and public life.* London and New York, Routledge.

Mbigi, L. 1997. *Ubuntu: The African dream in management.* Randburg (Johannesburg), Knowledge Resources.

McCarthy, C. 1990. *Race and curriculum: Social inequality and the theories and politics of difference in contemporary research on schooling.* Philadelphia, Falmer Press.

McClintock, A. 1995. *Imperial leather: Race, gender and sexuality in the colonial contest.* New York, Routledge.

McFalls, E. L., and D. Cobb-Roberts. 2001. Reducing resistance to diversity through cognitive dissonance instruction: Implications for teacher education. *Journal of Teacher Education* 52(2): 164–172.

McKinney, C. 2005. *Textbooks for diverse learners: A critical analysis of learning materials used in South African schools.* Pretoria, Human Sciences Research Council: Child, Youth and Family Development Research Program.

———. 2007. Caught between the "old" and the "new"? Talking about "race" in a post-Apartheid classroom. *Race, Ethnicity and Education* 10(2): 215–231.

McLaren, P. 2006. *Life in schools: An introduction to critical pedagogy in the foundations of education.* New York, Allyn and Bacon (fifth edition).

Mdluli, P. 1987. Ubuntu-Botho: Inkatha's "People's Education." *Transformation* 5: 60–77.

Meiring, P. G. J. 1975. Nationalism in the Dutch Reformed Churches. In T. Sundermeier (ed.), *Church and nationalism in South Africa.* Johannesburg, Ravan Press: 56–66.

Meyerson, D. E. 2003. *Tempered radicals: How everyday leaders inspire change at work.* Cambridge, Mass., Harvard Business School Press.

Michie, J., and V. Padayachee (eds.). 1997. *The political economy of South Africa's transition: Policy perspectives in the late 1990s.* London, Dryden Press.

Milchman, A., and A. Rosenberg. 2003. Two kings of uniqueness: The universal aspects of the Holocaust. In N. Levy and M. Rothberg (eds.), *The Holocaust: Theoretical readings.* New Brunswick, N.J., Rutgers University Press: 444–450.

Mirel, J. 2002. Civic education and changing definition of American identity, 1900–1950. *Educational Review* 54(2): 143–152.

Mitscherlich, A., and M. Mitscherlich. 1975. *The inability to mourn: Principles of collective behavior.* New York, Grove Press.

Moodie, T. D. 1975. *The rise of Afrikanerdom: Power, Apartheid, and the Afrikaner civil religion.* Berkeley, University of California Press.

Mouton, F. A. (ed.). 2007. *History, historians and Afrikaner nationalism: Essays on the history department of the University of Pretoria, 1900–1985.* Vanderbijlpark (Johannesburg), Kleio.

Nauright, J. 1996. A besieged tribe? Nostalgia, white cultural identity and the role of rugby in a changing South Africa. *International Review for Sociology of Sport* 31(1): 70–84.

Nel, P. G. 1982. The university as cultural centre. In P. G. Nel (ed.), *Die Universiteit: Verlede, hede en toekoms* [The University: Past, present and future]. Roodepoort (Johannesburg), CUM Books: 61–78 (69).

Nieuwoudt, J., and E. Nel. 1975. The relationship between ethnic prejudice, authoritarianism and conformity among South African students. In S. Morse and C. Orpen (eds.), *Contemporary South Africa: Social psychological perspectives.* Cape Town, Juta.

Noonan, S. J. 2007. *Leadership through story: Diverse voices in dialogue.* Lanham, Maryland, Rowman and Littlefield Education (with Thomas Fish).

Nyatsumba, K. M. 1997. *All sides of the story: A grandstand view of South Africa's political transition.* Johannesburg, Jonathan Ball.

Nyerere, J. 1967. *Education for self-reliance.* Dar es Salaam, Tanzania, Government Printer.

Oberholzer, C. K. 1959. Problems and trends of education in South Africa. *International Review of Education* 5(2): 129–141.

Orpen, C. 1973. Socio-cultural and personality factors in prejudice: The case of white South Africa. *South African Journal of Psychology* 3: 91–96.

Paasche, K. I. 2006. *An analysis of South Africa's education policy documents: Self-definition and the definition of the "Other."* New York, Edwin Mellen Press.

Pillay, S. 2005. The demands of recognition and the ambivalence of difference: Race, culture and Afrikanerness in post-Apartheid South Africa. In S. L. Robins (ed.),

*Limits to liberation after Apartheid: Citizenship, governance and culture.* Oxford, James Currey.

Ponterotto, J., and P. Pedersen. 1993. Preventing prejudice: A guide for counselors and educators. *Multicultural Aspects on Counseling* Series 2. Thousand Oaks, Calif., Sage.

Posel, D. [undated]. Getting the nation talking about sex: Reflections of the politics of sexuality and "nation building" in post Apartheid South Africa. Johannesburg, University of the Witwatersrand, Wits Institute for Social and Economic Research.

Posner, G. 1991. *Hitler's children: Sons and daughters of the Third Reich talk about themselves and their families.* New York, Random House.

Potgieter, C. 2002. *Black academics on the move: How black South African academics account for moving between institutions or leaving the academic profession.* Pretoria, Center for Higher Education Transformation.

Prah, K. K. (ed.). 1999. *Knowledge in black and white: The impact of Apartheid on the production and reproduction of knowledge.* Cape Town, Centre for Advanced Studies of African Society.

Price, R. 1991. *The Apartheid state in crisis: Political transformation in South Africa, 1975–1990.* Oxford, Oxford University Press.

Ramphele, M. 2008. *Laying ghosts to rest: Dilemmas of the transformation in South Africa.* Cape Town, Tafelberg.

Reichel, S. 1989. *What did you do in the war, daddy? Growing up German.* New York, Hill and Wang.

Reid, W. A. 1999. *Curriculum as institution and practice: Essays in the deliberative tradition.* Mahwah, N.J., Erlbaum.

———. 2004. Curriculum as institution. In J. Terwel and D. Walker (eds.), *Curriculum as a shaping force: Toward a principled approach in curriculum theory and practice.* New York, Nova Science: 89–100.

———. 2006. *The pursuit of curriculum: Schooling and the public interest.* Greenwich, Conn., Information Age (edited with an introduction and postscript by J. Wesley Null).

Ritterhouse, J. 2006. *Growing up Jim Crow: How black and white Southern children learned race.* Chapel Hill, University of North Carolina Press.

Rockefeller Foundation. 1978. *South Africa: Time running out.* A report of the Study Commission on U.S. Policy Toward Southern Africa. Berkeley, University of California Press.

Rose, B., and R. Tunmer (eds.). 1975. *Documents in South African education.* Johannesburg, A. D. Donker.

Russell, D. E. H. 1997. *Behind closed doors in white South Africa: Incest survivors tell their stories.* New York, St. Martin's Press.

Sackmann, S. A. 1991. *Cultural knowledge in organizations: Exploring the collective mind.* Thousand Oaks, Calif., Sage.

Saint-Maude, W. 1931. *War, wine and women.* London, Cassell.

Schivelbusch, W. 2003. *The culture of defeat: On national trauma, mourning, and recovery.* London, Granta Books (translation by J. Chase).

Schrieff, L., C. Tredoux, J. Dixon, and G. Finchilescu. 2005. Patterns of racial segregation in university residence dining-halls. *South African Journal of Psychology* 35(3): 433–443.

Sereny, G. 2000. *The German trauma: Experiences and reflections, 1938–1999.* London, Penguin Press.

Shor, I. 1980. *Critical teaching and everyday life.* Chicago, University of Chicago Press.

Sichrovsky, P. 1988. *Born guilty: Children of Nazi families* (translated by J. Steinberg). New York, Basic Books.

Soule, S. A. 1997. The student divestment movement in the United States and tactical diffusion: The shantytown protest. *Social Forces* 75(3): 855–882.

Sparks, A. 1991. *The mind of South Africa: The story of the rise and fall of Apartheid.* London, Mandarin.

———. 1996. *Tomorrow is another country: The inside story of South Africa's negotiated revolution.* Sandton, Struik.

———. 2003. *Beyond the miracle: Inside the new South Africa.* Johannesburg, Jonathan Ball.

Spies, F. J. du T., and D. H. Heydenrych. 1987. *Ad Destinatum II, 1960–1982: 'n Geskiedenis van die Universiteit van Pretoria.* Pretoria, University of Pretoria.

Spitz, R. 2000. *The politics of transition: A hidden history of South Africa's negotiated settlement.* Johannesburg, University of the Witwatersrand Press.

Stanley, L. 2006. *Mourning becomes . . . post/memory, commemoration and the concentration camps in the South African War.* Manchester and New York, Manchester University Press.

Steinitz, L. Y., and D. M. Szonyi. 1979. *Living after the Holocaust: Reflections by children of survivors in America.* New York, Bloch (second edition, revised).

Steyn, M. E. 2004. Rehabilitating a whiteness disgraced: Afrikaner white talk in post-Apartheid South Africa. *Communication Quarterly* 52(2): 143–169.

Stoler, A. L. 2002. *Carnal knowledge and imperial power: Race and the intimate in colonial rule.* Berkeley, University of California Press.

Stone, J. 2008. *When she was white: The true story of a family divided by race.* New York, Miramax Books.

Straker, G. 1992. *Faces in the revolution: The psychological effects of violence on township youth in South Africa.* Athens, Ohio University Press.

Stultz, N. 2003. Review of *The Afrikaners: Biography of a people* by H. Giliomee. *International Journal of Historical Studies* 36(3): 651–654.

Suransky-Dekker, C. 1998. A liberating breeze of western civilization: A political history of fundamental pedagogics as an expression of Dutch-Afrikaner relationships. D.Ed. dissertation, Department of Curriculum Studies, University of Durban Westville.

Thaver, L. 2006. "At Home," institutional culture and higher education: Some methodological considerations. *Perspectives in Education* 24(1): 15–26.

Thompson, J. H. 2006. *An unpopular war: From afkak to bosbefok voices of South African national servicemen.* Cape Town, Zebra Press.

Thompson, L. 1985. *The political mythology of Apartheid.* New Haven, Conn., Yale University Press.

Tibbits, F. 2006. Learning from the past: Supporting teaching through the Facing the Past history project in South Africa. Prospects: *Quarterly Review of Comparative Education* XXXVI(3): 295–318.

Tomaselli, K. G. 2006. *Encountering modernity: Twentieth century South African cinemas.* Netherlands, Rozenberg, and Pretoria, University of South Africa.

Tredoux, C., J. Dixon, S. Underwood, D. Nunez, and G. Finchilescu. 2005. Preserving spatial and temporal dimensions in observational data. *South African Journal of Psychology* 35(3): 412–432.

Tubbs, N. 1996. Becoming critical of critical theory of education. *Educational Philosophy and Theory* 28(2): 42–54.

Tutu, D. 2004. *God has a dream: A vision of hope for our time.* New York, Doubleday.

[University of Pretoria] Ad Destinatum. 1960. *Gedenkboek van die Universiteit van Pretoria.* Johannesburg, Voortrekkerpers.

Vandeyar, S., and J. Jansen. 2008. *Diversity high: Class, color, character and culture in a South African high school.* Washington, D.C., University Press of America.

Van der Westhuizen, C. 2004. The games people play or the impact of university incorporation on the attitudes, beliefs and perceptions of college lecturers. *South African Journal of Higher Education* 18(1): 153–164.

———. 2007. *White power and the rise and fall of the National Party.* Cape Town, Zebra Press.

Van Niekerk, S. 2006. *Apartheid was nie sonde nie* [Apartheid was not sin]. Privately published.

Van Woerden, H. 2001. *The assassin: A story of race and rage in the land of Apartheid.* New York, Metropolitan Books.

Van Zyl Slabbert, F. 2006. *The other side of history: An anecdotal reflection on political transition in South Africa.* Johannesburg, Jonathan Ball.

Verwoerd, W. J. (ed.). 2001. *Verwoerd: So onthou ons hom* [Verwoerd: This is how we remember him]. Pretoria, Protea Books.

Vestergaard, M. 2001. Who's got the map? The negotiation of Afrikaner identities in post-Apartheid South Africa. *Daedalus* 130(1): 19–44.

Villet, B. 1982. *Blood River: The passionate saga of South Africa's Afrikaners and of life in their embattled land.* New York, Everest House.

Waldmeir, P. 1997. *Anatomy of a miracle: The end of Apartheid and the birth of the new South Africa.* London, Viking.

Walker, C. 1990. Building a nation from words: Afrikaans language literature and ethnic identity, 1902–1924. In C. Walker (ed.), *Women and resistance in Southern Africa to 1945.* London, James Currey.

Walker, M. 2005. Race is nowhere and race is everywhere: Narratives from black and white South African university students in post-Apartheid South Africa. *British Journal of Sociology of Education* 26(1): 41–54.

Weiss, L., C. McCarthy, and G. Dimitriadis (eds.) 2006. *Ideology, curriculum, and the new sociology of education: Visiting the work of Michael Apple.* New York, Taylor and Francis.

Wessels, L. 1994. *Die einde van 'n era: Bevryding van 'n Afrikaner* [The end of an era: The emancipation of an Afrikaner]. Cape Town, Tafelberg.

Willis, P. 1977. *Learning to labor: How working class kids get working class jobs.* Farnborough, Saxon House.

Wineburg, S., S. Mosberg, D. Porat, and A. Duncan. 2007. Common belief and cultural curriculum: An intergenerational study of historical consciousness. *American Educational Research Journal* 44(1): 40–76.

Witz, L. 2003. *Apartheid's festivals: Contesting South Africa's national pasts.* Bloomington, Indiana University Press.

Wolf, C. 1980. *Patterns of childhood.* New York, Farrar, Straus and Giroux (formerly *A Model Childhood*, originally published in 1976 as *Kindheitsmuster*).

Woods, M. 2007. *Knowledge in the blood: New and selected poems.* Dublin, Dedalus Press.

# Index